AMERICAN FLY FISHING

Books by Paul Schullery

Author

The Bears of Yellowstone

The Orvis Story (with Austin Hogan)

Freshwater Wilderness: Yellowstone Fishes
and Their World (with John D. Varley)

Mountain Time

American Fly Fishing

Bud Lilly's Guide to Western Fly Fishing
(with Bud Lilly)

Editor

Old Yellowstone Days

The Grand Canyon: Early Impressions

American Bears: Selections from the Writings
of Theodore Roosevelt

The National Parks

Theodore Roosevelt: Wilderness Writings

Island in the Sky:
Pioneering Accounts of Mount Rainier

Contributing author

The Sierra Club Guide to the National Parks:
Rocky Mountains and the Great Plains

Wildlife In Transition:
Man and Nature on Yellowstone's
Northern Range

Paul Schullery

AMERICAN FLY FISHING

—— *A History* ——

NICK LYONS BOOKS

AUTHOR'S NOTE

Though I was supported in this project by the Museum, and though I frequently refer to the Museum in this book, I must make it clear that the opinions I express in the book are not necessarily shared by the Museum staff or Trustees. The wide assortment of opinions, judgments, and other interpretations I offer in this book are mine, and are not offered on behalf of the Museum. In funding work of this sort, the Museum is providing writers (I and others now working on other projects) with the opportunity to conduct historical research as individuals. The goal is to further knowledge rather than to promote any particular perspective.

Portions of this book previously appeared in *The American Fly Fisher*, *The Flyfisher*, *Rod & Reel*, *FlyFishing News, Views, and Reviews*, and *Sporting Classics*. Most of the passages are quite short, amounting only to a few sentences or paragraphs, but more extended portions of Chapters 10, 11, and 15 first appeared in different form in *The Flyfisher*, *Sporting Classics*, and *Rod & Reel*, respectively.

Printed on acid-free paper.

Printed in the United States of America

10   9   8   7   6   5   4   3   2

Library of Congress Cataloging-in-Publication Data
Schullery, Paul.
American fly fishing.

Bibliography: p.
Includes index.
1. Fly fishing—United States—History.   I. Title.
SH456.S32   1987   799.1'2   87-11189
ISBN 0-941130-32-0 (N. Lyons Books)

The American Museum of Fly Fishing was incorporated as a nonprofit educational institution in 1968. First housed in rented quarters in Manchester, Vermont, the Museum purchased its own building in Manchester in 1983, where informational exhibits on fly-fishing history are now open to the public all year. Exhibitions, research, publications, and the world's largest public collection of historical fly-fishing artifacts are all made possible by public support. For more information, write to American Museum of Fly Fishing, Box 42, Manchester, VT 05254.

for Steve

Contents

Acknowledgments

This book is the result of research I have been conducting intermittently for the past ten years and intensively for the past two. I am grateful first to the officers and trustees of The American Museum of Fly Fishing for the opportunity to spend five years working for that excellent institution. It is because of that work that I have been able to study fly-fishing history in depth. I am especially grateful for my acquaintance with museum officers Gardner Grant, Leon Martuch, and Leigh Perkins, all of whom have made history of their own, and all of whom improved my perspective on the culture and history of fishing.

The final research and writing of this book was supported by a generous grant from The American Museum of Fly Fishing in 1985–1986. Supporters of this grant included Gardner Grant, Leon Martuch, Alfred Pellicane, Leigh Perkins, Leigh Perkins, Jr., David Perkins, Nathaniel Reed, and the general fund of the Museum.

The foremost influence on my thinking about fishing history has been Museum trustee David Ledlie, for five years my Assistant Editor, and now Editor, of *The American Fly Fisher*. His knowledge and perspective have benefited me in many ways in the preparation of this book.

Numerous other writers, some of whom I have also known as friends, have been influential in the formation of my own viewpoints. I make every effort to acknowledge their contributions in the text, but must mention a few specifically here. Those I have been able to communicate with directly are Ken Cameron, Martin Keane, Mary Kelly, Jack Heddon, Richard Hoffmann, Austin Hogan, Nick Lyons, John Merwin, John Randolph, Stanley Read, and Craig Woods. Those who have especially influenced me only through their writings about angling history are Arnold Gingrich, Charles Goodspeed, John Waller Hills, R. B. Marston, John McDonald, George Reiger, Charles Wetzel, and that team of masterful bibliographers, Thomas Westwood and Thomas Satchell. We rarely know the full number of people whose writings have influenced us, and I am sure there are many others besides these, but these are the ones whose works I am most aware of being affected by.

David Godine first suggested to me that I write a history of American fly fishing, and Craig Woods provided the initial impetus and encouragement for this project.

John Merwin, my successor as director at The American Museum of Fly Fishing, administered the grant and provided logistical support.

JoAnna Sheridan, Registrar at the Museum during my directorship, helped in early stages of my research through her organizational efforts in the collection and library.

Alanna Fisher, now Registrar of the Museum, frequently provided me with materials from the Museum files during the course of my writing.

The manuscript was read and commented on by Jim Brown, Ken Cameron, David Ledlie, Nick Lyons, and John Merwin. Their notes and criticisms materially improved the final product, but I am responsible for any errors that remain.

Of course the library of The American Museum of Fly Fishing was a mainstay in my work. Though not as rich in books as some other collections, its files of manuscripts and assorted "ephemera" have made it one of the premier documentary treasures of fly fishing. As well, the Museum's collection of artifacts—hundreds of rods, hundreds of reels, tens of thousands of flies, and countless other items—was a constant source of information and curiosity.

The staffs at the following other libraries and societies were helpful during my research trips: The American Antiquarian Society; The Bancroft Library, University of California at Berkeley; The Beinecke Rare Book Collection, Yale University Library; The Fearing Collection, Harvard College Library; Ohio State University Library; Montana State University Library; University of Washington at Seattle; Williams College Library; Yellowstone Park Reference Library. I am also grateful to the owners of private libraries who let me use their collections.

Others who provided me with assistance, information, or documents are Larry Aiuppy, John Bailey, Robert Behnke, Dennis Bitton, George Grant, Dale Greenley, John Harder, Alec Jackson, Donn Johnson, Martin Keane, Mary Kelly, Hermann Kessler, Verlyn Klinkenborg, Bud Lilly, Leon Martuch, A. J. McClane, Cliff Netherton, Al Pellicane, Datus Proper, John Randolph, Steve Raymond, Tom Rosenbauer, Gary Saindon, Steve Schullery, Helen Shaw, Pat Trotter, and John D. Varley.

My wife Dianne Russell helped with transcription of library materials on various research trips.

My brother Steve introduced me to fly fishing fifteen years ago. I can only begin to express my appreciation to him on the dedication page.

The Fly Fisher's Choice

There was a time when one could think quietly and coherently. I was younger then and thought hard. Today it is difficult to think at all. There is no room or time left for cogitation. The speed is so great that before words can be put into print they are obsolete. The haste which prompts the desire to hurry what one may have to say, on any subject, leads to a distortion which may soon lead to complete confusion. This applies to fly fishing, particularly to trout fishing, and on a greater scale to fly fishing for salmon. This terrific impulse, at the present time, is toward "who did this or that first!" Is that important?

GEORGE MICHEL LUCIEN LaBRANCHE, from a
manuscript fragment written late in his life,
now at The American Museum of Fly Fishing.

Once, in a sincere but probably unsuccessful attempt to hint at the richness of the fly-fishing experience as I have known it, I wrote that "calling fishing a hobby is like calling brain surgery a job." The same thing could be said about any other kind of fishing, I suppose, and I'm sure there are people who feel just as strongly about sailing, photography, stamp collecting, or mushroom hunting. I'm a little too egalitarian, and a little too acquainted with some of these other passions, to announce that fly fishing is the best thing there is. But I'm sure enough of myself to announce that it's the best thing there is for me (at least among those pursuits we so inadequately label as hobbies), and I'm well enough informed to know that many people feel just as I do. This book is, most of all, for us. It may also interest the non-fly-fisher, and I would be glad to see it do so, but I expect it will be most likely to reach those already involved in the sport.

Fly fishing has over several centuries gathered around itself a mystique, an aroma of almost magical sophistication, that causes it to attract or repel prospective participants more intensely than other types of fishing. I suppose that much of this part of its character resulted from fly casting, wherein the angler does not cast the weight of the lure, which traditionally has been too light to cast any meaningful distance (being merely a wispy insect imitation on a small hook), but instead casts the weight of the line. Fly casting looks prohibitively graceful to the newcomer, and no doubt intimidation in the face of learning this fundamental skill has been a leading cause of the sport's not being taken up by more people. Throwing a lure that has enough

1

weight to drag a couple hundred feet of line along behind it is comfortingly easy after watching some veteran fly caster work sixty or more feet of fly line through graceful rolling curves, placing a fly precisely where it should go.

Upon this fairly simple differentiation between fly fishing and other types of fishing, several centuries of anglers have constructed an edifice of legend and lore, so that this subsport within the greater sport of fishing has grown into a separate thing, especially in the minds of many of its adherents. It may be a little arbitrary of me to further set aside for attention only those fly-fishing events that have happened in the New World, but every book must have its limits, and American fly-fishing history seems easily able to justify a book such as this one. A lot has happened to us, and we've been very busy.

One of the points I make in this book is that fly fishing gives us lots of choices. We can decide to use only dry flies, or to learn entomology, or to fish only for large fish with weighted streamers, or to restrict or liberate ourselves in any way we want as long as we keep an eye on the laws involved. Fly fishing offers us some enchanting subpursuits, such as its literature, the crafts of rod building and fly tying, and an assortment of social opportunities. Those too are ours if we choose to take them. Some do, some don't.

History is one of the least accepted of fly fishing's side attractions, and that has often puzzled me because the history of fly fishing encompasses all the other elements of the sport. The study of its history illuminates more than the past; it reveals how we came to think as we do today. In the ten years that I have seriously studied fly-fishing history I have found entertainment and instruction that for me could be surpassed only by actually going out and fishing.

One reason that fly-fishing history has such limited appeal is that it has most often been written in a manner that makes it seem pretty simple and orderly. One popular approach is the Parade of Famous Dead Anglers, wherein we are introduced, one by one, to various authors and what each of them left to posterity. Professional historians would not call that history; they would call it literature review. It has not always been that incomplete—John McDonald, Charles Goodspeed, and a few others have given us notable exceptions—but a lot of it has.

When I first came to fly fishing, and before I started looking into its past for myself, I liked the history in this light form. Here at last was a simple story, full of good, smart people who worked together for centuries to give me this grand sport. But as soon as I looked a little closer I found not history but a sort of idealization of history—a startling blend of fact, myth, and hero worship. It was great fun, but it was ultimately unsatisfying because it was so simplistic and even unbelievable.

Austin Hogan, who was Curator of The American Museum of Fly Fishing before I became Director there, used to lecture me on fly-fishing history and its audience. ''Fly fishermen are hedonists, Paul. You've got to sugar-coat history for them or they just won't pay attention.'' He said it with a tired resignation that almost persuaded me to do it, but I couldn't. I soon discovered that I was hardly the only person with hope that fishing history could be taken more seriously. Besides Austin, who had devoted decades to the subject, there were many others working on various aspects of the sport. Austin had already located some of them and persuaded them to contribute to the Museum's journal, and in the five years I was editor of *The American Fly Fisher* I probably did nothing better for it than to find several others, including some genuine card-carrying historical scholars.

We are engaged by this topic mostly because we love fly fishing and this is a fulfilling way of participating in it. We are fascinated by the sport's complexity as much as we are puzzled by the ways in which its history has been, just as Austin feared, sugar-coated. Why is it, for example, that fly fishermen are compelled to announce that fishing has, in the words of one writer, a "literature the like of which no other sport can boast?" Where in the world did we ever get such an odd notion? Certainly not from the hunters, or dog fanciers, or turf enthusiasts, all of whom have distinguished literatures they are just as proud of. Our literature may be the best as far as we're concerned, but then we'd rather read about fishing than about anything else.

Or why, to echo an aging George LaBranche, are we so concerned about who did things first? Another point I try to make in this book is that hardly anyone really did something first. An accompanying point is that doing something first is not nearly as significant as doing it and having others realize it's a good idea and start doing it too. In Chapter 15 there is a small parade of fly fishermen, over a period of half a century, each of whom was the "first" to catch a bonefish on a fly. The last, Joe Brooks, did it in 1947, but with the difference that he saw to it that the world found out, thus helping start a new part of fly fishing.

What interests me here is influence. We often hear that Lee Wulff was the first to use animal hair in a dry fly when he developed the first Wulff flies in 1929. In 1888 Charles Orvis reported on floating flies tied in North Carolina, flies made entirely of deer hair. *Forest and Stream*, in May of 1922, pictured a floating dragonfly imitation using hair wings. Norman Means, a well known Montana fly tier, developed his practically unsinkable "Bunyan Bugs" using horse-hair wings and was selling them by 1927. There are others who used animal hair either before or at the same time that Wulff did, but it was Wulff, not all the others, who made the idea stick in the popular mind, and thus had a major effect on the way we fish. Again, as interesting as the curious early developments are, it comes down to who had the real influence.

I have devoted much of a chapter to the great publishing boom of the 1970s, listing which books seemed most influential, but even there I have probably not done all I should have because the most influential force in publishing since 1970 has not been any of those authors named. It has been Nick Lyons, who, through his work with Crown Publishers and later on his own, has not only shepherded dozens of new books into print but has reprinted a host of equally important older books.

One last example of the subtleties of influence. As I was finishing up the manuscript of this book, I learned within a few days of the deaths of two fly fishermen, Vincent Marinaro and Tony Skilton. Marinaro wrote the eloquent and brilliant *A Modern Dry Fly Code*, certainly one of the most stimulating and perceptive of American fishing books. His writings have influenced the thinking of many thousands of fishermen, including numerous other writers. Tony Skilton was for many years Director of the Orvis Fishing School. He wrote little, but he taught thousands of people to fly fish, introducing them to the possibilities of our sport, stirring who knows what creative impulses in the minds of many young fishermen. These two men, good friends, both worked hard in fly fishing, and both reached out farther than most of us could dream of. I am not prepared to say which will turn out to have had the greater influence.

That is the main reason why, though I consider the first three parts of this book history, I would rather call the final part commentary. The sport has changed rapidly in the past forty years, and many developments are still too fresh for us to be sure how they will settle out. That does not stop me from offering interpretations and opinions, but it does make me cautious about early judgments on what it all will mean.

Entire books, many in some cases, have been written about such subjects as fly-design theory, or casting technique, or the craft of building cane rods. All the hundreds of people who have written fly-fishing books wouldn't have spent hundreds of pages on a single specific topic if it could be summarized in a paragraph (though some of them would have been better off to write the paragraph). For that reason, I see it as my responsibility to identify important directions rather than list all the theories and ideas. There are already some nice books on specific historical topics—fly reels, bamboo rods, fly patterns, books, and so on—and I am not trying to replace them, but to provide a synthesis of those topics and many others.

I want very much to persuade you that fly fishing history is worth your attention, not so that you will think as I do but so that you will add this one rich dimension to your appreciation of the sport. If you are reading this book you have already decided that it is worth at least some attention, and so I suppose my fondest goal for the book is that it reinforce your decision.

Before I start, though, I must also tell you about the choices *I* have made. First, I have not written a history that will be fully accessible to a total stranger to fly fishing. I have written this book as a fly fisher writing about fly fishers, so there is an informality, and a partiality, that would be missing from a strictly constructed "definitive" history.

My first choice for a subtitle was *How a Sport Came to the New World, and What Has Happened To It Since*, a title rather more whimsical and less comprehensive than *A History*. Though I intend to cover the necessary ground so that this might be considered a reasonably complete survey of our history, I am going to do so in a spirit of open-ended inquiry that may disappoint those expecting the last word on the subject of American fly-fishing history. Like all other elements of fly fishing, its history contains many unanswered questions; I may have contributed the most in this book on those occasions when I have managed to identify or clarify those questions, regardless of the fate of their answers.

What this means for the reader is that I am assuming you know something about fly fishing. I'm realistic enough to know that someone absolutely new to the sport is not likely to read its history first; most likely he will read manuals, magazines, and advertisements for some time before becoming interested in history. And so I'm not going to devote much attention to definition of simple terms, assuming, for example, that you have some idea what a fly is (and hoping your idea will be enriched by the book). In making this choice, and recognizing the realities of how long a book of this sort might be and still attract any audience at all, I am just being realistic about what seems to me to be most worth discussing. That, as many fly fishers would tell you, is a hard thing to decide. For the more I study the history of fly fishing, the more I think of Laurence Sterne's timeless lament, in *Tristram Shandy* (1759–1767), on the hopelessness of concluding any historical study:

> When a man sits down to write a history . . . if he is a man of the least spirit, he will have fifty deviations from a straight line to make with this or that party as he goes along, which he can in no ways avoid. He will have views and prospects to himself perpetually soliciting his eye, which he can no more help standing still to look at than he can fly; he will moreover have various Accounts to pick up: Inscriptions to make out: Stories to weave in: Traditions to sift: Personages to call upon: Panegyricks to paste up at this door: Pasquinades at that: . . . To sum up all; there are archives at every stage to be look'd into, and rolls, records, documents, and endless genealogies, which justice ever and anon calls him back to stay the reading of:—In short, there is no end of it. . .

One

PILGRIMS, PIONEERS, AND A MAN NAMED PORTER

1

Old World Origins

I doubt not, that the use of the fly among the mountains,
or wherever the trout are found, is nearly as old as the first
knowledge that trout were delicate eating.
REV. GEORGE W. BETHUNE,
notes to *The Complete Angler* (1847)

Considering how long anglers have been talking and writing about it, we still know frustratingly little about the origins of fly fishing in the Old World. There are the well-known independent accounts from nearly two thousand years ago, the most trustworthy being that from Macedonia reported by Aelian; but there is no clear connection with any such early fly-fishing practices and what surfaces in the historical records of Europe and England during and after the twelfth century.

The best historical research now suggests that there was no one source of fly fishing; it has long been popular to consider the 1496 British tract *The Treatyse of Fysshynge wyth an Angle*, long attributed to a Dame Juliana Berners, a fountainhead from which all subsequent fly-fishing practice sprang.[1] That simple an approach to fly-fishing history would make professional historians nervous even were it not now so thoroughly disproved, for both the internal evidence of the *Treatyse* itself and the widespread opportunities for recreational fishing in medieval England and Europe argue strongly against such a singular origin for such an intuitively attractive practice as fly fishing. But we no longer are dependent on unfounded suspicions to doubt the primacy of the *Treatyse*. Thanks mostly to Richard Hoffmann, a Canadian medievalist, a far more exciting and believable picture of early fly fishing has emerged, a picture international in scope and wonderfully varied in attitudes revealed. Fly fishing was widespread on the European continent by the time of the *Treatyse*, and those continental traditions differed, socially and technically, not only from each other but from the British tradition as well.

These early fly fishers are fascinating. We know little about the individuals, but they are us, six hundred years ago and more.

The harder we look, the older our fly-fishing tradition gets. This does not necessarily mean that if we look hard enough we will find that fly fishing goes back forever, practiced by anglers even mistier than the ones we now strain to see. Historians (I will use the term in this book to mean professional scholars, not sporting

7

writers) have identified a perceptual shift that occurred in the 1100s, by which human society lessened its distrust of nature and became more inclined to seek enjoyment in the natural world; outdoor recreation in medieval Europe may have received a boost at this time. But in any event it does not yet appear that historical research into fly fishing is in danger of coming up against some Original Fly-Fishing Event, before which the sport simply did not exist.

Perhaps the finest collection of evidence for European fly fishing is from Germany, where at least since the early 1200s writers have mentioned the catching of trout and grayling with the *vederangel*, or feathered hook. This is a particularly broad literature in that it reveals fly fishing as practiced not only for sport and subsistence but by rich and poor alike. Hoffmann has summarized the work of a German scholar, Hermann Heimpel, who wrote in the 1960s:

> From texts recording local custom in a broad band of territories from the Swiss lowlands to Styria and dating from the 1360s through the late sixteenth and seventeenth centuries, Heimpel establishes the *Federschnur* or *Federangel* as the classic technique for commoners to fish for their own purposes (not for trade) in the lord's private but natural waters, and he identifies this device as the artificial fly.[2]

Though there is evidence of sport fishing in France by the 1200s, it does not deal with fly fishing as do some early works from Spain. Thanks (again) to Richard Hoffmann, by way of a first English translation in *The American Fly Fisher* in 1984, we have an extraordinarily important fishing tract, Fernando Basurto's *The Little Treatise on Fishing*. This work, published in Zaragoza in 1539, was part of a much larger work, a *Dialogo* to the author's patron. It is in the form of a dialogue between a commoner-fisherman and a nobleman-hunter over which of their sports is the better. By emphasizing the moral harms of hunting, the fisherman convinces the hunter to take up fishing. Here we had not only the first known use of dialogue in an angling treatise—the form Walton immortalized—but also a justification for fishing different from the British one; in the *Treatyse*, the angler prefers fishing because other sports, particularly hunting, hawking, and fowling, are more physically taxing and dangerous. For this and other reasons, it is clear that this Spanish tradition is distinct from the British one.

Basurto gave explicit descriptions of many items of tackle, but his fly fishing is of most interest to us. He used a jointed rod, probably wood with a whalebone tip; he imitated stream insects with silk-bodied flies, though it is difficult to know exactly what feathers were used to hackle the flies or just how they were attached. As Hoffmann has pointed out, Basurto's instructions for presenting the fly are more detailed than those in the other early tracts. In part, Basurto recommends "throwing down the stream and going up the stream with reasonable speed so that the feather goes along the top of the stream, for in such a manner the trout eat real flies and so we fool them with artifical ones."

The Basurto text shows that sport fishing did not originate with its author. It also shows that sport fishing, and in some cases fly fishing, was known to many other fishermen besides the authors of the documents themselves.

For centuries, historians and fishermen have puzzled over a line in the *Treatyse* that credits some information in that book to "bokes of credence." Some writers have assumed the author of the *Treatyse* was engaging in credibility-building by claiming to have done homework in earlier books, and that no such books exist. Indeed, many people have assumed that after all these years of searching no such books *could* exist. Since discovery of the *Art of Angling* (1577) in the 1950s, and even more certainly since the discovery of the Basurto tract, fewer speak confidently about the impossibility of finding more books. No such books have yet been found, but a clear and sizable documentary trail exists, one that has only recently been traced carefully, and it shows that the *Treatyse* is indeed only part of a long tradition of fishing practices.[3]

In 1980, W. L. Braekman, a Belgian historian, published his review of some dozen manuscripts from various British libraries and archives, documents that date from the 1300s and 1400s; they are of varying lengths, and many were previously unidentified. They discuss several aspects of fishing technique, and complement already-known material, such as the poem *Piers of Fulham* and the epic *Wallace*, as evidence that there was a well-established sport-fishing tradition (even fly fishing) long before the *Treatyse* was published in 1496. Even the *Treatyse* has long been known to have existed in manuscript form as early as 1450, but no earlier than 1406.

So it was that at the conclusion of the fifteenth century, British and European fly fishers were practicing their sport in ways well established by centuries of practice. We don't know to what extent the traditions may have been interconnected in that century; we can't tell if the British tradition, for example, owed its origin to some movement of information from the continent in some earlier century. There were ample opportunities for exchange of information between these British and continental fishermen. The degree to which these still poorly known fly fishers were in debt to one another for their theory and tackle should be an important subject for future researchers.

What we do know is that something happened to turn this rich and inquiring set of traditions into something less broad. For some reason still not understood, it was in the British Isles that the fly-fishing tradition—not merely the literature but the vitality of technical innovation—thrived and grew. While by 1650 British fly fishers were on the verge of a literary flowering that would include Walton, Franck, Venables, and Cotton, the European anglers were drifting not only into greater obscurity but even into oblivion. As it would turn out, European anglers would eventually, by the 1800s, often look to England for leadership in fly-fishing thought. But that is ahead of the story of the Old World foundations of American fly fishing.

The Treatyse of Fysshynge wyth an Angle, though not an especially original document, has been an influential one. For centuries, even in the 1900s, leading writers have praised it as a summary of the sport; no other work has approached Cotton's "Instructions how to angle for trout and grayling in a clear stream" (published first with the 1676 edition of Walton's *Compleat Angler*) in being praised as seminal and definitive.

Of course such praise sounds (and is) absurd to the modern angler who wants to know something about AFTMA line ratings, monofilament leader tapers, deer-hair poppers, or dozens of other practical things. But it is true that the *Treatyse*'s instructions did rule British fly fishing, at least as it was published, well into the time when American colonists were doing their first fishing.

We must rely, more than we should want to, on scanty evidence for our understanding of fly fishing in England before the late 1600s. Just because the *Treatyse* is the first known published work on fly fishing in England, and just because we know that the *Treatyse* was based on a gathering of information from some century or two of fishing tradition, does not mean that the *Treatyse*'s instructions were typical of England in 1500. For all we know the *Treatyse* represented a minority view. The comparison is not entirely trustworthy, but what regional fisherman today would write a book, based on experience in one state or fishing area (the Catskills, the Yellowstone area, Maine, or others), that was truly representative of fishing tackle and techniques throughout the country? For all we know there were scores of unlettered fly fishers across England, some using streamer-type flies, some using a hundred or more patterns developed in their locality. I hope not to overemphasize this problem—our too-frequent reliance on slight evidence, or on evidence from published sources only—but we must be aware of it; witness how totally the research of one person—Richard Hoffmann—has in less than three years radically altered our perspective on medieval European sport fishing by identifying a relatively small number of previously unknown or neglected fly-fishing traditions. We must tread carefully in these ancient fields.

That said, we must rely mainly upon the *Treatyse* and subsequent books for what we know about the fishing practices that were common among the ancestors of American settlers.

You more often made than bought your tackle. Your rod was of two or three pieces, sometimes with the butt section hollowed to hold the tip. Your line was horsehair and you made it yourself, dyeing it if one or another theory of camouflage appealed to you. The rod's length probably depended most upon the size of the stream you were going to fish. On a small stream you might be content with a twelve-footer; on a large one the rod might be all of twenty feet. Your line, usually no longer than your rod but certainly no more than twice as long, was attached to a loop at the rod tip. You had no reel; in playing a fish you had to do your best to keep the rod tip high because the bend of the rod was your only way to tire the fish; you had no extra line to give it, and if you had spent much time building your rod you would probably be reluctant to follow the advice of some fishermen (including Walton) and toss the whole rig into the water and let the fish tow it around until tired out.

The famous ''jury of twelve'' flies listed in the *Treatyse* ruled fishing literature for a century and a half and have never completely disappeared, but wherever you got your information, even if you earned it the hard way by experience, you were almost certainly imitating stream insects. Like the unknown author of this mid-fifteenth century fragment from the British Library, you probably understood that various flies emerged seasonally:

> . . . in June, iuly an agust in the vpper part of the water with an artificiall flye, made vppon your hooke with sylke of dyverse coloures lyke vnto the flys which be on the waters in these monethes, and fethers of a cok or capons necke, iayes fethers be good & pecokes and popiniayes.[4]

Whether you were hidebound in following the rule of certain flies for certain months (a system that later became more restrictive than it probably was in 1500), you knew that your best bet was to take a careful look at the emerging insect of the day, or, in the words of another fifteenth-century manuscript, ''ye must loke what colowre that the fley is that the trowgth lepythe aftir and ye same colowre must the federisse be and the same colour must the sylke be of for to bynde the federysse to your hoke.''

Today we tend too much to think of these early anglers as simple primitives. That's partly because they lived in a nontechnical age and partly because these little written passages, with their oddly inconsistent and (to us) poor spelling, make the writers sound kind of dense. These people lived much closer to the natural world than we do; many spent their entire lives within a few miles of a trout stream, and were probably more finely tuned to natural processes, by necessity, than we could now imagine. If they approached nature with a mixture of superstition and misunderstanding that now seems laughable to us, we must remember that the mixture was based on long observation. They lacked science, but they weren't stupid. Modern fishing historians have pointed out that, despite the crude woodcuts in the *Treatyse*, these early anglers had the capacity to make finely tapered rods, excellent and even delicate hooks, and flies that either floated or sank. They knew what they were doing, and they did it quite well.

On the other hand, they had to deal with certain limitations that most modern fly fishermen would probably find intolerable. Perhaps the worst was wind, which, with a relatively limber rod of fifteen feet and a light horsehair line even longer, could effectively resist many casts. Not having any alternative but to go home, fifteenth-century anglers learned to work with the wind, either in some form of "blowline" fishing—that is, letting the wind carry the fly and line out and more or less bounce it on the water—or by fishing from whatever direction and by whatever manner the wind would allow. The line itself was another limitation; as A. J. McClane has reported, horsehair, at its best, is not as strong as silkworm gut or nylon. A leader of two strands of hair may test two-and-a-half pounds or less. Though Cotton, writing in the late 1600s, said that the fisherman who couldn't take a twenty-inch trout in a clear stream with two hairs "deserves not the name of an Angler," I am more inclined to agree with McClane that "a two-hair trout was no easy mark." Cotton was apparently an exceptionally talented angler himself, and in this remark he may have anticipated, unconsciously, many later generations of experts who have written with too little memory of what it's like to be a beginner.

The period roughly coinciding with the 1600s gave us a much better look at fly fishing. From Mascall, in his *A Book of Fishing with Hooke and Line* (1590), Dennys, in *Secrets of Angling* (1613, with an important 1620 edition with additional notes on fly fishing by William Lawson), and Markham in *Second Book of the English Husbandman* (1614) we learn that tastes in rod design and hook construction were evolving and flies were undergoing at least some experimentation, as when Mascall recommended cork bodies. But it was later in the century, with the works of Walton, Cotton, Franck, Venables, Barker, and Chetham, that we suddenly have a more completely open window on how fishing was done. Together they portrayed their fly fishing, from Franck (who will resurface, if somewhat hazily, in the next chapter) on salmon fishing; to Venables on the utility of upstream fishing; Barker, Franck, and Walton on the occasional use of the "winder," or reel; and several of them in greatly expanding the list of fly patterns then in use.

By 1700, and in some places much earlier, the British fisherman could buy a made rod, perhaps eight to twelve sections that were spliced together with thread for the season, obviously a product of considerable craft. He (they seem always to be males in these early books) may have owned a reel, but probably did not use it for fly fishing unless he went for salmon. He may even have known of silkworm gut, which was in limited use by the 1660s though it seems not to have become a popular commercial item until much later, perhaps even the mid-1700s. He had learned that certain styles of flies were most popular in certain regions. He was paying more and more attention to aquatic entomology (or, like many modern fly fishers, was paying more attention to those authors who themselves studied entomology); Chetham, whose first edition of *The Angler's Vade Mecum* appeared in 1681, even recommended examining the naturals under a microscope. He could buy his other tackle—flies, reels, lines, and so on—from any number of merchants, apparently a big change from 1500 as far as we can tell. He was supported by the knowledge of many experts in fishing writing and the fishing tackle trade, and he therefore needed less personal familiarity with the waters and the fishes than his ancestors two centuries earlier may have.

I realize that in this brief profile of angling at the time of early American colonization I have left out much. Most important, I have left out the sporting code that accompanied and defined the sport itself. I will have more to say of it later. For now it is enough to say that since our first published fly-fishing books, those intriguing and often frustrating Old World texts that ask more questions than they answer for historians, a sporting ethic has been at the center of fly-fishing instruction. You learn, these authors assert, not merely mechanics but a code of behavior, a code that is typically a reflection of the greater manners and mores of the age. Fly fishing's evolution has often been the testing and refinement of that code as much as it has been of more mundane developments in the technology of catching fish. In no place has this coevolution yielded a more fascinating tale of fishermen and their adventures than in the New World.

2

The Colonial Angler

*And what sport doth yeeld a more pleasing content, and
less hurt and change than angling with a hooke!*
CAPTAIN JOHN SMITH (1616)

I imagine that many history-minded fly fishers have at one time or another daydreamed about the satisfactions and excitements of being transported back to seventeenth-century America for a day, with a full vest and a favorite graphite rod perhaps, for the incomparable fishing that could be had then. The dream may have ranged from the salmon streams of New England to the limestone country of southeast Pennsylvania, and maybe even to the Rocky Mountain wilderness or on to the steelhead rivers of California. But I suspect that some of the time the dream concluded with more sober considerations: what would be the most reliable automatic weapon to have slung across the back of my vest?

That is more or less the same conflict of sport and dread that has dominated the fly fisher's understanding of what Colonial fishing must have been like. For here, more than any other part of the story I can think of, fishing historians and professional historians are in almost total disagreement. Fishing historians, including even such outstanding ones as Charles Goodspeed and John McDonald, have told us that sport fishing did not really become popular in the New World until half a century after the Revolution, that up to that time Americans were too busy building cabins, killing bears, and fighting off Indians to spend time at such a frivolous activity. Goodspeed, whose wonderful *Angling in America* (1939) documents numerous sport-fishing references in the 1700s, concluded that "the unceasing vigilance and unremitting toil by which pioneer life was protected and sustained left little time for relaxation," but he was talking there more about the 1600s and early 1700s than the later 1700s. Most other writers have echoed that sentiment, though some have generalized much more broadly and told us that it was well into the 1800s before sport fishing took hold. They were wrong.

What has set fishing writers off on the wrong track has been a shortage of the kinds of evidence they are accustomed to, and a simplistic understanding of Colonial culture. Americans wrote no fishing books to speak of before the 1800s, and left relatively little other documentary record, and most of that record was not searched out by fishing writers anyway. There is little in the way of evidence for sport-fishing tackle trade before the mid-1700s, and even less in the way of surviving tackle. Writers in the late 1800s and early 1900s, living in eras when there were many fishing magazines and books, assumed that no publications meant no sport. Then there has been the religious problem: those early colonists were Puritans, and didn't approve of having fun.

The most careful writers have always known it wasn't that simple, but that, roughly, is the argument as it is most often heard. It is wrong, but the reasons for its error are interesting enough to discuss as a way of introducing Colonial sport fishing and our first-known fly fishers of the late Colonial and early National periods.

In England, where we know fishing was common (though, as in most places, sport was also a means of gathering food, and it is always difficult to separate the two in recreational history), only a few books were published in either the 1600s or 1700s. The sparsely populated colonies, if they needed a book on fishing, could rely on British books for information on how to make tackle and baits.

But the shortage of published works on fishing is poor evidence; historians, were they so sarcastic, might point out that this is about the same as assuming that because nobody published books about sex in America before the 1800s, nobody was engaging in it. Fishing, like sex, was not a publishable topic; book producing (and practically all periodical publication) was reserved for other subjects. For example, in the years 1682 to 1684 in Boston, almost all of the 130 books produced were religious in nature. Religious publishing remained dominant in most colonies well into the 1700s, with an assortment of almanacs, government documents, and educational aids taking up most of the other press production. But, as we will see momentarily, there are other kinds of documentary evidence than books and pamphlets.

Some writers have pointed out that strict religious codes prevented colonists from having pastimes like fishing. That is perhaps the most incorrect assertion of all. First, modern scholarship has shown that even the New England Puritans were not as stiff-necked as older texts have portrayed them; they enjoyed many a good time. Second, the various other colonies had different sets of rules anyway, and some colonies were commercial, rather than religious, in the first place. Third, even the most professedly religious colonies quickly lost their Christian domination. The religious element may have controlled the press, and even the government, but they soon saw themselves outnumbered in the community at large. The religious colonies quickly became commercial colonies. In Boston, by the 1690s the tavern had replaced the church as the focal point of town culture, and the churches could not have seated more than twenty-five percent of the city's population. What would those other seventy-five percent do on Sunday?

The other argument, that colonists had no time for fishing because they were too embattled by bears, Indians, and other survival problems, is also in error. Indian wars were brief, and in most cases local, and only affected colonists for the duration of the struggle. Most colonists after 1640 spent most of their time in no fear of such conflict. By 1720, the inhabitants of the five major colonial cities—Boston, Philadelphia, New York, Newport, and Charles Town—constituted only eight per cent of the total population. The rest lived in smaller settlements or were scattered out across the countryside. Depending upon one's personal interests and obligations, one could find more or less time for fun. Recreational enthusiasms arrived with the first pilgrims, and they enjoyed themselves as soon, and as often, as they could.

We need to know much more about what really went on among Colonial fishermen. We have only begun. I can think of no other subject in American fishing history so in need of attention, or so rich in its possibilities for discovery, as the Colonial angler. What we know already assures us that they were there, and that they knew as well as we how to enjoy fishing, but there is little flesh on the bones; we know too few names, too little about their tackle and their exploits, and much too little about their connections with their European counterparts.

From what we know, New York showed the earliest popular interest in sport fishing. By the early 1630s, Collect Pond (later Freshwater Pond), according to historian Carl Bridenbaugh (in his *Cities in the Wilderness*), had "become the usual scene for open-air outings of fishing parties and 'unprofitable fowlers.' " The Dutch had no outward objections to a good time, and when the English eventually assumed control there was little change in the pace of recreation. As Bridenbaugh said, "New York was undoubtedly the gayest of colonial towns." Fishing and hunting were both common pastimes, and sportsmen no doubt roamed farther and farther afield as time went on and the cities grew. The 1700s produced numerous references to outings by individuals and groups in the area of New York City, either solely for fishing or for fishing, picnicking, and other social activities.

Boston, though it early (in the 1640s) established laws to protect common rights to public fishing waters, has left less trace of sport fishing in the 1600s. But judging by the pace of recreation there in the early 1700s, earlier fishing must have been going on. It was a prosperous colony with many citizens of ample leisure. Shooting was so popular by 1710 that the authorities, alarmed by numerous accidental shootings of citizens, were compelled to outlaw target and pigeon shooting in the city.

Charles Goodspeed pieced together the stories of several eighteenth-century Massachusetts anglers, including Reverend Ebenezer Bridge, who enjoyed the fishing around Chelmsford in the 1750s, and John Rowe, a Bostonian and today the best known Colonial angler by virtue of his extensive diaries from the 1760s and 1770s that describe many fishing trips. The existence of gentlemen like Rowe (who listed some of his companions in his diary; they were all persons of substantial social standing), suggests that fishing was not only acceptable and common, but had class. Rowe, for example, imported his fishing rods from England.

I have always had high hopes for the historical possibilities of Virginia as a fishing colony; it was established by a different social group, the leaders of whom were burdened with neither religious objections to recreation nor with too demanding a work load. Virginia has yielded sufficient evidence of sport fishing to show again that it was popular, but has not been as productive as I have hoped, perhaps because it became such a bastion of other sports, especially "the turf," as horse racing was long known. Jane Carson, in her *Colonial Virginians at Play* (1965), suggests that "fishing was almost as popular as hunting, for food and for sport." The prominent early writer Robert Beverly was fond of both sports and enjoyed them at every opportunity in the first decades of the 1700s, and judging from his circle of friends he was not unusual. In his *The History and Present State of Virginia* (1705), he reported: "I have set in the shade at the heads of the rivers angling, and spent as much time in taking the fish off the hooks as in waiting for their taking it." In 1700, in announcing a possible new school in New Kent County, *The Virginia Gazette* reported that "among other things, the fine fishery at the place will admit of an agreeable and salutary exercise and amusement all the year."

It may be that the shortage of fly fishing from Colonial Virginia is actually the result of fishing not having been as common there as in other colonies. If those settlers, who still considered themselves Englishmen and had British sporting attitudes, had not learned to associate fly fishing with anything but trout, they might have had few opportunities to fly fish unless they lived near the mountains.

But it is from Pennsylvania that the richest historical legacy has been given us of early American angling. The Quakers have been badly misused by popular writers who suggest that fishing was not acceptable in early Pennsylvanian society. The Quakers of Philadelphia did oppose "rude and riotous" activities (gambling, stage plays, fireworks), whose various purveyors and supporters had only to move a few miles from town in order to get away with their worst; but the traditional sports, including fishing, hunting, fowling, skating, and swimming (sometimes even racing) were not frowned upon. They were, in fact, often quite fashionable. Philadelphia saw the organization of no less than five different fishing clubs before the Revolution. These clubs were at least as much social as sporting, but they relied in good part on the skills of the members as fishermen for the success of their banquets, and this could in no way be confused with subsistence fishing; these men were prominent citizens.

The first and by far the most famous was of course the Schuylkill Fishing Company, founded in 1732. It was followed by the Society of Fort St. David, the exact date of whose origin is in question, the Mt. Regale Fishing Company in 1762 (whose members included Colonel Henry Bouquet and Richard Penn), the White Oak Barges in 1767, and the Liberty Fishing Company the same year. Some people belonged to more than one, but surely here is ample evidence of enthusiasm for angling.

The Penns themselves figure repeatedly in early American fishing history. William Penn once observed of the Indians, enviously, that "We sweat and toil to live; but their pleasure feeds them; I mean their hunting, fishing, and fowling." His daughter shared his apparent interest in recreational fishing; writing to her brother, then in England, in 1737 (from Philadelphia), she said:

> My chief amusement this summer has been fishing. I therefore request the favour of you when Laisure Hour will admit, you will buy for me a four joynted strong fishing Rod and Real with strong good Lines and asortment of hooks the best sort . . .[1]

Apparently, like Rowe in Boston, she could not find suitable tackle in the New World.

Estates lists and other obscure sources reveal that rods, lines, and hooks were occasional property, as one would expect, in the 1600s and early 1700s, but it is in Philadelphia that tackle sales and advertisements have surfaced in numbers. Goodspeed's sleuthing among Colonial newspapers turned up numerous brief mentions of tackle for sale in the *Pennsylvania Gazette* in the 1730s and 1740s, evidence of a growing trade, and possibly evidence of a more urban angler less inclined to make his own gear, and possibly even evidence of a growing tackle trade in England, from where much of the stuff was probably imported.

Such was Colonial fishing as we have so far recovered its records. People fished for fun and for food, and often for both, much as they do now. In the 1700s they began to show more interest in store-bought tackle, and the increasing growth and sophistication of Colonial society gave more people leisure and resources to enjoy the sport. Travelers' journals from the 1700s frequently mention fishing incidentally, such as the diary kept by the famous naturalist Peter Kalm, who in 1749 described the Mohawk River not far from Albany, New York:

> The whirlpools, which were in the water below the falls [Cohoes Falls], contained several kinds of fish; and they were caught by some people, who amused themselves with angling.

I notice that Philadelphia, which has given us the most evidence of sport fishing in the Colonies, was by all historical accounts the primary port of entry for emigres from Europe until near the end of the 1700s, and that these people and their cultures flourished in the lush valleys and along the now-famous trout waters of south Pennsylvania, and that a high degree of personal freedom in Pennsylvania permitted great latitude in personal recreation. It was Pennsylvania that gives us the fullest record of fly fishing in the first years of the new republic, to which we now turn, and it was in south and west Pennsylvania—not the Catskills, Adirondacks, Poconos, or any of the other famous fishing grounds—where in the next century a young Theodore Gordon grew to love the outdoors.

3

First Traces

Walked out Fishing this Morn Took great Plenty of small Trouts, Salmo . . .

JOSEPH BANKS, Newfoundland (1766)

The search for the first American fly fishers has been a long one. Since the 1930s, when Charles Goodspeed assembled his *Angling in America*, there seems always to have been at least one antiquarian or avid fishing writer sorting through the huge documentary resource of pre-1800 America in search of the slightest vagrant reference to fly fishing. Goodspeed, Charles Wetzel, and Austin Hogan spent many years at this task, haunting the oldest libraries and historical societies, but the rate at which new material is still surfacing shows that only a small part of the evidence has yet been sifted. We have a lot to learn about early American fly fishing.

It is a subject rich in those shadowy figures that add so much charm to historical study. There is no knowing how many seventeenth-century colonists fly fished without ever leaving a trace of evidence, but some of the first possible fly fishers were not even colonists. They were only visitors from the Old World.

Richard Franck was the first of these problematic anglers. Franck, best known in fishing circles for his book *Northern Memoirs* (written in 1658, published in 1694), was an expert fly fisher of difficult personality (Arnold Gingrich, one of angling literature's most forgiving chroniclers, called him a ''crazy coot''). He was, in the words of modern British writer Bernard Venables, ''a dark and rigid man, a man of a vast and prolix pomposity, a prater, a pedant, a coxcomb of dreary absurdity. He was a Cromwellian trooper and a stringently religious man. It is odd that he was an angler.'' But angler he was, and by all accounts a good one. The evidence that he visited America is much less conclusive than the proof of his fishing skill, but it is probably sufficient.

Having been a supporter of Cromwell, Franck may have found the political climate in England unhealthy after Cromwell's death in 1658. That at least is how Goodspeed and others have suspected that he came to America in the period between then and the late 1680s. Proof that he did come here is confined to references made in two other books. One is his *A Philosophical Treatise of the Original and Production of Things*, published in London in 1687, with the subtitle ''Writ in America in a Time of Solitudes.'' The other is a book he is generally believed to have written, *The*

A
Philosophical
TREATISE
OF THE
ORIGINAL
And
PRODUCTION
OF
THINGS.

Writ in AMERICA *in a Time of*
Solitudes.

By R. FRANCK.

LONDON,
Printed by *John Gain,* and are to be sold by
S. Tramnsh at the *King's Head* in Corn-
hill : and *S. Smith* at the *Prince's Arms*
in St. *Paul's Church-Yard.* 1687.

Title page from Franck's *Philosophical Treatise*, indicating that he lived in the New World.

Admirable and Indefatigable Adventures of the Nine Pious Pilgrims, which was published in London in 1708, the probable year of Franck's death. The subtitle of that book includes the phrase "Written in America, in a time of Solitude and Divine Contemplation," and there are several places in the text that suggest a knowledge of America.

That's it; that is the extent of what we know, though there is no reason more information couldn't exist, perhaps in passenger records of transatlantic voyages or in some yet-unnoticed journal of a colonist who encountered this singular man. The best that can be said now is that he was almost certainly here, and he was an enthusiastic fly fisher. It is pleasant to imagine that he found time, amid the solitude and divine contemplation, to cast a fly.

The second figure is no more substantially represented in the historical record. Richard Brookes, an authority on medicine and nature who produced or translated a number of popular books between 1721 and 1763, also wrote the extremely popular *The Art of Angling*, which went through more than ten editions in various forms between 1740 and 1800. Again we are dependent upon internal evidence from one of his books, *A System of Natural History*, published in 1763, for our only proof that he traveled in America at some time before that year. Brookes wrote competently, if not with especial originality, about fly fishing. Perhaps he fly fished here.[1]

It is impossible—at least it has been impossible for most of the writers who have discussed early American fly fishing—to deal with these earliest and least known years of American fly fishing without at least some mention of native American uses of lures. Anthropologists have gathered a great assortment of lure-like devices and fish decoys from among native American societies, and some of the first references to these devices, usually reported in travelers' journals, have found their way into the story of American sport fishing. The most famous is probably the journal of William Bartram, a pioneering naturalist who wrote of the American Southeast as he saw it in the late 1760s. Bartram observed southern Indians fishing for largemouth bass (he called them ''trout''), and his account of their technique is worth giving in full because it typifies several others:

> They are taken with hook and line, but without any bait. Two people are in a little canoe, one sitting in the stern to steer, and the other near the bow, having a rod ten or twelve feet in length, to one end of which is tied a strong line, about twenty inches in length, to which is fastened three large hooks, back to back. These are fixed very securely, and covered with the white hair of a deer's tail, shreds of a red garter, and some particoloured feathers, all which form a tuft, or tassel, nearly as large as one's fist, and entirely cover and conceal the hooks; this is called a bob. The steersman paddles softly, and proceeds slowly along shore, keeping parallel to it, at a distance just sufficient to admit the fisherman to reach the edge of the floating weeds along shore; he now ingeniously swings the bob backwards and forwards, just above the surface, and sometimes tips the water with it; when the unfortunate cheated trout instantly springs from under the weeds, and siezes the prey. Thus he is caught without a possibility of escape, unless he breaks the hooks, line, or rod, which he, however, sometimes does by dint of strength; but, to prevent this, the fisherman used to the sport is careful not to raise the reed suddenly up, but jerks it instantly backwards, then steadily drags the sturdy reluctant fish to the side of the canoe, and with a sudden jerk brings him into it.

Primitive by modern standards, I suppose, but it still sounds like great fun. The rod, described as ''reed,'' was probably some southern cane; more properly we might call it a pole rather than a rod. Just what a bass took the bob, slowly swinging just above the water, to be was probably just as uncertain then as are the bass's response to modern lures.

Why a wide variety of references to native American use of lures should receive so much attention from fishing historians is partly obvious and partly unclear. The obvious part is that you have to start somewhere, and these are surely the oldest references we have to an established lure-fishing tradition in the New World. The unclear part is just how these mainly subsistence fishing practices relate to the development of sport fishing, especially fly fishing. I wouldn't be surprised if some day it was shown that some of our early fly fishers adopted some of these techniques, and that lure makers got some ideas from them as well. In a few later cases, such as the Muddler Minnow and some of the hairwing Atlantic salmon flies, there is little or no doubt that Indian fishing practices were directly adapted. But most of the time the connection is more tenuous. British fishermen by 1800 were no strangers to a variety of lures, and fishermen in any age are simply likely to dream up something on their own, happily ignorant that it has been dreamt up before. In any event, these native American fishing practices, like the possible fly-fishing activities of early British visitors, are only preface for the more substantive records of the first-known fly fishers in the New World.

The evidence as it stands so far suggests that fly fishing had its first American adherents in the more populated, earliest settled areas of the country. There is a duality within this growth: some of it occurred in the major cities of mid- to late-1700 America, and some of it occurred as British officers stationed in the New World sought means to practice their favorite sport in a wild setting. Both of these traditions, one apparently based more on the activities of resident Colonials and the other the result of an expanding British military presence, have left exciting proof that fly fishing was an established pastime by the eve of the Revolution.

The British had taken control of both Quebec and Montreal, formerly French, by 1760. It appears that over the next century there was a growing sport fishery on Canadian streams, so that most of our early works on salmon fishing, for example, are from the pens of visiting British officer-sportsmen. The officer-sportsman remains a common "type" on the American sporting scene, whether British or American, into the late 1800s, when his visibility lessens. It is one such gentleman, Sir William Johnson, Superintendent of Indian Affairs for North America, who has been put forth as our first-known fly fisher. Johnson was established on the southern edge of New York's Adirondacks by the early 1760s, and in 1769 he obtained some land on Sacondaga Lake, building a lodge there in 1770. It was a summer home, and he fished the waters thereabouts frequently. He was without question an enthusiastic fisherman, and it takes little imagination, given his background, to assume he used flies, but no record survives that he did. Austin Hogan's attempt to establish Johnson as our first fly fisher, including a claim that he was fly fishing as early as 1761, has met with uniform rejection from historians, who agree it seems likely but who maintain that there is no proof. Regrettably, later writers have reinforced and embroidered this intriguing episode in American angling history so that Johnson is much more full and complete a fisherman in print than he is in actual historical record.

The first known account of fly fishing in the New World, just recently identified by *American Fly Fisher* editor David Ledlie, is from 1766. The angler in question was a young naturalist named Joseph Banks, a wealthy passenger of the *Niger*, a British ship sent to Newfoundland to protect British fisheries interests in 1766. Banks, who would eventually become a prominent naturalist (only twelve years later he would be president of the Royal Society), accompanied the expedition as an opportunity to further his scientific career and investigate nature in Labrador and Newfoundland. His diaries were not published until 1971, and they are revealing. In August of 1766, he made an entry about fishing (not the first) that revealed his methods:

Joseph Banks in about 1779, a portrait by John Russell printed in the 1971 edition of Banks' journals.

> So much for Salt water fish the Fresh are in great Plenty tho but of 2 sorts Trout and Eels the first of which offered good Diversion to an angler biting Very well at the artificial Particularly if it has gold about it with this Peculiarity in the rivers that they are to be caught in abundance no where but in the tide and at no time but from about two hours before highwater till Ebb in Pools indeed they always bite but best in sunshining weather I have seen no large ones none I believe above half a Pound in weight but am told that in some Parts of Nfland they are Very Large.

Wishing him only a finer regard for punctuation, we can wonder at these tidewater

An arctic char drawn by the British illustrator Sydney Parkinson from a specimen caught by Joseph Banks during his 1766 visit to Newfoundland, printed in the 1971 edition of Banks' journals published by the University of California and Faber and Faber.

Sir John Johnson, portrait by an unknown artist, from the Public Archives of Canada. *Courtesy of David Ledlie.*

trout (Banks collected and preserved both brook trout and Arctic char), imagining them to be migrants that fed in both fresh and salt water. His description of the "artificial" is perhaps not indisputably that of a fly, but under the circumstances it is far more likely a fly than any other sort of artificial lure.

The legacy of Sir William Johnson does not end with his death in 1774. His son, Sir John Johnson, took up the Loyalist cause at the outbreak of the Revolution and, though he lost his father's properties in New York, ended up as Superintendent of Indian Affairs for British North America after the war. He settled (with a handsome land grant from the Crown) about forty miles from Montreal, where he was visited by a traveler named Robert Hunter, Jr. in 1785. Hunter reported in his diary, finally published in 1943 (and recently brought to the attention of anglers by David Ledlie), that life on Johnson's lands was full of sport, including fly fishing. Hunter himself saw the proof, as in this excerpt from his June, 1785 diary, describing an outing not far from Johnson's home:

> I took a walk after dinner. It's astonishing the number of bass I saw playing in the current. They often catch three dozen in the course of half an hour with a fly. I think they are the finest fish I have tasted in America.[2]

A lot of people feel the same way today, and many of them would be amused to know that the second reliable reference to fly fishing in the New World was not for trout but for bass.

In the mid-1780s, other British visitors were also apparently sampling the fly fishing of the north. Colonel John Enys and two fellow officers traveled from Montreal to Lake Champlain, where they found good salmon fishing at the mouth of the Saranac, much to the amazement of the locals:

> This was the first salmon these people had ever seen and they were equally astonished to find these fish in the Saranac River, and to see them caught with a slender rod; they very much wished to see our baskets and it was not without some difficulty we made them believe we caught them with the flies we showed . . .[3]

I agree with David Ledlie, who has studied early northeastern fishing history far more than I, that the British influence in Canada quickly established a sport fishery; these few references are suggestive evidence at least. Late 1700s paintings of Canadian river scenes frequently feature salmon fishers using rods. These and other random pieces of evidence (such as a salmon fly with Hereford hairwing, described in a 1795 inscription in a Newfoundland Bible and reported by several modern fishing writers), do not prove that the sport fishery was large. But they do establish its existence. We know that in the first decades of the 1800s the sport fishery did grow and become quite widespread. Its magnitude before that remains to be determined.

The other tradition of fly-fishing development in America worked its way out from the coastal ports. Our knowledge of it is in some ways better, and in some ways worse, than our knowledge of the British officers, naturalists, and other visitors who fly fished here. The first good records are commercial, being advertisements for fly-fishing tackle. Charles Goodspeed's many years of reading in old newspaper files turned up most of these.

The Boston Newsletter, November 4, 1773, reported that:

> Jeremiah Allen Informs his friends and the Publick, that he has received per the *Dolphin* in the Hard-Ware Branch . . . Bambo, Dogwood, Solid Joint, and Hazel Angling Rods, Hair and Silk Lines, Best Kirby & common Hooks, Kirby Hooks on Gimp & Hair, Snap Hooks, Landing Nets, Flies, Goose Floats, Corks, Fly Line Gimp, Brass Winches, Span-Tops for Rods . . .

But again it is Pennsylvania that has shown us the most evidence from these early days. Philadelphia, the town that supported several fishing clubs with hundreds of members total, had several full- or part-time fishing-tackle outlets. The best known was Edward Pole, whose advertisements in *Dunlap's Pennsylvania Packet* in the 1770s revealed a wealth of tackle variety; he offered a wide assortment of lines, "Trolling wheels for rock, trout or perch, with or without multipliers," several types of wood rods (including cedar, hazel, and dogwood), and "Artificial flies, moths, and hackles, with suitable lines of any length." He even stocked silkworm gut, still a fairly new product to some English fishermen. The reference to multiplying reels is real evidence that Pole kept up with British developments; the earliest surviving reference to multipliers in all of fishing literature is only 1770, whereas the items quoted above are from 1777.

Pole not only provided a full line of tackle, he catered to anglers on the stream at his tavern The Wigwam, which was located on the Schuylkill not far from town.

Pole had to sell off the tavern in 1788, but the tackle trade must have been fairly good, because his business went on. Pole was succeeded at his tackle trade by George Lawton, who lasted at least into the new century; fly fishing researchers Bob and Gary Saindon have recently turned up an invoice for an order of tackle from 1803, an assortment of gear sold by Lawton to one Meriwether Lewis, who was stocking up for an extended transcontinental trip with his fellow officer William Clark. They bought no fly-fishing tackle from Lawton, but he thoughtfully included his most recent tackle list with the receipt, and it is obvious from it that he had improved even on Pole's excellent selection of items. Now there were not only "Plain and Multiplying Brafs Wheels," and "Horfe hair, filk, hardeft, filk-worms gut, Indian Grafs, Hempen, Cotton, Layout, and Angling Lines," there were many kinds of lures, including "Artificial Flies, Moths, Hackles, Minnew, Chubbs, Grafshoppers, Dilderries, Frogs, Mice, Birds, Cadds, &c. for Trout and other Fifhing." It is hard to tell which of this list were artificial; actually, some may have *been* live baits, as frogs, minnows, and the others would have been easy to keep on hand as they are now in bait stores. But what a collection, and how I'd love to rummage through his shop for a few minutes!

That business was good in Philadelphia is clear from Pole's competition. Pole was in business by 1774, and shared the trade with a William Ransted, who also sold a good variety of tackle. It is also to Philadelphia that we owe knowledge of the first probable American fly tier of record. Manuscripts published in the *Pennsylvania Magazine of History and Biography* in 1974 establish Davis Hugh Davis, a Quaker who kept the George Inn from 1773 to 1778, as a skilled tackle manufacturer:

> He was famous for making fishing tackle deep-seas, fly feathers etc. His operations for fastening the hooks & other light work was carried on during school hours, 8 till 12 & 2 to 5, after taking his rounds . . .

Further evidence that at least a little tackle making was going on this early is found in one of Pole's advertisements, in which he says he has "Ready Money for White Horse Hair," an offer that Lawton later expanded, expressing interest in "any quantity of Carolina Reeds, White Horfe Tails, Silk Worms Gut, &c. &c." It could be that some lines were being woven, or hooks being snelled, this early, or the hair could have been sent back to Pole's suppliers in England for production.

All of this information about fly-fishing tackle asks one important question: Who used it? I think it's safe to assume members of the fishing clubs bought a lot of it. There was plenty of good fly fishing available within a couple days travel of Philadelphia, as well as throughout the rest of the state. There just aren't many names yet to go with the trout and the tackle. There are a few, such as George Gibson, who started fishing the streams of Cumberland County—the Letort and others—in the early 1790s and became one of our first fly-fishing correspondents when sporting periodicals appeared. Gibson could have afforded to buy tackle, and certainly did not fish alone, though it appears from some of his published articles that he dealt with a fair number of baitfishers and anglers who viewed fly fishing skeptically. But there are too few for us to know how common fly fishing was, or what the reigning theories and techniques were.

4

A Sporting Journalism

Of this literature, which is better known as "American Sporting Literature," Mr. Porter may be said to be the founder and the head . . .

GEORGE WILKES (1858)

There is magic in an old outdoor magazine. You notice it, start to leaf through it, and suddenly it's half an hour later. In any old magazine we are amused by the advertising hype, amazed by the prices, and led from page to page in hope of new discoveries of old tackle. We are as well attracted, once we adjust to whatever style was fashionable at the time, to the thinking of the writers. And we are often surprised by what we read; so much that we thought was new is just recycled, periodically (so to speak), generation after generation. Magazines have such a short life expectancy that they disappear from our attention and their contents are lost until some historian or other documentary wanderer comes upon them in an attic, library, or museum, and then they are almost new again, reaching out to an audience their publishers never imagined.

Serious fishing historians have known for many years that it was in the periodicals, not the more durable books, that the development of fly fishing was most thoroughly chronicled. The books are a little like milestones along the way; the periodicals— millions of pages of chaotic flow of information, debate, and promotion—are the paving stones. A book may represent the opinions of one person, perhaps a person who held a minority viewpoint; the periodicals not only review the book, they offer in their endless stream of articles all the other prevalent opinions that were being discussed in writing at the time (though even the periodicals are incomplete, finally, because only a small portion of anglers in any generation write anything at all about their sport; the periodicals are simply more reliable because they are more comprehensive). Books come down to us as past perspectives, and in that they influence later generations perhaps even more than they influence their own, as each subsequent writer mentions earlier books and spreads their message. Periodicals die quickly most of the time; they reflect their own age more specifically. They, along with tackle catalogs and a broad array of other kinds of materials—patent records, unpublished manuscripts and diaries, business directories, a huge assortment of artifacts from rods to flies to clothing, and personal interviews of surviving fishermen—yield to us a better understanding of any generation of fly fishers than do the books those fly fishers might have written.

American fly fishers become far easier for us to know and study in the early 1800s because they wrote more. They may have written more partly because there were more of them, but it was also because publishing was becoming easier. Advances in printing technology, an increase in the size of the publishing trade, and an assortment of commercial interests (especially more sporting-related trade) combined to awaken in the New World a sporting journalism that would quickly grow to rival that of England. Starting about 1820, a few magazines—*The American Farmer*, *Farmer's, Mechanic's, Manufacturer's and Sportsman's Magazine*, and others, some of which were really newspapers—published the occasional sporting item. Then, in 1829, the demand and commercial prospects became sufficient for an entire journal devoted to sport, and soon others would follow.

The first was the *American Turf Register and Sporting Magazine*, founded in New York by John Skinner; the first issue appeared in September 1829 and the magazine went on as a monthly until its demise in 1844. Like most of the earlier sporting magazines, it was most heavily devoted to the turf. Hunting, fishing, and other activities were covered frequently, but most of the charming, even beautiful engravings that served as frontis for the *Turf Register* were portraits of famous studs and champions. As Skinner put it:

> But though an account of the performances on the American turf, and the pedigrees of thorough bred horses, will constitute the *basis* of the work, it is designed, also, as a Magazine of information on veterinary subjects generally; and of various rural sports, as Racing, Trotting Matches, Shooting, Hunting, Fishing, &c. together with original sketches of the *natural history and habits of American game of all kinds* . . .

It was, thus, a sporting miscellany in which fishing was often only an incidental topic, and fly fishing only incidental within that. But it was an important start, and contained much of great interest to fly-fishing historians.

It was followed in 1831 by another journal, one of greater influence and eventual prestige. This one also came out of New York, from what one writer has called "a dingy attic print shop at 64 Fulton Street," and it was *The Spirit of the Times*, even broader in its scope: "A Chronicle of the Turf, Agriculture, Field Sports, Literature, and the State." The needs of readers were different then than now; it is impossible to imagine quite this mix of topics under one cover today. The *Spirit*, in its various incarnations over the next thirty years (it has a convoluted publishing history, compounded by the quick appearance of several other journals with nearly or exactly the same name), appealed to all sorts of recreation interests; an article on trout fishing might appear next to a critique of a recent play, which might share its column with a poem on the governor's table manners. It was wide open.

It was also welcome, some sign that sportsmen of many types had for some time felt the need for just what these early journals offered. Openly imitative of *Bell's Life of London*, one of the foremost such publications in England, the *Spirit* at its peak (1856) was claimed to have had forty thousand subscribers. Before the Civil War that was a monumental circulation for such a journal; I suspect the number was exaggerated but I do not doubt the magazine's popularity.

The moving force behind this journalistic establishment—at various times responsible not only for the *Spirit* but also the *Turf Register* and at all times the most admired and imitated of sporting editors—was William Trotter Porter, known affec-

William Trotter Porter in about 1836. *Courtesy of The American Museum of Fly Fishing.*

tionately in journalism circles as "York's Tall Son." He is still one of few American sporting journalists to be the subject of a book-length biography, Francis Brinley's worshipful but enormously informative *Life of William T. Porter* (1860). Porter was born in 1809 in Newbury, Vermont, and was from childhood fascinated by both the outdoors and publishing. He was only twenty-two when he established the *Spirit*, but was already experienced in the printing trade (having shortly before, while working at another print shop, given a young Horace Greeley his first job).

Brinley (who was, incidentally, Porter's brother-in-law), Norris Yates, and more recently David Ledlie have adequately chronicled Porter's career. For our purposes it is sufficient to say that he established and maintained a standard of quality that was looked to by most others in the new field of sporting journalism, which added other publications, such as *The Southern Sportsman*, *The American Sporting Chronicle*, and the *New-York Sporting Magazine and Annals of the American and English Turf* as the 1830s and 1840s went on. Many of these magazines lasted only a few issues, as has always been true of such ventures. As Noah Webster had put it not many years earlier, "The expectation of failure is connected with the very name of a Magazine."

William Trotter Porter, an engraving that appeared in the first number of *Porter's Spirit of the Times*, September 6, 1856.

The fly-fishing journalism in these first periodicals is a striking mix of old and new. In some years, I am sure, there were more words about fly fishing lifted from British publications, both books and magazines, than there were contributed by American writers. At first there was fairly heavy reliance on just a few correspondents. George Gibson, mentioned earlier, was one of these. Gibson had fished widely in his life, but loved his home county in southern Pennsylvania, where he was a regular with fly rod on the Letort, Silver Spring, and Big Spring. He and at least a few others corresponded with both the *Turf Register* and the *Spirit* about their exploits. It becomes clear from these short reports that there was by 1800 (and presumably earlier) a thriving little group of fly fishers working those streams and also working on their own fly patterns. Gibson occasionally discussed his own choices; he did not believe in a fly for each month, but was likely to use certain flies for certain waters, and he was an avid fly-changer. One of his experiences, reported in the *Turf Register* in 1838, will serve as typical:

> It is nonsense to believe there is a colour for every month [this was still a common notion, since the time of the *Treatyse*]—it is not so—for in fishing three mill pools on the same stream, on the same day, I have found, that to be successful, I had to change my fly and the colour of it at each pool; and in fishing in the same places a few days after, the only fly trout would rise to, was a small grey one, and to such a one they would rise freely in all the pools. In the early part of the season when the trout is poor, he will run at any thing; but towards June he becomes a perfect epicure in his feeding at such time.

We will have more to do with the hatch-matching theories and fly patterns of these early journalists in a later chapter. For the moment I offer this example of their wisdom to point out that they were thinking, creative, flexible fishermen. In fact, even in this case, as quoted above, Gibson was not lecturing; he was reacting to an earlier article reprinted from the *London New Sporting Magazine* in the *Spirit*, in which the author had offered some opinions he disapproved of. What I find most impressive about sporting journalism's transatlantic exchange of views in the nineteenth century is its intensity. Even these first American journalists were intimately acquainted with the fly-fishing theories of the Old World. They did not operate in a vacuum. When, for example, Stewart's *Practical Angler* appeared in 1857, with its codification of upstream fishing, one of the British reviews was reprinted—it was a long review, with full consideration of the upstream-downstream debate—in the *Spirit* before the year was out.

Sometimes the exchange was more than literary. In 1832, Gibson, an army general who lived most of the time in Washington, D.C., received from Sir Charles Vaughn, who had just completed a stint as British ambassador, a large collection of Irish and English flies, along with a large collection of other fishing gear. Porter saw the hoard and raved about its quality in the *Turf Register*.

At other times the interchange was not so straightforward. In several issues of the *New-York Sporting Magazine and Annals of the American and English Turf* in 1833 there appeared an extended essay on fly fishing, quite a careful one in fact, that purported to be by a long-time resident of Scotland who had emigrated to New York. Actually it was just a slightly reworked pirating of Salter's *Angler's Guide*, published in London in 1823. Some editors were desparate for material, and didn't mind doing such things.

But these first periodicals had a huge influence on developing fly fishing. By the time of the Civil War they had introduced fly fishers to the first group of angler-

Title page from one of Frank Forester's very popular books, first published in 1856.

The ornate title page of the *Turf Register* was in the tradition of British sporting publications. Though horses and racing were minor features of this engraving, they actually dominated much of the space in the periodical itself.

celebrities we would produce. Frank Forester, whose real name was Henry William Herbert, was an ex-Britisher who became the most widely read sporting writer before the Civil War. His pen name was given him by one of Porter's brothers when Forester first wrote for the *Turf Register* (just then acquired by Porter) in 1839. Herbert, ironically, was embarrassed to be a sporting writer, hoping to make a greater name for himself in romantic fiction; yet it was only his sporting writing that would give him fame, at last. Charles Lanman, our first great travel writer, frequently appeared in the pages of these journals, and, like Forester, worked much of his article material into a string of tremendously successful books. Captain Jonathan Peel (''Dinks'') wrote the excellent appendix to Forester's *Fish and Fishing* (1859) as well as contributing to the *Spirit*.

There are many such early names. In a sport that is often quite personality oriented, it is surprising that these early characters—William Post Hawes, George Gibson, ''Meadows,'' Alfred Brook, and many others—have been so thoroughly forgotten. They participated in a great exploration, and began the transition from British to American fly-fishing practice. They represented a fusion of old and new, and experienced a tension that later nineteenth-century fishermen would finally resolve. They were at least as effective, and probably much more widely read, in our first sporting periodicals than a few of them would be when they wrote books.

I mustn't give the impression, though, that these early fishing writers offered only advice on techniques. They offered much more. They and their work constituted the

Henry William Herbert, ''Frank Forester,'' the most popular writer in our first generation of sporting journalists.

foundation of sporting society, with its various sub-societies, including a fly-fishing fraternity that would eventually become practically its own subculture in this country. They helped establish a network for the dissemination of information. More than one early correspondent confessed complete ignorance of fly fishing, as did this writer in the *Turf Register* in June of 1830:

> I wish, Mr. Editor, that some of your correspondents would give us an article on fly fishing, with instructions as to the handling of the rod, for I confess that I never saw a trout killed with the fly in my life, although I have killed many a dozen with the worm.

But they taught many other things. They taught sportsmen that they were not alone, that they had common interests. They taught, both by example and by aggressive preaching, that there was such a thing as a sporting code, and that gentlemen did not ignore it.

They taught things that now might (or should) make us a little uncomfortable. Here is Porter on fly fishing:

> Fly fishing has been designated the royal and aristocratic branch of the angler's craft, and unquestionably it is the most difficult, the most elegant, and to men of taste, by myriads of degrees the most exciting and pleasant mode of angling.

"Men of taste" were presumably men of education and class; fly fishing has had snob appeal since the 1600s, and Americans were quick to latch onto that just as they latched onto multiplying reels, silkworm gut, and tapered lines.

But most of the time I see something much more affirmative and hopeful going on in these first decades of American sporting writing. There is a general self awareness appearing, as sportsmen realized their place in the world of sport and in the bigger world as well.

They became aware, for example, that they were looked down upon by some of their British counterparts. The British book *The Angler's Souvenir*, by Paul Fisher (1835), contained this biting dialogue between two British anglers:

> Simpson: "Have you ever seen any American books on angling, Fisher?"
> Fisher: "No. I do not think there are any published. Brother Jonathan is not yet sufficiently civilized to produce anything original on the gentle art."

Brother Jonathan didn't appreciate that kind of talk; remember that in the previous fifty years we had twice been at war with Great Britain, and were not always kindly disposed to the mother country's moods. American anglers had expressed their dissatisfaction with British fishing methods even earlier than 1835. An 1832 correspondent to the *Turf Register*, writing from New Hampshire, complained that English flies were "not good for catching Yankee trout":

> I soon ascertained that the patent English line and *artificial fly* would not do. Our fish are too Republican, or too shrewd, or too stupid, to understand the *science of English* trout fishing. I therefore took the common hook and worm, with a simple line and light sinker, and a rod cut on the spot; they then understood, and we readily caught in a short time, twenty-three fine *brook Trout.*

John J. Brown, a New York tackle dealer who published the workmanlike *American Angler's Guide* in 1845—a book heavily dependent upon British books ranging from Cotton to Hofland—took time to respond to Fisher's taunt in the 1851 edition of his little *Angler's Almanac*, with a hint of democratic sentiment lacking from some more gentlemanly statements of the day about fly fishing:

> From the foregoing extract it would seem that John Bull has a rather poor opinion of Brother Jonathan's literary and piscatorial attainments. Now we would courteously inform Mr. Bull that there are several works on fishing in this country, and that we are so civilized that we do not become gentlemen before we can use the rod—that we commence using the fishing rod at the same time that our schoolmaster begins with the birchen one—that the practice grows with our growth and strengthens with our strength, and though we do not find leisure to give our whole attention to it, that our numbers are *legion*, and among them some quite as scientific in literary and piscatorial attainments as those who angle on the other side of the Big Pond.

Brown's outburst was prophetic; any fishermen who wanted to see Americans establish themselves as virtuosos in the various arts and crafts of fly fishing would be fully satisfied by 1900.

But there were other awarenesses emerging. One was of the fragility of the fly-fishing resource. Even in these first periodicals we hear complaints of wasteful over-fishing and other abuses. A writer in the *New York American* in 1837 objected to "the cruel practice of catching and destroying very small trout, in many cases but one remove from the embroyo," calling the fishermen who did this "pseudo Sports-men." Another correspondent, in the *Spirit* in 1840, protested against catching trout on Long Island in the early spring before they were in good condition, and concluded with what may be the first published recommendation for fly-fishing-only restrictions:

> We wish it were possible to put a stop to *pond* fishing on the Island until May-day, by which time the trout would be active, rosy and in good condition for the table, and then allow them to be taken with the fly only.

Exactly why he recommended the tackle restriction is unclear, but his reasons may just as likely have been social as biological.

Later in the nineteenth century, sportsmen would form an important force in the conservation movement; these were early stirrings, and the growing sporting press was getting its first practice as an important forum and pulpit.

More than any of these more serious concerns, though, the sporting press was a combination of cheerleader and master of ceremonies for what was above all a celebration. Articles and books were full of good feelings toward other sportsmen. There was the occasional dispute or insult, but the vast majority of what was written was warmhearted and brotherly in tone. There was a discovery going on, of fellow sportsmen, of new ideas, of new fishing grounds, of new writings, and of all the other things that go into making fly fishing, in the words of Lee Wulff, "the most social of all the solitary sports." It was under this golden glow of fraternalism and good sportsmanship, guided and promoted by the likes of Porter, Herbert, and all the others, that fly fishing developed a national identity. It was in this good-humored atmosphere that writer after writer extolled the pleasures of fly fishing, starting America's literary development of fly fishing's idyllic image.[1] As one 1837 writer, who would be echoed by hundreds of others either more or less eloquent, put it in the *Spirit*:

> Happy must that man be, the thread of whose life is a "silken line;" and who finds nothing more crooked in existence than the hook upon which he wreathes his fly.

5

All that Art and Taste Can Accomplish

The best rods were formerly imported from England, and made of hazel or hickory, but they were little adapted to our modes of fishing, and have consequently grown into disuse. American rod makers have introduced great improvements in the article within the last ten years, and can now turn out rods which, for workmanship and beauty of finish cannot be surpassed. They are made to suit the tastes of all Anglers, from the single ferruled rod for the novice, at the cost of from $2 to $5, to the more expensive one of the scientific Angler, varying from $5 to $50.

JOHN J. BROWN, *American Angler's Guide* (1845)

In 1825, according to a curious little book called *Long Island Miscellanies* (1847), Grover C. Furman and Garrit Furman were ''both merchants in the city of New York.'' They also seem to have been sportsmen, and the Furman name is associated with fishing and fish culture in New York throughout the nineteenth century. As near as has been determined, one of these men, probably Grover, was the one who received, either by purchase or gift, a fly rod in 1832, inscribed to ''G. C. Furman, New York, 1832.'' It was a gorgeous rod by the standards of any generation, but for some reason he simply put it away. One hundred and thirty-nine years later, after an improbable journey through time—which, notwithstanding trunk lids and screen doors, is the worst enemy of old tackle—it came to rest on the workroom table of The American Museum of Fly Fishing in Manchester, Vermont. It is extraordinary that it survived at all; that it is still more or less brand new is miraculous. As Dick Finlay, then curator of the Museum, put it, ''a computer would be required to determine the odds against its survival over the 140 years of its existence.''[1]

I doubt that it is American built. Were it even ten years younger I would wonder, but 1832 is just a little too soon. Even in the 1830s it appears that fly fishers who wanted the best equipment bought imported tackle from England. I imagine that

32

England was the source of the Furman rod.

It is twelve feet long. It is a five-piece rod, though there is one spare fourth section and three spare tips, a total of nine pieces.

All sections but the tips are stained almost black (because anglers then as now knew better than to wave a flashing rod over spooky fish); the wood is probably hickory or ash. The metal fittings are nickel silver, an alloy also referred to as German silver by many early writers, that being the finest material. The reel seat, about a foot up from the base of the rod, is two simple sleeves (the lower one has the inscription) under which the foot of the reel slipped. There is a narrower ornamental ring of nickel silver an inch or so above the reel seat, and the bottom few inches of the butt are encased in a handsome extended cap of nickel silver as well. The female ferrules, however, are painted as dark as the rod shaft to reduce risk of flash. The male ferrules, which consist of simple sleeves of nickel silver from which protrude a tapered wooden "dowel," are bright nickel silver, but they will be invisible inside the female ferrules when the rod is assembled.

The guides are the traditional ring-and-keeper type, informally called "floppy" or "loose ring" because they swing freely, that being the dominant guide type before the Civil War.

The outfit of the angler in this Currier & Ives print is fairly typical of before the Civil War: high boots, rod with the reel well up from the butt, and a "ground spike" in the butt of the rod so that the rod could be stuck upright in the ground, reducing risk of harm to it.

Perhaps the most famous of all Currier & Ives fly fishing scenes, this one is said to show Daniel Webster fishing a Long Island pond. Published in 1854 and entitled "Catching a Trout/We Hab You Now, Sar," it shows Webster playing a brook trout. Some writers have maintained that this picture is proof of the legendary giant brook trout of Long Island that Webster was long believed to have caught, although the fish in the picture looks no more than two pounds. The picture is now of greatest historical interest for its depiction of angling gear and garb; Webster is fishing a cast of four wet flies, and the fish has taken the tail fly, or "stretcher," that being the fly on the very end of the gut "cast."

The rod has what at first appears to us to be an unwieldy, clumsy shape. The butt is as thick as a pool cue, but it tapers rapidly so that the second section is not much thicker than the butt section of a modern fiberglass rod. From there the taper is gradual and graceful to the tips themselves, which are barely larger than pencil lead. All the lines are clean, and all the pieces are beautifully rounded; modern woodworking technology could not have built this rod with any more craft than its builder did. The tips are all made the same: the thickest forty percent is the same stained wood as the other sections, but the rest is pale orange, probably lancewood, it being the preferred rod-tip material. The lancewood portion is actually two short pieces of lancewood spliced together; such splices were common in those days. Counting the tip-top, the tip section (just a little over two feet long) has seven guides.

Such a rod, loaded with a horsehair or horsehair-and-silk line, could not do as much as a modern rod can; the fly fisher was still often at the mercy of the wind, and the softness of the rod's flex could not push even a heavy wet horsehair line far against a strong breeze. But at twelve feet the rod gave its excellent line-handling opportunities, and made a variety of specialized casts, like predecessors of our roll

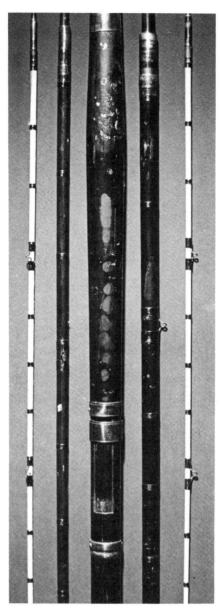

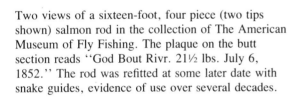

Two views of a sixteen-foot, four piece (two tips shown) salmon rod in the collection of The American Museum of Fly Fishing. The plaque on the butt section reads "God Bout Rivr. 21½ lbs. July 6, 1852." The rod was refitted at some later date with snake guides, evidence of use over several decades.

cast, a pleasure. An experienced caster could work a trout stream thoroughly and with a grace we might envy using such a rod, and does not need our sympathy.

Certainly only a small portion of American fly fishers had such fine equipment. Not only would there have been cheaper grades of tackle available, there was always the choice of making your own. As our best modern casters, such as Lefty Kreh, have shown, with a little work on your timing you can cast a fly line with almost anything from a broomstick to a car aerial. The home rod builder could make himself a rod of twelve to fifteen feet from a judiciously trimmed and tapered stick. It might not have the smoothness of the best English rods, and it might lack their cosmetic appeals, but at that length it was more than good enough to push out a trout-fishing cast of thirty feet or so, and that was about all he needed. With a little extra effort he could attach simple metal ferrules, or, as was often done back then, the sections could be spliced together. Splicing, now an almost completely forgotten craft in rod building, was often the most common way of attaching the sections. In its simplest

A fly rod splice, showing the fitting together of the two bevelled sections prior to wrapping. Such spliced rods were commonly assembled at the beginning of the season and left mounted until the fishing was finished in the fall.

form, it consisted of joining two sections by giving them, instead of ferrules, matching bevels at their ends that when pressed together joined them into one smooth piece that was then wrapped with thread, often for the season.

By the early 1800s, reels were an accepted part of fly fishing but were usually quite simple. Opinions differed on what was best, but there was an undertone that has never changed. Then, as now, at least a few writers realized that a fly reel was more than a convenient storage spool for extra line. William Schreiner summed up that realization in his *Schreiner's Sporting Manual* in 1841:

> An indifferent reel is worse than useless, and only calculated to spoil your sport and temper; a penurious spirit has encouraged the manufacture of many such, and heretofore almost excluded a good article from our stores; but I am happy to inform my readers, experience has wrought a great change, and that none but the best are now good enough for the majority of purposes.

Though I suspect that Schreiner was overstating the part about the ''penurious spirit'' it was true that about that time it became easier for Americans to get top-quality fly-fishing tackle. It became easier mostly because they began building it themselves.

Modern master fly tier Poul Jorgensen tied these replicas of four early American trout fly patterns given by George Washington Bethune in his 1847 edition of *The Complete Angler*. From the left, they are a dropper fly (brown wing, red floss body, black hackle); a palmer (black hackle, black mohair body); a white moth (white owl wing, white ostrich herl body, white hackle); and a red palmer (seal's fur body, ''red'' hackle). *Courtesy of The American Museum of Fly Fishing.*

In the ads for tackle in the June 3, 1832 issue of *Spirit of the Times and Life in New York*, four of the various sporting dealers specifically offered tackle. "Abr'm Brower" of 230 Water Street, carried not only a broad selection but an impressive volume:

> Grass, Gut silk, and Hair lines of English and American manufacture . . . A large assortment of Canton and Calcutta, Bamboo Fishing rods with or without Joints, for Fly and other fishing . . . Also steel Fish hooks and a large assortment of fine Limerick hooks; several thousand Savannah canes, for fishing and reed making, all of which may be had wholesale and retail . . . N.B. Just received—a large quantity of superior, fresh Silk-worm guts, which he offers for sale on the most reasonable terms.

T. W. Horsfield, No. 52 Fulton Street, had "Trout, Herring and Salmon Flies . . . Hooks fastened on gut, gimp, grass, hair silk and flax lines, gut leaders, a variety of artificial baits, such as shrimp, Minnow, &c." Horsfield had some unusual items for that time, when a great many Americans still believed that salmon would not take flies in the New World. Brower and Horsfield were joined in those advertisements by Charles R. Taylor, 1½ Maiden Lane, and a man named Lewis at No. 3 Wall Street, but the ads in any one periodical do not give a complete representation. We also know of Samuel Bradley, who opened a shop in Boston around 1800 (and whose business, under various owners and names, would last more than 175 years), and Andrew Clerk, another Boston shopowner who claimed an establishment date of 1820

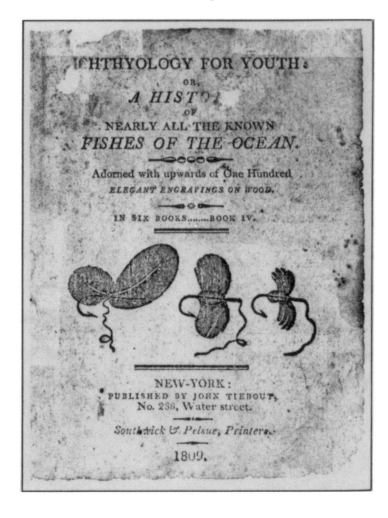

Perhaps the earliest known American representation of the steps in tying a fly, published in a children's book in 1809 and taken from an older British work. *Courtesy of The American Museum of Fly Fishing.*

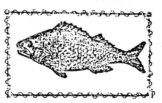

FISHING TACKLE

Of all Sorts, at the Old Experienced TACKLE SHOP kept by

GEORGE R. LAWTON,
SUCCESSOR TO
EDWARD POLE,

No. 32, Great Dock-ſtreet, between Front and Second-ſtreets, near the Drawbridge, Philadelphia. Where may be had a large complete and general aſſortment of all kinds of FISHING TACKLE, for the uſe of either Sea or River, viz.

FLY, trolling, bottom bag, and all other ſorts and ſizes of fiſhing rods, either hollow or ſolid, plain or ringed,
Plain and Multiplying Braſs Wheels,
Horſe hair, ſilk, hardeſt, ſilk-worms gut, Indian Graſs, Hempen, Cotton, Layout, and Angling Lines,
Deep-ſeas, for Sea or River Fiſhing, ready fitted,
Trimmers for Pike Fiſhing,
Cork Floats, a variety with either Gooſe or Swan Quills,
Artificial Flies, Moths, Hackles, Minnew, Chubb, Graſshoppers, Dilberries, Frogs, Mice, Birds, Cadds, &c. for Trout and other Fiſhing.
Beſt Silk-worms Gut, Indian-graſs and Weed.
Leads of various Patterns, for Black Point and other

Fiſhing,
Beſt Kirby and Common Fiſhing Hooks of every Size, either Looſe or ready Hung, on Silk, Hair, Silk-worms Gut, Indian-Graſs, or Weed,
Double and Treble, Spring and Dead Snap Pike, and Eel-hooks wired,
Box, and Plain Salmon, Jack, Pearch, and Trout-ſwivels,
4, 8, 10, & 12, Stave Round and Flat Pocket Reels, ready fitted,
White and Yellow Gimp, for Pike Fiſhing,
Fiſhing Baſkets and Apreas,
Dram Bottles and Flaſks, covered with Leather,
Caſting Minnew, Landing, Scoop, and Crab Nets, &c. &c.

Carolina reeds for reed makers or fiſhing rods by the thouſand or ſingle one.
Allowance made to country ſtore keepers and others purchaſing quantities to ſell again.

Any orders from town or country, will be as carefully attended to, and as duly executed as if perſonally preſent.
All kinds of Fiſhing Tackle, repaired and made to any pattern.
From an experience of upwards of thirty years, and the complete and general aſſortment of Fiſhing Tackle kept at this Shop, it is expected that purchaſers can be ſupplied better and on more reaſonable terms, than any other ſhop in the United States, as he always has a large ſtock on hand.
At the ſame place may alſo be had a general aſſortment of

FOWLING TACKLE.

N. B. Gentlemen going on parties of pleaſure, in the Fowling or Fiſhing way, either to Black Point, Sea or River, or any other place, may be completely furniſhed with any kind of Fiſhing or Fowling Tackle, at the ſhorteſt notice.
N. B. Ready money for any quantity of Carolina Reeds, White Horſe Tails, Silk Worms Gut, &c. &c.

Lawton was successor to Edward Pole, who was selling fishing tackle in Philadelphia in the 1770s and 1780s. This advertisement was attached to an invoice dated 1803 and made out to Merriwether Lewis, just then outfitting an expedition with William Clark to explore the upper Missouri River and points west. *Courtesy of Gary Saindon.*

(and would later be absorbed by Abbey & Imbrie, the business lasting more than a century). John J. Brown, now mostly remembered as the author of one of the first and most successful American fishing books, his *The American Angler's Guide* (1845), opened his tackle shop at 122 Fulton Street in New York about 1845, changing his location a few times before disappearing from city directories after 1858. Brown offered a full line of tackle. Imagine entering his shop and browsing among just these items he advertised in 1845:

FLIES

Trout, perch, pickerel, basse, salmon and herring Flies, of every size and description, on gut, hair, flax and gimp.

SQUIDS, BAITS, &c.

Pearl, ivory, bone and tin Squids, of various sizes and shapes, for Blue-Fish, Basse, Pickerel, Salmon, Black-Basse, and other kinds of Angling; artificial Minnows, Grasshoppers, Beetles, Frogs, Mice, Shrimp, Wasps, &c. &c.

Notice that he sold flies for ''basse,'' and lures for both ''Basse'' and ''Black-Basse.'' ''Basse'' were probably what we call striped bass. Fly fishing, already, was being used for quite an assortment of fish.

But when it came to actual tackle making rather than tackle selling, there are two other names that stand above all these others in the last decades before the Civil War. One is Conroy, and the other is Welch, both of New York.

Conroy and Welch weren't the only two making tackle in the 1840s, but they were the most renowned; they both were able to match in quality and appearance the 1832 rod now at the Museum in Vermont, and therein lies one of early tackle making's most interesting tales. Mary Kelly, a leading tackle-history researcher, seems to have first pieced together this story from the pages of the periodicals, so I will give it in her words. It is revealing, I think, in showing how fast American craftsmen moved into tackle making and made it their own:

> There was quite a stir in the *Spirit* in 1849 about who could make the better rod— cost & time being no object. The correspondents on the subject finally made a wager. Judges were selected, and Ben Welch and John Conroy were instructed to begin building. Eventually the rods were completed. Presented to the judges, but without markings, it was a blind test. After careful study and much testing, Welch's rod was considered superior. That surprised many, Conroy's reputation at the time being that of America's premier maker, his rods sought after by every serious and/or wealthy angler (Conroy also had snob appeal).
>
> Ben Welch, on the other hand, had a reputation as turning out less expensive, less desirable rods. However, Welch was considered an excellent to superior maker of trolling rods, and also made reels.[2]

In tracing the development of Conroy's fame we are led, inevitably and instructively, back to the hero of the previous chapter, William T. Porter. Porter, a leading arbiter of good taste in all things sporting, had published more or less constant references to Conroy's tackle in the *Spirit* in the 1840s.

It is always difficult to judge statements in the sporting periodicals (of any day) about the quality of one manufacturer's tackle compared to that of another. Friendships and commercial arrangements often interfere with objectivity, leaving the reader unsure of how much to believe. It is true, though, that Conroy was almost always praised, as in these comments by pioneer hatchery developer Theodatus Garlick in 1857:

> The very best of fishing tackle of every variety, can be procured from Mr. Conroy, New York. His rods are unequalled, and so I may say of all his fishing tackle. Very many rods are sold as Conroy's which are not of his make. I would therefore advise persons wishing good rods and tackle, to make their purchase of Mr. Conroy himself, and they will not be disappointed.

And, for contrast, just to show that not everyone is ever happy all the time, here is a dissenting opinion from a fisherman who made a trip to the Adirondacks (Hamilton County was then the destination most in vogue in that region) of New York in 1854:

> Tuesday, June 7th. We had tolerably good fishing today and it is pleasant to stay here. I may as well note that all the tackle we have had from Conroy's is most unreliable; the hooks miserably secured and the leaders of irregular sized gut.

All that this disagreement may mean (unless somehow Garlick was right and the gentleman in the Adirondacks had bought some bogus Conroy tackle) is that fishermen often disagree. But in another way, the rods and reels of that time were not seen the way modern fly fishers see their gear. The lines were not as solidly drawn between the various kinds of fishing as happens now. The differences can be seen in both rods and reels.

Neither rods nor reels were quite so specifically defined as they are now. A twelve-foot rod that was used for trout might similarly be used for light baitfishing or perhaps even trolling. An eighteen-foot rod that was used for salmon might also be used with metal lures for bluefishing or taking striped bass. It was this flexibility that brought about one of the period's most successful rod designs. The idea was not original with Porter, but he and Conroy were responsible for design and production of a sort of rod for all seasons. Porter announced it in the *Spirit* in 1843, and the text was reprinted in Brinley's biography of Porter in 1860 and elsewhere later:

> We do not deem it necessary to have a rod for trout, bass and salmon fishing; we have had for years half a dozen excellent rods, but very rarely use but one for any kind of rod-fishing; indeed, the two largest bass we ever caught were taken at the same instant with an extremely light and fragile London fly-rod, not heavier than a tandem-whip. Conroy has recently got up a new *general rod*, from a pattern we furnished him eighteen months since, which answers every purpose, either for fly, salmon, bass, black or pickerel fishing. He has immortalized the writer of this article by giving it the name of "Porter's General Rod." The idea of the rod in question was suggested by circumstances occurring in the use of a very fine one, made expressly for us some years since, by our venerable old friend Leutner. It has four joints for bass or pickerel, and five for trout or salmon fishing, with three extra tips. It can be put together as to make a rod either ten or sixteen feet in length; you may make out of it a light hand-rod for fly-fishing, or a heavy, powerful rod, sufficiently strong to play a thirty-pound salmon or bass, at the end of a hundred yards of line! Instead of rings on one side, "Porter's General Rod" has fluted guides on both sides, through which the line can play; the sockets of the joints are double instead of single, that end of the joint fitting into the double sockets having double ferrules around it. There is no difficulty in taking this rod apart from the swelling of the wood when wet, while at the same time you may use it all day without tightening the joints; it can never get out of order with fair usage. Its weight is about three pounds only; the smaller joints are of lancewood, and the ferrules, guides, tips, sockets, etc., are of German silver. Conroy informed us a few days since that he had more orders for this rod than for all others added together.

Fluted guides, later called "trumpet guides," were small tubes with the ends widened like the flaring bell of a trumpet. A double ferrule was a new development in rods; it was a ferrule much like those on modern bamboo rods, with a metal sleeve the size of the rod section to which was attached the "male" portion (the part that entered the other ferrule), another sleeved section. It left no wooden dowel exposed, and was much more waterproof, as Porter suggested. Later in the century Hiram Leonard would perfect this waterproof ferrule, but the idea was older than Leonard.

This generalized approach to rods was applied to reels as well. The reel of America and England in the late 1700s and early 1800s was attached to all sorts of rods; it was a versatile, unspecialized piece of equipment. A big one, with a capacity of two hundred or more yards of heavy line, might yield and retrieve line on a salmon river, a trout lake, and a saltwater bay in the course of a season.

America's most important contribution to tackle development in the period between 1800 and 1860 was certainly its reels. The most renowned reel builders were the famous Kentucky watchmakers who, starting with George Snyder before 1810, applied the precision and craft of watchmaking to the production of what many consider the best reels in history. These reels were almost always multipliers, and it seems likely that the application of the watchmaker's craft to reels probably had a lot to do with multipliers increasing in popularity; they have never entirely escaped the stigma of mechanical unreliability, but a good many prominent fly fishers, including John Brown, George Washington Bethune, and Jerome V. C. Smith, were devoted to them. Others thought them an abomination, and such disagreements raged over other subjects as well: Should there be a click? Should the reel be located a foot or two up the rod, right at the end of the butt section, or moved from place to place to suit the circumstances? (Reels were moving to the ends of at least some fly fisher's rods in both England and America by the 1830s.) Snyder, Milam, Meek, and other Kentucky builders have probably gotten too exclusive credit for the improvement of American reels. East Coast builders, including Conroy and Welch, were also building excellent reels of great beauty and durability. Ironically, though the tradition of finely machined multiplying reels would continue through every subsequent generation of American fly fishers, from the Vom Hofes of the late 1800s to the Bogdans of today, the main direction of fly fishing for most anglers would indeed be the simpler reel. What is now considered the first patented American fly reel was William Billinghurst's 1859 single-action skeleton frame model that by its construction announced two rules that would become fundamental in fly reels for a century: it must be light, and it must be well ventilated so the line can dry.[3] But Billinghurst's reel (which has been characterized as looking like something that fell off a birdcage) is almost of another era than the one we are considering in this chapter. The pre-Civil War fly fisher was still a generalist. His rod and reel did not limit him to one kind of fishing, but left him independent of the limitations of any one style of fishing. His sense of independence was no doubt increased, judging from the patriotic pronouncements he made in print, by virtue of his tackle now being American made and, in a heartwarming number of cases, even better made, than British equivalents.

Fifteen years after G. C. Furman acquired the lovely fly rod described at the beginning of this chapter, Daniel Webster wrote a letter to his son, which said, in part:

> I found in the gun-room an unopened box. Nobody knew whence it came, nor exactly when. It was found to contain the most splendid angling apparatus you can imagine. There are three complete rods, all silver mounted, with my name engraved; beautiful reels, and books of flies and hooks, and quantities of other equipments. The maker's card was in the box containing the books, &c. He is Mr. Welch, of New York.

It was in June, and Webster was an ardent fisherman, so his letter to Welch was as excitedly grateful as it could be:

> Dear Sir,—
>   On my arrival here, on the 8th instant, I found an unopened box, whose contents no one knew; nor could I ascertain whence it came, nor, with any accuracy, the date of its reception.
>   You know what the box contained, and can therefore well judge of my surprise, as I found no explanation, and no clue, except your card, and a short memorandum in writing. Such a rich and elegant apparatus for angling, I am sure, I never saw, either at home or abroad. The rods and reels are certainly of exquisite workmanship, and richly mounted; the flies truly beautiful, and the contents of the books ample,

abundant, and well selected. Poor Isaak Walton! Little did he think, when moving along by the banks of the rivers and brooks of Staffordshire, with his cumbrous equipments, that any unworthy disciple of his would ever be so gorgeously fitted out, with all that art and taste can accomplish for the pursuit of his favorite sport!

It was not quite the miracle of the Furman rod's survival, but it was still a matter of great excitement at the Museum when in 1977 one of those three rods also surfaced, this time in the hands of a Webster descendant in Virginia. It was not a fly rod, but a twelve-foot, heavy four-piece rod probably made for trolling or heavy saltwater fishing. The tip was missing, but the other three pieces had their ferrules, all a soft burnished silver, worn smooth from years of handling. Webster, unlike Furman, did not let his rod gather dust in storage. But for all its worn fittings, scratches, and other signs of hard use, it is still obviously the product of great craft; Webster's excitement was justified, and so was ours when, after two years of discussion and some hasty fund-raising, the rod and leather case arrived in Manchester.

Taking the butt section (I did not dream of mounting the other sections on it) in my hands, one gripping it firmly below the reel seat (with its elegant script engraving, "Daniel Webster, Marshfield, Mafs.") and one above, I was chilled by the thought of who else had held it thus, 142 years earlier. It was easy to see that Webster and his many anonymous companions on America's rich fishing waters had every reason to love and treasure their tackle as much as we do today.

The base of the reel seat on the Daniel Webster rod in the collection of The American Museum of Fly Fishing. *From a photo by C.M. Haller.*

6

The Fly-Fishing Exploration

This is to be my last letter from the Mississippi valley, and my passion for the gentle art of angling, will not allow me to leave the great river without recounting a few fishing paragraphs, as mementoes of my journey thus far.
CHARLES LANMAN, "in my canoe, July, 1846,"
from *A Summer in the Wilderness* (1848)

The quickness with which fly fishing spread to the farthest corners of North America has always seemed to me to give the lie to the notion that only a few gentlemen-sportsmen on the East Coast were interested in fly fishing. There were several types of fly-fishing explorers, and indeed the gentlemen were one of them, but they were accompanied, even preceded, in their explorations by others.

One group was the settlers themselves, those people who first moved into a region. Like their ancestors who fished the waters near the Colonial communities, these people often mixed recreation with subsistence fishing and were as likely as anyone else to be fond of flies. John Brown, whom some later writers looked down upon as a "poor tackle maker without classical education or social position," was a champion of fly fishing as being a relatively simple pastime accessible to anyone. In his *Angler's Almanac* for 1851 he commented on the availability of fly fishing to all people:

In the months of April and May the raftmen and lumbermen from the Delaware are seen in the fishing tackle stores of New York selecting, with the eyes of professors of the art, the red, black, and gray hackle flies, which they use with astonishing effect on the wooded rivers of Pennsylvania. Those brothers of the angle who have never cast a fly are advised to pluck up courage and at once do so; it will add greatly to their enjoyment. Take our word for it, less skill is necessary to success than is generally imagined and pretended by fly fishers.

Talk like that certainly did not endear Brown to all the other writers who were just then busily asserting that fly fishing was, in the words of William Schreiner,

43

"justly esteemed the *beau ideal* of angling." As it turns out, though, it is not this local element that gives us most of our early accounts; they give us few, in fact. The exploration was conducted, in print at least, by other groups.

In the early decades of the 1800s, especially the years between 1830 and 1870, the traveling sportsmen were often the explorers. These people reported on their sporting outings with such regularity that it would almost be possible, by a statistical analysis of the fishing trips they reported in the periodicals and books, to draw a series of maps showing the outward progress of popular fly-fishing waters.

The movement began, as we have seen, in the waters nearest the Colonial towns. It is easy to envy the angler who spent his days on the ponds around Boston back when you could have a pond to yourself, or wandered the shady banks of Arch Brook, which Hermann Kessler, for many years art director of *Field & Stream*, tells me, "ran south through a wooded area which is now Central Park, is flowing through a sub-basement of an Episcopal Church on East 50th or 51st Street, and continues underground until it empties into the East River." There are still reports that a few trout hang on somehow in these subterranean streams, but it's their ancestors I think of.

The first American fly fishers worked their way out from the settlements. By the first decade of the nineteenth century they were secure in the limestone country of southwestern Pennsylvania, the streams and ponds of Long Island, and the waters near various settlements in New England. Their Canadian counterparts were equally well established in many northern waters, including some requiring considerable effort to reach.

It would take—and would be worth, I think—an entire book to describe this exploration in detail. What is important about it is not who fished where first, though that is always intriguing, but how quickly new waters became well-known waters. Improvements in transportation through the nineteenth and twentieth centuries, especially the locomotive in the second half of the 1800s and the automobile after about 1910, quickly made fly fishers mobile enough to fish quite far from their homes; an angler in 1860 could range many times as far from home in search of weekend sport as could an angler in 1790.

Consider New York. This report on fishing near the city appeared in the *American Turf Register* in August of 1838, and it pretty well describes the proportions of fishermen heading in each direction in a typical year in the 1820s, 1830s, and 1840s:

> Notwithstanding the present month is emphatically the shooting season in this section, we doubt if the proportion of anglers is not greater by twenty to one. There are hundreds upon hundreds of our citizens scattered about the country within 200 miles of us, and probably there is not a brook, river, or pond, within that circle, in which they have not wet a line. The largest proportion are whipping their flies over the placid ponds of Long Island, where the run of trout this season is of unusually fine size. Two or three parties, made up principally of "old hands," have lately made a descent upon the rivers of Sullivan and Montgomery counties, in this state, with immense success. The Williewemauk, Calikoon, and Beaver-kill, are three of the finest trout streams in this country; they are comparatively unknown to city anglers, and are less fished than others of like pretensions within our knowledge. The trout are large, very numerous, and of the most delicious flavour. The rivers referred to lie between 30 and 60 miles back of Newburgh. To reach them from town, take any of the North River steamers to Newburgh, and the stage to Monticello, where you will find some good trouting. Five miles farther on, at Liberty, you will reach Big Beaver-kill. Make your headquarters at Mrs. Darby's, and you will be sure to find excellent accommodations, and capital fishing. You will reach the Williewemauk, seven miles further on, where Mrs. Purvis will take very good care of you.

"Trout Fishing in Sullivan County, N.Y.," the frontis woodcut from John Brown's *American Angler's Guide* (1845).

The Catskill streams were just far enough away from the city that they did not receive serious attention from numbers of fly fishers for several decades after closer waters, such as on Long Island, were popular. Like the Poconos in Pennsylvania, they were not popular as long as anglers could find plenty of good fishing much closer to home. By 1850, access to the Catskills was greatly improved, as reported in this communication to the *Spirit* on June 22, 1850:

> Beaver Kill, flowing into the Pepacton branch of the Delaware, formerly reached after a fatiguing journey via Newburg and Monticello, is now easy of access, being within six hours of Chehocton (or Hancock), the most beautiful village on the line of the Erie road. And still nearer to that town, crossed by the new plank road leading to Walton, is the Cadosea, a brook wherein Mr. N. P. Willis took a hundred trout (or less) in three hours (or more) last June.

By that time the railroad had opened the great New York fishing country west of the Hudson and given fly fishers access to "a hundred little brooks and 'kills' bearing unpronouncable Indian and Dutch names," and showing just how quickly transportation improvements could open up a fishing country.

But it was Long Island that attracted them first, and inspired Frank Forester to describe it as "the Utopia of New York sportsmen."

> The natural formation of Long Island is not indeed such, that we should look to it, if strangers to its qualities in this respect, with any high degree of expectation as a mother of trout streams; and yet it is probably surpassed in this particular by no region of the world.

Forester proves, in that statement, why he is no longer regarded as an especially accurate journalist, but Long Island fishing was in fact very good. Though recent research has pretty much discounted the old tale of Daniel Webster catching a sea-run trout variously reported at between nine and fourteen pounds, there were five and six pounders, brook trout that grew fat in the ponds of the small mills that were built on several streams, and others that spent some of their time feeding and growing in the salt water off the mouths of the streams.[1] The sporting press sang the praises of the ponds at Smithtown, Babylon, Islip, Fireplace, Patchogue, and so on, and the names of the favorite fishing hosts, such as Snedicor and Carman, were household words for fishermen. In the 1830s, the trip was made by coach; yet another New York Furman, Gabriel, described a delightful three-day 110-mile journey in 1835 with stops to "look at the trout stream filled with the speckled beauties." By the mid-1840s the same journey could be made by rail in a few hours, at the breakneck pace of thirty miles an hour.

It seems curious to us now, but in the 1840s and 1850s, when the Catskills were at last attracting serious sporting attention from fly fishers, another area of New York, the Adirondacks, was receiving much more press coverage in New York City though it was twice as far away. I suppose there were several reasons for this. For one, it was just about as easy to get there, up the well-settled Hudson Valley and the Mohawk to the southern edge of the great recreational area. For another, the Adirondacks were relatively unspoiled in the early 1840s, while the Catskills were already heavily logged. For another there is the imponderable element of personal preference; the travelers who sought out the Adirondacks, and who eventually made it the most famous vacation destination in Victorian America, were influenced by more than desire for good sport; they were influenced by social fashions and Victorian esthetics. The Adirondacks, with their placid, wild-yet-safe settings (involving lakes more than streams), became by the 1880s the home of hundreds of high-cost lodges, public and private. The Adirondack wilderness struck a stronger chord in the American traveler's psyche than did the Catskills. Just as later the Catskills would come to dominate much of fly-fishing writing, the preeminence of the Adirondacks in the 1850 to 1880 period is interesting but it does not prove much about the quality of the fishing or the skill of the fishermen. In all ages, we fly fishers are ruled mostly by the fashions of the times.

The fishing exploration of that great region now mostly enclosed within Adirondack Park in northern New York moved fast. Remember a few chapters back when Sir William Johnson established himself on the southern edge of the Adirondacks? An 1852 diary of a fishing trip to the same area, published in the *Spirit* on March 4, 1854, observed that even that outpost had been bypassed already:

> As we go North it becomes more mountainous. We pass the "fish house" on our way, so called from its being a sporting retreat of Sir William Johnson's in the olden times. It is on the banks of the Sacondaga river. There are a few trout here now, and the deer have gone long ago.

Austin Hogan believed that George Washington Bethune, one of the period's most literate and well-read anglers (and editor of the famous 1847 edition of the *Compleat Angler*) may have been fly fishing at Piseco Lake as early as 1836; Bethune was in any case one of the founders of the celebrated and lionized Piseco Lake Trout Club whose doings were reported in books and periodicals in the 1840s and 1850s. But Hogan gives Porter, once again moving through early-nineteenth-century sport like a fatherly guide to the whole movement, credit for starting "the first onrush" to the Adirondacks of sportsmen. Like Long Island before it, the Adirondack region would soon be well known, and its chief destinations, such as Piseco, the Saranac Lakes, Raquette Lake, Tupper Lake, Blue Mountain Lake, and dozens of others entered the language of American fly fishing.

As so often happens, there was actually a series of waves, or "onrushes," to the Adirondacks. The most famous of all occurred immediately following the publication of William Henry Harrison Murray's little book of stories, *Adventures in the Wilderness* in 1869. Murray's portrayals of camp life and sporting adventure attracted huge numbers of new outdoor enthusiasts, invalids seeking better health, and various other crowd-joiners just as it brought groans of despair from those who had been

By the late 1800s the Adirondacks were the home of many luxury resorts, such as this one on Lake George. Fishing was only one of many pastimes for visitors, many of whom preferred the gambling casinos and boating parties.

enjoying the relative isolation of the region for decades and dreaded the flood of what the press called "Murray's fools." But by the time of Murray's book the best waters were known and mapped in the minds of many fly fishers, and the exploratory quest of fly fishing had moved on.

Boston fly fishers were attracted to the Adirondacks, but also had easy access to many other waters. Cape Cod was a Long Island-equivalent for early-nineteenth-century Bostonians, and though the correspondents from there complained that the streams were too overgrown for fly fishing on the scale of that practiced on Long Island, the streams and ponds of the Cape did yield much good sport to fly fishers in the 1830s and 1840s. It was the same fish—the brook trout—and it was often as large.

Though it isn't possible to tell for certain that he used flies, it is Massachusetts that gives us an extremely early fishing guide, one John Dennison, known locally as Johnny Trout. Dennison, according to the *Turf Register* (August 1832), had "been a trout fisher for twenty-odd years, and has probably killed more trout than any one person in the United States. He has been and is employed, by the frequenters of the trout streams from Boston and all parts of the country, to show them the sly places where the fish congregate, and also to catch them a mess, when all their exertions have failed . . ." Dennison's home waters are not given, but I suspect from the context of the article that he lived somewhere near Cape Cod Bay rather than inland from Boston.

Fishing writing was frequently guilty of a rather joyous boosterism in those days. There was always interest in promoting tourism and related business, but there was

An 1870 illustration from *Harper's New Monthly Magazine* showing a crowd of "Murray's Fools" boarding a steamer for the Adirondacks in search of adventure and good health. The man in front appears to be reading a book, probably intended by the illustrator to be Murray's *Adventures in the Wilderness* (1869).

perhaps even more than now a conviction among fly fishers that each lived in the best fishing region of all, and if not the best then the most underappreciated. A November 1838 correspondent to the *Turf Register* proclaimed the glories of the Lancaster, New Hampshire, area, and in the process gives us a notion of how continuous the sport-fishing effort was along the East Coast:

> Fishing and sporting parties are almost as common in this section as they are at Nahant, Boston, or any where along the coast, from the Gulf of St. Lawrence to the "low and mucky ground" at New Orleans. And in all the world over—(pray back up the asservation, ye anglers,) in all the world over there is not a better place for the purpose than this country affords.

A debate between this correspondent and Frank Forester, who earlier said the same thing for Long Island, would have been interesting. But, though already in the 1840s there were stirrings of alarm over the damage to trout waters from dams, logging, netting, pollution, and simply overfishing by greedy sportsmen, the fishing was still in most places outstanding, especially from the viewpoint of modern anglers.

Maine was likewise well known and promoted by the 1840s, when a correspondent to the *Turf Register* echoed the New Hampshire enthusiast just quoted:

> In Maine, there is noble trouting in the whole month of July, as well as in that of June, and in part of May. Three kinds of the genus *Salmo* are caught there: the large Salmon-trout, that have given Sebago Pond a high celebrity, the brook trout, haunting every stream that ripples among the fine old woodlands and turfy meadows of that yet only half-reclaimed wild territory, and the fine species which is found in the large sea-pools that are formed by the flow of the tide, on the margin of old Ocean, in the neighborhood of Saco and Kennebunk.

He went on to caution the newcomer, however, about expecting to find good fishing just anywhere; advice from experienced anglers was important.

Of all of Maine's trout (the state did not yet have smallmouth bass, those arriving in 1869), the giants of the Rangeley region have most often caught the imagination of fly fishers. The fish were probably caught on flies as early as the 1840s, but came to prominence shortly after the Civil War, when George Shepard Page brought several five- to eight-pound fish to New York, where after a good bit of skeptical quarreling by fishing writers the fish were scientifically identified as brook trout after all. In 1864 Samuel Farmer, who may have been using bait, caught sixteen fish weighing a total of 100 pounds. Of course few fishermen then returned their fish, so the trout-rush to the Rangeleys in the 1870s and 1880s had much the same results it had elsewhere. But for the big-fish stillwater angler of that time, the Rangeleys must have been heaven.

As a more or less irrelevant but enjoyable aside, I offer a great American regional fish story from the Rangeleys, this one preserved by Austin Hogan. Hogan, who, along with A. I. Alexander and Samuel Lambert, researched the region well, tells of John Danforth, a Rangeley guide who claimed to make "trout knock themselves out by casting his fly to fish under thin glare ice."[2]

The Atlantic salmon seems to have been the most perplexing of the popular fly-caught species, because for a long time there was great confusion over it. There was confusion over its range (John Brown, who almost certainly had never been west of the Alleghenies, said it was common in the Mississippi), but there was even more confusion over whether or not it would take the fly at all. In January 1832, in the *Turf Register*, William Porter made a rare miscue in commenting on sporting conditions in the New World. He announced that fly fishing for salmon had not been successful:

> Fishing for the salmon has not, we believe, been a successful sport in our country. We have heard of a few attempts in the waters of Maine, where this fish is so abundant, but of no success. Those with whom we have conversed on the subject, could not recount a single instance in which this noble fish had been known to rise and strike at a fly.

As we saw in Chapter 2, salmon were taken on flies in the late 1700s, and were still being taken in Canada when Porter wrote. What makes Porter's comments so strange is that in his own magazine, the year before, a correspondent had reported that "they have been taken in the Penobscot, about 18 miles from the sea, and, I presume, may be taken in any of the rivers of Maine."

But of course salmon fishing was much more widespread than that. As it had been in the 1700s, so it was in the 1800s—the leading salmon fishers of the north were British officers and tourists. They had not missed the opportunities, and were fully aware of the great sport in the streams entering the North Shore of the St. Lawrence. In 1816 and 1817 the traveler Frederic Tolfrey visited Canada, a visit reported in his important but largely neglected book *The Sportsman in Canada* (1845). Shortly after his arrival at Quebec he fell in with a charming sportsman, a Major Browne, whom he discovered was already "as well acquainted with the habits and peculiarities of the Yankee salmon as if he had amphibiously been born amongst them" from many years of experience. Major Browne's tackle was such an eye-opening experience to Tolfrey that his account of it deserves quoting:

"First Salmon of the Season in the Hospital Pool," an engraving from Tolfrey's *The Sportsman in Canada* (1845). *Courtesy of David B. Ledlie.*

Whereupon the kind-hearted Major inducted me to a *grenier* at the top of his domicile, a long and lofty apartment—three garrets rolled into one in fact—and here did I behold what in the plenitude of my ignorance I conceived to be some mis-shapen hop-poles, but which the Major dignified by the name of "salmon rods." He took one down from its exalted position, and placed it in my hands. To say the truth, it was an unsightly tool, but all doubts as to its excellence were soon dissipated the moment I poised and tried it; and from the hasty opinion I was enabled to form by a cursory handling of this gigantic pole, I was convinced it was a rod of great power, yet so perfect were the proportions that it appeared to be under perfect command, and to possess all the qualifications of a smaller and a lighter one . . .

Having allowed me due time for examination, the worthy Major first broke the silence:—"That rod, M. Tolfrey, is the *na plus ultra* of salmon-rods. I made it myself, and a better never threw a line: you will perceive that there are only two joints (barring the whalebone top) in it, and they are spliced in the middle. This is the rale secret for making a rod throw a fly dacently. Your dandy London rods, with their four or five joints and brass sockets and ferules, are of no use here: they are mighty pretty to look at, but you will find that they snap like a reed with a lively salmon at the end of 'em in the Jacques Cartier River."

It wasn't strictly true, of course, that London tackle wouldn't hold up. Lieutenant Campbell Hardy, Royal Artillery, who wrote *Sporting Adventures in the New World; or Days and Nights of Moose-Hunting in The Pine Forests of Acadia* (1855), warned against using the local tackle:

Rods and lines are always best brought from England: those procurable at Halifax or St. John's being, though strong and serviceable, roughly made, and the rods liable to warp. The salmon rod should be, at least, eighteen feet in length; of its pliability I will say nothing, as every angler has his own taste in this matter . . .

Reels are best purchased in England, those purchased across the Atlantic being generally loosely-made, catchpenny articles, hastily put together for sale in British America, by the Yankees.

Sounds like the lieutenant encountered some of the cheap reels so many American writers complained about too, and did not see the work of Welch or his fellow craftsmen.

There is a small shelf of these British accounts of salmon fishing, and they are one of the least appreciated literary legacies of nineteenth-century angling. Walter Henry's *Events of a Military Life* was made up in part of material that had appeared in the *Turf Register*. The book was first published in 1843, and it tells of his years with the British 66th Regiment, with whom he was surgeon. He first took Canadian salmon on a fly in 1830 on the Malbaie, a river on the North Shore ninety miles from Quebec. Henry, like the others, did not fish alone but in company with locals; the fishing was well known and long established. Other writers, including Sir James Alexander, Major William Ross King, and Captain Richard Dashwood, support that fact.

But Americans were fishing Canada too, and probably none are now as well remembered for their accounts as is Charles Lanman. Lanman was a phenomenal traveler for his day, author of thirty-two books, many on his travels. He was frequently chasing the frontiers of sporting adventure, whether on Canadian salmon streams so raw they were not yet named, or drifting along on the upper Mississippi, or on dozens

"The Upper Pool at the Goodbout," an engraving from Alexander's *Salmon Fishing in Canada* (1860).

THE UPPER POOL AT THE GOODBOUT   [Frontispiece

Title page of a particularly historic copy of Alexander's book, with the signatures of two former owners, Charles Blackwell and Theodore Gordon, now in the collection of The American Museum of Fly Fishing.

Chas. Blackwell *1860*
Theodore Gordon 1891

SALMON - FISHING

IN CANADA

BY A RESIDENT

EDITED BY

COLONEL SIR JAMES EDWARD ALEXANDER
KNT. K.C.L.S. 14TH REGT.
AUTHOR OF ' EXPLORATIONS IN AMERICA, AFRICA, ETC.'

WITH ILLUSTRATIONS

THE CHUTE-EN-HAUT

LONDON
LONGMAN, GREEN, LONGMAN, AND ROBERTS
MONTREAL : B. DAWSON AND SON
1860

of better-known trout waters from the South to Maine. Writing in the *American Whig Review* in 1847, he offered his theories on fly pattern:

> Our books tell us, that a gaudy fly is commonly the best killer, but our own experience inclines us to the belief, that a large brown or black hackle, or any neatly-made gray fly, is much preferable to the finest fancy specimens.

Hardy was offended by the local patterns he saw:

> Every river in Nova Scotia and New Brunswick, has its particular fly, or series of flies adapted for salmon fishing. Some of these flies, particularly those used in the dark streams of Nova Scotia, would be considered monstrous, both as regarded their gaudiness and size, by a sportsman of the Old World.

"West Falls," from an 1899 *Century Magazine* article about fishing the Nepigon.

Feathers of golden pheasant, Canadian wood-duck, and macaw, show conspicuously amongst the broad plumage of the tail of wild or domestic turkey, on their wings. Their bodies are composed of masses of many-colored pig's wool, deeply buried in which, are broad bands of tinsel.

Others, particularly those for the Atlantic rivers of New Brunswick are smaller, less gaudy, and more carefully made. The dubbing giving place to floss silk, and the turkey wings modestly brightened by a fibre of golden pheasant or scarlet ibis.

Tolfrey agreed more with Lanman, saying that "the less gaudy the fly the greater will be the chance of success."

Thanks to Lanman and many other writers, by 1870 the fly fishing exploration of the East was essentially complete. There were still unfished salmon streams and other waters far to the north, and there were probably still some virgin waters here and there in the New England wilds, but by 1870 the traveling fly fisher had plenty of sources of information on the good fishing spots. Genio Scott's *Fishing in American Waters* (1869), Thaddeus Norris's masterful *American Angler's Book* (1864), Robert Barnwell Roosevelt's two books *Superior Fishing* (1865) and *Game Fish of the North* (1862), and Charles Hallock's *The Fishing Tourist* (1873) and *The Sportsman's Gazeteer* (1877) were among the growing number of guides to these best-known waters of North America.

But by that time a remarkable number of the other great fly-fishing waters of North America had already been pioneered. The vast and diverse fishing grounds between the Alleghenies and the Pacific were opened to the first fly fishers often as soon as the first settlers arrived. Even the South, with its more isolated trout waters and slow tidewater streams, received the fly fisher's attention. I'm going to speed up the travelogue, jumping from region to region, to suggest that even while the Adirondacks, Rangeleys, and Catskills were being settled, adventurous fly fishers were casting their lines on far wilder waters, waters whose present owners have no idea that their region's sporting tradition is more than a century old. Here we meet a broader variety of explorers, many not primarily sportsmen, some perhaps not sportsmen at all.

In 1846, Charles Lanman, on the upper Mississippi, hooked not only trout but pike and bass on his flies, and reported it all in *A Summer in the Wilderness* (1847). Much earlier than that, 1830, Cincinnati had formed its first angling club and sport fishing was well established in the Midwest.

In 1847, a pioneering explorer of a different sort, Wilford Woodruff, was making his way with a party of fellow Mormons toward Utah. Near Fort Bridger in what we call Wyoming, he found time to fish. Woodruff, who would eventually become president of the church, had acquired his rod in Liverpool, England, but had apparently never used it in America. His diary was recently noticed by Ralph Moon, who published the relevant passages in *The American Fly Fisher* in 1982:

> I threw my fly into the water and it being the first time that I ever tried the artificial fly in America or saw it tried, I watched it as it floated upon the water with as much interest as Franklin did his kite . . .
> . . . and as he received great joy when he saw the electricity descend on his kite string, so I was highly gratified when I saw the nimble trout dart at my fly hook, and run away with the line. I soon worried him out and drew him to shore.

Though he said little about it in his published works, James Swan, who lived for many years in what became the state of Washington, most of the time on Puget Sound, had fly-fishing gear with him. In his book *The Northwest Coast* (1857) he commented that he "found that flies were of no account" among some of the trout he encountered.

The various survey parties associated with the great railroad explorations of the early 1850s were more successful. George Suckley caught dozens of fish, including many sea-run cutthroats from streams near Puget Sound in 1853 and 1854. A fellow member of the railroad survey, Captain George B. McClellan, also caught cutthroats, and left a cranky note about an unsuccessful outing he had not far east of the Cascade Range at a lake in the Yakima Valley. According to his notebook, there were fish to be seen, but "the wretches would not rise to the fly." This brings to mind the oft-repeated tale, which has many forms, of some important British official—an officer or diplomat—who is said to have recommended discarding British possessions in what is now the American Pacific Northwest because the salmon were not good sport fish. The earliest telling of the tale I have seen was in the *Spirit* in July of 1852, from a western correspondent using the nickname "Chinook:"

> After reaching fresh water, the salmon of the Columbia no longer feeds, as is the case with the European salmon, and no persuasion will ever persuade it to rise to the fly, a circumstance perhaps, we are indebted to the peaceful settlement of the boundary question; for it is said that the officers of the British Man-of-War Modeste, which was sent at about that time to look around, became highly disgusted, and that Capt. Gordon wrote home to Lord Aberdeen that the d——d country wasn't worth having, for the salmon would not bite.

Eventually West Coast anglers would learn to take all the Pacific salmons on flies, some quite consistently, and would realize that the steelhead, another great fish for flies, was not a salmon at all; it is still easy to encounter not only confusion among West Coast natives over the various salmons but outright disbelief that any of them can be taken on flies.

A writer in the *Spirit* in November of 1857, writing under the title of "Trout-Fishing in the Territories of Nebraska, Washington and Oregon," told of a variety of experiences on the West Slope of the Rockies and in the Puget Sound area, and related that his fishing companion lamented the absence of fishing tackle outlets on the West Coast:

> To such of your readers as may probably condemn the unsportsmanlike practice of fishing with salmon-roe, meat, or grasshoppers—to those who have no patience with any other mode of trout-fishing, except by the scientific whippings of an artificial fly—"Pog" begs to remark, that he would like to know what else a poor devil of a Piscator is to do, there being no fishing-tackle shops on the Pacific, near the 48th parallel, when his flies are all used up, and his fly-rod most irretrievably broken?

Tackle did have to come a long way. Another adventurer, down in Oregon, reported to the *Spirit* the next month that he had made a trip from Jacksonville, down near the California border, to visit a friend in the wilds of the Umpqua only to discover that sporting civilization had preceded him:

> The journey is over, and we are on the banks of the Umpqua, at the gate of our friend Capt. ———. On stepping upon the porch of his cottage a sight presented itself which made my heart to knock against my "seated ribs"—a sight unseen before for many days; there in the wilds of Oregon, against the side of the house, was suspended a regular Conroy rod, with a lancewood tip, a silk and hair line on the reel, a gut leader and a Limerick hook, garnished with grey wings and a red hackle.

At the invitation of the Captain, the traveler took the rod to the river and caught five trout, up to two-and-a-half pounds, in an hour.

California has left us a number of accounts from the 1850s and 1860s, including some by British sportsman. A British sportsmen's account from *Bell's Life of London* was reprinted in the *Spirit* in 1850; he told of taking many large salmon on fly-fishing gear. Judging from his descriptions these were almost certainly king salmon; some weighed over forty pounds. Contrary to popular belief, salmon fishing and steelhead fishing with flies have been popular with at least some anglers on the West Coast ever since. The sporting periodicals of the 1870s and 1880s contain numerous accounts of salmon (some of which may have been steelhead) taking flies freely. At first these fishermen simply used large trout and salmon flies brought from the East, but gradually local patterns developed.

This race across the nation has not been intended to show that fishing was going on everywhere by some date, but to suggest that a start had been made, and made at a surprisingly early date, in many places. Even Montana had been fly fished by 1860, the year that a government naturalist, J. G. Cooper, collected various fish specimens in the state. He commented on the qualities of "Lewis's trout," a form of cutthroat:

> This fine trout abounds in the headwaters of the Missouri, up to their sources on the eastern slope of the mountains, and a few were taken at and near Fort Benton by the soldiers, all of them large ones. They bit readily at almost any artificial fly; also at insects, meat, pork, and even leaves and flowers, after they had been tempted with grasshoppers. Officers and men, nearly all who were not on duty, would crowd the banks of the beautiful mountain streams, and catch as many as the whole command of three hundred men could eat every day, and with tackle of all kinds, from a rude stick with a piece of common twine and a large hook, to the most refined outfit of the genuine trout-fisher.

The Michigan grayling, as drawn by the famous sporting illustrator James Beard and published in Alfred Mayer's *Sport with Rod and Gun* (1883).

We must be impressed by the energy required of whoever managed to get a ''refined outfit of the genuine trout-fisher'' all the way to Fort Benton in 1860. Colorado probably had fly fishers earlier than that, and was receiving attention from sporting journalists by the 1860s, as was the wilder country of Michigan, where the grayling was first formally acknowledged to exist in 1865 and was virtually gone by 1900. Even the Yellowstone country, atop its forbidding and long-resisting plateau, had been fished with flies by 1870, the year that the Washburn-Langford-Doane expedition (a mixed party of prominent Montana citizens and a military escort) explored the present park area. At least two members of that expedition, Cornelius Hedges and Warren Gillette, tried flies, though both seemed to have much greater

''Englishmen in Colorado: Fishing for Breakfast,'' from the London *Graphic*, 1872. The American west was a popular sporting resort of European adventurers following the Civil War.

success with grasshoppers. Within a few years even this new wilderness would see its share of fly rods.

I wouldn't try to push this notion too hard, but I see an ending of sorts in the 1870s. There were perhaps still unfished waters, probably quite a few in the West, but there were hardly any uncaught sport-fish species, at least in fresh water. The greater part of the exploration—the real pioneering, which sometimes involved serious risk—was over. Second-generation fly fishers inherited waters known and studied, while in the East anglers settled ever more firmly into habits developed by several previous generations using the same streams and ponds. What had been an exploration—loosely it could be compared to the exploration of the country—was now a process of settlement, of developing greater familiarity with regions fished often before. Traveling by fly fishers continued to increase, but now it was encouraged not so much by the urge to fish virgin waters as by the urge to fish waters of growing fame, waters touted by countless hotels and rail lines.

More than an ending, though, I see the 1870s as a beginning. Once the waters were explored, and once the fishermen were settled in to their home waters, the flies their fathers brought, and the tackle and techniques as well, would have to be modified, even rejected. As Hardy pointed out in discussing the salmon flies of Canada, every stream had its favorites. Like England, where regional differences in fly style were pronounced by the time of Walton and became much more so by the early 1800s, America was now at the stage of regional refinements. I realize that it started earlier in Pennsylvania than in, say, Montana, but by 1870 it was under way. I also realize that a region rarely functioned in isolation from the ideas and developments of other regions. The sporting periodicals and traveling fishermen saw to it that interchange went on pretty continuously. But, as we'll see later, a regional fishing tradition can be a stubborn and insistent thing, and local developments can thrive with no outside support for decades.

Fly fishing in America had made great strides toward becoming *American* fly fishing by 1870; our rods and reels were our own, American fly patterns were popping up here and there, and, thanks to a vital and blossoming press, we were becoming increasingly self-aware. But it was not until the full array of fly-fishing waters was peopled—that is, not until America's waters were supplied with anglers to challenge and enthrall—that the potential for a uniquely American style of fly fishing, a style that kept only of the Old World that which was technically useful and ethically appropriate, could be fulfilled.

Two

THE VICTORIAN FLY FISHER

7

The Tackle Revolution

A true and tried rod of graceful proportions and known
excellence, which has been the faithful companion on many
a jaunt by mountain stream, brawling river, or quiet lake,
and has taken its part, and shared the victory in many a
struggle with the game beauties of the waters, at last comes
to be looked upon as a tried and trusty friend, in which the
angler reposes the utmost confidence and reliance, and which
he regards with a love and affection that he bestows upon
no other inanimate object.
JAMES HENSHALL, *The Book of the Black Bass*, (1881)

A seductive line of reasoning says that the great tackle revolution of the 1800s, especially of the years after 1860, was the result of the need to be able to cast dry flies. It is an unfortunate oversimplication; in the 1800s a number of concurrent and complementary developments changed the character of fishing tackle, and no one of those developments could easily be given precedence. Were it not for improvements in lines, improvements that were under way early in the century, modern dry-fly casting would have been more difficult; without the development of stiffer, more authoritative rods, false casting and dry-fly precision-casting would also have been harder. It would be no safer to say that the development of stiffer rods enabled anglers to create the modern dry fly; so much was changing that no one part of the change is safely pointed out as somehow the initial impulse of it all.

Fly rods actually went through two major changes in the 1800s. The first was brought about in good part by an increase in imported exotic woods to England and America. John Waller Hills, in his engaging *A History of Fly Fishing for Trout* (1921), summarized progress that occurred in the late 1700s and first half of the 1800s:

No more is heard of hazel, the universal favorite of early fishers, and still less of eccentric materials such as crab tree, juniper, medlar, blackthorn and yew. Ash and deal alone survived, and they were only used for butts. For imported materials took their place, hickory, lancewood, bamboo and greenheart. Hickory, an American wood, is mentioned as a rod material in Sir John Hawkins' edition of *The Compleat Angler* in 1760, and again in Snart's *Practical Observations on Angling in the River Trent*, published anonymously in 1801. It became the common material for trout rods. Lancewood, from the West Indies, began to be used during the period. Greenheart, a native of the West Indies and South America, but coming chiefly from British

61

Guiana, now so universal and invaluable, was not used for rods until the end of the period, though its fine qualities for other purposes, such as shipbuilding, were known long before.

I wonder if some British fisherman in the New World told John Hawkins about hickory, or if he learned of it in some British lumberyard after it was imported to England. The increase in world trade in the 1800s introduced many other woods besides these to American rod builders. By the 1880s Americans were aware of many other less-important woods with exotic names—purpleheart, lemonwood, snakewood, and the like—and rods of these woods do occasionally surface in museums and private collections. But a few woods dominated. Hickory and ash were preferred for the heavier sections before the 1870s (and by many anglers even after), and lancewood came to dominate the tip sections at the same time. Greenheart, not well known in this country until well after 1840, maybe even 1850, was the only one of these woods to hang on, at least in the Old World, after the bamboo revolution took hold. Tradition-minded (and often very practical) British anglers still use greenheart; when Hills wrote, there was still considerable question in England over whether bamboo was superior to greenheart.

Concurrent with the increased availability of new materials, and giving impetus to experimentation, was a growing interest in stronger casting tools, especially for trout fishing. W. C. Stewart's *The Practical Angler* (1857) codified the upstream fishing techniques that had been discussed by various writers for many years. Among other things, an angler's need to be able to cast in any direction at will—despite prevailing winds—certainly increased enthusiasm for stiffer, more powerful rods.

But it was the second big change in fly rods that took hold and that has charmed generations of anglers. That change was the introduction of the split-bamboo rod.

The first fly-rod builders we know of who recognized the extreme fiber density of the outer layer of bamboo were British. By splitting the cane, taking long thin strips of those densest outside fibers and gluing them together, these craftsmen could produce strong sticks. By the first decade of the nineteenth century, a few British rod builders were making rod tip-sections of three or four such strips glued and then bound with thread wraps for additional security against unreliable glues.

Throughout the 1800s and to a lesser extent since then, builders have experimented with ways to join these strips. Some have put the densest fibers—those nearest the surface—in the center of the combined bundle of strips. Most have put them on the outside. The numbers of strips have varied. The earliest recorded rods, or sections of rods, used three or four strips. In the period 1870 to 1900, American builders experimented with practically every number up to twelve but eventually settled on six (eight was second most popular, but much less popular than six). In that period they worked almost always with Calcutta cane, distinguished from the Tonkin cane used later by irregular dark splotches here and there on the finished rod.

Though it is unclear how the transatlantic crossing was effected, at least a few craftsmen in America were experimenting with split-cane rods by the Civil War. By the 1870s there would be considerable competition and animosity among those claiming priority for one or another of these builders, but most votes go to Samuel Phillipe, of Easton, Pennsylvania, as the first to build at least partial rods with split cane, usually less than five strips but gradually increasing to six.

This story, as interesting as it is for its personalities, involves more hair splitting than even most history-minded anglers would find worth the trouble. Honors have been awarded by later writers for the first man to make a complete six-strip rod, the

Samuel Phillipe, as pictured in James Henshall's *Book of the Black Bass* (1881).

first to make a complete trout rod, the first to make a complete six-strip salmon rod, and so on. Fishing historian Mary Kelly, who as usual has penetrated the murk of tackle history further than others, hesitates to put forth any individual as certainly the first:

There were in America in the years before Leonard began making rods at least 6, possibly 16, highly skilled rodsmiths working with split cane (The 6–16 spread is because the proof-positive dates have not yet been determined for when all these rodmakers began work).

By his own account, Leonard built his first rod in 1871, of ash and lancewood, by which time both Ebenezer Green, of Newark, New Jersey, and Charles Murphy, also of Newark, had built split-cane rods.

An 1877 advertisement circular from Hiram Leonard; notice that he offered greenheart rods. *Courtesy of The American Museum of Fly Fishing.*

BANGOR, ME., May 1, 1877.

DEAR SIR,—

I desire to call your attention to my manufacture of FINE FISHING-RODS, and particularly those made of SPLIT BAMBOO (for which I was awarded a MEDAL and DIPLOMA at the CENTENNIAL), which during the last six years have proved unsurpassed in all those qualities — combining an elasticity nearly equal to that of steel, with lightness and great strength and durability — that go to make up as near as it may be possible a perfect rod.

Every rod bearing my name is mounted with my PATENT WATER-PROOF FERRULES, and is warranted against imperfections in material and workmanship.

The REELS of my make are the lightest, strongest, handsomest, and most durable ever made.

I keep constantly on hand a full line of FISHING TACKLE, and tie ARTIFICIAL FLIES to any desired pattern.

Below please find list of prices, which CANNOT BE EQUALLED.

SPLIT BAMBOO RODS, SIX STRANDS,
THREE JOINTS, WITH FULL GERMAN-SILVER MOUNTINGS.

Salmon, 17 feet	$50.00
(For each additional foot in length $5.00.)	
Grilse, 14 feet	40.00
Trout and Bass	30.00
" Twelve strand but	35.00
" Five joints (Trunk Rod)	35.00
Ladies' rod, weight 4 1-2 to 6 oz., Ornamented handles, Price, $25.00 and upwards.	
Trout, of Green-heart, with Split Bamboo tips	25.00

REELS.
(Patent applied for.)

Salmon	$25.00
Trout	10.00
" Ladies' (very light)	10.00

I shall make a specialty of adjusting Reels and Lines to match balance of Rods.

I feel greatly indebted to a large number of our most enthusiastic and experienced anglers for the encouragement I have received by their appreciation of my efforts to furnish them a superior article in my Split Bamboo Rod, and I take this opportunity to thank them.

Heretofore I have found it difficult to execute all orders as promptly as I could desire, but with increased facilities now at my command I shall be able to meet the wants of all my patrons.

Soliciting your orders, I am,

Very respectfully,

H. L. LEONARD

Hiram Leonard in the 1860s. *Courtesy of The American Museum of Fly Fishing.*

Green did not make rods commercially, or if he did the output was inconsequential. Murphy, however, a combative little man of considerable skill, had a more noteworthy ''first'' in that he made more headway than the others in establishing himself in the business of building split-cane rods. He sold them at some point through Andrew Clerk, in New York, and the surviving samples are excellent rods; these were finished, finely made products; their tapers may look odd to the modern fisherman, but they were superbly made. Though there are several variations on the story of how Leonard came to learn about cane rods, and though he could have seen the work of any number of American (or British, for all we know) rod builders, I agree with Ken Cameron, who states that the resemblance between the Murphys and the first Leonards is too strong not to mean something.

Leonard is the giant figure of American rod building. He has taken on an almost messianic image, a backwoods genius who emerged from the Maine woods with his disciples to establish the bamboo rod as the final step in the development of the rod-maker's craft. Cameron and Mary Kelly, both skeptical of incautious adulation, have significantly revised that image in recent years, respectfully pointing out that behind the legend there is a very interesting, if not really extraordinary man whose greatest gift may have been in taking the crafts developed by Murphy, Green, Phillipe, and whoever else, and making a labor-intensive craft into a lucrative industry. Where most if not all of the other early rod makers worked in small shops or in their homes, Leonard was quick to recognize what was most important about a remark Robert Barnwell Roosevelt had made in 1865 in *Superior Fishing*. Roosevelt had said that split-bamboo rod sections were ''beautiful, and expensive, but are almost unattainable . . .'' Roosevelt went on to explain why he preferred cedar to bamboo, and we

The fly fisherman pictured in Genio Scott's *Fishing in American Waters* (1869) used a rod much lighter in appearance than those pictured only twenty years earlier, with the reel much nearer the butt.

don't know if Leonard actually saw the Roosevelt remark, but Leonard had the savvy
to know its truth. In his own career as a rod builder, though he deserves great respect
for his leadership, that leadership has not been fully appreciated. It was more commercial than esthetic, I think. Cameron put it best:

> It was Leonard's genius, I believe, not to be the artificer of a handicraft, but of
> machines—and to recognize the mechanical genius of those ''assistants as competent
> as himself''—Payne, Philbrook, Edwards, Thomas, the Hawes brothers, *et al.* They
> all invested their genius, and, for all the beauty of the product, their real accom-
> plishment was not in the rods themselves, but in the machines that made the rods.[2]

This is not cynicism speaking. Had Leonard and his later imitators not developed
fast milling machines and ferrules that could be made quickly from tubing (rather
than fashioned painstakingly from flat sheet stock), and in other ways applied the
principles of the Industrial Revolution (at least those principles that allow good things
to be made faster) to rod building, the bamboo rod would have remained the toy of
the rich few who could afford to ask a man to put a few weeks of time in on making
one. Many later builders—and hundreds of hobbyists—have of course taken that
narrower course, and they have built beautiful rods; but they have not supplied
thousands of fly fishermen with rods they could afford.

Not that Leonard's own rods were cheap. They were out of reach for most
fishermen. In 1877 a seventeen-foot salmon rod, three piece, six-strip bamboo, was
fifty dollars, a huge amount for your average sportsman. Even his greenheart rod
with bamboo tip was twenty-five dollars. Leonard did not move down to the Catskills
in 1881 because he wanted to participate in what is now fondly (and sometimes
myopically) seen as a great regional angling tradition. He didn't move there for the
good fishing. He moved there for the same reason that he had, for several years,

The Leonard factory in the 1890s. *Courtesy of The American Museum of Fly Fishing.*

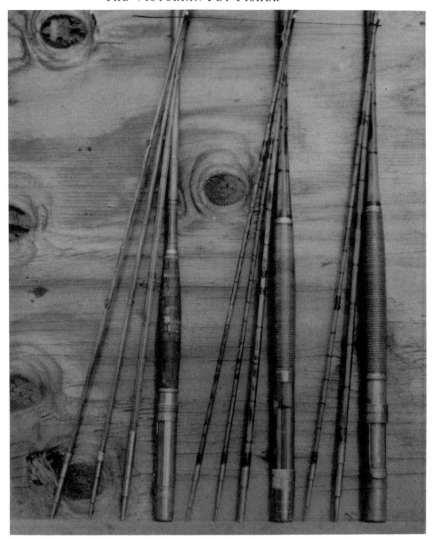

Three Leonard bamboo rods from before 1900. The two on the left are older, with
the more gradual taper from the handle (which was rattan wrapped, rather than
cork rings) to the rod itself. The center rod has alternating strips of bamboo and
cedar from just above the handle clear to the butt cap. The two older rods are of
Calcutta cane, with its characteristic ''splotches'' of darker color; the rod on the
left is of Tonkin cane, more uniform in color. *From the collection of The
American Museum of Fly Fishing, photo by the author.*

sold rods in New York City: the money was a lot better. We may say that Leonard,
Payne, Thomas, Hawes, and the others of that small, exclusive group of builders of
''classic'' rods before 1930 were at the peak of their craft, and produced the best of
all rods. But we could, and I think with more accuracy than cynicism, also say that
they were so few because their market—the people able to buy the best—were a
small percentage of the fishermen buying rods. In 1890 Leonard may have sold as
many as one thousand rods; that must have pretty well taken care of the New York
sportsmen who had become his devotees.

But Leonard maintained no monopoly on any portion of the rod market, even in
the 1870s. The years between the Civil War and 1900 were ones of great boom in
tackle making, and dozens of makers—many forgettable, a few outstanding—ap-

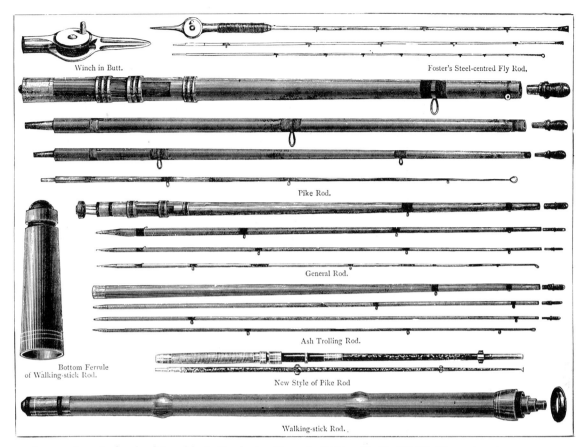

An assortment of rods pictured in J. Harrington Keene's *Fishing Tackle* (1886). The rod on top retains the ground spike popular in earlier years, and most of the rods come with "ferrule plugs."

peared in various parts of the country. Much more than before the war, tackle companies became an important part of the fly-fishing subculture. The magazines, also experiencing an explosion in popularity, reported on the doings and inventions of their regular advertisers with enthusiasm. John Krider of Philadelphia was producing masterful ten-strip rods, the construction of which still impresses rodbuilders. Thomas Chubb of Post Mills, Vermont, seems to have started out as a wholesaler making tackle parts only for other manufacturers and dealers, but eventually he established his own extremely popular line, including a number of rods the average fisherman could afford better than he could Leonard's. Chubb's factory, which was burned repeatedly by accident, would be considered huge by most modern rodbuilders; his output must have been enormous. Charles Orvis, also of Vermont, had been in business since 1856, and had been building bamboo rods since (probably) the late 1870s. Orvis never produced rods in the thousands, but they were good rods, less expensive than Leonard's, and added the Orvis name to the list of most-respected manufacturers of the day. If anything, there were more manufacturers to choose from than today. You could pay what amounted to a small fortune for Leonard's best, or you could send Sears and Roebuck or Montgomery Ward a couple dollars and they'd send you a three-piece, six-strip, nine-foot bamboo rod, a simple Hendryx reel, and a cheap line. Either way you could go catch trout.

Those cheapest rods must have been produced in incredible numbers, judging from the frequency with which they show up in garage sales, antique stores, and the hands of hopeful, uninformed people who bring them to the American Museum of Fly Fishing with high hopes they've unearthed a priceless relic.

Charles Orvis late in life. *Courtesy of The American Museum of Fly Fishing.*

An 1888 view, from the company's catalog of that year, of the Thomas Chubb rodmaking operation in Post Mills, Vermont.

So by 1890, if you were an enthusiastic fly fisherman you probably owned a split-bamboo rod. In those early decades most manufacturers always rounded the six "corners" off the rod, making it round because people had become used to round rods for a few centuries and because the makers had not yet realized that in paring off those corners they were removing many of the best, densest fibers. The rounding-off continued into the 1900-to-1920 period with some builders, especially those who built cheap rods and advertised them as some miracle fiber (you may also have still owned some solid-wood rods, especially if you also fished for salmon and liked the heft of an eighteen-foot greenheart better than that of a bamboo rod of equal power). It was probably nine to eleven feet long (though Leonard was selling smaller rods by then, as were other makers, especially for women). Typically, the entire length of the rod had intermediate wraps, almost always red, of a few turns of thread every inch or so to reinforce the sometimes unreliable glues that held the strips together. The handle might have been covered with turns of rattan, but it was more probably cork, either a sheet wrapped around the handle core or narrow rings of cork slid over

The Thomas Chubb factory in Post Mills, Vermont, in 1874.
From the Thomas Chubb Collection, The American Museum of Fly Fishing.

The Kosmic name remains one of the most mysterious in American tackle-making history; several of the most prominent names in bamboo rodbuilding were at some time associated with the company, but the dates of involvement of various individuals, and their influence on the company's work, are still being studied. In this 1890 ad the Kosmic rodbuilders were at the beginning of their association with the great sporting goods firm of Spalding.

the core and shaped to suit. The sheet was cheaper, and worked well. The fittings —ferrules, guides, trim, reel seat, and so on—might have been the finest nickel silver or the cheapest plated brass. Snake guides had replaced the older, less-efficient forms.

Your choices for a reel were as broad as they are today. On the one extreme, and probably the most common for the average fisherman, were a variety of budget reels, such as those built by Hendryx and Meisselbach after the early 1880s. The Meisselbachs were inexpensive but not really cheap; they occupied a position like that held by the Pflueger Medalist series in recent decades: reliable ''workhorse'' reels that require little maintenance and last more or less forever. That may be why so many Meisselbachs turn up these days, besides there having been so many made. On the other extreme were the costly and beautiful machines of the Vom Hofe family (Frederick started in the late 1850s, his sons and grandsons carrying on the business in his best tradition), and though most of their trade was in larger reels, such as those for salmon fishing, they did build some wonderful small models for lighter fish. These reels were the heirs, at least in quality, of the earlier Kentucky tradition, and have served as models for some of the best twentieth-century reels, such as those built by the Walkers.

For the technologist and mechanical historian, this period, say 1860 to 1900, is an interesting one in reel development. Not only were makers producing some precision machinery in terms of gearing and overall tolerances, they were experimenting

The Orvis 1874 reel came in two models that differed only in width; the larger was considered a bass reel. The handsome walnut case had a compartment for the detachable handle.

with many types of "clicks," "drags," and "brakes" in order to develop efficient, reliable systems for line control during the fighting of a heavy fish. In any historical period, including even our own, most of the time it is true that the reel "is just a place to keep the line," but it has always been true that reels must be built not for most of the time; they must be built for those few—some would say too rare—moments when a big fish takes or when a fish of any size is hooked on unusually light terminal tackle.

Though there were relatively few direct imitations made of it at the time, one reel has come to symbolize the maturing of the American fly reel into a distinct piece of tackle, a reel to be used especially for fly fishing rather than the general-purpose reels of before 1870. That reel is the Orvis 1874 model, now widely regarded as the prototype of the modern American fly reel.

The Orvis reel had no one feature that made it different from all earlier reels. It was instead a clever and handsome combination of many useful ideas. It was, like most modern reels, ventilated (with many small holes in the sideplates), narrow spooled (for faster retrieve of line), and mounted upright on its foot. A number of contemporary and earlier reels, such as the 1859 Billinghurst, the 1869 Ross, and the 1872 Fowler, had some of these same features, appearing in a period of rapid evolution in reel design. Stewart, in his influential *The Practical Angler* (1857), had emphasized the importance of the new reels:

> Reels have been greatly improved in shape of late years; they are now made much deeper, and not so broad, thus allowing the line to be run off more easily, and be wound up more quickly.

Even earlier, wooden trolling reels had applied this principle. We do not know to what extent Orvis was influenced by all these precedents and examples; he was by all accounts an inventive and practical man whose background in machine work may have simply inspired him to see what was needed. His reel, which sold for $2.50 in its handsome walnut box, was not offered until about 1876 (a prototype sent to Charles Hallock at *Forest and Stream* had received good press but had been politely criticized for lacking a "click," which Orvis then added). An aluminum model sold for $3.50, and there was a bass model, about twice as wide, that sold for $3.00. Hallock had encouraged Orvis to add a salmon reel to the line, but it never happened.

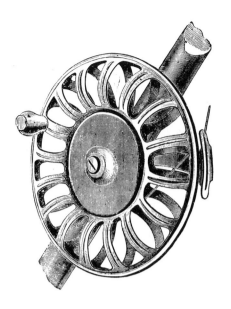

The Follett reel, like the earlier Billinghurst and several other late nineteenth century reels, was side-mounted on the rod; it was not used strictly for fly fishing. Its price has appreciated immensely since this 1882 advertisement appeared.

A reel that was more influential at the time—at least judging from the number of later reels that resembled it—was the famous Leonard 1877 ''raised pillar'' reel. Invented by Francis Philbrook, the reel's most important feature was probably its raised pillars, those being the cross bars that attached the two side plates of the reel. The pillars were all mounted beyond the main plates, thus allowing for greater line

A rare early Leonard reel, possibly a pre-1877 patent prototype. In the final 1877 model, the mottled hard rubber side plates pictured on this reel were replaced by metal. Leonard popularized the ''raised pillar'' design that placed the cross-bars, or pillars, of the reel above the sideplates, thus increasing the reel's capacity. *From the Leonard-Hawes Collection, The American Museum of Fly Fishing, photo by the author.*

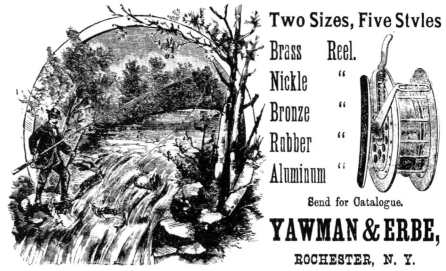

An 1884 sporting periodical ad for the Yawman & Erbe automatic reels, which came in many materials. The fanciful engravings of the day graced many ads; in this one the angler (who is not using an automatic reel) seems to have fought a large trout or salmon to a standstill in a small waterfall.

capacity. Few reels were built this way after 1900 or so, but the idea was popular then and remained a hallmark of reels from Leonard-Mills (the Mills Company of New York became sole distributor of Leonard tackle in about 1879) well into this century.

The late 1800s also witnessed the birth of the automatic reel. Martin and Yawman & Erbe were two of the leading manufacturers, producing great numbers of surprisingly reliable automatics. The automatic, looked down on by most trout fishermen (with some notable exceptions, such as those fishing from the famous Au Sable riverboats on Michigan streams), has been a staple for many fishermen and is still popular among bass fishermen and others whose greatest need is for line control rather than line capacity. Of all the late-nineteenth-century fly reels, these pioneering automatics may be the most mechanically appealing; some were elegantly engraved or stamped (if stamping can be elegant, these were).

The flood of new American tackle did not entirely push out the British products; anglers in North America also took advantage of the best from a variety of Old World manufacturers, especially solid-wood rods and fine fly reels. Americans have a century-long love affair with Hardy reels.

The tapered fly line long predates American fly fishing. Seventeenth-century British anglers knew of lines that were made entirely of horsehair that at its thickest may have been more than a dozen strands but that trimmed down gradually to three or fewer at the fly. It was understood that there was a gradual tapering of the tackle from the rod butt in the angler's hand to the terminal leader. Also by the 1600s, at least some were using lines made partly of silk. All-hair, silk and hair, and other materials were employed well into the 1800s, when line-making technology advanced sufficiently to allow the development of lines made only of silk. The late Myron Gregory, in recent decades the most dedicated student of fly-line history, summarized the progress of the nineteenth century a few years ago:

The all-silk line didn't become popular until sometime between 1870 and 1880. They were, at various times, produced by a variety of methods. A taper could be produced by mechanically changing the number of threads being introduced as the line was woven. The threads themselves were also sometimes tapered for a line to be constructed by a prearranged formula. Women employees in the mills were also used to either add or subtract threads manually from the thread weave to produce a taper. They could watch, for example, six or eight braiding machines at one time, each of which took several hours to make a line.

After the line was braided, it was placed in boiled linseed oil to soak. After becoming saturated with oil, the line was dried in an oven, then it was put through a series of hair brushes, and over stone polishing wheels to smooth and polish the line's surface. The oiling and polishing process was repeated a minimum of 16 times to produce a line of good quality and took place up to 24 times for a superior line. From the start of manufacture to the moment of packaging for sale involved a period of six to seven months.

These lines were a vast improvement over the older hair or hair-and-silk lines, mostly because they could be made heavy enough to allow casting into a fairly stiff breeze. Actually there were some individuals and manufacturers experimenting with linseed-oil-soaked silk well before the 1880s, but it was in the last decades of the century that the oiled-silk line took hold and became the standard in this country.

I'm just as glad I missed the silk line era. When working at the museum I had the opportunity to try peeling any number of ancient dried silk lines from their reels, and the wiry tackiness of those old lines did not fill me with excitement for the old days. The lines required a lot of care, regular—almost daily, if you really wanted them to last—drying after fishing outings, and a level of solicitousness that would easily bore the modern fly fisherman accustomed to the nuisance-free plastic lines of today. Still, I know several veteran fishermen who stare wistfully off into some happier past when they discuss the casting qualities and stylishness of the best silk lines. Anything that helped Halford, Skues, and dozens of other great anglers develop their most important theories dare not be disregarded too lightly.

Silkworm gut, which had been introduced to angling readers by several authors starting in the early 1700s (though in use earlier by a few people), dominated fly-fishing leaders by the time of the Civil War. Flies (which will occupy most of our time in the next few chapters) were tied ''snelled'' to gut, usually on a short snell with a loop, which was then attached to the looped end of a gut leader anywhere from four to nine feet long. Several Americans tried to raise the silkworms and commercially produce gut, starting at least as early as the 1860s, but none were successful.[3] There was occasional resentment that we were dependent upon Spanish and British merchants for this critically important link in the tackle assembly. A correspondent to *Forest and Stream*, October 25, 1888, offered what was probably the most cynical view, certainly a minority view, of the situation:

> I once bought of a man new in the business ten hanks of as good gut as is often seen in this country at a price that was akin to burglary, but his second bill rectified all previous errors and made me think the dealer should be indicted for manslaughter. London is the chief market to which most, if not all, of the dealers in fishing tackle are obliged to go for their silkworm gut, whether it be Spanish, Indian or Chinese. Unless the dealer has a factory in Spain, separate and distinct from the castles in Spain, which some dealers have; and it would appear to a man up a tree that if the London dealers have the first whack at the gut crop they are intelligent enough to take the cream of it.

A London dealer responded in a later issue, pointing out that the market just didn't work that way, which was probably true most of the time. Gut, though a big improvement over horsehair, was limiting in several ways. It was wildly variable from lot to lot, as well as within each lot, so that a sturdy-looking section might be brittle or simply weak. The dealer and the angler paid their money and took their chances. It was, by our standards today, inconvenient in that it required careful soaking before use. It had neither sufficient strength for truly large fish (like adult tarpon) nor sufficient strength in its smallest sizes (which were rarely small enough) for fishing tiny flies. But it was an improvement, and millions of fishermen used it happily and with great success their whole lives. That is saying a lot for any product.

Two things strike me about the great tackle revolution of the late nineteenth century. One is that by 1900 the most important advances in rods, reels, and lines had been made and the pace of improvement slackened. It is true that the great bamboo rod builders, those underpaid craftsmen so well profiled in Martin Keane's *Classic Rods and Rodmakers* (1976), continued to refine and improve rods—a slightly better ferrule here, a tougher varnish there—but they were working in the main in a craft whose fundamental rules were already laid out. The biggest exception may have been the efforts by several companies, culminating in the achievements of Wes Jordan at Orvis in the 1940s, to develop an impregnation process that would protect bamboo much better than varnish did, but even here the fundamentals of rod building were not affected. If the rods, reels, and lines of 1900 were in any way inadequate to their owner's needs, the shortcomings were insufficient to demand further improvements of the manufacturers. Any age that feels that good about its fishing tackle is to be envied.

The second thing that has always seemed appealing about this era is the extent to which fly fishing was an international pastime. The American fly fisher of 1890 was a walking world map with a rod of Asian bamboo, a line as likely English as American, Norwegian or English (or even American) hooks, a fly that might contain feathers and furs from any of dozens of places whose names he might not find pronounceable, wading stockings or boots of likely foreign manufacture (if he didn't just wade wet in warm wool pants), and a leader and snell, both of gut but not necessarily both from the same continent, depending upon which dealer had provided them. But most intriguing, I think, was not his gear; it was his emotional baggage, that peculiar and frequently stirred brew of notions and wisdoms, British and American, that guided his fishing from cast to cast. To understand what was going on in our imaginary angler's mind when he went fishing in American waters, as much as we need to appreciate his rods, reels, and other tackle, it comes down at last to the fly.

8

Victorian Glories

In America, "fancy flies" are more numerous than the imitations, especially since their introduction as a lure for black bass.

MARY ORVIS MARBURY, *Favorite Flies and Their Histories* (1892)

In 1892, the Houghton Mifflin Company published *Favorite Flies and Their Histories*, a large book compiled by Mary Orvis Marbury. Mary was the daughter of Charles Orvis and head of the Orvis fly-tying operation. The book was and is the premier monument to a now-belittled era in American fly tying. It contained in its 500-plus pages thirty-two color plates illustrating in vivid chromolithography some 290 fly patterns. Fly patterns have advanced since then, but fly pattern illustration may never have had it as good since.

The book was a huge success, going through at least six printings in America and England in four years. It has been given credit, more than any other one event, for helping standardize the tangle of fly-pattern names and dressings that had by then become the curse of American fishermen and fishing tackle dealers. It was a magnificent book—it is still absorbing and enlightening reading—and it strengthened Orvis's already strong position as a leading arbiter of fly pattern form and definition. Not the least, it gave Mary a lasting place in the pantheon of famous angling writers. The British journal *Fishing Gazette* announced her death in 1914 with the headline "Death of the Most Famous but one Female Angling Author." Not that there was all that much competition, or even many competitors (there were a few by Mary's time), it was still an extremely high compliment, especially coming from across the ocean, to be ranked near the supposed author of the *Treatyse*.

One day not long after my arrival at The American Museum of Fly Fishing as its new director, I was exploring some of the shelves of the collection storage room. I came across a large, handsomely made but obviously aged box—cedar, it appeared to be—that didn't seem to be a tackle box or any other type I might have recognized. Carefully lifting the hinged top, I saw what seemed to be the top ends of dozens of small mortised picture frames. Each end had written on it, by hand, some phrase, such as *BASS DD* or *TROUT Q*. When I slid one from the box, I saw one of the, if not *the*, greatest treasures in the history of American fly fishing: the original flies, mounted in appropriate order, from which the chromolithographs in Mary's book had

Very few photographs of Mary Orvis Marbury have survived. This one appeared with her obituary in the *Fishing Gazette* in 1914. *Courtesy of The American Museum of Fly Fishing.*

75

been made. You could take (as I did later, when having them photographed for the Museum's journal) one of these frames and place it next to the appropriate plate in the book, and see just how faithful the artists and printer had been to the original. Their fidelity was outstanding. The originals, now pushing ninety, were still brilliant, some more so and some less so than the plates in the first edition of the book. Nothing else I have found has given me such a penetrating sense of connection to the late-Victorian angler of America.

Modern fishing writers have an unfortunate tendency to view the era of the gaudy Victorian wet fly as some sort of embarrassing and slightly silly misstep in the Great March Toward Imitation. The view of fly fishing as progress toward better and better imitations of trout foods is both narrow and dull. Fly tying as a craft has much more than that to offer us, and is at its most stimulating when respected for the many directions it can go, in any age, at once.

Today, without doubt, the colorful wet flies that grew to popularity in the late 1800s would seem odd in the fly boxes of most fishermen, at least trout fishermen. But then, in their own time and historical context, they were exciting and entirely successful. More than that, they were the first important movement, broadly achieved, by American fly tiers toward independence. Before we mounted large-scale assaults on the mysteries of imitation, or formalized an American approach to floating flies, we did this. We made the wet fly our own, as much as something so well established by centuries of European use could be made new and distinct. Nothing else we did in fly tying before 1900 so fully reflects the American fly fishing tradition of that day as these grand, colorful fly patterns so perfectly assembled and preserved by Marbury and her contemporaries.

This chapter, then, is not a sidelight in the history, a delay before we get to the growth of imitation. It is a celebration of something of value that has been not only discarded but disrespected.

The two fishing writers who have done the most helpful thinking about this period are Austin Hogan and Ken Cameron. Both suggest that a kind of reaction against British formality and imitative theory was going on. Hogan saw the American angler of the 1870s and later as glorying in his independence:

> His fly box caught on fire, the dominant Scarlet Ibis became a symbol of his allegiance to the non-imitative and his gutta percha hip boots a symbol of his prosperity.[1]

Cameron took the analysis further, applying his greater knowledge of the cultural traditions of England:

> The English tradition was ''classical,'' authoritarian, bound to a structured society and closed waters; the new American tradition would have to be the opposite, the flies as different from English models as the fast-moving, rocky, woods-lined American rivers were from the American's idea of an English chalk stream. (Because of a relative lack of information, the fact that England also had fast-moving, rocky, woods-lined rivers was ignored on both sides of the Atlantic.) American fly-fishing was to be egalitarian, innovative, Romantic; if tradition was an Englishman, Innovation would be Yankee—Twain's Connecticut Yankee, remaking the British archetype with American ingenuity. Ironically, of course, it was the English whose ingenuity and scientific dedication would come up with the real innovations of the period.[2]

I think that is a sound analysis but for two points. First, I wonder to what extent the well-known but hard-to-identify ''average guy'' really gave a hoot about expressing his independence from a British cultural tradition that, after a century of independence, he knew virtually nothing about. Second, I'm opposed to Ken's final statement because it implies that British developments in insect imitation were innovations while the gaudy American flies were not. Both developments were the products of creative minds, and both were widely influential and highly successful. It is one paradox of fly fishing's historical view of itself that imitation theory has always held center stage while all other traditions and approaches are less important when in fact they are often more common but less written about. I will return to this internal tension later. For now there are more colorful matters to be attended to.

There is a language problem here in that ''fancy'' did not originally mean ''gaudy.'' It has come to mean gaudy to most modern readers because some of the most famous fancy flies were gaudy, and because the term fancy does evoke an image of overdressed, or at least frivolous, appearance. Hills said that to the British way of thinking a fancy fly was ''an article which was a fair copy of an insect but could not be connected with any particular species or genus or group.'' Under those terms I suppose many would call the modern Adams dry fly a fancy fly. Mary Marbury, quoted at the beginning of this chapter, seemed to think that fancy meant something more like gaudy. It has been the gaudy ones that have come to be identified most closely with the trout fishing of the late 1800s in America, and that are probably the most important part of the movement I am discussing here, but I will try to abide by Hills's definition anyway. The American fancy fly was more likely to be colorful than not, more likely to be truly ''fancy'' in the modern sense of frilly or colorful. We have little solid information on how many anglers thought they were imitating something specific,

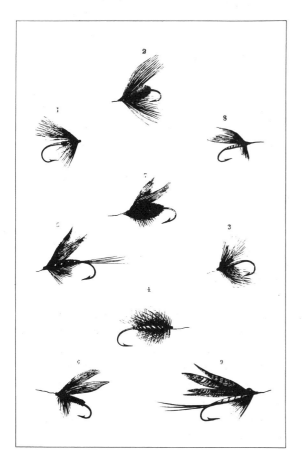

The flies in Norris's *American Angler's Book* (1864) were all British in origin.

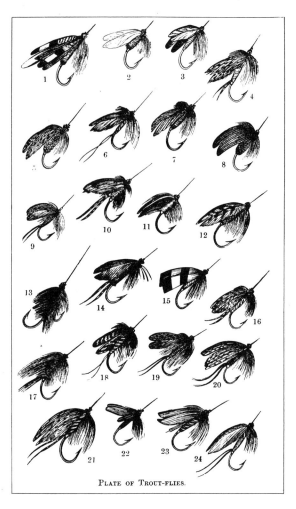

PLATE OF TROUT-FLIES.

Genio Scott pictured many flies in his *Fishing in American Waters* (1869), most of which were not named. The only named patterns in this group were: 2, the Coachman; 11, the June-fly; 20, the Yellow Professor; 21, the Gray Professor; 22, the Black Gnat; and 23, the Blue Professor.

how many thought they were imitating some general life form, and how many didn't give much thought to it at all because the things seemed to work, didn't they?

The American game fish made the movement to colorful wet flies easy. The American brook trout, as modern studies have shown, is much more catchable than the European brown, possibly the natural result of the latter having been fished hard for many centuries by savvy anglers who would tend to remove the most catchable fish from each generation. But the growth of fancy flies was more than a response to the ease with which brook trout could be taken. North America's fish fauna are more diverse than those of England or even Europe, and the number of sight-feeding game fish that would quickly come to the attention of fly fishers is correspondingly greater. Besides the trout there were many warm-water fish, most especially the basses that by the mid-1800s were an important part of the recreational fishery throughout their range, and that by the end of the 1800s had been spread to countless new waters. The combination of bass, trout, and other fishes set Americans off on a fishing adventure unlike anything that could have occurred in Europe, and what with the general ease of taking these fish on flies, the craft of fly tying responded with many new patterns. John Gierach, a Colorado fly-fishing writer, has caught something of what happened back then in his observation on the nature of the modern bass bug, which he describes as "a folk art response to what a largemouth bass actually is: a big, nasty, hungry, gape-jawed fish whose typical feeding opportunities are almost too numerous to list."[3] The American fancy fly was, similarly, a folk art

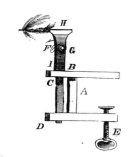

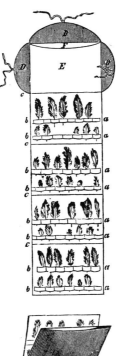

A fly tying vise and fly tying
materials wallet pictured in Frank
Forester's *Fish and Fishing*
(1859).

response to a variety of fishes whose feeding habits did not constrain the fly fisher to worry overly much about accurate imitation of fish food types.

This is not to say that such worrying would have been totally trivial. As we will see in subsequent chapters, at least some American fly fishers almost from the beginning concentrated on the possibilities of accurate imitation. Nor is it to say that these fish are always easy to catch. The brook trout can become a difficult fish (whether spooky, selective, or whatever the difficulty may be ascribed to) in late summer when the water is low, clear, and smooth. But it is to say that for nineteenth-century Americans, the average day's fishing was much easier than it is today. As the British writer Parker Gilmore put it in the 1880s, when the situation had already begun to change on some hard-fished waters, American fish "are not troubled with the fastidiousness of appetite which in Great Britain causes it always to be a source of doubt whether the water is in proper order, the wind in the east, or thunder overhead, either of which, or all combined, too frequently cause the most industrious to return, after a long and laborious day, with an empty basket."

It should be no surprise that under such circumstances the same mixture of theory, whimsy, and random experimentation that has so often ruled the creation of salmon and steelhead fly patterns should also rule in early American trout and bass flies. If you don't need to worry that the fly look like anything in particular, you would quickly reach the point where you enjoyed making it look pretty, or ugly, or just different. If you were a Victorian fly fisher blessed with a wealth of exotic feathers and brilliant furs and silks (made available by the same world trade that brought you greenheart and Calcutta cane), you could hardly be expected to be content with simple brown hackles or drab-winged flies with neither flash nor color.

There were hundreds of fancy flies, many of which lasted only a few years or gained only local or regional popularity. Marbury's book, and other less grand but still impressive books (Orvis and Cheney's *Fishing with the Fly*, 1883, contained 127 patterns), featured many that faded quickly but a few that even yet evoke that era for the well-read angler: Royal Coachman, Professor, Silver Doctor, Parmachene Belle, Scarlet Ibis. What is perhaps both confusing and revealing about these flies is that though there were hundreds of lesser-known patterns that were more or less truly American in origin, practically all of the best-known fancy flies had some British ancestor. The Royal Coachman is a variation on the much older British pattern called the Coachman; New York tier John Hailey developed it in the late 1870s and it was named and marketed by Orvis at that time. The Professor, with its yellow body and red tail, was apparently originated by John Wilson, a quirky but renowned writer and teacher of philosophy in Edinburgh in the 1820s and later (one indignant biographer marveled at Wilson's "eccentric habit of running off without notice on walking- and fishing-tours of the Highlands"; it was evidently on one of these outings that the fly was developed). The actual origin of the Doctor family of flies is unclear, but it was certainly British. The Parmachene Belle was created by Henry P. Wells, one of the more influential writers of the late 1800s (*Fly Rods and Fly Tackle*, 1885; *The American Salmon Fisherman*, 1886). Wells reported that it was developed in the Rangeley Lake region in the late 1870s, and its construction was the result of one of the most unusual imitative efforts of any time:

> That the large trout looked upon the artificial fly not as an insect, but as some form of live bait, we agreed was probably the fact. Upon this theory, that combination should be most successful which most closely reproduced the colors of some favorite trout-food. Why, I cannot now recollect, but the belly-fin of the trout itself was selected as the type.

As long as fishermen use the fly there will be arguments over whether or not this reasoning made sense. It is interesting to us, besides its unorthodox approach to imitation, because it suggests that at least some fishermen were aware of the unlikelihood that fish always took artificial flies in the belief they were insects. Last on my short list above was the Scarlet Ibis, the fly that several fishing historians have used as the symbol of this era. Bright red, obviously an imitation of nothing trout would normally eat, the fly's origins are unknown but probably Old World.

This summary of the fancy fly asks more questions than it answers. First, the declaration of independence embodied in these "American" flies is an ambiguous one. They were largely based on British (or Scotch, or Irish) patterns; what kind of independence is that? In fact it could be a substantial one, because they were not only dressed up, they were often enlarged for American waters. More, they were not used, as near as can be told, as discriminately as were their British forebears; they were "favorite flies," and an angler might swear by one and be willing to use it constantly for all fishing conditions (as Wells claimed he would do with the Parmachene Belle if he had to). More than that, under the influences of commercial fly tying they changed in other ways. Ken Cameron, in a perceptive examination of late-nineteenth-century fly-tying advertisements and techniques, has pointed out that high-volume production and two-dimensional portrayal (as in the lovely portraits in the Marbury book) both tended to flatten the flies into essentially two-dimensional objects where in many cases the original British patterns may have had not only a wide hackle spread but split wings.

But all this begs another question: just how popular were the fancy flies? The answer is hard to find. Marbury's book was the result of hundreds of letters the Orvises sent out to fishermen all over the country, asking for their personal and regional favorites. The results do not indicate that the fancy fly ever had complete domination. Here are the top dozen, each with a tally of the number of votes it got.

This isn't the best kind of evidence we might want—Marbury's correspondents would be, I imagine, the most likely to be up on commercial fashions, for one thing—but it's about the best we get:

Coachman	58	Grizzly King	23
Brown Hackle	44	Royal Coachman	19
Professor	38	Queen of Waters	19
Montreal	28	Silver Doctor	18
Black Gnat	25	Cowdung	18
White Miller	24	Scarlet Ibis	15

Hardly more than half of these flies are gaudy, but some of the others were likely fancy. I suppose several of the others were not being tied or fished as their British originators intended. The vast majority are, indeed, clearly British in origin. But the favorite-fly approach to fly fishing had not really peaked in 1892; both the Royal Coachman and the Parmachene Belle were fairly young then, fifteen years or so old. Another survey, reported by Larry St. John in his underappreciated *Practical Fly Fishing* (1920), involved some two hundred "prominent anglers" who were polled by the magazine *American Angler* in the late teens. A point system was adopted, and each angler was asked to name his three favorites. Each first place choice got three points, each second got two points, and each third got one. Here are the top twelve, a quarter of a century later:

Royal Coachman	93	Black Gnat	31
Coachman	56	Grey Hackle	27
Parmachene Belle	54	Montreal	26
Cahill	45	Cowdung	21
Professor	43	Silver Doctor	20
Brown Hackle	43	Queen of Waters	18

Here the Royal Coachman and the Parma Belle have had time to take better hold in the angling market and fashion. If anything, fancy flies have advanced in popularity; the Royal Coachman's lead is extraordinary. By the time of St. John's book the question of popularity is confused by the rise of other fly types—dries, streamers, bass bugs—so that the whole search becomes muddled ever more. It seems clear, though, that 1900 was no magic date for the peaking of the fancy fly movement; I don't see much evidence that it peaked before 1920.

There is another question that these fly patterns ask, and though it involves in a distant sort of way a subject that will be taken up more fully in the next chapter, I will ask it here anyway. It is this: How important was the fly's appearance to the angler who favored fancy flies? The evidence, from the dialogues in periodicals and the occasional discussion in books, suggests to me that they did care. A number of authors, ranging through the 1800s in America, did not favor bright flies merely because they were pretty. There was a repeated conviction that certain colors were most attractive to fish. The editor of *Forest and Stream*, himself no slouch in natural history, put one of the most popular theories of the day in print in that magazine on December 5, 1889:

When we come to fish, most varieties that are taken by artificial lures, show that same fondness for bright colors, and red seems more attractive than any other. The majority of artificial flies have red in their composition; for instance the Abbey,

Montreal, royal-coachman, grizzly-king, professor, red-hackle, red-spinner, Howard, soldier, scarlet-ibis, and many others too numerous to mention. In fact this color is so attractive to chub, pickerel, perch and rock bass, that anglers often have to use flies dressed with more sober colors, when fishing for better fish. The trout and bass that are found in the wilder districts, seem to have this fondness for red more fully developed—or perhaps in much fished waters they become better educated and more refined in their tastes.

Black Bass have a great weakness for black and yellow. Professor Mayer's ''Lord Baltimore'' and W. Holberton's ''Lottie'' are two instances of this. In the early part of the season these two flies will kill more black bass than all the others, and are the most deadly flies that the angler can use.

A strange fact is the partiality that Maine trout seem to show for the ''Jenny Lind'' fly, a combination of bright red, yellow and blue—as unlike any natural fly as one can possibly imagine. Bluefish and Spanish mackerel are attracted by red squid, and striped bass, shad and weakfish are often taken on bright colored flies. In waters where pollock abound, the principal lure used is a big red and white fly.

This, however good it might have turned out as scientific discourse, was not the statement of someone who was interested only in finding prettier flies to fish with. There was more to the fancy-fly movement than esthetic whimsy; the flies were perceived to work best, and it was true then as it is now that we often catch the most fish on the fly we most trust.

The last question is an old one, one that many fishing historians have asked about six centuries of fly fishing: What did the fish think these flies were? It has always been an unsatisfying inquiry to try to justify a full-dress wet fly, which looks like the emerged dun of some mayfly, as an adult that has sunk. Adults just don't seem to sink in such numbers that fish would take them all for adults that had sunk. There has never been an easy answer for this question, and the fancy-fly movement only makes it more complicated. No doubt there are many answers. Fish take flies for many reasons. They may indeed have thought the fly was a sunken mayfly adult. They may have mistaken it for an ''emerger'' or some nymph, or some life form like nothing that the angler thought he was imitating, such as a minnow or some drowned terrestrial insect. Undirected feeders in many American waters often saw all sorts of food; a red, white, and blue fly would no more surprise them than an electric aqua dragonfly or a yellow-and-black bumblebee. The issue of imitation has always occupied fly fishers, and part of its endless attraction has been the imponderable uncertainty of just how much it matters to the fish in the first place.

The fancy flies that appeared in waters all over America in the late 1800s have of course not all disappeared, nor will they as long as wild waters exist. It is perhaps an oversimplification to call it a ''national'' movement because anglers in each locale most often developed their local specialities with relatively little concern over whether or not they would work elsewhere. It was part of that regional specialization I mentioned in Chapter 6 that began as anglers were challenged by the diversity of American waters. But however we define it, the fancy fly was a major step in American fly tying, a step made no less important by the reaction against it that resulted in an American approach to imitation.

9

Imitation's Forgotten Prophets

The entomology of American fly-fishing is yet to be written. Miss McBride, some years ago, contributed a few pleasing and instructive articles to a weekly journal on this subject, and so far as my knowledge extends, her attempt was the last one made by an American writer; but, as more than two hundred years elapsed from the time of Walton to the date of Ronalds' work on English piscatorial entomology, our angling authors may be pardoned, if a decade or two elapses in the production of an American text book on this fascinating subject.

WILLIAM HARRIS, in the notes to Foster's
The Scientific Angler (1883)

The great obstacle to understanding various theories of fly construction is language. The terms "imitative" and "nonimitative" are in some respects unsatisfactory. The imitative fly is generally perceived to be one that was constructed to counterfeit some specific insect (we will consider other fish foods in a later chapter). The most that can usually be said of the nonimitative fly is that it is the opposite of the imitative. But surely it must imitate something; all the millions of fish taken on these flies cannot have consumed them without mistaking them for food. The nonimitative fly usually has been constructed like the imitative one; it may very well have looked a lot like a bug or some other food to the fish.

More recently, and just as troubling semantically, large groups of flies have been called "attractors." Austin Hogan complained to me about the looseness of this term, saying that "all flies are designed to attract and so the word attractor . . . is ambiguous and entirely without meaning." The term attractor is another attempt to deal with the problem already established by the terms imitative and nonimitative, and the term probably works most of the time. Most fly fishers know that when they hear a fly described as an attractor they are hearing about a fly that for one reason or another is thought to "attract" fish by some means besides resembling some specific life form. But that is pretty arbitrary when you consider how many fishermen commonly will use a Quill Gordon, Hendrickson, Red Quill, or other traditional established imitator to prospect, thus turning the most determined imitators into attractors (if not nonimitators).[1]

These language problems are not going to go away, and probably can't even be solved. They are part of the confusing language of fly fishing that bewilders so many beginners. Again, Austin Hogan objected to calling a streamer a streamer *fly* because a streamer is a streamer, period, not a fly:

> Joe Bates started the streamer *fly*, which it never was and never will be. Neither is a nymph a fly but a nymph and nothing else. If it doesn't imitate only God knows what it is. The departure from classic meanings is a product of our idiot fringe . . . Fortunately I have never heard anyone call an Atlantic salmon fly anything but a fly. Here the logical is also illogical but acceptable by years of usage.

George Washington Bethune, scholarly editor of the first important American edition of Walton, and pioneer essayist on American fly fishing. *Courtesy of David B. Ledlie.*

Austin recognized the essential whimsy of these terms, but most modern fishermen rarely give them thought. The lines between bass flies and bass bugs (some bass "bugs" imitate frogs), the question of why bonefish are fished for with "flies" that imitate fish and crustaceans, and other interesting little tangles don't matter as long as the fish hit the thing, whatever we call it. I don't suppose the lack of interest is harmful to anyone, but I also believe that Austin had grounds for being annoyed by it.

The smartest of our early fly-fishing writers knew about these semantic traps, and also recognized the greater practical traps that they represented. Nineteenth-century fishing literature, both Old World and New, is full of reconsiderations and rejections of formalized, simplistic systems of fly-pattern use. George Washington Bethune was one of the most articulate, well read, and thoughtful fly fishers in American history. In the extended notes to his 1847 edition of Walton's *Compleat Angler* Bethune analyzed the problems of system as well as anyone before 1900:

> The reader may be aware that anglers differ widely in their theories respecting the choice of flies, some contending that the nicest possible imitations should be made of the fly *on the water*, or rather that on which the trout is feeding at the time; others holding directly the reverse, and asserting that no imitation deserving the name can be made, and that when the natural fly is abundant the fish will reject any resemblance of it which may be thrown to him . . . It also seems to be established that salmon do not take flies from being deceived by their resemblance to the natural, in some places the most gaudy colors being in repute, in others, as in Wales, those of sober brownish hues. So also as to the adaptation of colors to the time of day, the color of the water, &c., one successful angler will lay down to you a set of rules, another, equally successful, directly the reverse. In fact, almost every practised fly-fisher has a creed and system of his own, though the advocates of exact imitation speak with artistic contempt of all who differ from them; and are in their turn ridiculed as pedantic pretenders, or mad with too much learning. The truth, as in most vexed questions, lies between the extremes. If nature be violently contradicted, the trout are too keen-sighted not to detect the clumsy trick, and the success of certain flies at certain seasons, and not at others, proves that the fish have some rule in feeding.

Bethune had a broad vision; he understood what many still don't, that a lot of things work a lot of the time, and that some may work more than others but none seem to work all the time. And what a marvelous phrase was "mad with too much learning."

But all this disagreement was the result of raging controversy among the well-established British writers. Again, let me indulge my admiration for Bethune's ability to synthesize:

> . . . the anglers of our day are divided into two schools, which may be conveniently distinguished as the *routine* and the *non-imitation*. The former hold that the trout should be angled for only with a nice imitation of the natural flies in season at the time, and that, therefore, the flies seen on the water, or found in the belly of the fish, are to be carefully imitated. To this school belong the older writers, from Venables down, and Taylor, Blaine, Hansard, South, Shipley, and Fitzgibbon, &c., &c. The *non-imitation* school (which reckons among its adherents Rennie, Professor Wilson, Fisher, of the Angler's Souvenir, &c., &c.), hold that no fly can be made so as to imitate nature well enough to warrant us in believing that the fish takes it for the natural fly; and, therefore, little reference is to be had to the fly upon which the trout are feeding at the time.

Bethune tended to "lean to the non-imitation theory, but would not carry it so far as to reject all the notions of the *doctrinaires*." The more careful thinkers of the 1850s, 1860s, and 1870s, agreed with him. Thaddeus Norris, in his *American Angler's Book* (1864) took a course of cautious agreement, though he was a sort of agnostic on the question of how well we can know what the trout actually take the fly to be. His fellow writer and sometime rival Robert Barnwell Roosevelt, writing in *Game Fish of the North* (1862), was equally equivocal:

> . . . one half the most skillful fishermen assert that the fly, as for instance, the scarlet ibis, need resemble nothing on earth, or in the waters under the earth, and that the sharp-sighted fish are never deceived by thinking ours the natural insect, but take him for some new and undescribed species. As for myself, to use the quaint language of the editor of the "Knickerbocker," "sometimes I think so, and then again I don't, but mostly I do."

But the direction of fly fishing writing in the Old World had been made certain by publication of Alfred Ronalds's *The Fly-Fisher's Entomology* (1836). Competing theories as entrenched as these do not disappear, and never have, but what did happen, both in England and much later in America, was the production of ever more sophisticated tracts on imitation theory (nonimitation, by definition, does not require sophisticated tracts in the first place; the risk someone reviewing fishing literature runs is overestimating the dominance of imitationists on the basis of their greater output of instructional and theoretical books. Their school of thought demands more books). Ronalds set a course for fly fishing that has never been changed significantly, and over time the imitationist approach has accumulated not only a great volume of instructional literature but various social trappings; quite often the nonimitationist is seen as primitive, unsophisticated, or simply unfashionable.

American writers were aware of British developments, and borrowed heavily from them. Most early book authors, including Brown, Norris, Scott, and Forester, took British patterns wholesale, only modifying some of them. They have taken a lot of criticisms by later writers for their apparent laziness, but they knew their limitations. They usually expressed regret (even if they thought strict imitation unnecessary) that Americans did not have a book the equivalent of Ronalds's. Some even knew that an American book would have to be much larger to handle the far more diverse insect fauna of North America. More than that, their recommended patterns, even if borrowed straight from British books, caught fish by the ton. It is true that American insects were not always exactly matched by British flies (as Halford, Moseley, Skues,

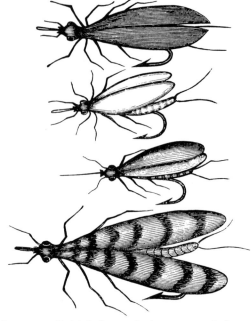

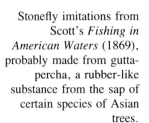

Stonefly imitations from Scott's *Fishing in American Waters* (1869), probably made from gutta-percha, a rubber-like substance from the sap of certain species of Asian trees.

and a parade of others would show, neither were British insects), but most of the time they obviously matched up well enough.

The periodicals between 1830 and 1920 show occasional, if possibly isolated, instances of imitation going on here and there. Some were accidental, such as George Gibson, writing in the *Spirit* in August of 1849. He told of a drab fly whose wing came off while he was catching a fish on Big Spring in Pennsylvania (near Carlisle). The fly had nothing left but a mohair body, but that was enough to catch many more fish, so many that his fishing partner came over and got the wings trimmed from *his* fly as well. It could have been an inadvertent nymph imitation.

Some were surprisingly purposeful and modern. Several writers before 1900 displayed a keen understanding of nymph fishing techniques and imitation. In July of 1886, an article in *The American Angler* described cisco (also called lake herring) fishing near Buffalo, New York. The anglers tied what was certainly (and knowingly) a mayfly emerger imitation, sank it in a deep pool with a small sinker, and pulled it to the surface to imitate the surfaceward motion of the natural. It worked well. In the previous year, on August 8, the same magazine published editor William Harris's report on imitations of emerging caddis on the Yellowstone River near Livingston, Montana:

> I was somewhat surprised at the fly-fishing methods of the resident anglers of Livingston. Casting the fly is not the practice, albeit every fisher uses a cast of from three to six flies weighted with a split shot, with which they plumb the depths, bringing the flies by successive short, quick jerks to the top of the water, and then allowing them to sink: then repeating the operation, which is very similar, hence successful, to the rise of the caddis and other ephemera from their watery home to assume the butterfly form.

As early as the 1850s, American writers were recommending casting flies (most used two or three, but some used as many as twelve in a "ladder" of flies that swept a whole riffle like an instant hatch) on "a length of shotted gut." Weighted lines and flies are not new, nor are arguments over whether or not such sport is truly fly fishing. Neither, these examples show, are attempts to imitate insect appearance and behavior (we'll see more examples in the next chapter). There were a number of fly fishers who put more than casual effort into imitation, however, and most of them have either been forgotten or disregarded. By introducing some of them here I don't mean to suggest that these are the only ones; at least one other, Theodore Gordon, will get his own chapter soon. I offer these as significant leaders, and as examples of just how far imitation theory went before it took hold and became a part of widely respected fashion in American angling.

The first was also the least known, and as far as can be told was *not* of much influence on other fly tiers. But she is extremely interesting, one of the most intriguing characters in nineteenth-century fly tying. Her name was Elizabeth Benjamin, and we owe what we know of her to the discovery, by Austin Hogan, of a letter written in the 1930s by her son, then eighty-one years old.[2] According to this letter, which was written to someone who wanted information on fishing history, Elizabeth Benjamin was the wife of a conductor on the Elmira, Williamsport & Northern Railroad. She spent her summers, with her husband and son, at Ralston, Pennsylvania. The letter from her son, Joseph Benjamin, described the fishing situation there on the eve of the Civil War, when his mother became involved in fly tying:

> Ralston is located between Elmira & Williamsport on Lycoming Creek, a small hamlet in a valley between hills and mountains; about 1858 and 1860 it became known as one of the best places for catching large speckled brook trout in that section of the state, parties would come to Ralston, from the big cities loaded down with all kinds of fancy fishing tackle, but usually returned home with empty baskets, one day my mother noticed a man by the name of Conley who kept the only tavern in the place would go fishing every afternoon about sun-down a short distance from our house, and always returned with a mess of trout that would make every one set up and take notice.
>
> My mother got so interested in Mr. Conley's success she waded out in the creek unnoticed by Conley, and observed that the largest trout would always jump for certain kinds of flys when lighting on the water, believing she could imitate the kind of flys the trout were taking, she mentioned it to my father, and they worked nights making nets; and would wade out in the creek and catch the flys place them under glasses on a table until they would "shed their coats."
>
> In order to make the imitation flys to resemble the genuine ones, it was my job to procure certain kinds of fethers obtained from roosters, chickens, ducks, pigeons and bird nests, the feathers were shaped by my mother; fastened by hand to fish-hooks with different colored silk thread; many tourists coming to Ralston soon found out the flys they had was not especially adapted to that locality for good trout fishing, and when they learned of the success of others who had purchased my mothers hand made flys, they paid her fabulous prices for all she could make.

When Austin published his report on this letter he suggested that Elizabeth Benjamin was catching nymphs and hatching them out, but the letter seems unclear about that; it sounds as if she could have been catching duns and watching them change to spinners. It appears from the letter that she was catching flies that were "lighting on the water" rather than emerging from it. In either case it is a fascinating story, one of the most unusual items Austin turned up in his many years of research. Elizabeth reminds me of a remark by Hugh Sheringham in his perceptive introduction to the 1921 edition of Ronalds's book. Sheringham, in reflecting on our dependence on written tradition for our knowledge of imitation history, speculated that "perhaps— which is not impossible—many a district has had its 'mute inglorious Ronalds' working patiently away on a firm basis of sound knowledge."

There was nothing mute about the best-known American writer on imitation in the 1860s. Robert Barnwell Roosevelt was a colorful and clearly spoken sportsman;

in a sport not known for a shortage of eccentrics and strong personalities, he must be near the top. Congressman, Minister to the Netherlands, reformer, novelist, New York State Fish Commissioner, naturalist, and one of New York's most gossiped-about social lions, Roosevelt deserves much more than the lame introduction he so often gets as ''Teddy Roosevelt's uncle.''

His two best known books, *Game Fish of the Northern States of America and British Provinces* (1862) and *Superior Fishing, or The Striped Bass, Trout, and Black Bass of the Northern States* (1865), were among the most important of the nineteenth century; he and his chief rival, Thaddeus Norris, whose *American Angler's Book* was the only clearly more-respected work, taught generations of Americans to fly fish.

Roosevelt's contribution to angling entomology is mostly contained in two chapters of *Game Fish of the North*. One is on flies and knots, including how to tie flies, and the other is a brief tour of the world of aquatic insects, an informal popularization of the insect classifications of the day. Neither is comprehensive, but both are important introductions for American readers. It is true that he relied heavily on Ronalds, but he also revised Ronalds's patterns so that they could be tied with easily available American feathers. He was a naturalist, and by inclination was fascinated by insects; his chapter on them is unfortunately short on advice about applying the information given to fly-fishing techniques; though he discussed nymphs, for example, he had little to say about how to imitate them. Like Ronalds he knew to imitate a full range of insect types, including stoneflies (with wings ''from the mottled feather of a brown hen made full, and to lie flat''), caddisflies, bluebottle, ant, and a large assortment of mayflies. He told of a new development, ''a Limerick hook now made with the shank turned over so as to form a loop into which the gut is inserted and the trouble of tying the gut is avoided,'' thus introducing for many readers the revolution of the eyed hook that would by 1900 take control of serious imitative fly tying.[3] Snelled flies were worthless once the gut that had been tied into the fly broke; the eyed-hook fly could be reattached as long as it lasted. Snelled flies would endure well into the 1940s in many parts of the country; in 1910 Charles Orvis's son told a customer that ''it is certainly much easier to attach regular snelled flies than the eyed hooks and this is the reason that the regular snelled flies will largely be used.''

Perhaps most important, though he admitted abdicating most of his responsibilities to his readers because he did not prepare a systematic entomology (he claimed he had intended to), Roosevelt was the first to put into book form a rough ''hatching'' narrative that introduced some of the major fly types and their emergences. His discussion was confined mostly to the waters of Long Island, apparently his favorites. In *Superior Fishing* he chided Norris for going after easy sport with unschooled trout of the ''rarely visited forest'' instead of facing the challenge of going to Long Island ''to tempt the dainty trout with finer imitations from the well-fished pond of the cultivated country.'' Norris had been a strong advocate of using only a few general patterns that, Roosevelt claimed, worked well as long as you stuck to backwoods trout.

On the one hand Roosevelt was not sympathetic with the obscure classifications of the professional entomologists. He gave them a jab for their excessive nomenclature:

> As they are principally minute objects, wise men wisely concluded the deficiency should be made up in length of name, and but one class appears under the weight of less than four syllables.

On the other hand, that is a fairly gentle jab after all, and Roosevelt was obviously very interested in insect natural history. No doubt his book started a lot of other anglers grubbing around in the shallows, and his work was, in the words of Arnold Gingrich, "a significant start."

In the 1870s American angling entomology benefitted from the work of yet another fascinating—though utterly dissimilar from Roosevelt—character, Sara McBride. She too was largely the product of hard-fished waters (most of these early angler-entomologists shared one of two, and sometimes both, backgrounds; either they were British or they did most of their fishing on difficult waters). She was the daughter of John McBride, a famous fly tier of the 1840s and 1850s, and seems to have begun to tie flies in the early 1860s. An ad in *Forest and Stream* on May 4, 1876, described her as "having been for the past twelve years associated with my father, John McBride, in the manufacture of fishing tackle . . ." What little we know of her life was mostly ferreted out by Ken Cameron and presented in an article on "The Girls of Summer" in *The Flyfisher* in Winter 1977.

We don't know much. She appears on the fly-fishing scene about 1876 and disappears in about 1881. In that time she published several highly acclaimed articles on fly tying and fly-fishing entomology. For detail and accuracy they were not approached by an American writer for more than fifty years. She published in *Forest and Stream*, the Rochester (New York) *Express*, and *Rod and Gun* (a reprint of the *Express* material, it was reprinted in *The American Fly Fisher* in the Spring of 1978). Her series of articles in *Forest and Stream* were adapted by Charles Hallock for publication in his *Sportsman's Gazeteer* (1877), where he described her work as "a valuable contribution to the angling literature of America." She was likewise praised by others, including Mary Marbury, and in 1876 was awarded a bronze medal for her flies at the Centennial Exposition. She was, in short, one of the most respected fly tiers of the late 1870s, and she was read by many later tiers, including Theodore Gordon.

Advertisements for her flies stressed that she based them on imitations of nature; in the 1876 ad mentioned above she offered to copy any fly from the natural.

Her entomological essays ran through the orders of insects of interest to fly fishers. She gave a better balance between mayflies and other flies, stressing the utility of caddis especially. She spent a lot of time in the stream—Caledonia (now Oatka) Creek south of Rochester, the site of Seth Green's famous trout hatchery and the home, even then, of difficult fish—and raised nymphs in her aquarium so that she could observe their metamorphoses, which she understood and portrayed well. It is unclear from her descriptions if she was tying nymph imitations, or to what extent she may have intended her flies to float, but her adaptations of British patterns and her own developments were regionally important. It is a shame she did not continue, and almost as great a shame that we do not know what became of her.

The trouble was, almost certainly, that in most places such attention to imitation still was not necessary; McBride was not the first to lecture an unwilling audience, and she would not be the last, even though when we last hear of her, about 1881, the first brown trout were on their way to America where they would change the fishing dramatically.

The famous 1883 shipment of browns from the Old World was not the first; shipments arrived two or three years earlier, coinciding nicely with growing news of the dry-fly rage and related developments in eyed-hook technology and fly-line improvement. The demise of the brook trout due to environmental degradation of many

John Harrington Keene, about 1888. *Courtesy of David B. Ledlie.*

kinds had been bemoaned in the sporting periodicals for many years; writers were claiming this was the last generation of trout fishers. By the late 1880s, browns were moving in to various waters, some already deserted by brook trout and others soon to be so if only because of competition with the hardier, savvier brown. The neglected entomologist of the 1880s arrived about then too.

His name was John Harrington Keene, and of all the neglected fly-fishing thinkers of the 1800s, he is probably supreme. He made more proposals, of better sense, on more subjects, than any other pioneering fly tier of the century in America. One reads his descriptions of midge fishing, of extended- and hinged-bodied flies, of gauze wings, of beetle imitations, and much more with a feeling that American fly fishing has not paid sufficient attention to its own masters.

Keene came to America in the early 1880s. His father was Queen Victoria's chief water keeper at Windsor Park for twenty years, and young John was consequently exposed to the latest and best thinking in British fishing through his life there; he discovered his ''Daiphine,'' a type of scale-wing he used widely for flies, while cutting up some scales from rudd (a common British forage fish) his father had caught ''for the royal household.''

The next chapter deals with the floating fly, but it is impossible to entirely separate at this stage developments in imitation and those in floating flies. Part of the creed of the imitationist was wrapped up in the new ethic of floating-fly fishing. Keene was the most articulate and persistent writer on floating flies in America in the 1880s, and in his book *Fly-Fishing and Fly-Making* (1891 edition) he outlined the reasons for preferring the upstream method of fishing. Some of the reasons apply mostly to dry flies, but some are broader than that:

> The first question which presents itself is, ''Shall I fish up stream or down?'' To this I reply, with all the emphasis of which I am capable, ''Upstream, by all means, *whenever possible*.'' There is every reason for it, but here are a few, briefly put: (1.) Trout invariably lie with their heads up stream—*ergo* take their food in that position. (2.) Trout cannot see the angler more than a few feet behind them, whilst they can and do see many yards in front. (3.) The vibration of the water, caused by the movement of the advancing angler, if wading, does not penetrate up stream as it does down stream. (4.) The water is not ''roiled'' or muddled for the fish by wading up stream.

He elaborated on these and other points in that book, improving on what Stewart and others had been telling British and American readers for some time; nobody had done such a good job with it for Americans before, and I don't think it has been much improved on since.

Keene came to the attention of American fly fishers through his articles first. *The American Angler* published more than twenty articles by him in 1885; another dozen or so appeared in *American Field* in 1887 and 1889. Thanks to the research of David Ledlie, who tracked down most of these items, we now have a record of Keene's work that tells us how broad his learning was. Many of the articles were devoted to fly tying, at which he obviously excelled. He promoted eyed hooks, explained various specialized techniques that had not been discussed in American books, and generally gave his audience an unequaled opportunity to understand the details of fly tying (portions of these articles found their way into his books, the most important of which were *Fishing Tackle, Its Materials and Manufacture*, 1886 and *Fly-Fishing and Fly-Making*, 1887). He was also a competent illustrator, doing most or all the artwork for his books and articles.

Fig. 91.—JOINTED BODY FLY.

J. Harrington Keene's jointed-body fly, from *Fly-Fishing and Fly-Making* (1891).

Fig. 73.—IMITATION JUNE-BUG.

Keene's june-bug imitation, from *Fly-Fishing and Fly-Making* (1891).

Fig. 79.—BLACK ANT, SCALE-WINGED.

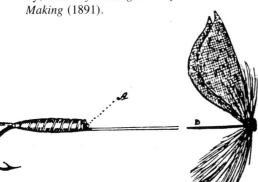

Fig. 80.—SCALE-WINGED MIDGE FLY.

Fig. 67.—THE INTERCHANGEABLE FLY.

Keene's interchangeable fly allowed the substitution of different wings and hackles on different bodies, from *Fly-Fishing and Fly-Making* (1891).

Three of Keene's scale-wing imitations, from *Fly-Fishing and Fly-Making* (1891).

Fig. 82.—GRASSHOPPER, SCALE-WINGED.

Keene brought from England the latest attitudes toward imitation (he was either a friend or at least correspondent of Halford's). He lived for some years in Manchester, Vermont, on one of the tougher late-season streams in the East, the Battenkill, and in the neighborhood of the Orvis family. David Ledlie has wondered if there was some disagreement between him and the Orvises, and there is evidence to support the idea. Mary Orvis Marbury conspicuously ignored Keene in her book, and he occasionally wrote less than flattering things about their flies. In his chapter on tackle in George Oliver Shields's *American Game Fishes* (1892), he commented on the popular "grasshopper-fly" that Orvis sold, saying that "it certainly resembles no grasshopper in this sublunary sphere."

In the *American Field* for May 14, 1887, he gave the natural history of the mayfly, following it through its life stages (he raised nymphs in an aquarium). He also discussed, less accurately, the life of the caddis. Among his suggestions for fly tiers in the late 1880s, besides those already listed above, were: a detachable wing system for interchanging wings on bass flies; double-wing dry flies; keel-type flies; stripped herl for quill-bodied dry flies (not original with him, but perhaps the first mention of it for an American audience); rolled wings for down-wing flies; wood-duck flank feathers for fly wings; cork-bodied mayfly with mallard-feather wings mounted in

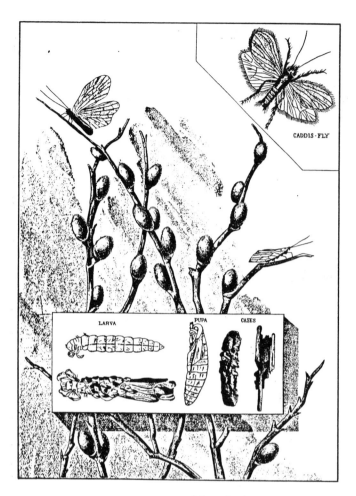

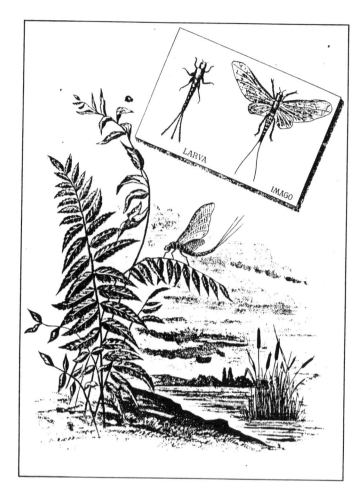

Mary Orvis Marbury's rendering of caddisfly life stages, from *Favorite Flies and Their Histories* (1892), showed several forms of caddis cases but referred to the flies as "duns."

Mary Orvis Marbury's rendering of nymph and adult mayflies, from *Favorite Flies and Their Histories* (1892).

what would later become known as the "fan-wing" style; a mayfly spent spinner with an extended body using buoyant hog bristles as a core; four hackle-tip wings; a june bug imitation; and an assortment of midges, stoneflies, and grasshoppers, all carefully illustrated and convincing.

Keene's books did well, and he undoubtedly did much to spread the word about imitation. He was part of an increase in interest that occurred in America in the 1880s and 1890s, and was probably the strongest single voice in those years. But he was realistic if not skeptical of how quickly Americans would accept any code of imitation even though they were encountering finicky brown trout in more and more of their streams. In the *American Field*, April 27, 1889, he seemed to give an almost audible sigh of resignation:

> It is doubtful however whether for many years to come the exact imitation theory of fly making will obtain, in this country, as it has done in certain sections of the old world.

He was right, and he was wrong. It appears now that he may have had more influence than he thought. When he wrote that, other American writers, propelled by the twin forces of brown trout selectivity and British fly-fishing fashion, were showing serious interest in imitation. It would be another British writer transplanted to America who first attempted to take all the diffuse interest and information and codify it.

Though Mary Marbury presented a brief discussion, with illustrations, on angling entomology (heavily dependent upon Sara McBride's earlier work) in her popular *Favorite Flies and Their Histories* (1892), and though any number of American writers talked about imitation in articles in the periodicals, it fell to another Englishman, Louis Rhead, to attempt the first full codification of American trout stream insects.

Rhead has been uniformly belittled by later angling entomologists, who in their attempts to show his mistakes (and, I fear in some cases, thereby highlight their own contributions) have thrown the baby out with the bathwater. Louis Rhead was one of the most creative, fresh-thinking, and stimulating of American fly-fishing writers, a man of extraordinary gifts. Reading him now, like reading Keene, leaves one with the feeling that we fly fishers are sometimes pretty dense. Not only do we ignore these rare talents when they come along, we later reinvent everything they did and claim it as new.

The problem with that attitude is that we probably didn't ignore them at the time. Keene and Rhead were widely read and respected; Rhead was one of the most energetic anglers in American history at promoting and marketing his ideas and his flies, for many years selling a line of flies and lures through William Mills in New York. What it so often comes down to is this: it is hard to know how many fly fishers in an age adopted practices proposed by any writer because practically all fly fishers do not leave a written record. Fishing theory and fly trends are difficult to trace, and so many good ideas (such as the hinged-bodied fly) are truly reinvented time and again while other good ideas (such as weighted nymphs fished in imitation of emergers) seem always to be known about but occasionally reannounced by new writers. Old flies often seem to fade from popularity not so much because they lose effectiveness as because they are replaced by more fashionable new flies, whether the new flies have proven more effective or not. Fly fishers are not simple in their tastes, and favor certain tackle, certain techniques, and certain attitudes for reasons other than might have been most common among an earlier generation.

Louis Rhead came to America in 1883. He was best known as an illustrator and artist, an extremely popular and productive illustrator of books. His work earned him numerous awards, including a gold medal at the 1904 St. Louis Exposition. He was eventually responsible for several books, all illustrated by his striking line drawings or paintings, and he wrote regularly for the magazines. His books were *Bait Angling for Common Fishes* (1907); *The Book of Fish and Fishing* (1908); *American Trout Stream Insects* (1916); and *Fisherman's Lures and Game Fish Food* (1920). He edited

In *Forest & Stream* in 1922 Louis Rhead showed how to tie a good imitation of a freshwater shrimp, a remarkably modern series of drawings that would not be out of place in a book from the 1980s. *Courtesy of David B. Ledlie.*

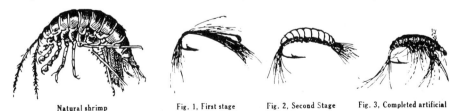

Natural shrimp   Fig. 1, First stage   Fig. 2, Second Stage   Fig. 3, Completed artificial

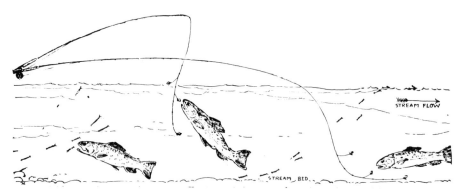

In *Forest & Stream* in 1922 Louis Rhead anticipated the technique now known as the "Leisenring Lift," by which a nymph is fished from the bottom to the top of the stream. Note trout feeding on nymphs rising to the surface. *Courtesy of David B. Ledlie.*

Rhead's two-hooked, hinged-body crayfish imitation, featured in *Forest & Stream* and in his book *American Trout Stream Insects* (1916). *Courtesy of David B. Ledlie.*

two others, *The Speckled Brook Trout* (1902) and *The Basses, Fresh Water and Marine* (1905). Though he discussed imitation in several works, his major effort was *American Trout Stream Insects*, a book based on several years of trout fishing in the Catskills.

On the one hand the book is a marvel for its time. Rhead illustrates dozens of mayflies, caddisflies, stoneflies, craneflies, and others, most in color; an angler-entomologist would not so skillfully combine writing with illustration again until Ernest Schwiebert produced *Nymphs* (1973). On the other hand the book was ultimately more frustrating than helpful. Rhead, despite criticisms and advice from fellow fishermen, chose to ignore scientific nomenclature:

> After a careful study of the various British books on trout insects and their artificial imitations issued to date, I deem it wise to brush aside the science of entomology, which is of no actual service to our purpose, and to lay before the angler a plain, simple plan whereby he can obtain just enough information to understand easily the general characteristics of the insects he is likely to observe trout feeding upon while wading a trout stream, to the end that he may have with him a fair imitation that will be most successful in luring trout.

Though it certainly was a dangerous departure from British practice (and perhaps also from practical realities), just ignoring science in itself was not necessarily fatal to Rhead's plan. It looks as if Rhead was actually ignorant of entomology, and did not even know how far it had advanced at that point in America. But it would have been possible, and maybe even popular, to write an angler's entomology that merely introduced the types of insects and then presented likely imitations for each, giving the times of their emergences and any other relevant information. It is there where Rhead really failed, however wrong he may have been to ignore scientific entomology.

Rhead was not content to codify existing patterns and add a few more; he created an entire new selection with virtually no regard for several centuries of accumulation:

> I have tied the various artificials as I think they will best imitate the natural insects, without any reference whatever to the artificial flies made and sold by American and English fly-makers, although I have made a careful study of all the works on trout flies. I have no hesitation in pinning my faith on the angler who uses these new patterns, if used as directed in the accompanying charts, as against the expert who angles with the popular native "fancy" flies or even the imported English dry flies.

Fly-pattern development, for all its chaotic lack of system, has always been slow to absorb and permanently accept a new pattern; it was the height of naiveté (something

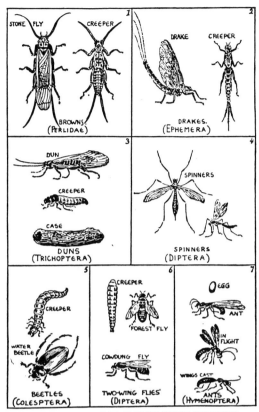

SPECIMENS OF SEVEN DIFFERENT ORDERS OF INSECTS

In his book *American Trout Stream Insects* (1916), Louis Rhead introduced his readers to the general form of the important stream insects but did not follow scientific nomenclature beyond that level.

he accused American commercial fly tiers of for their fancy flies) for Rhead to imagine he could simply replace centuries of accumulated tradition and favored patterns.

Even had it been possible, it could not have been done by the flies he offered. They were anything but uninteresting; his artist's perspective gave him a radically different view of insects, and some of these were probably at least as lifelike as anything else available. But they did not look like flies were thought to look; they looked (and sometimes were) ungainly, or at least strange, as if they had been created by a skilled hat maker rather than a fly tier. Even if some of them worked well (and anglers did not flock to offer testimonials), they were too much at once for anglers to accept. Rhead grossly underestimated not only the effectiveness of popular flies, but the reluctance of fly fishers to give up cherished favorites.

Why, then, should Rhead be remembered better than he is? Because he did much more than write a failed imitationist tract. He provided a huge amount of information on fly fishing, much of it provocative and original. *American Trout Stream Insects*, for all its mistakes and occasional arrogance, contains a wealth of valuable information.

More, Rhead's articles are as striking as Keene's in their modern sound. We have often been told that the nymph was introduced to America by Hewitt in the 1930s, yet here was Rhead, writing in *Forest and Stream* in the late teens and early 1920s on nymphs and how to fish them. A brief note in August of 1922 reported that his nymph fishing was very successful that year. In May he presented a remarkable essay on "Fishing from Bottom to Surface," in which he outlined what later became known as the "Leisenring lift" technique, complete with his customarily excellent drawings showing his "pump-lift" technique. Listen to the titles of some of his other articles:

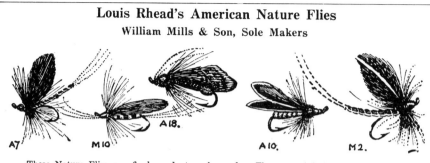

Louis Rhead's American Nature Flies
William Mills & Son, Sole Makers

These Nature Flies are finely and strongly made. They are tied from patterns made by Mr. Rhead to imitate natural flies collected and painted by him while on the streams of New York and Pennsylvania.

Mr. Rhead states that the same varieties of flies are found on most of the trout streams of the United States and lower Canada, and that the forty patterns he submitted are the best out of hundreds of natural flies collected by him.

Those marked with * are the ones he selected as the most popular and successful varieties..

April Patterns	May Patterns	June Pattern	July Patterns
*A- 1 Needle Tail	*M- 1 Green Drake	*J- 1 Female Greeneye	*K- 1 Golden Drake
A- 2 Brown Buzz	M- 2 Brown Drake	J- 2 Male Greeneye	K- 2 Pinktail Drake
A- 3 Short Tail	M- 4 Mottled Drake	J- 4 Greenback Drake	K- 4 Spottail
*A- 4 Brown Drake	M- 5 Cinnamon	*J- 5 Yellow Tip	K- 6 Olive Drake
A- 5 Longtail Drake	M- 6 Sandy	J- 7 Lemontail	*K- 7 Orange Stone
A- 6 Soldier Drake	M- 8 Gray Drake	*J- 9 Chocolate Drake	*K- 9 Redhead Gnat
*A- 7 Sailor Drake	*M-10 Yellow Sally	*J-14 Pointedtail Drake	K-10 White Miller
*A- 8 Red Bug	M-11 Flathead	J-16 Emerald	K-12 Plume Spinner
A- 9 Long Horn	*M-12 Alder	J-19 Hairy Spinner	K-13 Golden Spinner
A-10 Cowdung	*M-17 Golden Spinner	J-20 Gold Body Spinner	*K-17 Orange Miller
A-16 Shad Male	A-17 Shad Female	A-18 Shad Female (with eggs)	

Each pattern is tied on one size hook only, which is suitable for natural size of fly. Average size about No. 10.

PRICE $2.50 DOZEN

SUPPLEMENTARY SERIES—NEW TINY NATURE FLIES

To fill the demand for a smaller fly which is exact imitation of the natural insect, made on size 12 hooks.

April Patterns	May Patterns	June Patterns	July Patterns
A11 Brown Dipper	M7 Tiny Ruby	J3 Dark Claret	K3 Little Celt
A12 Pale Claret	M9 Dark Olive	J6 Silver Sedge	K5 Ruby Tip
M3 Olive Speckled	M13 Maple Fly	J8 June Orange	K8 Green Spinner

$2.50 per dozen

METAL BODY FLY

Set of six metal body flies. Good for all season, all weather. All localities. Steady diet. Most killing trout flies ever made.

Price $1.00 Set

METALBODY FLY

LATEST NEW TROUT FLIES

New set of six **Humpback Nymphs** suitable to surface, middle and bottom waters. Good all through the season.

Price $1.00 Set

NYMPH

New set of four "Reverse" Downstream Dry Flies Just drop them on the surface; they float downstream until taken by trout.

Price $1.00 Set

REVERSE DRY FLY.

In the 1920s and 1930s, William Mills of New York catalogued a series of Rhead's lures and flies. Note the "humpback nymphs," possibly Rhead's attempt to imitate emergers, and the "reverse dry flies," to be fished downstream.

"Downstream Dry-Fly Fishing"; "Tying the Fresh Water Shrimp" (his illustrations are excellent); "Unsinkable Cork Body Stone Flies"; "Trout Insects for Early Fly Fishing."

It is hard to place Rhead in the development of American fly fishing because some of the things that he concentrated on most—especially his commercial attempts to establish his many "nature lures," as he called his various original flies and lures—were so unsuccessful and even hurt his reputation. He not only criticized the major commercial outlets of flies, he took on such established and admired figures as George LaBranche. He did not have to do much of that to have no friends left to write anything kind about him in later years. The offense of simply discarding the fly patterns and insulting everyone was not just a personal affront to those being slighted. It was an arrogant step because it implied that he could do better *all the*

Many of Louis Rhead's excellent line drawings that illustrated his books were more or less self-portraits, including these two from *The Speckled Brook Trout* (1902), ''A pool where the big fellows lie,'' and ''Dashing down stream (Beaverkill)'' (see next page).

time, as if all his flies were improvements. One of the biggest differences between Rhead and Preston Jennings, who twenty years later finally produced the first accepted angler's entomology and fly-pattern collection for America, was that Jennings had the wisdom to borrow from the best and accumulate a set of flies that was the work of fishermen of the previous forty years.

It may be even harder to measure Rhead's successes than to analyze his failures. He certainly stimulated many anglers in their own work; Montana's George Grant, one of the pioneers of modern hackle-weaving techniques, has said that he found Rhead's books extremely stimulating and helpful, fifty years ago when he was learning about trout stream insects and fly-tying theory in what was nearly a regional vacuum as far as published information. As well, whether or not they used Rhead's "nature lures," anglers could benefit from his portraits of natural insects and his information on when they emerged.

Rhead remains one of the more interesting enigmas in American fly-fishing history. If he behaved as he wrote, he was probably not a pleasant person; he displayed in his writing an overbearing assertiveness that reminds me of Edward Hewitt's. But he was undeniably an original thinker, and among his other contributions his very differentness—his unorthodoxy and independence from hoary tradition—may have provided later angler-entomologists, those who finally got it right, something to react against and try to improve on.

Like Rhead, the progress of imitation in American fly fishing is difficult to comprehend. It depended mostly upon whom you asked, or who you read, whether or not it was important. All the while that Theodore Gordon was writing his gracious little notes in *Forest and Stream* (roughly 1900 to 1915) encouraging fellow American fly fishers to tie accurate imitations, many other writers were advocating fancy flies, or claiming that fly pattern meant nothing at all. It is plain that imitation, though it had a foothold by the time of Keene's writings, had not made great progress by the time Rhead's book on insects was published. There may have been more people seriously interested in entomology, but they were still a small percentage of those fly fishing.

Imitation got its biggest boost from a type of fly that has only been peripherally dealt with in this chapter, the dry fly. For some imitationists, including both Keene and Rhead, imitation quite often *meant* dry-fly imitation. Because the story of the dry fly and its arrival in America needed special attention, I did not integrate it into this chapter but have saved it for the next.

10

The American Floating Fly

Probably the reason dry fly fishing has not been practised to any great extent in this country is because of the character of our streams, as well as the fact that our trout are not so highly "educated" as are those of the much fished chalk streams of England. It may be asserted that dry-fly fishing had its rise with Mr. Halford, author of "Dry-Fly Fishing in Theory and Practice," "Dry-Fly Entomology," and other works, a man of sufficient wealth and leisure to ride a hobby to its stable.

O. W. Smith, *Trout Lore* (1917)

The entire history of floating flies has been challenged in the past ten years by fishing historians on both sides of the Atlantic. The leading revisionist in England has been Jack Heddon, a studious authority on British angling writing who has stirred a lot of excitement by going against the established dogma of the dry fly as an invention of the 1800s. In this he has necessarily taken on the best-known historical sources, themselves now as entrenched in popular conviction as the story they tell. Most of all, a challenge of this sort is a direct criticism of John Waller Hills's *A History of Fly Fishing for Trout* (1921), wherein much of what is now considered gospel in angling history originated.

This is not an American story, so I won't dwell on it. But it merits summary because the same problems of historical interpretation have cropped up in American fishing history.

The established view is that the modern dry fly developed in the early 1800s, receiving first full description in G. P. R. Pulman's *Vade Mecum of Fly Fishing for Trout*. The 1851 edition, according to Hills and many later writers, was the first to give a complete description of the dry fly, that is, a fly kept dry by false casting, cast upstream over a rising fish. The problems of historical interpretation could be said to spread outward, like rings of the rise, from this statement. They start, in fact, with the description itself, because Hills and others indulged in wishful reading by finding false-casting in the description at all. What Pulman was recommending was not false-casting to dry the fly. Here are his words:

> Let a dry fly be substituted for the wet one, the line switched a few times through the air to throw off its superabundant moisture, a judicious cast made just above the rising fish, and the fly allowed to float towards and over them, and the chances are ten to one that it will be seized as readily as the living insect.

First, Pulman is talking about false-casting to dry the *line*, not the fly. He has just told us to put on a dry fly, so there would be no need to dry it anyway. Then, Pulman seems to be talking about putting it over more than one fish (''them'') rather than a specific one. Hills knew what he was looking for, but he didn't know how it fit into historical process. He was a product, writing in the 1920s, of the great Halfordian revolution, an event that not only made the dry fly popular but developed a tight, narrow definition of what dry-fly fishing actually was. In earlier editions of the book, Pulman had described (as did several other authors of the 1700s and 1800s) floating a fly over a fish. But Hills did not consider that fully dry-fly fishing because it did not meet the Halfordian definition, lacking false casting. Hills's hasty reading of Pulman's line-drying instructions convinced him that he had found the point of origin of the important practice that was nearly a religion by 1920.

The point that has been made repeatedly by recent writers (and, incidentally, by Roderick Haig-Brown in 1946 and by Al McClane as early as 1965) is that though anglers before the 1860s and 1870s (the years when the modern dry fly was being formalized in England) did not fulfill the requirements of Halford's definition of ''dry fly,'' they were fishing flies on the surface. They may not have understood the concepts of split wings, or stiff hackles, or upstream casts over rising trout, or any other specific element of the Halford code, but they were fishing on the surface. Hills formalized the conviction that they were not dry-fly fishing in his *History* partly by quoting some of the better-known early books that seemed to talk of floating flies, such as Barker's and Mascall's, and then writing them off mostly because they did not meet the Halford definition. Half a century later, Arnold Gingrich, in *The Fishing in Print* (1974), did the same thing:

> There had been frequent mentions of the taking of trout with flies ''on top of the water,'' going back over nearly two centuries to the time of Col. Robert Venables. But most of these citations of surface-takes by trout were either as phenomena or desiderata, rather than to a recognized and purposive practice.

With that, Gingrich echoed Hills, though to my ear, and to the ears of Jack Heddon and others, the citations are obviously quite purposive. What they are not, however, are descriptions of dry flies in the modern sense. These early men knew, it is clear from their many mentions of it, that the fly should sometimes be kept on the surface.

That is why I used the term ''floating fly'' at the head of this chapter instead of ''dry fly.'' The former is less loaded (though Halford himself used it to mean dry fly) than the latter. One of the most creative, even brilliant, analysts in the history of floating flies was Vincent Marinaro. In his book *In the Ring of the Rise* he offered a definition of dry flies that is far more useful to historians than the narrower Halfordian concept:

We must begin with the proposition that no matter how dry the fly is, it must touch the water and be exposed to the air at the same time. If this idea is carried out to its logical conclusion, all of us must agree that if the smallest portion is exposed to the air no matter how deeply submerged the fly may be, it is still a legitimate form of the dry fly.

These are the murky waters of sporting definition, and they mix subjective preferences with objective realities; we can decide to call any lure anything we like, whether we can convince anyone else to agree with us or not.[1] The important point for this chapter is the distinction that Marinaro makes, by implication, between the two fundamental types of trout flies: those that are completely submerged and those that are not. Hills and his followers proposed that it wasn't until the pre-Halford stirrings of the early 1800s that fly fishers came to employ the latter group intentionally, and sought to find ways to refine the floatability of that group. Heddon, McClane, Cameron, I, and others propose that the Halford dry fly is more accurately perceived as a refinement of a long-standing type of fishing that involved having some portion of the fly poking above the surface. We have done a reasonable job of establishing our case through consideration of the evidence of British works before 1850, but I will now show, in any event, that something similar took place in America.

There are two separate approaches to floating flies as they grew to popularity in America in the 1800s. Each has subsets, but they are distinguished just as are the British ones. The first approach was that adopted by many fly fishers with little or no connection to the Halford school, fly fishers who in the years between 1830 and 1880 somehow kept their flies on the surface. The second approach grew out of the formal dry-fly school that flourished in England in the period after about 1870 under the leadership of Halford. By the 1880s, the formal dry-fly school was getting well known in America, so that by about 1890 it is usually difficult to tell whether a writer who described floating flies was working independent of, or as a part of, the British dry-fly tradition.

By now, I suspect, those readers who have some familiarity with American fishing history as it has usually been written must be at least puzzled, because ''everyone knows that the dry fly came to America in 1890 when Theodore Gordon wrote to Halford, right?'' I apologize for shaking readers loose from such sturdily constructed moorings, but it must be done; American dry-fly history has fared no better than British dry-fly history at the hands of writers who, for the most part, knew before they started what they wanted to prove.

Not surprisingly, the first references that I have found in American sporting writing to flies floating, or to fish feeding on natural insects on the surface, are British in origin. On May 19, 1832, for example, the *Spirit of the Times* reprinted an article from *Bell's Life of London* in which the author discussed some of the problems of trout fishing, the ''principal'' one being ''heavy falls of rains, by which the streams and pools became so clouded that the fish cannot see the flies playing on the surface.'' The author was talking about natural insects, but I offer it to suggest that fly fishers have not failed to notice, in any age, that trout rise to take floating naturals. That was also obvious to J. V. C. Smith in his 1833 book *Natural History of the Fishes of Massachusetts*, in which he described surface feeding to midges:

It frequently happens, in a calm time, that the surface is covered with an insect so small that they could not be perceived by the fish if it was at all agitated by the wind. At such times the trout are rising in all directions, apparently in sport, but upon examination they will be found to have fifty or more of these little specks collected in the throat.

Smith reported that he was frustrated in his attempts to imitate something so small, and leaves us to wonder if he tried to imitate them with a floating fly. But I offer this, like the previous one, to suggest only that some fishermen were perceptive enough to understand surface feeding.

A couple of 1833 articles exposed American fishermen to floating flies. First, from *The American Turf Register and Sporting Magazine* for August, from a long article by the British writer "Sylvanus Swanquill" (who gets my vote for the sappiest of angling pen names), these passages about a fly he has just cast:

> Whish! goes the line through the air, as gentle as a butterfly's flight; down drops the little greendrake on the curl of the water like a snowflake, only rather softer; and see! here it comes tripping up the stream with its little wings expanded, and looking as innocent as any real ephemera that ever dropt into the water . . .
>
> Don't he walk the waters like a thing of life? Mayflies themselves that are bobbing up and down at his elbow take him for one of their own kin, and wonder how the deuce he manages to go sailing along against the wind and the tide that way.

Here is a floating fly dragging on the surface. That it remained on the surface a long while becomes clear later when a swallow comes down and takes the fly *from* the surface.

That same year, in the *New York Sporting Magazine and Annals of the American and English Turf* for July, a pirated British essay thinly disguised as American discussed floating flies carefully:

> Having ascertained the quarter from which the wind blows, take your place on the windward side of the river, and if there is a good breeze, it will not only assist you in throwing your line, but when you draw it toward you after being delivered, will cause your flies to float well upon the surface, and create a little wave or ripple on the water, thereby assisting the deception, and enable you to fish or whip with your line over deep still pools, which often contain very large fish. In order to ascertain what kind of fly to begin with, examine the water; you will probably soon be directed to flies floating thereon, by seeing the fish rise at them . . .

Of course there are some language problems inherent in such statements. A fly could conceivably be called "floating" by these people if it were just beneath the surface; it would still be "floating" over most of the river's depth. But this is all such a good description of floating flies, even to the wisdom of fishing on a breezy day that ruffles the surface and obscures the floating fly's outline to the fish.

As well, I cannot prove, nor would I suggest, that Americans in any number actually applied these principles after reading the articles. What I suggest instead is that such principles are more or less intuitive to someone who has observed trout feeding on surface insects.

There were several ways known to British and American anglers for keeping a fly on the surface (even if it could not truly float on its own). "Dapping" the fly on a tight line was one, blowline fishing (in which the wind was allowed to whip and bounce the fly on the surface) was another. Yet another was practiced in both Old World and New by the 1840s, and it involved a multiple-fly rig. A writer in the *Spirit* on February 22, 1840, described the technique used on a Long Island pond. The fly on the end, called the point fly, or tail, or stretcher, was fished weighted and sunk, forming a kind of drifting anchor to allow the upper fly, often known as the dropper or bob fly, to skim the surface:

> In the expectation, then, of being obliged to cast to windward, I affixed a small shot to the head of my lowermost fly, so as to form a good substitute for the necessary member (this little fixture, I suppose you know, is a mighty assistant in making a cast in the wind's eye). The snell to which this headed fly was attached, was about two feet long, and in the loop, where it was joined to the end of the leader, I slipped another snell, of about 9 or 10 inches long, with a second fly.
>
> This I have always found to be a killing rig; the upper fly skims lightly over the surface, while the lower one is a foot or so beneath it; and it is with the latter that I have generally been most successful.

It appears he caught more fish on the sunk fly than on the upper one, but the practice was not uncommon, and apparently was successful with both flies at least some of the time.

Some of the most interesting early accounts of surface flies and surface-feeding fish that I have found involve Atlantic salmon. Fishing for Atlantic salmon with floating flies has been rediscovered by several generations of Americans, and was practiced in interesting ways by British anglers as well before it was "invented" by Hewitt and Monell after 1910 or so. A series of articles in the *Turf Register* between 1839 and 1842 are revealing. In the March–April issue, the writer and his companion, fishing a Canadian salmon stream, had this experience:

> We found that a fresh batch of fine trout had made their way up the river, low as it was, which afforded us capital sport, rising greedily at our salmon flies, and very lively and strong on the line, but we could see no salmon until late in the evening, when we noticed a very large one sucking in some small flies in the middle of the stream. We both covered him, endeavoring to tempt his palate by various flies resembling those on the water, using at the same time a single gut casting line, but all in vain. At last, just before starting for home, I tried one more cast over him— he rose like a young whale, and I found myself fast . . .

They saw the fish feeding on surface insects, but we can't be sure they floated their imitations. The same author offered a clearer case in the August 1842 issue, though, in another description of salmon fishing:

> However, I dared the combat and threw out my fly as a gauntlet. The gage was soon taken up, for scarcely had the simulated insect alighted on the water when a huge mouth swallowed it, and I found I had got hold of a tartar.

The rise of a salmon can often be seen, even if the fly is slightly submerged, but this sounds to me like a fly that floated, as the author said, "on the water." There is no question, in any case, that the author knew that salmon could be tempted to break the surface of the water for a fly. On another occasion, described in the May–June 1839 issue, he told of taking a salmon on a fly that was not even touching the water:

> On Friday morning, I prepared a most captivating Grouse's hackle, with a small black head, two parti-colored antennae, and the most natural tail imaginable. Waiting till the shadow of a large maple fell on the hole, I then took off my shoes—stole quietly along the rock and sat down. After a little I dropped the new fly within a couple of inches of the water, and bobbed it up and down, as if the insect meditated

alighting, but did not much relish the thought of wetting its delicate wings and feet.

No salmon that ever swam could resist the temptation. Up came my friend with open mouth—darted his huge muzzle out of the water, and took the fly in the air, and then disappeared in the depths of the eddy.

Odd approach, but it worked.

One of the most interesting of all the early accounts was quoted in Chapter 6. Wilford Woodruff, with no prior knowledge of American fly fishing and no known connection with later fly fishers, dropped a fly on a trout stream near Fort Bridger, Wyoming, and "watched as it floated upon the water."

That was his first cast, and he reminds me of several authors who observed that you often got your fish on those first casts when the fly had not yet gotten soaked and sunk. One could argue whether or not this is a technique of floating-fly fishing or is merely hoping for the best on the first few casts, but it was known to catch fish, and was described in full, even to false-casting, by Thaddeus Norris in his great *American Angler's Book* in 1864. This has been recognized by most writers since the time of Gordon as the "first" description of dry-fly fishing in America:

Thaddeus Norris, a portrait published by the Derrydale Press in 1931. *Courtesy of The American Museum of Fly Fishing.*

> If it could be accomplished, the great desideratum would be to keep the line wet and the flies dry. I have seen anglers succeed so well in their efforts to do this by the means just mentioned, and by whipping the moisture from their flies, that the stretcher and dropper would fall so lightly, and remain so long on the surface, that a fish would rise and deliberately take the fly before it sank.

At about the same time, Theodatus Garlick, in his *A Treatise on the Artificial Propagation of Certain Kinds of Fish* (1857), recommended that "flies should be dropped very gantle [sic] on the surface of the water, and should not be suffered to remain stationary at one place, but is to be drawn along by a trembling motion communicated to the rod by means of the hand; great care should also be taken, not to let the line drop on the water, but simply the flies, and a portion of silk gut leader, and these so gently as not to create suspicion." Again, we can't be positive, but throughout his directions Garlick specifies *on,* not in, the water.

After the Civil War, as fly-fishing writing and tackle production increased, many more accounts appeared. Here are some:

"Podgers," writing in *Forest and Stream* on November 19, 1874, about fishing for either salmon or steelhead on the Navarro River in California:

> The fly lit lightly on the water, and danced along the surface, with no results. My friend smiled and the standing committee guffawed. Paying no attention, I made a second cast at a good distance. My fly had scarcely touched the water before there was a flash, a swirl, and, as I threw up the point of my rod, I felt a weight as if I had hooked a saw log . . .

F. L. King, reporting in *Forest and Stream* on December 4, 1873, on bass fishing near Rochester, New York:

> It is seldom that I let my flies sink below the surface of the water. It is not necessary with this fly [his own pattern, humbly named the King], but the instant that it touches the water, if they are at all inclined, it is greedily taken, in fact I have seen them jump clear out of the water to seize the supposed prize. It looks too much like bait fishing to let them sink below the surface . . .

J. L. Mullaly, in his patent (#139,180) for an ''improvement in angling flies,'' May 20, 1873:

> A fly thus constructed [with the hook turned up under the wings, rather like a modern keel hook] will be found more deceptive and consequently more serviceable than those commonly employed. The hook being concealed will be readily and unsuspectingly taken by the fish. The wings will form a sort of float and the hook operates as ballast, so that the fly retains its natural position on the water, and even if it should become inverted it will right itself readily.

James Henshall, bass fishing in *Forest and Stream*, August 26, 1880:

> The angler should endeavor to cast his flies as lightly as possible, causing them to settle as quietly as possible, and without a splash. After casting, the flies should be skipped along the surface in slightly curving lines, or by zigzag movements, occasionally allowing them to become submerged for several inches near likely-looking spots. If the current is swift, allow the flies to float naturally with it, at times, when they can be skittered back again, or withdrawn for a new cast.

Lewis B. France, on fishing for trout in Colorado, in *The American Angler*, August 19, 1882:

> I tried my gray hackle with all kinds of bodies, the professor, the coachman and everything I could lay hands on, I danced the flies over his head, across his back, I let them float and I skittered and dropped them, but that trout never moved.

These references increase in the 1880s and 1890s, and they reveal a variety of surface-fishing techniques being experimented with. I have no idea what percentage of fly fishers were involved, but obviously those who read the magazines were regularly exposed to interesting ideas. In 1886, Wakeman Holberton's patented fluttering fly was introduced, designed to ''seam the surface with an attractive wake, and its expanded wings will create a fluttering motion.'' In 1888, Charles Orvis reported to *Forest and Stream* on a fly developed in North Carolina ''made by cutting narrow strips of the skin [of deer] with the hair left on, and wrapping the same around

Wakeman Holberton's advertisement, in 1886, for his fluttering fly, a reverse-tied pattern that, according to the advertisement, was almost guaranteed to be an improvement on old-fashioned flies. Reverse-tied flies resurface, so to speak, every so often but never seem to catch the imagination of most anglers.

the hook a few times, and tieing [sic] well at the end. The Indians tie them to perfection and use some sort of cement or varnish making waterproof the thread. They use various colors and lengths of hair from different skins . . . The effect of this reversed method is very perceptible in swift water. Every little move in drawing back as it floats down gives it the appearance of a live worm trying to get out of the water.'' This is the earliest sure reference I have found to Americans using deer hair in a floating fly that was probably designed for trout, but I don't assume it's the first. George Dawson, writing in Orvis and Cheney's *Fishing with the Fly* (1883), recommended what sound like floating flies for Atlantic salmon, though the "rise" of a salmon is often visible even to flies a few inches below the surface.

> The rule with some anglers is "to let the fly sink a little;" my rule is never to let it sink at all. When a fish strikes I want to see him. There is no movement that so thrills and delights me as the rush of the salmon for the fly. To me, half the pleasure of a rise is lost if I don't see the head and shoulders of the kingly fish when he leaps for the lure.

The examples I've given, and others I've found, seem sufficient evidence that at least some American anglers were experimenting with floating flies of many kinds in the years before the Halford dry fly became popular. The rise of the formal dry fly was also well reported to American anglers.

I assume that almost as soon as the formal "dry fly" made its way into the British sporting press it also appeared in the American press. The exchange of information was often even more direct than that. The famous American fishing writer Reuben Wood, on a visit to England in 1883, was taken to the Kennet by Robert Marston and *shown* dry-fly fishing, according to Fred Mather in *Men I Have Fished With* (1897). Eighteen eighty-three is, in any event, the year of the first reference I have yet located in an American source to "dry flies." H. P. Wells was quoted in *Fishing with the Fly* on the subject:

> I am inclined to believe that more important than fishing up or down stream, more important than wearing brilliant or sober-tinted clothing, more important than wading or fishing from the bank, more important than a dry or a wet fly, more important than being yourself visible or concealed, more important, indeed, than any of the different cautions of the books, is to have your leader absolutely invisible, or, if that is impossible, then at least that it present to the trout no unusual or unfamiliar appearance.

That same book contained other references to floating flies, such as W. David Tomlin's repeated mentions of fishing with a "Floating May-fly," a term used by several early commercial outlets to distinguish their dry flies (Orvis advertised "cork body floating" flies in the *American Angler* in 1881).

But most important in 1883 was the appearance of the first American edition of David Foster's British book, *The Scientific Angler*. Edited by a well-known American angling writer and editor, William Harris, the book contained a complete summary of dry-fly fishing. There is even a curious footnote by Harris about trailing a fly across the surface so as to "leave a wake behind it like a sternwheel steamer." But it is Foster's presentation that mattered most. There was talk of which insects, when they fall into the water, "float buoyantly along" and which don't, a discussion of why legs in a floating fly "should be ample and full" (to promote flotation), and several succinct pages on how to fish the flies. It's all there: false-casting to dry the

Fig. 86.—WINDING BODY OF "EXACT IMITATION" FLY.

Fig. 85.—"EXACT IMITATION" FLY.

Fig. 87.—HOW TO FIX LEGS OF "EXACT IMITATION."

Three stages in the production of J. Harrington Keene's "exact imitation" dry fly, from his book *Fly-Fishing and Fly-Making* (1891). The core of the body is horse-hair, the legs are hackle feathers clipped very short.

flies, making sure the wings on dry flies "cock" properly as they float along, the virtue of being able to fish dry flies both up and down stream, the importance of avoiding drag . . . it is impressively complete. It also must have been influential. I am sure, anyway, that the copy I have read was; it resides in the library of The American Museum of Fly Fishing, and at the head of the title page appears the signature of a former owner: Theodore Gordon.

The dry-fly revolution that really got rolling with the appearance of Halford's first book, *Floating Flies and How to Dress Them* (1886) got plenty of attention in American books and articles. J. Harrington Keene's three different series of articles, in 1885, 1887, and 1889, mentioned in the previous chapter, all discussed dry flies at great length, with detailed instructions. Keene's book *Fly Fishing and Fly Making* (1887) also contained material on dry flies, especially the enlarged second edition (1891), which was evidently popular. Robert Marston's essay "Dry-Fly Fishing," originally published in the *Fishing Gazette*, was reprinted in *The American Angler* on June 27, 1885. This was a remarkable essay, more open-minded than many dry-fly treatises in that it recommended both up- and downstream fishing as the occasion required (explaining how to throw some slack in the line so a downstream drift was practical). Halford's own words, excerpted from his 1886 book, were reprinted in a series of articles in *The American Angler* starting in January, 1889, and his book

Cork-bodied floating fly pictured in Keene's *Fly-Fishing and Fly-Making* (1891).

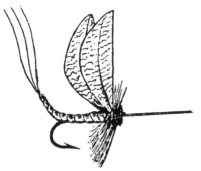

Fig. 71.—CONCAVE-WINGED MAY-FLY WITH CORK BODY.

Keene's pattern for a pair of mayflies (top) and a reverse-tied fly (similar to the 1886 Holberton patent) appeared in the May 21, 1887 edition of the *American Field*. There was some controversy over the originator of the reverse-tied fly, and Keene, writing in the *American Field*, May 18, 1889, pointed out that Foster Brothers of England had developed such a fly in about 1882. *Courtesy of David B. Ledlie.*

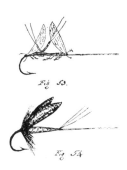

could be purchased directly from *Forest and Stream* by 1888 (it cost twelve dollars, more than twice the price even of Thad Norris's huge *American Angler's Book*).

William Mills of New York was selling Halford-style dry flies by 1888, as were the Kewel Brothers of San Francisco. Orvis started selling them about the same time. Thomas Chubb got into the market shortly thereafter.

So by 1890 the dry fly was no secret in America. It continued to get occasional attention in the press through the 1890s and first decade of the new century from such popular writers as Louis Rhead, George LaBranche, Mary Marbury (who featured a page of the Halford flies in color in *Favorite Flies* in 1892), William Harris, and, of course, Theodore Gordon, who started writing regularly for an American audience after 1900.

Not that the fly was widely appreciated; it is difficult to tell just how well known it was at any point. Louis Rhead, writing in *Outing* in 1908, could still claim that "dry fly fishing is comparatively unknown among our anglers—at least in practice." Emlyn Gill, in his little *Practical Dry-Fly Fishing* (1912), reported that a New York tackle dealer told him in 1911 that "there were not more than one hundred real dry-fly fishermen in the United States."[2] And good old James Henshall, in *Favorite Fish and Fishing* (1908), had predicted that the dry fly would not "find many adherents in this country," and went on to object to the already-rising snobbery of the dry fly, entering "a protest against claiming for it a higher niche in the ethics of sport than wet fly-fishing."

Of these three, Henshall would have been the most trustworthy. Rhead and Gill were New York fishermen of fairly narrow (if exclusive) acquaintance, men likely to apply a Halford or Hills type of definition to what was a "real" dry-fly fisherman. They would have had little contact with (or interest in contact with) the "other" type

Keene's hackle-point spinner, from *Fly-Fishing and Fly-Making* (1891).

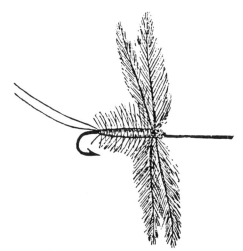

Fig. 72.—FORM OF FLOATING FLY.

of floating-fly fisherman mentioned earlier. I wish we could know where Orvis, from his peculiar geographical neutrality in Vermont, and with his carefully cultivated set of correspondents all over the country, sold dry flies, and how many people bought them. But even that would only be a beginning, because it would not tell us how many people were tying their own and fishing them without regard for the opinions of New York dealers.

What is usually seen as the culminating event in the development of dry flies in America, at least in their early stage, is the publication of two books, Gill's 1912 book mentioned earlier and George LaBranche's 1914 book *The Dry Fly and Fast Water*. There were three, really—the third (second in order of appearance) was Samuel Camp's little *Fishing with Floating Flies* (1913)—and I suppose nitpickers could include a small 1912 booklet privately published by Louis Rhead, also on dry flies. But now that we've witnessed the development of two overlapping schools of thought, those of imitation and dry flies, we run into a puzzling problem with these books. None of the three are especially avid about imitation. The era between 1900 and 1915 is usually seen as the period in which Americans, especially Gordon, laid the foundation for an American theory of imitation and dry-fly usage, but the books did not reflect an imitationist stance. Indeed, the best of them by far, LaBranche's, was totally disinterested in Gordon's style of imitation. Just as Americans were still, in 1915, predominantly committed to general and fancy flies, they were inclined to use general and fancy flies for their dry-fly fishing, or to rely on whatever British patterns were handy. Besides that, LaBranche popularized an enduring American approach to dry flies that is not all that different from fishing ''blind'' with wet flies, in that it involves casting, repeatedly, to likely spots. He was, in the words of Marinaro, the ''principle architect of the early American style of fishing the rough mountain waters . . .''

This internal conflict among the supposed pioneers of American dry-fly fishing is fascinating. There were Keene, Gordon, Rhead, and others each preaching his own personal brand of imitation, and there were others, including LaBranche, going their own ways and having at least as great an effect on fly fishing. That said, it is virtually impossible to continue without turning at last to American fly fishing's most intriguing character, a person whose historical persona is so charming and engaging that he has become the symbol of the best of an entire sport. That person, of course, is Theodore Gordon.

11

Theodore Gordon

Though once a real person, he has become our myth.
JOHN MCDONALD

Theodore Gordon has become the central figure in the history of American fly fishing. For all the wonderful things that have been written about the other "giants" such as Thaddeus Norris, Lee Wulff, Ray Bergman, and so on, it is from Gordon that the modern tradition is most often said to flow. He has been glorified more with each passing generation, until within the past ten years he has been given credit for, among other things, the invention of the streamer, the original study of angling entomology in America, introducing the dry fly to America, introducing the nymph to America, originating an American style of dry-fly tying, originating the American approach to imitation, and being, finally, "the father of modern American angling." Such a figure, so enshrouded in the love and legend of a sport, will not be lightly tampered with; I have already stirred up considerable resentment by suggesting that much of this legend is just that—legend. I have not done this lightly, or without an understanding of what Gordon has come to mean to us. He is unrivaled in his importance as a symbol, and he is rarely matched in his qualities as a writer and angling thinker. But he has been unfairly jerked from his context by our half-century binge of admiration.[1] We needed a Theodore Gordon to fill out the lore of American fly fishing. We were lucky, though, to find that he fit the bill so beautifully. He was in practically no sense the original we have given him credit for being, but he was still remarkable.

In a more strictly organized history of American fly fishing, I might just have placed Gordon in context wherever his contributions merited it. I have not done it this way because Gordon, whatever his historical significance relative to his contemporaries, has become extremely important to us later. The reasons for that situation are in themselves interesting enough to cause me to break him out of the narrative and examine his story. Besides, a look at Gordon's work provides a nice sort of cross-check on fly fishing in his time.

What I propose, then, is first to sketch his biography briefly and then to consider the various elements of his contribution, both the technical and the less tangible ones.

Perhaps the two best sources of information on Gordon are John McDonald's introduction and notes in *The Complete Fly Fisherman: The Notes and Letters of Theodore Gordon* (1947) and Alfred W. Miller's ("Sparse Grey Hackle") research

Gordon as a teenager, about 1870; he was an avid hunter, collecting many of his fly tying materials from domestic game. *Courtesy of The American Museum of Fly Fishing.*

report in *Fishless Days, Angling Nights* (1971). Gordon was born to a reasonably wealthy family in Pittsburgh in 1854. His father is reported to have died of malaria the following year, and Gordon's childhood was spent in various parts of the South and in Pennsylvania, where he summered near Carlisle and became an avid outdoorsman. It was apparently during his youth that he also fished the Florida Keys, though probably not with flies. Even in his youth his health was bad, and he seems to have been subject to frequent respiratory problems, including pneumonia. After the Civil War his mother took him south on a more permanent basis. Among its other effects, this move has left us with little knowledge of his activities as a young man. We have few records, beyond his own occasional comments in his later writings, of what he did in the late 1870s and early 1880s. There is a faded picture of him as a teenager, posed with bird dog and shotgun in a Carlisle studio, and an 1885 portrait of the young man taken in Savannah.

As a young man he worked in accounting, bookkeeping, and securities, but his mother's fortunes failed, and so did his health. Sparse believes that by 1893 Gordon and his mother had moved to New Jersey, where he worked intermittently in brokerage offices and began ever more frequent and lengthy fishing trips, especially to the Catskills (he is also known to have fished Michigan and Wisconsin, not an unusually broad experience for a man of his time who was an avid sportsman). During this time his mother's health was also failing, and Sparse tells us that Gordon complained bitterly about what a burden she was. Gordon was apparently selfish and uncaring about this woman who had worked herself sick trying to raise him in comfort; much

This photograph of a dapper young Gordon was taken about 1890 in Savannah; it appeared with his 1915 obituary in *Forest & Stream. Courtesy of The American Museum of Fly Fishing.*

Gordon in about 1885, a photograph taken in Savannah. *Courtesy of The American Museum of Fly Fishing.*

of the evidence suggests that he was a cranky, uncompanionable person quite often.

By 1900 or shortly thereafter he had become a professional fly tier, dividing his time between relatives in New York and various Catskill rivers. He probably spent most of his last ten years, 1905 to 1915, living in various inadequate quarters in Sullivan County, near the Beaverkill, Neversink, and other rivers he loved.

Gordon corresponded with *Forest and Stream* at least rarely in the 1890s, but he did not begin to write regularly for an American audience until about 1903. He had already become an avid reader of fishing books, having several dozen of the best in his library, and he was already fascinated by imitation theory and the dry fly. In 1890 he wrote to Halford and received in return an encouraging letter and a set of Halford's own flies, an event given great press by later generations of fishing writers as the first appearance of dry flies in America.

It is one of the peculiarities of Gordon's career that he did not start writing for Americans until long after he was well established as a correspondent of the British *Fishing Gazette*, for which he wrote as early as 1890. Throughout his writing career, as John McDonald has pointed out, Gordon seemed to save his most sophisticated work for his British audience.

Between 1890 and 1915, he wrote hundreds of letters, many published as ''notes'' and ''little talks'' in *The Fishing Gazette* and *Forest and Stream*. It is these letters, both the published and a wonderful amount of unpublished material, that McDonald gathered with care and published as *The Complete Fly Fisherman*. The book initiated a reverence for Gordon that has increased steadily since it was published. During his life Gordon published no book, though he was at one point approached about publishing a collection of his ''little talks,'' and though there was reportedly a manuscript found among his possessions after his death (according to some accounts), a manuscript burned because of fear of infection by tuberculosis.

We owe McDonald much for giving us *The Complete Fly Fisherman*. It is one of America's truly great angling books. This is all the more impressive considering that it is just a chronological gathering of short articles and correspondence written more or less randomly over a quarter of a century. At first reading, the book surprises by the amount of information and breadth of knowledge it reveals, but it is much more than a miscellany. There emerges through its pages an angler's ethic and philosophy, both of which have increased in worth as time has passed. Gordon's contemporaries saw that wisdom in him and praised him for it; they seem to have been as much struck by those qualities as by his technical expertise. *The Complete Fly Fisherman* is not Waltonian; it is neither as pastoral nor as relaxed as *The Compleat Angler*. It deserves its own label. Later writers could do much worse than to be labeled Gordonian.

What survives, then, is a tragic story, of a promising young man whose misfortunes compelled him to live a simple life, one that if he might not have preferred it, was at least what we would have preferred for him. He became the total angler, devoting his entire energy to learning and understanding fly fishing. He lived the life that many dream they would like to live. The distance of time has softened the story's rough edges—his apparent meanness—and have left only the slightly out-of-focus image of the enfeebled recluse, coughing blood and shivering through the bitter Catskill winters, trying to tie enough flies to support himself and his sport. All the necessary romantic elements are there, down to a shadowy female figure, mentioned with frustrating brevity in his writings as "the best chum I ever had in fishing." Fittingly, her name is lost, and she survives only in two old photographs of her and Gordon fishing together. This woman completes the bittersweet image of the complete fly fisherman. It is American fly fishing's loveliest story.

The biggest problem in understanding Gordon has been keeping him in context. Most of the errors that have been made in judging him have occurred because writers knew little or nothing about Gordon's times besides what they read in his own writings; he would no doubt be appalled (if flattered) to see himself given credit for so many things he did not do.

It is also easy to overestimate his importance when reading *The Complete Fly Fisherman*, because there you find twenty-five years' worth of miscellaneous writings gathered under one roof, so to speak, and all together like that it is indeed a big batch of information. But that is not how Gordon wrote it, and, more important, that is not how his contemporaries read it. Very few Americans saw much of his best material, because it was published in England, and only a handful saw that sizable portion of the book that was letters to a few individuals. Gordon was part of a huge, chaotic flow of information to *Forest and Stream*, one of dozens of correspondents. He certainly wrote more, and infinitely better, than most of his fellow correspondents, but periodicals do not last, and it would be foolish to assume that readers of *Forest and Stream* between 1903 and 1915 realized that Gordon was giving them some greater whole in his loosely structured notes.

Gordon was, however, a great fishing writer. He was consistently engaging, and smart. He could be amusing ("Bed is a great institution.") and he rarely failed to be interesting. He rarely does even yet. The notes contain scores of fascinating little vignettes of telling experiences, of ruminations on trout vision or behavior, of considerations of some insect he saw and tried to imitate. He was on track far more often in his judgments than, say, Rhead, though I don't think his batting average of good judgment would rank much above Keene's. But beyond his fishing theory, his greater wisdom in what fishing is all about has rarely been excelled:

> It is just as well to remember that angling is only a recreation, not a profession. We usually find that men of the greatest experience are most liberal and least dogmatic . . . It is often the man of limited experience who is most confident.

> A visit to a first-class fishing-tackle shop is more interesting than an afternoon at the circus.

One can never learn all that there is in fly-fishing. Only men of limited experience think that they know it all.

It is the constant—or inconstant—change, the infinite variety in fly-fishing that binds us fast. It is impossible to grow weary of a sport that is never the same on any two days in the year. I am fond of all sorts of fishing, in fresh or salt water, in the interior of the country, or on the coast, but trout angling takes a grip upon the imagination. It is more of a mental recreation than other methods. There is always something in question, something to discuss.

But should it be an off day, when the fish are glued to the bottom of the stream, how hard we work to tempt them! We feel a certain animosity against the trout. "Confound them! They must rise at something." Fortunately our mood is easily sweetened and a little success goes a long way. If it was always easy to take trout, surely we would not be so fond of fly-fishing.

In all fly-fishing, the wet and the dry, we are constantly learning something, and this we fancy is the secret of the infinite charm which the sport possesses. If the trout will not take your dry fly, try a wet fly, or wet the dry one. If they fail to appreciate the wet dry fly, skim or bob your dropper fly. Try every known method, but always stick to the artificial fly.

It is in such undogmatic, inquiring, and gently enthusiastic language that Gordon established a remarkably modern attitude, in print at least, about American fly fishing. Whatever kind of person he may have been, the image his writings created is positive, honest, and creative. Few other fly-fishing writers are so regularly quotable. But for all this, we still must ask just what of his legend is true.

Some portions of it are easily disposed of. He had nothing to do with inventing either the streamer or the bucktail. Baitfish imitations were in use in England by early in the 1800s, and many writers in America mentioned them before Gordon wrote at all (see the chapter on saltwater fishing, or Joe Bates's review of streamer and bucktail history in his book *Streamers and Bucktails*). Gordon did develop a regionally popular pattern known as the Bumblepuppy, but it has not achieved national prominence and was only a small part of the evolution of baitfish imitations. I suppose this misconception comes from reading only Gordon's writings with no knowledge of what others were doing.

Gordon did not originate the study of angling entomology in America. His writings on entomology are brief though reasonably accurate; they did not approach either McBride's or Keene's, nor did Gordon claim any such knowledge. He was familiar with the writings of McBride, Keene, Marbury, Roosevelt, and other fly-fishing writers, and well knew that he was not adding anything to what they had done in the formal study of angling entomology. He repeatedly made statements like this:

I know so little of entomology that I do not pretend to instruct anyone. I only hope that a more competent person may take up the study of insect life in our trout streams.

Here we see what he did and what he didn't do. He did not write an angler's entomology, but he tirelessly preached its importance. He never stopped telling his readers to look at the insect and learn its ways, then imitate it.

But he did occasionally mention some specific emergence he had witnessed, or attempted to imitate, usually telling the readers that it was a caddis, or a mayfly, or whatever, and giving the times, dates, and locations. It would be worth the time for some enterprising Catskill angler to extract this information from the entire twenty-five years of articles and unpublished letters and see what kind of "hatch chart" it would turn into. Then it would be worth that same angler's trouble to go on and compare those flies that Gordon observed and recorded with the color portraits of flies in Louis Rhead's book *American Trout Stream Insects* and see how the two of them line up. Rhead also gave emergence dates, and perhaps between the two of them they may have given us a valuable resource that could then be compared with various modern works on the same subject. Even after this exercise, the best we can say for Gordon as an entomologist is that he tried his best to encourage others to care about the subject.

Gordon did not introduce the dry fly to America. Chapter 10 lists many who preceded him, including Halford himself, whose writings were reprinted in an American periodical before Gordon began writing. We can assume that it was from some of these writings that Gordon first heard of the dry fly.

I see no evidence that Gordon was an influence in American nymph fishing. A careful reading of his articles and letters will reveal a few mentions of nymphs (he even corresponded with Skues about them), not unlike those made by others before him, and even some comments on having "tied up a thing intended to resemble a large larva or nymph," but of such slight things are not a movement made. There is little to suggest that these remarks took hold, or that even Gordon understood the potential of such imitations. They are no more convincing than the earlier mentions, given in Chapter 9, of various nymph-imitation efforts.

The next two claims must be dealt with more or less at the same time. One of them is that Gordon originated an American style of dry-fly tying. The other is that he originated an American approach to imitation (I differentiate this from the more formal study of angling entomology because one need not know a bug's name to develop a good imitation of it). Here the story is more complicated. His concern for imitation, at least as expressed in his articles, is almost totally toward dry flies.

It is almost as hard to know exactly what insects Gordon intended his various patterns to imitate as it is to tell what Rhead meant his flies to imitate. Gordon was quite the generalist, and tied even the Quill Gordon to make it adaptable to many purposes. His real goal was to find ways to imitate local insects, adapting British patterns, either by changing their materials, their sizes, or their proportions, to serve the purpose. Even the Quill Gordon, but for its wood-duck wing, is a nearly direct copy in materials of a Halford pattern. So the question becomes how he transformed the British patterns.

Of course he did it by careful observation, but the result has been given credit for more originality than it seems to deserve. It is said that Gordon added stiffer hackles to British flies so that they would float on America's rougher streams.[2] Frank Elder, in his authoritative *The Book of the Hackle* (1979), pointed out that "almost every writer since the days of Halford has indicated that the essential part of the good dry-fly is stiff hackle." I recently examined one of the copies of Halford's *Dry Fly Entomology* (1897), the limited edition with one hundred dry flies tied to Halford's specifications, and I would have to say that the hackles were strong and bright on a lot of those flies. Gordon did emphasize stiff hackles, though, and they did become an important part of the "Catskill style" of dry flies. That was not a particularly original suggestion, however. But the Catskill style of dry fly itself, which grew from Gordon's work, must be his main claim to a contribution, so we had best look at it.

Harry Darbee, in his delightful memoir *Catskill Flytier* (1977), defined the Catskill style of today:

A Quill Gordon tied by Gordon. Note backward slant of wings, which were mounted ahead of the hackle. Note also long body and relatively small proportion of hook shank devoted to hackle. Gordon varied this pattern in many ways to suit his needs. *Courtesy of The American Museum of Fly Fishing.*

Roy Steenrod's famous Hendrickson. This particular fly was given by Steenrod to Preston Jennings in 1932, with the statement that the hackle was too long, and only the colors were to be considered representative. After Preston's death, the fly was given by Mrs. Jennings to Arnold Gingrich, who presented it to The American Museum of Fly Fishing. Note the changes from Gordon's Quill Gordon. In the Hendrickson, the wing is not slanted and is tied in with (rather than ahead of) the hackles, and a bare "neck" is left on the hook. *Photo by C.M. Haller.*

> . . . a good-sized hook, typically size 12 Model Perfect: a notably lean, spare body, usually of spun fur or stripped quill of peacock herl; a divided wing of lemon-colored, mottled barbules of woodduck flank feather; and a few sparse turns of incredibly stiff, clean, glassy cock's hackle, mostly either blue dun or ginger. The wings and hackle are set back from the eye of the hook, leaving an unusually long, clean "neck" at the expense of a slightly shortened body.

The operative word for these flies, the one that so often comes to mind, is the word Darbee used repeatedly: clean. They are almost Spartan in their trim simplicity, and are one of American fly tying's most admired esthetic standards. Their influence on fly tiers in other regions has been considerable, and by themselves they are a credit to the Gordon heritage. But about half their characteristics are not ones favored by Gordon. He did not prefer to divide his wings. He did not often leave a bare "neck" on the fly, and he was sometimes inclined to slant his rolled wood-duck wings back over the body, the way a mayfly's wings often cant back rather than just stick straight up.

Gordon is said to have taught Roy Steenrod and/or Herman Christian and/or Rube Cross to tie flies (Steenrod's claim seems strongest). If it was Steenrod, the secretive Gordon chose well, for Steenrod loved to teach fly tying, and went on to teach hundreds of others, and through Steenrod, George Parker Holden apparently learned of the flies and praised them highly in his very good books and articles. But somewhere between Gordon and the next generation, including at least Cross and certainly those since Cross, the Catskill dry fly evolved considerably; the wings split and became invariably vertical, and the neck was sometimes bared. On the Gordon flies I have seen, more space on the shank was devoted to the body, proportionately, and less to hackle, than on modern Catskill dry flies, even allowing for the bare neck (the bare neck appears only intermittently on the mass of commercial Catskill dry flies anyway). From all of this it appears that Gordon was catalytic but did not pass on to later generations a finished fly. He appears to have been a pivotal figure in establishing an approach to the dry fly, but his important start was taken and refined substantially by such later masters as Cross, the Dettes, the Darbees, and Flick.

The Catskill dry fly was one of the first American styles of dry flies, and it was eventually joined by many others, some of which were obviously influenced by, or derivative of, it. Gordon's contributions to dry-fly theory, at least those we can identify from hindsight, are two: he talked about dry flies and imitating American floating insects incessantly in his writings (and occasionally was invited to speak to fishing groups), thus exposing others to his interest, and he taught at least one person to tie dry flies in his style. His name was kept alive by those who knew him through personal contact—men such as Cross, Steenrod, and Christian in this country and Skues (his most faithful British correspondent) in England. Of his original dry flies, only one, the Quill Gordon, has risen to national prominence and endured. It is still one of the most popular of dry flies.[3]

Other claims are made for Gordon, and they are all of a type with the statement that he was somehow "the father of modern American angling" in that they are made with little or no knowledge of his times. His comments on stream degradation have been used to claim for him some originality as a conservationist or even as an ecologist. He was only one of hundreds of anglers who had been making such complaints for sixty years; many of the others actually did much more than did Gordon about the degradation. He may have "fathered" the Catskill dry fly, though he seems instead to have produced an intermediate stage of it between the British fly and the modern American fly, but he did not father any other kind of American angling—not bass fishing, or deep-sea fishing, or muskie fishing, or paddlefish fishing. It is this sort of overkill that has led us so happily to a mythic Gordon of Olympian stature.

At the time of his death, in 1915, his imitationist theories were still a minority position in American dry-fly fishing. As mentioned in Chapter 10, the first several books on dry-fly fishing in America were by his definition nonimitationist, and furthermore reveal little or no debt to (or especial knowledge of) his work.

Exactly how much disagreement there was between Gordon and some of his contemporaries is still being revealed. George LaBranche has often been described as a close friend of Gordon's who was heavily influenced by Gordon. LaBranche's admiration for Gordon was great (he said Gordon was "the best fly tier I have ever known"), but LaBranche's book reveals no such influence, of course, relying on techniques not promoted, and flies not favored, by Gordon. But the extent of LaBranche's alienation was not known until a manuscript fragment surfaced in the early 1980s, loaned by LaBranche's daughter to The American Museum of Fly Fishing. It was probably written in the early 1950s, not long after *The Complete Fly Fisherman* was published:

> Many things have been said recently in more or less permanent print about the personal relations of the late Mr. Theo. Gordon and myself. I had the pleasure of corresponding with him for many years but met him but three times, twice appointments [this word is unclear] on the river. I considered him a great friend and com-

panion. We discussed fishing naturally—and when I told him that I was fishing a
dry fly on any part of the water rather than confining my efforts to the still water of
pools, or slow running currents, he told me that I was belittling [this word also
unclear, but no other choice was apparent] the theory of dry fly fishing. He agreed
with G. A. B. Dewar and Halford that what I was doing was an affectation and that
the dry fly should be used on slow flowing water over rising fish only. I was upset
more than a little, but persevered with my idea.

It's worth pointing out that Gordon was not always that hidebound, and neither
was Halford. The latter wrote to Emlyn Gill in 1912 and told him that he, too, had
taken to occasionally dropping a dry fly on a likely spot to see if he could get a trout
to rise there.

But we do see in this fragment a more accurate portrayal of the relationship
between these two famous fishermen. They admired one another greatly, as two
superb craftsmen should but often do not because of jealousy and rivalry, but their
disagreements were fundamental.

The writings of later imitationists are of interest here too. When Preston Jennings
published his *Book of Trout Flies* in 1935, finally providing the usable system that
Gordon wished for and Rhead attempted, he had little to say about Gordon. Of all
the reviews of the book—and there were dozens that Jennings pasted in his
scrapbook—only one writer even mentioned Gordon's earlier work. That one was
the English writer G. E. M. Skues, so long a correspondent with Gordon (it is said
that when in 1940 Skues caught his final fish it was on a fly tied with wood-duck
sent to him many years earlier by Gordon; doesn't that close a lovely circle?). This
may strike us as a tragedy, that Gordon could be so quickly forgotten, but as far as
Jennings was concerned, there was no particular reason to remember him. The following remarks by Jennings are from manuscripts left by him and donated to the
Museum. They are part of a second book he was working on. They were probably
written in the few years after the appearance of *The Complete Fly Fisherman* in 1947:

> Quite recently, the present writer has read a biography of Theodore Gordon, who,
> to many represents the John the Baptist of American fly fishers, or the voice crying
> in the wilderness, making way for a new era . . . After perusing his writings, which
> were in the major part contributions to the English Fishing Gazette, only two state-
> ments could be considered as contributory to the art of fly fishing, the first, the fact
> that he realized that there were other fly-tiers in America and that he had no means
> of communication with them, which was understandable, as he had no factual knowl-
> edge, or language with which he could enter into an exchange of ideas. Secondly,
> he bemoaned the fact that so many artificial flies were named after the current Fish
> and Game Commissioner such as the ''Seth Green'' or the ''Rube Wood;'' however
> as his influence grew and he was able to sell flies of his own manufacture, he seemed
> to have forgotten his earlier ideals, and marketed two creations, both of which bear
> his name, the Quill Gordon and the Gordon.[4]

Jennings, who earlier in his life had written more generous things about Gordon,
was hardly fair to the fullness of Gordon's contributions as a writer and fly fishing
philosopher, much less to his contributions to the evolution of the Catskill dry fly,
but I think I understand why he was nettled. Jennings had slaved away (and was still
slaving away in the 1950s) to develop scientifically based flies and imitationist theories, and had produced a great milestone of a book, when along comes this wave
of adoration for Gordon's diffuse and totally unsystematic body of articles and letters.
It must have seemed to Jennings that American fly fishers had lost their perspective,
and perhaps they had. When *The Complete Fly Fisherman* appeared in 1947 there

was a great surge of interest in Gordon; a resurrection had occurred that seemed terribly important to the readers of these notes and letters from this mysterious, melancholy fisherman. That resurrection has had as much to do with sentiment as with any respect for Gordon's work as a fly-fishing theorist, but that only strengthens its hold on us. Though he was only one of the fishermen seriously working on dry flies in his day, he is the "father" of the dry fly. Once he caught our imagination he could be no less.

What we have, after all this re-examination, is a slightly more human Theodore Gordon, a believable historical character rather than a shadowy spirit-figure that haunts the opening chapters of so many modern fly-fishing books. He rarely claimed to be the father of anything, and his immediate contemporaries made few such claims for him. They knew he was a great writer, a singularly thoughtful fisherman, and an outstanding fly tier, one of the best of his time, but they did not think he was a saint. That all came later, from the imponderable perspective of distance and adoration.

He was just what fly fishing needed: a mystical, reclusive, gifted, tragic character, and I appreciate him even more for the ironies of his life.

One of them is that this man, credited with creating something uniquely American, was in constant touch with the British. They were his most receptive audience, and they were his constant source of inspiration. Out of his dependence upon the Old World grew his independence of it.

Another irony was Gordon's quarry. As he reached adulthood the brook trout was on its way out. It was replaced most often by the European brown. Had the brown not been introduced, Gordon's work would have been much less necessary and he might have met the fate of Keene, McBride, and those others who were too early to find a lasting audience. Not only was Gordon's Americanization achieved under the guidance of British anglers, its goal was to enable him to catch European fish. An odder declaration of independence is hard to imagine.

But there is one more irony, one that appeals to me most. It is what we have made of Theodore Gordon. He was by some accounts an unsociable fellow who preferred to live alone and practice his crafts in a privacy that was almost obsessive when it came to his fly tying. He only blossomed as a social person in his "little talks," which were cheery and consistently charming. He saved his good spirits for his writing, preferring especially that audience that was farthest away. He seemed not to seek publicity or recognition, and when approached about publishing some of his writings in book form, or about editing a fishing journal, he was lukewarm. He was a true recluse. The irony is that we have taken this solitary man and made him symbol for all that is social and brotherly about fly fishing. We have named one of our most effective and distinguished fly fishing organizations, a bastion of good fellowship, after him. We have made him our saint. And, had he been any less a hermit, or any more successful, we could not have done it. He had to be just the person he was, a lonely, unambitious sport, or we could not have done it. In fly fishing, whose literature is heavy with religious overtones, where rivers are "sacred" and "hallowed" and venerable figures are "father," and where great writings are treated like gospels, Gordon was a perfect martyr, just obscure enough for his achievement to lie fallow and forgotten for a tasteful interval before his resurrection as a new, different, and wonderfully useful person.

12

Angling Society

No greater revolution ever occurred than that which brought about the entire change in thought and habits of the American people touching outdoor life and the sports and types of recreation representative of it.
WILLIAM HENRY HARRISON MURRAY, ''Reminiscences of my Literary and Outdoor Life,'' in *The Independent* (New York) LVII (1904)

For all that we may read the books and articles of previous generations of fly fishers, and for all the attention and affection that we may lavish upon the tackle they developed, I think that we don't get most of our mental images of them from these words and artifacts. We get them instead from their art. Whether we think of the many Currier and Ives fishing scenes, the dozens of woodcuts and engravings in British and American books (many of the early ones in American publications were merely slightly altered British ones, replacing a background castle with a Colonial mansion, for example), the immortal portrayals of eastern angling scenes by Winslow Homer (nobody has improved on his interpretations of an airborne fly line), the quite mortal portrayals by many of his contemporaries, the hundreds of late-nineteenth-century photographic portraits of anglers (invariably formal and stiff, usually unsmiling) with their catch, or the glorious, almost lurid covers of the early-twentieth-century sporting magazines, we usually see our forebears in these published images. A remarkably high percentage of them seem to have worn neckties and dress coats.

These images are an important and underappreciated historical resource; they tell us much about angling practice and style, and they are at least as good a window on our sporting past as are the prose and the tackle.

One thing that has often struck me about them is the spirit of a sporting society that they convey. Certainly some of the pictures show solitary fishermen, but most do not. Most show us good friends fishing together, one perhaps handling the net for the other, or several gathered around a canoe, one with his foot on it like a hunter with a dead elephant. It has always been one of the pleasant paradoxes of fly fishing, so celebrated for its solitary pleasures, that fishermen love to get together.

The growth of fishing society, in its various formal manifestations, was rarely a fly-fishing movement. It was instead a sporting movement, so that the vast majority of organizations formed before 1920 were probably not even limited to fishing in general, but were "sportsman's" organizations. The organizations, however, had different purposes.

The first movement, as we've already seen, was the social club exemplified by the various societies that grew up near Philadelphia before the Revolution. These clubs flourished in many major population areas, so that a well-connected traveler in the 1850s could probably find like-minded sportsmen in many cities. The Cincinnati Angling Club, organized in 1830 and occasionally mentioned in the *Turf Register* or the *Spirit*, revealed how quickly gentlemanly recreation had reached the "Old Northwest," and similar groups could be found in most eastern cities. They fished by many means, and concentrated at least as heavily (and often more heavily) on the eating, drinking, and companionship of a fishing outing as on the sport itself.

Or perhaps that is an unfair statement, for the companionships were for them, as they still are for many of us, part of their definition of "the sport itself." In another way, however, they may have differed a bit from us in the extent to which casting tournaments were a part of the activities of many clubs; at least the sporting periodicals of the period 1870 to 1920 devoted a great deal more attention to such tournaments than they do today. Fly casting was an important part, at times the most important part, of these tournaments.

Casting instructor and historian Cliff Netherton has documented the development of the sport of casting in two large volumes, *History of the Sport of Casting, People, Events, Records, Tackle and Literature, Early Times* (1981), and *History of the Sport of Casting, Golden Years* (1983), both detailed collections of the publications and records of casting competition and technology, with extensive annotations. For our purposes no such detail is appropriate. What is significant is the speed with which casting became an integral part of fishing society. By the 1880s and 1890s, many of the leading clubs and societies were holding informal tournaments, and there were well-publicized national competitions sponsored by the best-known clubs. The New York State Sportsmen's Club is credited with some of the first, starting on the eve of the Civil War, but within two decades or so there were many competitions under the auspices of the National Rod and Reel Association, the Fly Fishermen's Club of Indianapolis, the Chicago Fly Casting Club, and, by the early 1890s, the San Francisco Fly Casting Club and the Golden Gate Angling and Casting Club (the first California fishing club may have been the McCloud River Club, founded about 1878). The now-venerable Anglers' Club of New York, formed in 1905, held its first tournament in 1906.

The best-known fishermen and fishing writers participated in these early tournaments, to a far greater extent than they do today (one could read today's fly fishing magazines for years without becoming aware of the thriving international competitions that still occur in fly casting under the auspices of the American Casting Association). Seth Green, the Leonards, Edward Hewitt, Thomas Conroy, Hiram Hawes, T. B. Mills, George Varney, and others are listed in these tournaments, revealing that not only were the best-known fishing writers willing to compete, so were some of the most prominent rod makers willing to send representatives to pit their products against those of the other leading builders. There was a keen competition, as well, between American and British anglers and manufacturers, a competition that probably did not decide much in favor of either, but even in its inconclusiveness revealed how quickly Americans had reached the highest levels of casting and rod-building craft.

By far the greatest influence on the formalization of American angling society was what was known at the time as the "club movement" aimed at protecting the sportsman's quarry. The deterioration of wildlife habitat in all parts of America had

The casting tournament became one of the most important social outings for fly fishers in the late 1800s, just as it became an important showplace for builders of tackle.

been observed and discussed in the sporting press and elsewhere (among pioneer foresters, wilderness lovers, birdwatchers, and other interest groups and professions), but now something was being done about it.

The development of a consciousness of conservation needs in wildlife management is one of the most fascinating historical subjects I have encountered. Following the Revolution, Americans rejected much of their British heritage of wildlife management as elitist (which it was) in favor of some more democratic principle, only vaguely defined in most cases, that gave the wildlife (fish are a type of wildlife, for this discussion) to everybody. All citizens, ideally, were equally entitled to pursue game. The system was admirable in intention, but flawed in execution, as everybody eventually showed that the notion of personal share of the resource was not agreed upon. Once Americans did not depend upon wildlife for survival—that is, once wild animals were no longer important as protein—a different kind of exploitation, for sport, replaced exploitation for protein, pelts, or other utilitarian purposes. In the years following the Civil War, as various outdoor recreations boomed (an almost spookily similar boom occurred following World War II), the resource upon which the boom was based collapsed, necessitating a rethinking of just what constituted not only good management but also good sport. Fewer and fewer anglers, for example, saw no harm in killing the hundreds of trout often reported in the magazines of the 1840s. Recent historians, most especially John Reiger, have pointed out that it was in most cases the sportsmen themselves who came to the rescue of the resources. This might seem natural to us now, considering that the sportsmen were the ones with the most to lose, but it is the sad truth that too often these days, the general public perceives management agencies as the only things standing between wildlife and complete annihilation by hunters and fishermen. Reiger has summed up the real state of affairs of the late 1800s in his important book *American Sportsmen and the Origins of Conservation* (1975):

> And it should be emphasized that, contrary to popular belief, sportsmen urged these restrictions upon themselves, for no individual, group, or government agency forced them to limit their ''bags,'' hunting and fishing seasons, or any other aspect of sport. If sportsmen failed to regulate themselves, no one else would, for they lived in a country characterized, first, by a Judeo-Christian tradition that separated man from nature and sanctified his dominion over it; second, by a *laissez-faire* economic order that encouraged irresponsible use of resources; third, by weak institutions, including the federal government, that seemed unwilling or unable to protect wildlife and habitat; and fourth, by a heritage of opposition to any restraint on ''freedom,'' particularly that vestige of Old World tyranny, the game law.

This is not to say, though, that sportsmen unanimously came around to the wisdom of moderation and regulation. The ''game hog,'' a term popularized in the 1890s by George Oliver Shields in his magazine *Recreation*, will always be with us, but he was made especially visible by regular attacks on his activities (Shields gloried in publishing photographs of excessive kills in the magazine, with short sermons on the stupidity and selfishness of the ''sportsmen'' guilty of the offense).

The protection movement took two forms. One was more or less an extension of the earlier social clubs. Wealthy sportsmen, appalled by the destruction of good sporting grounds, simply bought up their own ''preserves'' and kept everyone else out, thus unconsciously completing the circle back to the early British elitist traditions. Pennsylvania's Blooming Grove Club (1871), the Bisby Club in the Adirondacks (1877), and Long Island's South Side Club (1866) were three of the most impressive

The ''Lower Castalia Club House'' on the Castalia spring creek in northern Ohio, as pictured in *Forest & Stream* in May of 1891.

Lower Castalia Club House

in size, quality of sporting opportunity, and durability, but there were many others. Austin Francis, in *Catskill Rivers* (1983), has told the story of some of the more important Catskill clubs, and Ernest Schwiebert and Richard Hunt have given us a portrait of one of the most famous of the Pocono clubs, that now holding the Henryville waters of the Brodheads.

This resorting to private sport has had many results for American fly fishing, among them an irony: These private waters were the scene of some of the most brotherly of our fishing books, books rich in fellowship and Waltonian sentiments that were quite firmly restricted to a select few.

At the same time, had the privatization not occurred, some of our best fishing thinkers might have written much less. It is true that the private preserves were eventually to have a great influence on wildlife management by what was learned on them. Just as Gifford Pinchot, now thought of as the father of American forestry, received much of his first practical experience managing private forests, so did the great preserves provide managers with excellent classrooms for studying many aspects of game management. In any event, whatever sorts of value judgments modern social thinkers may apply to the sporting elitism of the fly fishers of earlier generations, those anglers did much more than simply hide in their own safe private holdings. Many of them were the loudest voices in the greater movement to protect public fishing as well.

There had been organizations of sportsmen aiming to protect fish and game even before the Civil War, but it was in the 1870s that the idea caught hold and became a powerful national movement. Suddenly sportsmen in cities all over the country were banding together. There were several hundred clubs by 1880 (how many depends upon how you define them, and if you include shooting clubs primarily interested in trap and skeet, for example). Their influence was quickly felt, and they began what has been more of a century of sometimes uncomfortable coexistence between sportsmen and managers. The vast majority of them were not fly-fishing clubs, but clubs of all kinds of sportsmen. The fly fisher, for all his growing pretensions to being the highest form of angler, was still not self-recognized as a type with strong special interests that would separate him from other fishermen.

There were early signs, though. Some of the preserves restricted certain waters to fly-only fishing, for example. More impressive were early attempts to restrict *public* waters to fly fishing only. Michigan businessman William Mershon waged such a campaign with surprising success in that state, actually managing to get the North Branch of the Au Sable set aside for fly fishing only in 1907. The restriction lasted until 1913, when a combination of interests forced the repeal of the regulation. One local complained that the fly-fishing restriction was ''an act to prevent the people who live in that section from catching trout, and permit them to be caught by the fellows from the cities who go up there.'' Lines were drawn here that would often appear later, between the perceived interests of the locals and the supposed needs of the ''fellows from the cities.'' Mershon, with considerable wisdom, had justified the restriction on the basis of too many small fish being killed. In an article in *Forest and Stream* on October 29, 1910, he stated that the goal was to reduce the hooking mortality of small trout:

> . . . if taken with the bait hook, a large percentage of them would be killed, whereas if taken with a fly, very few of them die. I know this to be a fact, for in former years when baitfishing was permitted, I used to see any number of dead fish floating past me, and in my fishing last year a dead fish was rare.

In this contest between fishing methods, we begin to see a new level of disagreement. Most earlier generations had favored fly fishing because it was more sophisticated, or because it was not cruel to worms (little was said about cruelty to trout). Now it was gathering adherents who recognized its potential for preserving trout populations.

But putting aside the occasional fly-fishing advance, what was happening was crossing all the boundaries of the sporting world. Sportsmen were flexing their muscles and growing in understanding not only of their power but their culture. There was a gradually improving public perception of the fisherman as a respectable person. I am not convinced that fishermen were ever as poorly thought of by all of society as they are sometimes pictured, but there is little question that their image was improving in the late 1800s. When George Washington Bethune, a learned minister, edited his important 1847 American edition of Walton, he found it advisable to identify himself on the title page only as the "American Editor," for fear of disapproval by his colleagues or congregation. Less than three decades later, as we have seen, William Henry Harrison Murray, who was at times among the most famous of all New England ministers, openly published books about his outdoor adventures, and by 1880 it was easy enough to be a sportsman and a leading citizen. Robert Barnwell Roosevelt, social rogue though he may have been, was some proof of that, but Rev. Henry Van Dyke was perhaps the best proof. His books on the outdoors, such as *Little Rivers* (1895) and *Fisherman's Luck* (1899), were immensely popular, but were only a small part of a distinguished career that included preaching, teaching, serving as ambassador to the Netherlands, a term as president of the National Institute of Arts and Letters, and at all times being a profoundly influential religious and civic leader. His gentle essays on days astream, with their mixture of childlike exuberance and literary allusions (though they may be heavy slogging for many readers today) were classics of Victorian recreational literature. Men of Van Dyke's social standing guaranteed fly fishing would never again have to climb the social ladder; it was on the top rung.

There seems in fact to have been a regular rush to fly fishing by distinguished citizens in the last three decades of the 1800s. William Cowper Prime, who was among other things president of the Associated Press, officer of the Metropolitan Museum of Art, and a leading art historian, produced *I Go A-fishing* (1873), which remained popular for several decades, though now it is practically unreadable for all of what Gingrich called its "incessant God-hopping" and its bulk of nonfishing material. Gingrich said that "trying to get to the fishing in Prime is like the proverbial attempt to pick flyspecks out of pepper with boxing gloves on." A good way to get a sense of who some of the more distinguished fishermen were in those days is to read Fred Mather's *Men I Have Fished With* (1897) and *My Angling Friends* (1901). Mather, who himself made a respectable career out of fishing and fisheries, profiled some of the leading angler-citizens, mixing in a few rascals and "old rustic" types for color (and relief from the apparently overwhelming virtuousness of his other subjects; fishing writing's self-worship may not have peaked with Mather, but it certainly hit its stride).

It is important to keep in mind, however, that not all of the organizations being established—even those without private waters of their own—were concerned with conservation. Perhaps the best example of the ambivalence of attitude among these societies was the Anglers' Club of New York, mentioned earlier for its involvement in casting tournaments. The Anglers' Club has been rightly celebrated for the many achievements of its members (Hewitt, LaBranche, Sparse Grey Hackle, Schwiebert, and many others) in fishing theory and literature, and the meetings of the club have provided many of fly fishing's leading thinkers with opportunities to share and trade ideas. But from its establishment in 1905 (and incorporation in 1906), the club has been determined not to take part in conservation issues. H. Ross Jones, a club member writing in 1972, explained the club's position:

> The·Club is essentially a simple lunch club. It has no fishing facility of its own and it makes a point of never taking a position, as a club, on any conservation or legislative matter which is apt to generate controversy. This is because the Club's membership is such a cross section of anglers—running the gamut from buck privates in the rear ranks to captains of industry—that it would be impossible for the Club to truly speak for all of them.[1]

In choosing to be a simple social club, the Anglers' Club was following in the footsteps of the earliest American fishing clubs. And in being a social club of New Yorkers able to recruit heavily from the "captains of industry," the club reflected the mood of the day, which was more than tolerant of the respectable citizen doing some serious fishing.

The editor of *Forest and Stream*, in reviewing a book on hunting by another prominent sportsman of the period, Theodore Roosevelt, in July of 1885, commented on the changing public attitude toward sportsmen:

> The fact is that people nowadays realize in some small measure the importance of the sports of the field and water, and have come to understand something of the benefits to be derived from a reasonable and reasoning indulgence in them. Now they are applauded—not too enthusiastically, but still applauded—a very few years ago they were barely tolerated, and a short time before that a man who went "gunnin' or fishin'," lost caste among respectable people just about in the same way that one did who got drunk.

This was a period of great flux in sport. Attitudes, techniques, philosophies, and public image were all changing rapidly. These things were happening simultaneously, so it is really difficult to distinguish cause and effect, but it is clear that the central forum and the leading impetus behind the changes was the sporting periodical.

The charming miscellanies of the 1840s and 1850s had shown the way, but their editors probably never dreamed there would be such an explosion in sporting publication as occurred in the 1870s and afterward. There were dozens of periodicals, and the volume of communication was huge. The *American Sportsman* appeared in 1871, followed by *Forest and Stream* in 1873 and *American Field* in 1874. Some lasted only a few issues, others disappeared, were reconstituted by new investors, and resurfaced with a new name. *American Angler*, now one of the primary historical sources for the late 1800s, appeared in 1881.

Their editors are the neglected heroes of American sporting history. They were the spiritual heirs of William Trotter Porter's grand tradition. They established, more than any of the best-known writers, the tone and direction of American sporting ethics and practice. Charles Hallock and then George Bird Grinnell at *Forest and Stream*, William Harris at *American Angler*, Shields at *Recreation*, and dozens of less-well-remembered men conducted and directed sporting society in their pages, preaching, cajoling, instructing, mediating, and guiding. Leafing through the *Angler* or any of the others, one is struck by the amazing diversity of opinion and variety of belief. The more one studies the periodicals, the less one is likely to see any part

George Dawson, whose book *Pleasures of Angling* (1876) was the first American book devoted entirely to fly fishing, typified the social fly fisher of the late 1800s. This engraving of him appeared in *Harper's New Monthly Magazine* in July of 1859.

of the American sporting tradition as a simple process. We have never been like-minded except in our enthusiasm for catching fish. In related questions, ranging from the best way to do so to the reasons why it matters so much to us, we have never been in much agreement.

Based on these foundations—a mixture of fraternal and political organizations with a sprawling network of publications—American angling society thrived and grew. The number of celebrities and authorities grew apace with the periodicals and books until even many newspapers could boast regular columns by local experts. George Dawson is sort of the prototype of these columnists, conducting a column in the *Albany Evening Journal* in the 1860s. Dawson is now credited with being both our first fly-fishing columnist and the author of the first American book devoted entirely to fly fishing, *Pleasures of Angling with Rod and Reel for Trout and Salmon*

Genio Scott, from an engraving in the *Spirit of the Times*, December 23, 1876. Like Dawson and many others, Scott wrote many cheery little articles on the joys and companionships of fishing. *Courtesy of David B. Ledlie.*

(1876). *Pleasures of Angling* was typical of many books of fishing tales of the period, very informal and usually short on instruction ("I have never been able to master an 'ology' of any kind," Dawson once observed) but long on good feelings for fellow sportsmen (it is some measure also of the fly fisher's stature that Dawson counted among his fishing companions two presidents and a vice president of the United States). There was time, in such books, for a few pages digression now and then on anything from politics to the guide's personality, making the books quite similar to

Railroads were leading promoters of fishing, and changed the fly fisher's world, giving him access to the best fishing on an entire continent. This is an 1882 ad for Michigan fishing. *Courtesy of The American Museum of Fly Fishing.*

A beautifully posed scene from the Adirondacks, about 1890. *From the Mary Orvis Marbury Collection, The American Museum of Fly Fishing.*

many of the rambling narratives that appeared in the periodicals. If you wanted to spend the first chapter or two recounting the rail, coach, horse, and canoe rides that got you to the fishing camp, your audience would be with you all the way. Travel —getting there—was still an important part of the fishing experience. Imagine a modern writer, wanting to tell about his steelhead fishing trip, spending the first few thousand words describing his cab ride to Kennedy Airport, his various landings at O'Hare, Denver, Salt Lake, and Seattle, his motel room near the Seattle Airport, and his drive by rental car up the valley of the Stilliguamish to the pool he fished.

But travel was changing too. By the 1880s the railroad had put a vast sporting resource within reach of anglers of even modest means, and the railroads did not miss the opportunity to persuade anglers to travel. Guide booklets poured from their offices: *Guide to the Health, Pleasure, Game and Fishing Resorts Reached by the Grand Rapids and Indiana Railway* (1882); *Pleasure Spots Among the Ozarks* (Rock Island Railroad, no date); *A Paradise for Gunners and Anglers* (Pennsylvania Rail Road Company, 1883); *Fishing Along the Picturesque Erie* (Erie Rail Road, 1903), and many more. There were special incentives and promotions, too. In 1910 the Denver & Rio Grande Railroad had a standing offer of a twenty-dollar gold piece for any fly fisherman who caught a rainbow weighing ten pounds or more along their line; according to the *Transactions of the American Fisheries Society* for 1910, they paid up ''about twice a year,'' with the largest fish usually coming from the Gunnison in Colorado.

In only a decade or two, sporting travel would of course experience another revolution as automobiles replaced trains and made the fly fisher even more mobile. By the 1920s the average angler could range as far in a week as his counterpart a century earlier might in a year of slow, time-consuming outings. The effects of this increase in mobility on American fly fishing were many, but perhaps most of all they probably tended to increase the versatility of fishermen who were exposed to other fishermen not only through what they read but also through what they saw.

For the fly fisher, the development of a virtual angling subculture in the late 1800s changed his (and I say "his" knowingly, because practically all fly fishers were still male) sport significantly. Ease of communication, combined with so much that seemed to need communicating (by tackle manufacturers, fly tying theorists, fisheries researchers, naturalists, and a horde of conversationalists who could never "master an 'ology' "), made the fly fisher's world a more dynamic one than it had ever been before. The growth of an angling society also increased interest among fly fishers in the possibilities for broadening their sport.

13

The Very Nicest Appreciation of Time and Distance

It is not easy to tell one how to cast. The art must be acquired by practice.

CHARLES ORVIS,
Fishing with the Fly (1883)

Part of the stereotype of "fly fishers from the old days" involves a gentleman in tweeds and starched collar wading his favorite trout stream, making stiff, precise casts, ever conscious of the imaginary book he is holding between the elbow of his casting arm and his side. No doubt many did fly cast in just this way, but a reading of the various instructional texts written in the late 1800s and early 1900s reveals that fly casters then, as now, worked it out to suit their own temperament. George Dawson included a "short essay on fly casting" in his book *Pleasures of Angling* (1876), in which he commented on individual style:

> In casting, attitude may not be everything, but it is a great deal. And what a multitude of attitudes anglers assume! Some stand erect as pillars, swaying neither to the right nor to the left, whatever reach of line they covet. Some sway to and fro, with every movement of their rod, like a tall pine in a tempest. Others throw themselves forward as if ambitious to follow their fly in person; while now and then one casts with an ease and grace of attitude and movement which would excite the envy and admiration of an athlete or a sculptor.

This variety of style was as common then as it is now. H. P. Wells, an advocate of using the elbow only slightly but the wrist a lot, criticized other approaches in his book *Fly Rods and Fly Tackle* (1885):

> I am aware that I am at variance with the precepts of many writers, as well as with the practice of many excellent anglers, in the direction that the elbow be invariably

133

close to the side. Some cast at arm's-length, and largely with the shoulder-joint. This is a thoroughly bad method, fatiguing, inefficient, and rivalling in *grace a duck on land*. Others cast with the elbow to or near the body, but just before the flies light extend the arm to its full length, *as though they were about to impale something on the point of the rod*.

Thanks to the arrival of heavier silk lines in the 1870s and 1880s, the fly fisher of a century ago had a reasonable array of techniques in his casting repertoire. Most instructional texts mentioned only a few, mostly the forward cast, some variation on a side-arm cast, and some form of roll cast, but much more detailed instructions were also available. Keene, being current on British techniques, listed these in the 1891 edition of his *Fly-Fishing and Fly-Making*: overhand cast; wind cast (a high backcast followed by a driving, low forward cast); underhand cast; flip cast (later writers called this the bow and arrow cast, wherein the angler holds the fly, pulls the rod into a bend, and "shoots" the fly a short distance by letting go of it); reversed flip cast; Spey cast (a variation on the roll cast involving flipping the fly, after it has completed its drift and is hanging below the angler, back in front of him before initiating the roll cast); and the switch cast (pretty much our modern roll cast).

Even this list was only the beginning. By the 1940s, when Frank Steel and John Alden Knight produced their popular books on casting, there were many more techniques and variations. Steel, in *Fly Fishing* (1946), listed the forward cast, side cast, steeple cast (which I have seen but still do not believe), Galway cast, Wye cast, L-turn side cast, roll cast, side roll cast, L-turn roll cast, Spey cast, combination roll and overhead cast, L-turn combination roll and overhead cast, dry fly roll cast, dry-fly switch cast, drag-curve cast, positive forehand curve cast, positive backhand curve cast, forehand negative curve cast, backhand negative curve cast, positive vertical curve cast, grasshopper cast, grasshopper positive curve cast, grasshopper horizontal curve cast, and vertical negative curve cast. The list has continued to grow as later writers explored specialized fishing situations, adding a variety of puddle casts, reach casts, and so on.

But in the late 1800s there were some interesting twists that are not as often encountered today. Perhaps the most important was a difference of opinion over how best to execute the simple forward cast. One school of thought, represented by no less than James Henshall, recommended that the forward cast was not a back-and-forth motion but a narrow elipse. Henshall preferred, while casting right-handed, to make his backcast travel over his left shoulder, so that the fly inscribed a long oval, going backward to his right and coming forward to his left. His explanation made sense:

> Sometimes these movements are made straight backward and forward over either shoulder, or over the head; but the best way is to make the backward movement over the left shoulder, and the forward over the right shoulder, the line thus describing an oval or parabola. By this method the flies are not so apt to be whipped off, and it is, withal, more graceful, more *en regle*.

Whether or not it was more graceful is open to question, but its advantages had been recognized in this country forty years before the above description was published in *Book of the Black Bass* (1881). In the *Spirit* on August 19, 1843, a writer had recommended the same technique, as did others later, also pointing out that such a cast reduced the chance of the fly hanging up on the line as it completed turning over on the backcast. Dawson had referred to the oval approach as giving the "line a

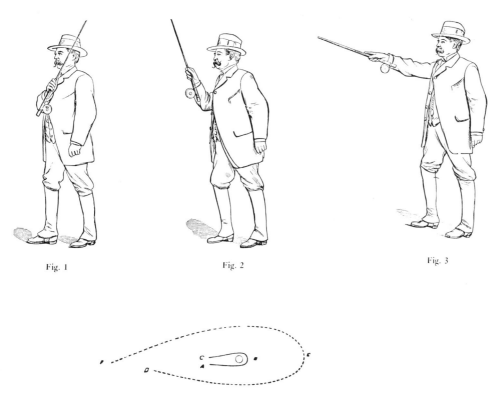

Fig. 1   Fig. 2   Fig. 3

James Henshall, from his *Book of the Black Bass* (1881), showing his cross-the-shoulder casting motion, and an overhead schematic drawing from the same book showing the path of the fly around the angler.

graceful sweep which is not only artistic but avoids the danger of lapping. To make an equally long cast with this movement, however, requires greater skill than with the other; for, without the very nicest appreciation of time and distance, the curved sweep of the line will prevent it from acquiring the direct position indispensable to a perfect forward projection.''

By the 1880s, with the advent of bamboo and silk lines, the tournament casters, even in the light-trout-fly category, were regularly hitting eighty feet and more. The salmon fly casters, using the large two-handed rods of fifteen or more feet, were going well over one hundred. The tendency in America between 1870 and 1920 was

From an early William Mills catalog. *Courtesy of The American Museum of Fly Fishing.*

A fanciful rendering of a kneeling caster, by Louis Rhead, from *The Speckled Brook Trout* (1902).

toward stiffer, more powerful rods, partly because casters wanted more distance. Increased precision and delicacy of presentation were important all along; Henshall claimed that "when the beginner can cast his fly into his hat, eight times out of ten, at forty feet, he is a fly fisher; and so far as casting is concerned, a good one."

The fly fisher of 1900, then, had a good armament of casting styles. He could push his line into a moderate breeze, he could resort to some sort of roll, side, Spey, or switch cast when the trees were looking over his shoulder, and he could fire a dry fly under low riverside brush with a sidearm cast. With those basics mastered, he could deal with most normal fishing situations as well as we can today. But wait, what about that deep run out there? Must be a good thirty yards to the best lies in that one, and all I have is my ten-foot trout rod. Wish I could cast just a little farther, get just a little more *umph* into it, don't you know?

Distance casting has been the most dramatic form of fly casting for a long time. A great many more people are interested in the athletics of the great distance casters of any age than know of the heroics of such casters as Frank Steel, first to score a perfect 100 in the dry-fly accuracy competition in 1932. There is something exciting, even exhilarating, in watching a good distance caster turn over a 130-footer across a steelhead river or even at a casting tournament. And those distances, more than anything else they mean, mean the double haul.

The double haul, or double-line-haul, or double pull, or any of its other names, has no clear point of origin. The first widely-published instruction to anglers on the well-timed tug on the line, either during the forecast or the backcast, that will increase line speed and distance, was possibly in the book *Salmon and Trout* (1902), a collection of several authors' writings. The instructions were given by Dean Sage, best known as a salmon fisherman and author of the sumptuous limited-edition book *The Ristigouche and its Salmon Fishing* (1888). Sage actually described the first half of the double haul:

An intriguing series of drawings by Rhead from *Forest & Stream* in 1923. The first of the series shows the angler (Rhead himself, it appears) lifting the line into the backcast. The second shows the line rolling out behind the angler; note the position of his left hand in this drawing. The third shows the forward cast being made; the left hand has moved from the angler's shoulder to below his waist, a perfect illustration of the "haul" used to speed up the line on the forward cast. Rhead illustrated the haul as well as it has ever been illustrated. *Courtesy of David B. Ledlie.*

The overhand or ordinary cast is made by lifting the line out of the water to the end where the fly is, and throwing it out behind to its full length before casting it forward. This is the most important part of casting, as, if not done, and there is a slack in the line at the time of the forward cast, the fly is frequently snapped off, and line and fly alight in front in a tangled mass far in direction and distance from where they should. In raising the line from the water, a little jerk should be given just as the fly leaves the surface, which makes it travel up and back much faster than it otherwise would, and prevents the line from hitting the ground or the water on the back cast.

That is an early instruction on hauling (I considered calling this chapter ''A Little Jerk''), but I doubt that the technique was anything new in 1902. Once silk lines replaced horsehair, and once snake guides replaced the old ring-and-keeper guides of pre-1870 rods, the friction-free line speed necessary for hauling was available. I personally know a number of fly fishers who discovered the value of hauling, either single or double, quite on their own. Martin Keane, the modern authority on classic rods, has told me that he sees no reason why casters well before 1900 might not have discovered the haul:

> Personally, I would not be the least surprised to discover some form of hauling either as we know it today or some abbreviated technique was used as far back as the 1880s particularly by tournament casters who it would seem did discover this technique possibly by having the line slip out of their hand on a back cast and then stopping it as it was getting away and noticing the extra load and additional energy produced by the rod at that moment.

I agree with Marty, partly because an examination of early casting photographs, such as those in Edward Samuels's *With Fly Rod and Camera* (1890), suggests to me that these casters were simply too proficient not to feel the line's pulls and respond to them.

But if they were using the haul, why was the technique so little known? I asked Cliff Netherton, our leading casting historian, this question, and found that he and I had been thinking the same thing. Casting was highly competitive, with manufacturers as well as individuals putting their reputations out for others to challenge. Any angler who developed the technique might be shy to share it except with his friends. A. J. McClane, who has had so much to do with progress in many aspects of fly fishing in recent decades, shared his opinions with me as well:

> . . . it could have existed in a modified form; overcoming water resistance with a single haul is a logical movement as a caster gains experience but that second pull may well have been no more than a slight ''tug'' which might go unnoticed. Instead of the underwear-ripping motions that Marvin Hedge used so effectively when I watched him at the Paris International in the late 40s—Bill Taylor, who was a great teacher (as Joan Wulff will testify) made a vest button pull of maybe four inches for some of the smoothest long casts imaginable. I suspect this modified style of a ''double haul'' was known to at least some of the early day rods when the double taper was in flower.

Al also suggested that once some of the tournament casters caught on, it was probably only a matter of time before others figured out what they were doing. I am not sure how fast that would have happened, but the modern double haul did not become formally recognized in a tournament until the 1930s. I have noticed, however, some intriguing peculiarities in the competition records from the 1890s and after.

In his small encyclopedia of casting, *History of Fly and Bait Casting* (1946), Harold Smedley thoughtfully lists casting records back as far as 1861. In the category "Trout Fly Distance—Heavy Tackle," there is a gradual increase in distances achieved, starting in the sixty- to seventy-foot range in the 1860s and 1870s, and slowly increasing to the nineties by the 1880s. That decade was dominated by Reuben Leonard, who won seven straight tournaments with casts as long as 102 feet. All the winners up to 1893 were New Yorkers, and in 1894 a Californian named R. R. Flint won with a distance of eighty-one feet. The next tournament listed was 1897, when San Franciscan W. D. Mansfield cast 111. In 1898 a Chicagoan, I. H. Bellows, won with ninety-eight feet. Then in 1900, A. E. Lovett of San Francisco won with 105 feet. Except for Mansfield's 1897 distance of 111, the record was still creeping up slowly, except that the Californians seemed to have something of an edge all at once (their clubs were new in the 1890s). Then, in 1902 Mansfield cast 134. Hmmm. The following year, T. B. Mills of the famous New York tackle company William Mills, cast 120, and for the next decade the casts rarely dropped below 110, though every year the winners were from Chicago or New York until 1915, when Mansfield was back with another 134. All this may mean nothing, but I doubt it. The West Coast was to take the lead in distance casting only two decades later when the modern double haul came into full view.

In the meantime there are occasional hints that it existed. In *Forest and Stream* in 1923 Louis Rhead wrote a two-part article on "Casting the Artificial Fly" that was illustrated by his always excellent drawings. In Part One (pages 242 to 243), there are two series of drawings, three in each series, showing the backcast and the forward cast. I do not know whether or not Rhead was himself aware of the haul— he does not mention it in the text of the article—but his drawings were perfect illustrations of it. In both series, just at the right point in the cast, the line hand executes a significant pull; in the backcast series, the line hand moves from his chin to his waist. It appears that the technique of hauling was appearing here and there among skilled casters. In an interview in 1973, Orvis's famous rodbuilder Wes Jordan, who grew up in the first years of the 1900s, recalled that he had discovered it himself: "I've put larger guides on my rods than other rod makers because I used to do the double haul when I was a kid. I didn't know about the double haul until I read about it and I had been doing it."

A number of people would claim to have invented it, but it appears to have surfaced formally in the 1930s. Marvin Hedge, we know, showed it to the world in 1934, having learned it from friends who used it around Oregon steelhead rivers in the early 1930s. Hedge unveiled it on a sweltering August day in 1934 at a St. Louis tournament, breaking the existing record by more than twenty feet. Hedge, building his own lines and spending hours rubbing them down with graphite to reduce friction (these were early versions of what we now call shooting heads), went on to contribute one of the great stories of British-American rivalry to fishing history. Vernon Hidy, who devoted considerable energy to recording western fly-fishing history, told the story in *The Creel*, the lovely journal of the Flyfisher's Club of Oregon, in July of 1964. Hedge was invited to Paris in 1937 by Charles Ritz, who had heard of his extraordinary casts. While there, Hedge beat Albert Godart, reigning European champion, by 9 feet, and then went on to London, where the record stood at 123 feet. Hidy's tale of Hedge's first cast must be quoted directly; it cannot be improved upon:

> When Marvin was called to cast by the officials of the British Casting Association, he noted that the position of the judges in their boat was rather short of the place his fly would likely land.

"Please move back," he called to them.

"*You* do the casting. *We* will do the judging," were the words which came back to him across the water. They would not budge.

Well beyond the judges, Marvin recalls, on a bank near where his fly would light if his cast was a good one, stood the Honorable Secretary of the B.C.A., M. H. Reisco, wearing a bowler hat and fingering a gold-headed cane in anticipation of the American's initial cast.

"My first cast," Marvin recalls, "went right over the judges' boat and out past the Secretary on the bank. He was pretty excited. He pointed at the fly in the water with the head of his cane. I heard him shout, 'Hey! I say there! It's sinking! It's *sinking!*' And by the time those fellows in the boat got out there they couldn't find it. It was my best cast of the day, about a hundred sixty-eight feet!"

Unruffled by this sticky wicket, the judges ruled "No Cast!" But Marvin, who had been told of the etiquette on the playing fields of Eton, Oxford and Cambridge, was very ruffled indeed.

"I could have pushed them out of that boat. I raised one record, it is true, but I had to be satisfied with a long cast of just one hundred fifty-one feet," he declares.

After seeing the champion perform, the British casting instructors began to advertise they had mastered and were capable of teaching *The Marvin Hedge System of Casting*.

One of the most pleasant aspects of British-American angling relations has been the occasional rivalry; these rivalries are good sport, and are rare compared to the many ways in which the two countries' anglers cooperate and communicate. They rarely are even as mean-spirited as Paul Fisher's 1835 taunt, quoted in Chapter 4, about "Brother Jonathan" not being sufficiently civilized to write fishing books. John Brown's response, also quoted in Chapter 4, was more typical of the tone of the rivalry. But even at that, I like to think that Brown, long forgotten by American fishermen by the 1900s, was able to look down (or up) from whatever spectral stream he was fishing that day in 1937 and watch Marvin Hedge drape his line across that boat.

Marvin Hedge's dominance of casting was brief. His 1934 record long cast of 147 feet was eclipsed by G. L. McLeod (149 feet) in 1936, and then in 1937 Dick Miller made a stunning cast of 183 feet. The exploits of these great competition casters are worth the books that Cliff Netherton has already devoted to them, and the achievements of the modern masters—from Jon Tarantino to Steve Rajeff—will be the subjects of the third book, now being written, in his series on casting history.

For the average fly fisher the names of the great casters are much harder to learn than those of the famous fishing writers (except in those few cases, like Lefty Kreh, where one is both), but they have quite often been leaders in rod development just as they are in casting theory. Jim Green's long association with Fenwick, Myron Gregory's work with Scientific Anglers, and Steve Rajeff's with Sage, are all good examples of the fruitful partnership of champion and industry.

The modern fly caster has more casts at his disposal, and more types of lines and rods for delivering them, than any of the previous generations. Modern casters also have more choices in casting style. The most distinctive example of the new choices in casting style is that promoted by Lefty Kreh, whose *Fly Casting with Lefty Kreh* (1974), a photographic guide to technique, has introduced a generation of anglers to an alternative approach to fly casting that goes directly against the tradition of the high backcast. Though not by any means the first book to use photographs to illustrate the sequence of motions in fly casting, this book did set a new standard for such productions. It also demonstrated the effectiveness of Lefty's low-backcast style, developed and refined while fishing open saltwater. Lefty, who has become the foremost spokesman for saltwater fly fishing, demonstrates his powerful style regularly at fishing conventions (where he is regarded as one of the best of modern instructors), and has had a huge influence on modern casting; many fishermen incorporate his style into their armory of techniques even if they only use it selectively.

The fishing-book boom of the 1970s saw the appearance of several other casting guides besides Lefty's including books by Rex Gerlach and Bill Cairns, but as usual, at least until the advent of instructional videotapes, most casting instruction appeared either in articles on specific casts or in books in which casting was only a chapter. The only problem a newcomer faces is in deciding which method of the many offered to adopt; there is still a tendency among the experts to offer their preferred method as the only really smart one, even though all the expert methods are demonstrably good at catching fish. In that, though, fly casting is a lot like fly theory, rod taper theory, and most other elements of fly fishing. If George Dawson could return today, more than a century after the publication of his remarks on fly casting quoted at the beginning of this chapter, he would still be amazed at the multitude of attitudes anglers assume.

Three

THE GEOGRAPHY
OF THE FLY

14

Flies That Aren't

*A friend in Texas, to whom I sent a bass-fly (an Abbey),
and who had never seen a "fly" before, enthusiastically
declared it to be "a fish-hook poetized," and thought that
a "Black Bass should take it through a love of the beautiful,
if nothing else."*

JAMES HENSHALL,
Book of the Black Bass (1881)

It seems not to have taken American fly fishers long to recognize the sporting possibilities of the nonsalmonids. By the 1840s, fly fishers were regularly taking the various basses and sunfishes, as well as pike and other occasionals, on flies in many parts of this country.

Despite their frequent appearance in fishing accounts, the basses especially were the object of debates over whether or not they would take a fly at all. That subject was debated in the sporting periodicals well into the 1880s, all the while that anglers were enjoying great sport with bass. A second debate was less easily resolved, that being the rivalry that developed between anglers over which was the more sporting fish, bass or trout. Like most good fishing arguments, this one is more or less impossible to settle, but it generated some heated opinions.

The positions of the combatants were probably almost as numerous as the combatants themselves, but a few stereotypes will serve our purposes here. There was of course James Henshall's claim that the bass was inch for inch and pound for pound the gamest fish that swims. Henshall's writings, especially his *Book of the Black Bass* (1881), were the best, most comprehensive and scientifically authoritative works on the bass for more than sixty years (how often can *that* be said of a popular fishing book?), and he championed a good cause, alerting thousands of fly fishers to the sporting possibilities of the basses just as those fish were finding homes in new waters in many parts of the country. Today people use the term "Maine smallmouth" as if the state and the fish were more or less created together on the same day, but it wasn't until the late 1860s that Maine received its first smallmouths. The largemouth has been an even more widespread success for fisheries managers. William Robbins and Hugh MacCrimmon, in their *The Black Bass in America and Overseas* (1974), summarized the fish's travels:

The bass's greatest
champion, James Henshall.

145

Few fish species have become naturalized by introduction over such a large geographical area of America as has the largemouth bass. From its original range which
encompassed less than one half of the area of the United States, part of southern
Canada and northeastern Mexico in 1825, the species has become established in
every State except Alaska and four Provinces of Canada.

Fisheries managers have of course altered our fishing in many ways by transplants:
Pacific salmon in the Great Lakes, rainbow trout in many states east of their native
range (and various genetically engineered variants of the rainbow), European brown
trout in countless watersheds, brook trout in many high-altitude western waters, and
so on. As much as I can I am steering clear of fisheries science in this book, if only
because it is a big enough topic that it truly needs a good history of its own (I'm not
volunteering; I'm just recommending). But I must point out that the bass, both in its
native range and in its huge new range, was an important force in the expansion of
American fly fishing. The expansion was not merely geographical, either. The bass
was an important factor in changing American approaches to fly fishing.

But before getting into just what it was the bass did, I must be fair to the viewpoint
against which Henshall wrote. Two examples will suffice to suggest that American
anglers were as divided on the bass question as on any other. First, from *The American
Turf Register*, for March 1831, perhaps the most famous early antibass sentiment:

> But there is no comparison, none at all, between sitting with your rod in a shallop,
> in one of the low, marshy lagoons of the south, surrounded by huge alligators sunning
> themselves lazily upon the blackened logs that float upon the turbid water, whose
> sluggish surface is not unfrequently rippled by the darting of the deadly mocassin
> hissing past you—and treading the verdant banks of some beautiful, rippling brook
> in New England; gurgling and leaping in its living course to the ocean, with its cool
> retreat for its watery tenant, ''under the shade of melancholy boughs,'' or amid the
> still water of an eddying pool.

That was, of course, a caricature, intentional or not, of typical bass waters, but
it echoes similar sentiments expressed by others. Here is a correspondent named
''Chester,'' writing in *The American Angler* on February 4, 1882, as part of a several-
months-long running debate over the relative sporting and personality qualities of
bass and trout:

> Enthusiasm and extra zeal has of late been manifested by the friends of the bass,
> and his habits and belongings are heralded with sentences heavy with superlatives
> and affirmations ''strong as dicers' oaths.'' Scientists have loaned their lore liberally,
> and have wasted the midnight oil in the bestowal upon this fish Latin and French
> names by the score, and these are beaten out of sight by your correspondent ''Asa,''
> whose nomenclature is certainly apt if not elegant, viz.: ''The Hog of the Waters,''
> and even the rhythm of poetry has invested him with a glamour that ought to give
> the bass grounds for his vanity, as a fit successor and co-biter of the trout.
>   Laden thus with so formidable an array of names, and possibly gorged with
> garter snakes, we are assured that he will rise to the fly quite as reliably as the trout,
> and is more than his equal otherwise. Sancho Panza invoked blessings on the man
> who invented sleep, and I have a deep respect for the discoverer of sausage, and
> can, therefore, admire any process by which garter snakes can be converted into
> good fish (I cheerfully admit this to the credit of the bass), but ask to be excused
> from admitting this porcine, snake-devouring rover of stagnant waters to any show
> of equality or right of heirship to the reputation of the glorious *Salmon fontinalis*.

One element of that argument, incidentally, was that an earlier correspondent had suggested that the bass might serve as a good replacement of the trout in waters where that fish had been cleaned out by overfishing. It is interesting to note that many of the first Americans who caught the new brown trout found it ugly, too. The native brook trout has not been easily replaced in our collective heart.

This is not, even after such a start, a chapter about bass. It is a chapter about the ways in which we have broadened the sport of fly fishing to meet newly perceived opportunities. I start with the bass because it has had so much to do with those opportunities, and in that way represents the many other fish we have sought with flies that were not really flies.

Flies, like the life forms they imitate and the fish they catch, are a product of their environment. The free wheeling approach to fly color and size adopted by American fly fishers in the nineteenth century was in good part the result of a fishing condition that led them in that direction; they did not have to do much more than use a fly that was pretty to them, because the fish, both trout and bass, were rarely discriminating. The development of the many types of flies and schools of fly tying in America since those times has been a response to the needs of many different fishing conditions. North America offered many fish types, and most climatic types from subtropical to Arctic. North America also offered a rich bird and mammal fauna from which to draw for fly-tying materials. It is no wonder that fly fishing has broadened its definitions in so many ways since it took hold in this country.

One of the most apparent and widespread developments in American fly tying has been the increasing use of flies that do not imitate real flies. "Fly fishing" has come to mean, to most people, at least, the use of a fly rod and fly line to cast something we still call a fly but that might imitate anything from a blob of stonefly eggs to a baby muskrat. There have been, and continue to be, disagreements among sporting theorists over just how far this stretching of traditional definitions can go and still be fly fishing, but it has always been true that at least some people called a great many different practices fly fishing. Variety, the blessing of the adventurous American fly fisher, is the curse of the fly-fishing philosopher. I don't think it need be, but among the confusing perceptual baggage of the sportsman is a powerful need to make sure things are being done "right," that is, according to a reasonable code of practice. The diversity of fly-fishing opportunities in North America challenge that code in many ways, some of which will be discussed later, but we must not think that we are the first to stretch the boundaries of fly fishing.

We were preceded in many ways by the British. By the late 1700s, and I assume earlier, they were taking pike—to say nothing of smaller nonsalmonids—on "flies." Taylor, writing in 1800, described pike fishing with a fly "the size of a wren."

The British also preceded us in intentionally imitating small fish; there is no question that the fly we call the streamer was well established in principle in Great Britain before it was "invented" in America. We have no way of knowing now just how often British fly fishers used wet flies (trout or salmon flies) to imitate small fish, but we do know that by the 1840s at least a few British anglers were tying specific fish imitations. Theophilus South (Edward Chitty), in *The Fly Fisher's Text Book* (1841), gave a matter-of-fact quotation from Richard Hely, an avid saltwater angler:

> I have fished a great deal in the tide-ways with the fly, and had admirable sport: mackerel, whiting, pollock, and sand-eels, may be taken in great quantities. The fly is a white feather, projecting considerably over the hook, and it resembles the herring fry, of which both mackerel and pollock are very fond.

Chitty lived for several years in Jamaica in the 1840s; I wonder if he also fly fished there. In 1844, James Wilson's *The Rod and the Gun* elaborated on a favorite sea-trout fly:

> We may here add, what we omitted in its proper place, that a singularly successful fly for sea-trout, large or small, may be made with silver tinsel enwrapping the whole body from head to heel . . . the wings, of a narrow elongated form, composed either of pure white or pale gray, or a mixture of both. It has a very glistening aspect in the water, looking somewhat like a small disabled fish, and sea-trout swallow it from a kindly fellow-feeling, believing it to be some relation of their own.

The 1851 book, *Fly-Fishing in Salt and Fresh Water*, possibly by a Mrs. Hutchinson, contained extended accounts of fishing with large "flies" from a boat. The flies were apparently intended to imitate fish (at least I can't imagine what else could have been meant), and the tackle was so heavy that the technique must have been more like trolling than fly casting, but it was tremendously successful:

> Most capital sea fly-fishing can be obtained off the coast of Connemara, viz., in Bertraghboy Bay, at the Skyard Rocks, at Deer Island, and off the Isle of Mweenish and the Isle of Arran. The whiting pollack [sic] that are to be met with there, take a large gaudy fly most boldly. I have with a fly taken some in those parts, as large as nine pounds. I used seven flies at once, and have frequently taken seven fish at the same time.

These were enormously large flies, judging from the author's description of two fish caught on one fly, "one of these fish being caught by the lip and the other by the tail." If the author did cast them, they must have had the glide angle of a shag rug.

Much more modest and castable flies were also in use, and appear now and then in various British publications. In Bickerdyke's *The Book of the All-Round Angler* (1889), there is an illustration of a large double-hooked pike fly, whose wing is made up of an entire peacock "eye" feather. In the same book Bickerdyke mentions that "an old Irish fisherman of Banagher told me that a fly made out of the tail of a grown calf was very killing . . . only the tip of the tail is used." The "bucktail" (which is often now tied with calf tail) is as indeterminate of origin as is the streamer.

Concern over the effectiveness of fish imitations must have been pretty common by the 1880s in Great Britain. J. Harrington Keene, writing in the *American Angler* on August 1, 1885, claimed that the Alexandra was "a grand killer of trout in Europe and is probably mistaken for a small minnow . . . In many waters its use is looked on as unsportsmanlike and is forbidden."

For these reasons I look with skepticism on any claims by any angler or on behalf of any angler to have "invented" fish imitations. Invention and origination are known reputation-makers, and there are plenty of honors to go around in fly fishing for coming up with new patterns and theories, but the imitation of a life form as widespread as the "baitfish" was probably as intuitive a process as the imitation of insects. "Everything of importance," Alfred North Whitehead once said, "has been said before by somebody who did not discover it."

Streamers (whether they were called that or not, and they rarely were before 1900) seem to have had many origins in this country. Like British anglers, Americans occasionally recognized that some wet flies could imitate fish. Robert Barnwell Roosevelt, in *Game Fish of the North* (1862), noted that the Scarlet Ibis resembled a fish:

As many of the Long Island trout yearly migrate to the sea, in which peculiarity they resemble the fish of the latter place, it may be that this fly is only a favorite with sea-going fish. A little tinsel wound round the body is supposed to improve its efficiency, as some fishermen suggest from a resemblance to the principal Winter food of the trout, the salt water minnow.

The standard work on streamers and bucktails is Joseph Bates's encyclopedic *Streamers and Bucktails, The Big Fish Flies* (1979). Joe, who has also been one of the world's foremost collectors of salmon flies, has traced the varied origins of streamers and bucktails, pointing out that though primitive bucktails were in use for smallmouth bass by the 1870s, the real movement to create the modern streamer was primarily a product of Maine. Joe is right; I've seen long-shanked bucktails tied by the Orvis Company in the early 1890s, and a number of others were experimenting with either bucktails (William Scripture, of Rome, New York, was tying them shortly after 1900, and receiving considerable attention for it) or streamers, or simply imitating baitfish with traditional trout and bass wet flies, but we owe Maine the most for starting one of America's important fly-tying traditions.

And, as usual, we owe this tradition to the environment as much as to the fly tiers. Maine's lake regions—the most famous being the Rangeleys—abounded in huge brook trout and in some cases landlocked salmon as well. These fish, often more than five pounds, fed on smaller fish, in some cases slender shiny smelt that had finally to remind someone of a dun saddle hackle. Fishing the lakes and the short streams between them was popular among sportsmen from New York, Boston, and other eastern population centers by the 1880s, but the most important streamer pioneers were their guides and other locals.

Herb Welch is given credit for being first (indeed, he is one of several Americans, along with Emerson Hough and Theodore Gordon, who have mistakenly been credited with "inventing" the streamer, a credit Welch apparently liked to give himself), and what he did was at least very important. Not only did he specifically tie imitations of fish, he had to hand-make hooks of sufficient length to do the job, apparently not having access to such hooks commercially. His first attempts were in about 1902, and by the 1920s he had been joined by others, including Joe Stickney, originator of the Supervisor and the Warden's Worry, and Bill Edson, originator of the famous Edson Tigers.

But for lasting fame no other Maine streamer tier has approached a housewife at Upper Dam, Mooselookmeguntic Lake. In August of 1970, a cooperative effort by a number of conservation and commercial organizations, working with the State of Maine, established a memorial and plaque at the site of her home. It read in part:

> Fishermen: Pause here a moment and pay your respects to Carrie Gertude Stevens. On July 1, 1924, while engaged in household tasks in her home across this portage road, she was inspired to create a new fish-fly pattern. With housework abandoned her nimble hands had soon completed her vision. In less than an hour the nearby Upper Dam Pool had yielded a 6 pound 13 ounce brook trout to the new fly that would become known throughout the world as the Gray Ghost Streamer.

Carrie Stevens's intentional smelt imitation was an instant success (the fish she caught that day won second place in that year's *Field & Stream* competition), and was soon followed by more than twenty other patterns that eager anglers purchased about as fast as she could tie them. The traditional feather-wing streamer has of course spread to all parts of the country: the excellent New York/Vermont patterns of Lew Oatman—his darters and shiners, especially; Edward Hewitt's Neversink

Edward Hewitt's Neversink Streamer was a simple, predominantly black pattern. *Photo by the author.*

Streamer; the light and dark (sometimes called Montana) spruce flies originated on the West Coast and in the Rockies; and countless others. Many, like most of Stevens's flies, never achieved more than regional prominence, but the feather-wing streamer was adapted to imitate (at least in the tier's mind), all kinds of shiners, smelt, bullheads, and immature sportfish. There were, predictably, soon streamer versions of older patterns, such as the Royal Coachman, and some of these maintained popularity for many years as well.

The same developments occurred in bucktails, though hair and feather were often combined in the wing of a single fly. The trim outline of a sparsely dressed bucktail has proven very successful—Art Flick's Black-Nose Dace may be the most famous today, but Sam Slaymaker's Little Brown, Brook, and Rainbow Trout patterns, and the Mickey Finn, popularized half a century ago by John Alden Knight, are also durable modern classics. Keith Fulsher's ''Thunder Creek'' bucktails, with their slim, bullet-headed silhouette, are a recent promising development in the bucktail form.

Perhaps nothing had so broad an effect on American fly tying, in fact, as the use of hair. Hair had been used in British flies for centuries, but mostly in dubbing rather than for other fly parts. Americans turned to hair for many purposes, and most of them did not involve insect imitations. One of them has become, in the minds of many, the most adaptable and broadly useful of all flies.

Though others were tying and selling a variety of trimmed deer-hair-head fish imitations long before, credit for establishing and popularizing the Muddler Minnow goes to Don Gapen of Minnesota. The fly is thought to be a modification of simpler Indian patterns, but that need not detract from Gapen's achievement in recognizing and marketing a great fly (in its second number in 1971, *The Flyfisher* published a delightful historical parody about a mysterious Ludwig Moedler, said to have originated the fly in the late 1800s; several later writers, as well as *Field & Stream* magazine, took the spoof seriously, quoting the article extensively). Gapen developed his muddler in the late 1930s on the Nipigon in Ontario, one of the best big-brook-trout rivers in North American history, and it has been refined and diversified ever since until now there is a family of muddlers, spuddlers, marabou muddlers, and other flies based on the trimmed-head concept. Many respected writers have acclaimed it the ''one fly to have'' if you're only having one. Luckily it is not necessary ever to have only one, but the muddler has certainly become one of those few flies that almost everyone does have.

And with the muddler we approach a line between the fish imitations and another fly type. These flies, though not fish imitations, and rarely even imaginable as insect imitations, have also been blessed by the fly fisher's whimsically perverse naming system. They are called bugs.

In fact it could be claimed that the muddler is more bug than baitfish, for it is often used to imitate nonpiscine creatures, from grasshopper to stonefly to crayfish to that mystical category of things known as bass bugs. But it grew out of a baitfish tradition, so we will leave it here with the others of that type, and move into the murkier waters of the bass fly fisher.

The bass *fly*, of course, goes back well into the 1800s, where it was most often an oversized and heavily dressed copy of a trout-fly pattern (though there were many popular wet flies developed just for bass). These flies were often intended for lake use, even trolling, and your first look at one today is usually a shock because of the bulk of it. The body was built up to a fat cylinder, often ribbed in heavy trim like the brocaded arm of an old couch, and the wing was dense and wide. No wonder the flies caused jokes about their being most effective if you could hit the bass on the head with your cast. Exactly how the bug grew from the fly is not precisely clear, partly because it grew from so many sources, but we do have some leads.

For example, the "bob" described in Chapter 3 by Bartram never disappeared through the 1800s. A writer in the *Spirit* in 1839 said that fishing the bob (the one he described is much the same in size as Bartram's had been) was actually "fly fishing on a larger scale," claiming it was even more fun. It seems never to have been accepted by fly fishers *as* fly fishing, but it did maintain popularity, and Henshall, when he wrote his *Book of the Black Bass* (1881), gave the method space, saying it was in "use at the present day in Florida, Louisiana, and Texas."

Another example: by the late 1800s lure fishermen were experimenting with an assortment of wooden-bodied lures for various warmwater fish, and surely fly fishers did not miss the possibilities of that investigation. The first "bugs" were probably an outgrowth of interest in bass and bass flies.

James Henshall is often credited with the prototype modern trimmed-hair bass bug, though it is not clear when he developed it. The bug had a fat body of alternating trimmed bands of black-and-yellow deer hair, yellow bucktail wings, and a yellow saddle-hackle tail. Cork-bodied bass bugs of many styles seem to have been a southern development, coming from the rivers of Arkansas and Missouri. A. J. McClane, in *The Practical Fly Fisherman* (1953), says that "native swampers made them up from beer bottle corks and turkey feathers. This was quite some time before the turn of the century." "Swampers" would be even less likely than most other fly fishers to leave much of a written record, so the tradition will always have fairly misty origins. But its development did not stay misty for long. Shortly after the turn of the century, the bass bug experienced a startling growth in popularity, and most of the enduring forms were created.[1] There have been hundreds, perhaps even thousands, but they follow a few main types.

The Coaxer, developed by a Chicagoan named William Jamison before 1910, may have been the first commercial bug; it had a cork body, red-felt wings, and a feather hiding the hook. It was soon followed by several others: The Wilder-Dilg, a cooperative effort between B. F. Wilder and Will Dilg, was apparently first developed about 1911 but not popularized until the 1920s; it had a cork body in front (usually pointed at the nose), hackle collar behind the body, and long feather tails. Also about 1910, Ernest Peckinpagh of Tennessee began to take bass on cork-bodied double-hooked flies he'd been using for some years for smaller panfish; by 1914 he was marketing his "Night Bugs" through a few commercial tackle dealers. Late in life, according to a letter he wrote to A. J. McClane in 1947, Peckinpagh credited Will Dilg, with the help of Cal McCarthy (whose flat-winged bug, the Cal-Mac, was another early favorite), with popularizing bass bugs through his articles in the 1920s.

From these uncertain beginnings the various bugs rose to great favor. In 1919, Orley Tuttle, who lived near Old Forge in the Adirondacks, was fishing for bass one evening when he noticed that large beetles that fell into the lake were quickly gobbled up by smallmouths. He soon tied up an all-deer-hair bug, with a body made of a large bundle of the hair tied down over the hook and the head trimmed to shape and the tail left longer. When he showed it to his wife, the story goes, she said, "Looks like the devil to me," inspiring Orley to name his creation the Tuttle Devil Bug. Tony Atwill wrote a fine short history of this bug for *Rod & Reel* in May/June 1979, and he traced the rapid progress of Orley's bug:

> By 1922, the Tuttles were selling 50,000 Devil Bugs a year. They ran Lottie's [Orley's wife] full-color ads in *Field & Stream* and expanded the line to include winged bugs, mouse bugs, trout bugs, and even a deerhair baby duck—death on muskies. With all the combinations of colors and models and styles, the Tuttles were marketing more than 800 different Devil Bugs, plus a few assorted handmade spoons and spinners. Devil Bugs were big time.

A selection of early bass bugs from the 1926 Von Lengerke & Detmold (New York) catalog. Reprinted in *Great Fishing Tackle Catalogs of the Golden Age* (1972).

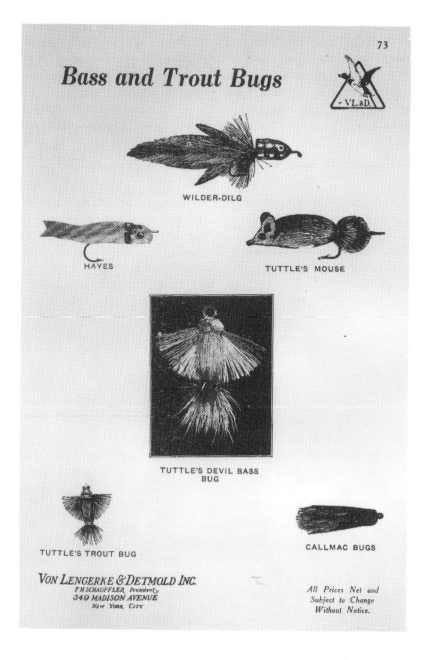

Two original bass bugs by Joe Brooks. The one on the right was a novelty item with an American flag that popped up when the fish hit it. *Photo by the author.*

So were a lot of others. Peckinpagh's assortments grew, as did those offered by the Weber Company, one of the real giants of commercial fly tying, based in Stevens Point, Wisconsin. By the 1930s there was a bewildering assortment of bass bugs available, possibly even more than there are today.

Many look clumsy by modern standards. Peckinpagh introduced one of the first poppers in the 1930s, increasing even more the attractive qualities of these flies, but a lot of them still look ungainly to us now. Their bodies were quite large in many cases, usually without the pleasant contours of modern synthetic poppers and "sliders," and the feathers were lashed on with conspicuous windings. None of this mattered to the bass, of course.

I am an enthusiastic admirer of Dave Whitlock and other modern masters of deer-hair fly tying, but at the same time the work done in deer hair forty or more years ago shows us most of the modern techniques. Joe Messinger's frogs and poppers, the mice from Weber and Tuttle, and the assortment of frogs and crayfish in books such as William Sturgis's *Fly-Tying* (1940) are all as finished and refined as any bass fisherman (or bass) probably needs. The foundation established by the pioneers of the bass bug is at least as strong as that established by the pioneers of dry flies and streamers.

There are still plenty of people with strong feelings about the bass-trout rivalry. Most now concentrate on the cultural or social differences between modern trout fishermen and modern bass fishermen. The modern "bassin' man," in stereotype, sits in his $10,000 bass boat complete with assorted electronic gear, an engine powerful enough to run his truck and pull his trailer, and a language almost defiantly abusive of grammatic convention. The modern "trout angler," in stereotype, stands (or hunches over) up to his Latin dictionary in a "storied" stream, mumbling about operculate gill plates, festooned with surgical appliances, carrying custom-made gear worth enough to have put his kid through college. Neither stereotype holds up, or, better put, both only hold up often enough to be reinforced in the public mind.

Nobody has written more intelligently, or more entertainingly, about these social fractures in modern sport fishing than Charles Waterman. Among the many reasons I would recommend his *A History of Angling* (1981) is that it contains episodes like this one:

> The bass, especially, drew the ire of former trout fishermen, a displeasure that has carried over 100 years. Even today, some Maine residents scorn bass as "tourist fish."
>
>   "Oh, bass are all right, I guess," a resort owner told me in 1970. "There's a man in Portland who eats the damned things!"

15

Saltwater Fly Fishing: The Century of Obscurity

It seems impossible to exaggerate the fishing possibilities of the west coast of Florida. With a fly rod the number of fish which may be caught is purely a question of physical endurance.

A. W. Dimock, *Forest and Stream*, June 26, 1890

The oldest record of saltwater fly fishing I have come across, including those given in the previous chapter from the 1840s and 1850s for Great Britain, appeared in the *Spirit* on October 7, 1843, reprinted from an unspecified issue of *Bell's Life of London*. The British writer of the article said that he had ''cast the fly for forty years and more, both in the ocean and the fresh,'' which would put his saltwater fishing back to around 1800 if the claim was accurate. I imagine that a thorough search of British periodicals and books would reveal more information, but I also imagine that saltwater fly fishing, like streamer fishing, is susceptible to frequent rediscovery. It appears to have been rediscovered regularly for about a century in North America.

There are numerous references in the period between 1830 and 1870 to fly fishing for shad and striped bass, though some of these suggest that the fishing was done while those species were on migratory runs into rivers. An extremely early possibility exists in Jerome V. C. Smith's little book *Natural History of the Fishes of Massachusetts* (1833), where Smith discusses fishing for sea trout (these would be sea-run brook trout). He was fishing for them at Poket Point (on the south shore of Cape Cod, opposite Martha's Vineyard), casting flies and bait into the bay from prominent spits, and he reported that in May striped bass might also be taken (though he did not say specifically that the bass were taken on flies).

Frank Forester recommended fly fishing for striped bass in his *Frank Forester's Fish and Fishing* (1849):

The fly to be used is any of the large Salmon flies, the larger and gaudier the better. None is more taking than an orange body with peacock and bluejay wings and black hackle legs; but any of the well-known Salmon flies will secure him, as will the scarlet bodied fly with scarlet ibis and silver pheasant wings, which is so killing to the Black Bass of the lakes.

Robert Barnwell Roosevelt, another oft-cited saltwater fly fishing pioneer, seems to have confined his bass fishing to estuaries and rivers rather than going to the fish in the ocean. In *Game Fish of the North* (1862), he described his methods:

The most scientific and truly sportsmanlike mode of taking striped bass must be admitted to be with the fly; which, unfortunately, can only be done in the brackish or fresh water. Like salmon, they will not take the fly in the salt creeks and bays, and thus, though the sport is excellent, it is confined to few localities, and those difficult of access. Fly-fishing may be done either with the ordinary salmon rod, or in a strong current with the common bass rod, by working your fly on the top of the water and giving a considerable length of line. The best fly is that with the scarlet ibis and white feathers mixed, the same as used for black bass; but bass may be taken with any large fly, especially those of gay color. Excellent sport is frequently had in this way from off some open bridge, where the falling tide, mixed with the fresh water, rushes furiously between the piers.

Modern striper fishermen know that the fish can be caught in saltwater, but Roosevelt's description is revealing in another way: his use of the term "fly-fishing" includes standing in one spot (such as on a bridge) and feeding line out into the current, then apparently holding it there and waiting for a strike. It does not become clear at any point that he was actually casting the fly, though he probably did when the circumstances permitted.

The written record of this early saltwater and brackish-water fishing (and I might point out that Joseph Banks, fly fishing in the New World in 1766, seems to have been fishing tide water) reveals a southward movement, from New England sport-fishing centers to the Chesapeake Bay and on to Florida, where saltwater fly fishing came to greater attention because of the great variety and size of species available. The fly fishing practiced in New York and New England continued from the Civil War on to today, but it doesn't yet get the attention given the more exotic southern fishing. That doesn't especially bother devoted enthusiasts of twenty-pound stripers and voracious bluefish off New England coasts, however.

Fly fishing in Florida may have been practiced earlier, but it seems to have become an important sporting activity in the 1870s and 1880s. As usual, there are a number of people put forward for the honors of discovering the sport, none of whom have an especially good case. It seems that various fishing areas—Homosassa, Biscayne Bay, Florida Bay, and so on—were each pioneered by a few people until it had all been explored with fly rods. *Forest and Stream* mentions bass fishing on the St. John's River as early as 1873. An angler named Huntington reported in *Forest and Stream* on July 20, 1876 that he was catching a variety of fish (bass, sea trout, and "skip-jacks") in the Homosassa region. The following year, on May 10, another brief note in *Forest and Stream* informed a Texas correspondent that sea trout were known to take flies in the Corpus Christi area of the south Texas coast (near present-day Padre Island National Seashore). J. C. Kenworthy, writing in *Fishing with the Fly* (1883), credited George Johnson, of Bridgeport, Connecticut, with developing fly fishing in the Homosassa region and by implication throughout the state. Kenworthy, under the pen name of "Al Fresco," wrote for the periodicals in the 1880s

An extremely early illustration of saltwater fly fishing in America, this engraving appeared in the May, 1891 issue of *The Century Magazine* with an article by Charles Holder. According to Holder's story, the angler, using a salmon rod, hooked a small "jack" (possibly jack crevalle) on a fly but became involved in a feeding spree by thousands of others.

and 1890s, extolling the sporting qualities and attendant delights of Florida fishing. Kenworthy, who by 1883 could list skipjacks (naming of Florida fishes was terribly confused, so that even today it is not always possible to tell what fish the early writers were referring to), ravallia, cavalli, snappers, sea trout, bluefish, catfish, and a variety of freshwater species as falling to his flies, enjoyed the simplicity of the tackle needed:

> Delicate mist-colored leaders are not a necessity, for Florida fish have not been educated or posted with regard to the tricks of the craft. They seem to recognize but little difference between a single strand of gut and a clothes line . . . With regard to flies, almost any of the more common ones will answer a good purpose. My choice for channel bass, cavalli, sea trout and bone fish [probably the modern ladyfish] is a large-sized gaudy fly with a large-sized hook.

James Henshall was another early fly-fishing explorer in Florida. He wrote about it in several of his books, but especially in *Camping and Cruising in Florida* (1884), where he reviewed his success in 1878:

> As might be imagined, fishing with the artificial fly can be practiced and enjoyed to the fullest extent, where fish are so abundant. I took many different species, both fresh-water and marine, with the artificial fly, in the vicinity of Fort Capron. While they did not run so heavy as those taken with bait, they were quite heavy enough for the fly-rod. For instance, I took crevalle of five pounds, sea-trout of ten pounds, red-fish of five pounds, blue-fish of four pounds, "snooks" or sergeant-fish of six pounds, bone, or lady-fish of two pounds, black bass of eight pounds, and tarpum [sic] of ten pounds, in addition to other species of less weight . . .

I used a twelve-foot, twelve-ounce, ash and lancewood fly-rod, and a remarkably good one, by the way, which I often found rather light for large fish. A grilse rod would be more suitable for fly-fishing.

I often took some of the aforementioned species while fishing for black bass and when using bass flies; but when fishing especially for the marine species, I used flies of my own tying, made without much regard to any particular pattern. I tied them on Sproat hooks from 4-0 to 6-0 in size, using a combination of colors, and usually with white or grayish wings, as the fishing was mostly done at dusk.

Bright feathers are easily procured in Florida from the numerous gay-plumaged birds, so that the angler will be at no loss for material for tying his flies. Two flies I remember as being particularly taking: one with upper wings of white ibis and lower wings of the mottled feathers of chuck-will's-widow; another with top wings of white egret and lower ones of pink curlew (roseate spoonbill). The coachman, oriole white and red ibis, silver gray, and other flies with white or light-colored wings, are good ones to pattern after in tying flies for this kind of fishing. They should be of good size, about the same as salmon flies.

Experimenting with fly pattern started quite early, but traditional salmon and bass flies remained popular well into the 1900s. Usually the alterations were simple, most involving longer feathers to imitate small fish. A British angler, Alfred Harmsworth, reported in *Forest and Stream* on January 5, 1895, that he had success with a "silver doctor, to which I had added a largish white feather."

A year later, on February 15, the same publication included a report from no less eminent an American fly authority than Mary Orvis Marbury. The Orvis family was involved in the resort business in both Vermont and Florida, which may have had something to do with Mary's visit, but she was plainly there to have fun too:

A few evenings ago I went out in a small rowboat with my brother, and we rowed into a big school of bluefish that were jumping in all directions. You felt as though you could wade out and catch them with your hands, they were so many and so near. They rose eagerly to the fly, and while the sun was setting we caught enough for our breakfast, all within sight of the house and the sound of the tea bell, which interrupted our sport.

The tea bell seems to indicate that some Florida fly fishing was getting pretty posh.

Marbury had published, in her *Favorite Flies*, a description of one of the first named saltwater flies, the "Cracker," tied by George Trowbridge, who reported various impressive catches, including a channel bass over twenty-three pounds.

Two fish have most often been associated with this southern fishing: the tarpon and the bonefish. Both were the subject of repeated rediscovery by fly fishers, though it was the bonefish that would be caught "the first time" by more anglers than any other American game fish.

According to the periodicals, at least a few bonefish (not ladyfish, with which they were often confused in naming) were taken on flies before 1900. On April 8, 1896, *Forest and Stream* ran a convincing account of bonefishing by a man whose pen name was "Maxie." He started by giving the appropriate scientific name of the true bonefish, and through reference to an earlier article in the magazine he made it clear that the fish he was catching fought as bonefish do (long runs, no jumps). He explained he had ten years' experience, and "derived more sport from using a medium weight fly-rod with large gaudy salmon or bass flies" than from using bait. He concluded by pointing out that the "bonefish" mentioned by Henshall in *Camping and Cruising* was actually the ladyfish.

Captain Bill Smith, pictured in 1939 with a bonefish taken on a fly and an Orvis rod. *Courtesy of The American Museum of Fly Fishing.*

From that beginning we follow a series of firsts, most reported by Joe Brooks in *Salt Water Game Fishing* (1968) and George Sand in *Salt-Water Fly Fishing* (1969). Sand credits a Florida man, Holmes Allen, with taking a bonefish on a fly in 1924 in the Keys, while fishing for snook; the hookup was not an intentional effort to take bonefish but the result of blind casting. Brooks says that the first was a Colonel L. S. Thompson of New Jersey, who caught several at Long Key in 1926 while fishing for baby tarpon; again the catches appear to have been accidental.

In 1939 a well-known Miami guide, Captain Bill Smith, having been criticized by George LaBranche for taking bonefish on a fly rod with a pork-rind lure and calling it fly fishing, tied some simple white flies and took a bonefish, resulting in his picture appearing in the local paper (forty years later Captain Smith donated more pictures and some of his tackle to the Museum, so at least this ''first'' will be documented).

Joe Brooks himself claimed to be the first to take a bonefish intentionally on a fly outfit, which he did in 1947. Brooks knew Smith, but Smith seems not to have told him about the earlier catch. In any event it was Brooks, not the earlier fishermen, who made the fish popular among fly fishers; Joe Brooks wrote widely and well about the bonefish, and explored bonefish waters in many areas of the South, starting the great trend toward fly-rod bonefishing. It still seems remarkable to me, however, that in 1949, after more than seventy years of continuous fly-fishing history in Florida saltwater, the Fishing Editor of the *Miami Herald* could be quoted (in Leonard's *Flies*, 1950) as saying that ''it was found, in June of 1947, that salt-water fish would take a fly.'' The editor, Allen Corson, had been with Joe Brooks on that first bonefish trip, and had assumed it all started there, no apologies to Henshall, Marbury, and all the rest.

The tarpon did not stay obscure. The fish was so grandly spectacular, and so huge, that once the first few large ones had been caught on heavy tackle it was a matter of considerable public interest every time someone did something new in tarpon fishing. By the early decades of the 1900s both Hardy's of England and William Mills of New York were selling a series of tarpon streamers, and the smaller fish steadily entertained fly fishers. In *Favorite Fish and Fishing* (1908), Henshall changed

Joe Brooks with one of the first permit ever taken on a fly. *Courtesy of The American Museum of Fly Fishing.*

his earlier weight estimate and said he had caught them as large as forty pounds, though he may have meant he did so on a later trip. However that may have been, forty pounds was a lot of tarpon for the tackle of that time, especially for the leader. Listen to this Canadian angler's account of catching baby tarpon in Jamaica, as reported in *Forest and Stream* on June 27, 1896:

> In six days' fishing in Jamaica I caught over 150 tarpon in fly-fishing, fish from 2 or 3 lbs. up to 7 lbs., the average, I suppose, being about 2½ or 3 pounds. Such perfect devils when hooked I never met. I was almost afraid of them. They come at you like tigers and take fly or bait right into the air as they leap, and if your rod tip is at the wrong angle, bang! she goes. I broke three or four rods, including a "steel" that I thought would stand anything.

The tarpon was soon the subject of books (the bonefish has yet had only one book devoted to it), the one of greatest interest in fly-fishing history being A. W. Dimock's *The Book of the Tarpon* (1911). Dimock's book featured many photographs of leaping tarpon, including some attached to a fly line (Dimock sometimes used flies, and sometimes bait, with the fly rod, but he helped pioneer the handling of such large fish on fly rods in any case). Henry Bruns, in his *Angling Books of the Americas* (1975), only slightly overstated things when he said that "these photos have never been surpassed." As far as every technical sense—clarity, for example —they surely have been surpassed. But as far as the excitement they evoke of these

A.W. Dimock, author of *The Book of the Tarpon* (1911), was a versatile saltwater fly fisherman. Here he is landing a redfish (on a demonstrably sturdy leader). *From an article "Salt-Water Fly Fishing" in* Country Life in America, *January, 1908.*

fishermen with their split-bamboo rods and small boats against a fish that was still a newcomer to sport, they are indeed unsurpassed.

The big tarpon, say the fish approaching one hundred pounds, was usually too much for fly tackle before World War II. Gut leaders, even at their best, were not up to the job, though bamboo rods and the fine reels of Vom Hofe held together well. The fish usually overpowered the fishermen, who were content (or tried to be) to have ''jumped'' the fish in the first place and enjoyed a brief moment of exhilarating connection before something gave. Here, from a letter written by the guide Jimmie Albright, on July 17, 1948, is a summary of typical tarpon fishing for the skilled fly fisher, even after nylon was introduced (but before it was refined, and well before various other technological advances changed the picture):

> Frankee [Jimmie's wife and fellow guide—she guided George LaBranche to his first fly-caught bonefish in the late 1940s] caught a 48½# tarpon on a fly and a #12 nylon leader and has entered it as a world record on fly fishing. We've caught a lot this summer including Lee Cuddy's of 46#. We lose all the big ones due mostly to frayed leaders and reels freezing.

But it could be done. In the early 1930s George Bonbright and his brother devoted themselves to tarpon fly fishing, and in March of 1933 Bonbright took a 136-pound, 12-ounce tarpon on his ''Bonbright'' streamer. He told the story in the August 1933 *Field & Stream*, leaving no doubt that his tackle was legitimate fly tackle, but some doubt whether there was any leader at all in the traditional sense; he seems to have attached his wire leader directly to the fly line, with none of the gut that was the curse of others. It was a smart move, and it allowed him to catch many fish of good size. His flies were sold by New York dealers on very large hooks—5/0 to 8/0. The fish took almost two hours to land:

> When we finally got the gaff into him, he hadn't a kick left. To be perfectly honest about it, I was in much the same condition.

It would be a later generation of Florida anglers, partly under the influence of Lefty Kreh, that would in the 1960s turn its attention to lighter tackle for catching the same large fish that Bonbright sought, but that would come after some significant leaps in technology helped them out. In the meantime, through the years before 1950 fly fishers on both coasts managed to have a great time anyway.

Though the saltwater fly fishing in the first half of the 1900s was almost all occurring on fishing grounds that had been known to at least some fishermen (though most didn't use flies), there is still a pleasant sense of exploration in the accounts. Here, for example, are fly fishermen taking sea pollock along the New Brunswick coast off the mouth of the St. Croix, as reported in *Forest and Stream* in January of 1920:

> The waters were green as an opal. Flocks of tiny ''Sea Geese'' fluttered and swam about us, while around the headlands the tides swirled with tremendous power. We headed into a wisp of fog through which the sun shone wanly. Then we heard them—that inimitable rustle and surge and splash of hundreds of large fish leaping after their food. Straight on to us they came, and in the wisps of fog we cast our flies and found that these fish were as wary and peculiar in their way as the far-famed salmon.

George LaBranche was an ardent saltwater fisherman, but did not try fly fishing in saltwater until late in life. He is pictured with his first fly-caught bonefish, taken at Islamorada, Florida, in 1947. The woman holding the fish is Frankee Albright, his guide. *Courtesy of Joseph Spear Beck.*

Or one of the West Coast's pioneer angling entomologists, Letcher Lambuth of Washington, describing coho salmon fishing off Vancouver Island at the mouth of the Cowichan. Like the previous fishermen, Lambuth and his friends fished from small boats. In this passage, from an account finally published in *The American Fly Fisher*, in the spring of 1975, he was using polar-bear-hair streamers, simple hairwing patterns two or three inches long:

> At the height of the run the fish will frequently be jumping in every direction as far as the eye can discern the splashes. Frequently the jumping fish will not take the fly. We explore for those disposed to feed by casting to the side from the slowly moving boat, allowing the line to swing into the wake and then stripping in. Sometimes the fly is taken when thus trolling. More often, as the fly is stripped in, the bow wave of the fish suddenly appears near the fly and the ensuing few seconds as the angler manipulates the fly and the fish makes up his mind to strike are moments of exciting suspense. Suddenly there is a boil or splash, a surge as the hook is set, and the reel whines.

Lambuth was by no means the first to take coho in saltwater; earlier writers, such as Sir John Rogers, in *Sport in Vancouver and Newfoundland* (1912), and A. Bryan Williams, in *Rod & Creel in British Columbia* (1919), also discussed the technique.

Some sportsmen fishing off the coast of North Carolina tried out trout fly-fishing tackle on bluefish with great success (they thought they were the first to do it, suggesting that it was still easily possible to be unaware of other saltwater fly fishermen). In an article in *The National Sportsman* in June of 1930, Rupert West told of their success on small bluefish using not only wet flies (including Royal Coachman and Silver Doctor) but also bass bugs.

Awareness of the fishing did grow, so that by midcentury, when Joe Brooks took what may actually have been the first permit on a fly outfit, and when Harold Gibbs was developing his great Gibbs Striper fly up in Rhode Island, the sport was poised for its first real leap in popularity in seventy years. The reasons for that leap are the subject of a later chapter, but the result was a whole new world of fly-fishing thought, as Lefty Kreh, Chico Fernandez, Myron Gregory, Dan Blanton, Lee Wulff, Stu Apte, Billy Pate, Joe Brooks, and many others ushered saltwater fly fishing into its most creative and productive era.

16

The Riddle of Anadromy

Why does a salmon rise? Why does a small boy cross the street just to kick a tin can?

LEE WULFF, *The Atlantic Salmon* (1958)

One of the nicest things about fly fishing is its tolerance of competing theories. It is possible to fly fish under an amazingly broad group of theories and still catch something, maybe even a lot.

Consider, for example, western nymphs. Polly Rosborough has developed an attractive and successful approach based on his famous ''fuzzy nymphs,'' emphasizing fuzziness as the key element in fly construction. George Grant, on the other hand, has accumulated more than half a century of gargantuan trout catches with an assortment of woven and hardbodied nymphs. Charles Brooks has emphasized the importance of tying nymphs ''in the round'' so that the ''legs'' are visible from any angle, and the late Dan Bailey developed his ''mossback'' series of nymphs with dark backs and light bellies on the assumption that fish may be able to distinguish one side of a nymph from the other. Other theories, as well as combinations of the above theories, abound. They all catch fish, though, as western guide Bud Lilly has observed, ''nothing works all the time.'' The success of so many competing fly styles invites other theorists to offer their opinions: the ''presentationist'' may see the success of so many different approaches as proof that what mattered most in the fishing of Rosborough, Grant, Brooks, Bailey, and their colleagues was not so much what the fly looked like as how good these men were at putting it in front of the fish in a persuasive manner. Fly-tying theory offers something for everybody. The ultimate irresolvability of the disagreements has a lot to do with the sport's endless charm for its enthusiasts.

The next step up—or down, or away—from theories that can be logically resolved would seem to be the bass bug. Here is a creation that only rarely resembles any living thing, or at least any that might spend time gurgling along over a bass pond. It may be white with red stripes and a fluorescent pink tail; it may trail half a foot of chartreuse saddle hackles after a balsawood body shaped like the Liberty Bell (Joe

Brooks tied one with a little American flag that popped out of the top when the bass took it); it may have pieces of rubber band sticking out at all angles; but however alien its appearance, we will probably not be able to resist painting eyes on it. After all, it *is* a bug. But even with the bass bug we know what we're trying to do. We're trying to convince a bass to eat the thing, knowing that bass are such admirable omnivores that they will eat almost anything if they're hungry, or disturbed, enough.

Salmon fishing takes this process—this attempt to resolve why a fish takes a fly and what we can do to make our flies more effective—even further from resolution. It takes it about as far as it can go, from something like biological theorizing as practiced by hatch matchers into a more mystical realm. Here are fish that rarely feed at all in fresh water (I am aware of the proven exceptions, and speak generally rather than absolutely), fish that for reasons yet to be·established—though we have lots of theories—will sometimes take artifical flies that often bear even less resemblance to natural life forms than your average bass bug. This degree of unknowing, this level of flexibility in theory and approach, has resulted in some of fly tying's grandest and most improbable products. It has generated every intellectual response, from intense near-scientific analysis to the sublime goofiness of those late-nineteenth-century British salmon fishers who believed that their elegant and complex salmon flies were actually imitations of butterflies, each pattern resembling only certain species of butterflies that were indigenous only to certain streams. Joe Bates, who has done much to celebrate the magnificence of the craft of tying traditional salmon flies, has also managed to maintain his perspective about it. In his standard work *Atlantic Salmon Flies and Fishing* (1970), he addressed the heart of the problem (if that is what it should be called) of the salmon fly this way:

> This makes me think of what goes on in a salmon's head when he, for example, streaks with violent surface wake after a gorgeous number 3/0 Jock Scott swinging past him in the current. Does he fail to take at the last second because he suddenly perceives that the Toucan veiling on the fly's body isn't applied exactly as it should have been, or that the Blue Chatterer cheeks are only blue Kingfisher?

The Atlantic salmon fly experienced, even more elaborately and with by far the most spectacular results, the same colorful changes as did American trout flies in the late 1800s. Fly tiers in the Old World responded to an increased availability of exotic feathers and furs with ever more elaborate patterns, the trend reaching its finest statement in George Kelson's *The Salmon Fly* (1895) and T. E. Pryce Tannatt's *How to Dress Salmon Flies* (1914). Kelson's book, with its excellent color plates and dressings for some three hundred patterns, became the salmon fly's equivalent to Mary Orvis Marbury's *Favorite Flies;* what the latter book did for the nineteenth-century American wet fly, Kelson's did for the late-Victorian salmon fly.

Tying these flies was not the simple process most trout fly tiers were familiar with. The construction of one such fly, with many elements and various specialized demands on the tier's skill (and patience) was a feat of craft beyond traditional fly tying (I should point out, by the way, that elaborate and colorful salmon flies existed prior to 1850, but were not the standard in most areas). The best craftsmen existed in what was nearly a guild, with some closely guarded techniques not lightly shared with others.

A development of this sort does not happen for simple reasons. It may be even more complicated than the reasons behind another type of sportsman deciding to have his shotgun engraved and inlaid at great expense. That process is purely ornamental,

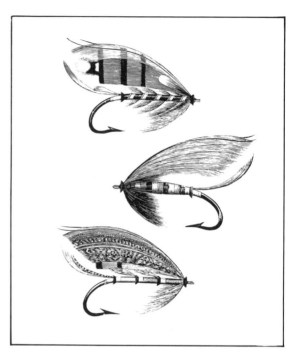

In the second half of the
nineteenth century, the Atlantic
salmon fly became the most
complex and challenging part of
the fly tier's craft. Pictured, from
Kelson's *The Salmon Fly* (1895),
are a Black Ranger (top),
Variegated Sun Fly (middle), and
a Beaconsfield (bottom).

while the salmon fly was, to the minds of many, not only elegant but somehow
functional. There were, indeed, fishermen who had to have blue chatterer rather than
kingfisher, and had to have it because they thought it necessary for successful fishing.
In this they were like the American trout fishermen who favored gaudy wet flies.
Yes, the flies were pretty, but they seemed to work, didn't they?

Looking back, however, these fishermen may remind us of the automobile mechanic who, when asked why he wore a tuxedo while working on cars, responded,
"Because I can afford to." American salmon fishermen did not long feel that they
had to spend what it took in time and money in order to have flies that elegant. More
important, they discovered that they did not need them in order to catch fish. The
full-dress salmon flies of the Victorian era have never disappeared from North Amer-

Fly fishing for Atlantic salmon on the Jacques Cartier, near Quebec, in the late 1820s
or early 1830s. *From Godfrey Vigne,* Six Months in America *(1832).*

Members of the St. Marguerite Club, one of many exclusive salmon fishing clubs in Canada in the 1890s, with a trophy. *Courtesy of The American Museum of Fly Fishing.*

ican rivers (much less from Old World rivers, where many a tradition has found sanctuary long after its apparent time was past), nor should we be anxious to see them go; they please their users, and they work, and that is about all that can be asked. But for most North American salmon fishermen they are not of importance in actual fishing except as the original forms of the much simpler hairwing patterns that were derived from them.

It is difficult to know just where the hairwing salmon fly originated; hairwing flies of various sorts, as we've seen in previous chapters, go back to the early 1800s, perhaps further. Joe Bates recorded the case of Colonel Thompson, who was involved in the development of the Trude hairwing trout fly in the 1890s, using a similar fly for salmon on the Restigouche in the 1920s. If this was indeed the first such use, its location was especially appropriate. The Restigouche was also the inspiration and source of one of our most sumptuously produced angling books, *The Ristigouche and its Salmon Fishing* (1888), published in Edinburgh with great care and filled with superb engravings of the best in Victorian sporting scenes and salmon flies.

Gradually the simplification took hold, so that today many of the most important traditional full-dress patterns have modern, reduced hairwing or featherwing counterparts. Ernest Schwiebert provided a good summary, with his customarily distinctive illustrations, of contemporary reduced salmon patterns in *Art Flick's Master Fly-Tying Guide* (1974).

The two things that were eventually most to distinguish American salmon fishing from Old World fishing were smaller rods and dry flies. Even today you may find an occasional angler on Canadian rivers using an ancient fifteen-foot greenheart rod (or its graphite counterpart), just as you may find a few using traditional flies, but Americans, with the assistance of their rod builders, gradually moved to lighter rods, even for wet-fly work. Edward Hewitt, in his *A Trout and Salmon Fisherman for Seventy-Five Years* (1948), was still recommending "for two-handed wet fly work, a rod about fourteen feet, weighing sixteen or eighteen ounces," but by then many others were using much smaller rods than that, in the ten- to twelve-foot range. For dry-fly fishing, the smaller size was more the norm.

Like so many other things we think we did first, we were probably either anticipated or duplicated in England. There are the occasional references, such as George Dawson's of 1883, mentioned in Chapter 10, or the earlier references in that chapter from the 1840s, but those of course were not to the formally defined "dry fly" that is at question here. The same sort of references occur in the British literature, the earliest that I know of being from 1867, reported in Herbert Maxwell's *Salmon and Sea Trout* (1896). Maxwell told of a Dr. Begg, who fished the North Tyne with flies with "fat, fuzzy bodies, generally of gray rabbit or monkey wool, enormously over-winged, on small single hooks." He held his rod tip high so that the flies swung across the current, "trailing along the surface of the water," a sort of simplified version of the riffling hitch popularized by Lee Wulff in the late 1940s.

Theodore Gordon has given us an early instance of dry-fly fishing for salmon with "real" dry flies. Writing for the *Fishing Gazette* in 1903, he told of having tied a fly for a fisherman who fished the Restigouche, where the "fly sat on the water like a boat" and was taken by a fourteen-and-a-half-pound salmon. Gordon commented that "if that salmon did not take that fly for a large moth or insect of some kind I am greatly mistaken." G. L. Ashley-Dodd, in *A Fisherman's Log* (1929), knew of dry-fly fishing on the Test in Great Britain almost as early:

> To the best of my knowledge the first serious attempt to fish for salmon with a dry fly originated with the late Major J. R. Fraser, C.M.G., in, I think, the year 1906.
> The idea of taking it up seriously was suggested to him by the not uncommon occurrence, on the River Test, of a salmon rising at and taking a May-fly when he was fishing for trout on the lower waters which are frequented by salmon.

Anthony Crossley, in his *The Floating Line for Salmon and Sea-Trout* (1939), reported raising (but not taking) salmon on a lake "at Garynahine in Lewis" as early as 1912, but repeated attempts in subsequent years were of slight success until he succeeded, many years later, in taking some salmon on dry flies in Iceland.

These accounts are only preface for the story of how dry-fly fishing became established and known in America, and that story is well told in George LaBranche's gracious little book *The Salmon and the Dry Fly* (1924) and Edward Hewitt's less gracious but no less informative *Secrets of the Salmon* (1922). It appears that Colonel Ambrose Monell, who introduced LaBranche to the fishing, took salmon on dry flies as early as 1912 on the Upsalquitch (part of the Restigouche system in Quebec and New Brunswick). Hewitt's book contained spectacular photographs of a twenty-four-pound salmon rising to a dry fly.

For LaBranche, as for many anglers since, the overriding concern was to have a fly that floated as high as possible; pattern theory was otherwise of little interest. He preferred heavily palmered flies, and he and Hewitt both liked Hewitt's famous Bivisibles for that reason. Though the Museum has in its collections some cork-bodied flies owned by LaBranche, he was not terribly enthusiastic about them. By the mid-1920s many others were working on salmon dry flies, so that when Charles Phair's *Atlantic Salmon Fishing* (1937) was published, Phair was able to report that there were at least three hundred dry-fly patterns for salmon. LaBranche's flies are

Long the most prominent name associated with Atlantic salmon fishing in North America, Lee Wulff promoted and pioneered many ideas, including the use of very short rods. *Courtesy of The American Museum of Fly Fishing.*

not popular today, having been replaced by the Wulffs and other hair flies that have the sort of high-riding qualities LaBranche would have applauded.

It was in the late 1920s that there appeared an angler who had an actual influence on American fly fishing that was greater than the imagined influence of Theodore Gordon. Lee Wulff's contributions to the sport have been so far ranging, and so diverse, that I considered devoting a separate chapter to him as well. I finally decided not to primarily because his contributions *were* so diverse; I could fit them in to the various parts of the story as I told it, in that way more fully suggesting just how much a part of the sport's evolution this man is. Fly fishing has had many singular characters whose work substantially altered the sport, but we have had nothing else quite like Lee Wulff.

His contributions to salmon fishing are typically impressive, but I introduce him here because he so perfectly epitomizes the direction that American salmon fishing took as opposed to Old World salmon fishing. Few Americans were able to carry the difference as far as Lee Wulff could, but that has mostly been because he is just that much better than the average fisherman.

Wulff learned dry-fly technique for salmon in the 1930s and probably did more than any other angler, both by example and through his writings, to popularize it on salmon rivers where it had never been seen before. The Wulff flies, named by Dan Bailey, have become standard patterns for both trout and salmon, surely among the most important dry-fly developments in this century. Wulff developed the first of the flies on New York's Ausable River for trout in 1929 (Dan Bailey and Red Monical developed several of the Wulff series in Montana); they were certainly not the first floating flies to use hair for wings, but they were the ones that mattered most in the subsequent popularization of hairwing dry flies. The Wulffs and many other dry flies—Joe Messinger's Irresistible, Harry Darbee's Rat-Faced MacDougall, the Bomber, and so on—revolutionized salmon fishing on this side of the Atlantic, while dry flies never caught on to any extent in the Old World.

Wulff also was a leader in the development of nontraditional wet flies for salmon. His experiments with nymph-type flies convinced him that they could be as effective as other wet flies (but no more effective, he decided). His popularization of the riffling hitch, a way of attaching leader to fly that allowed the fly to be worked across the surface with a wake often appealing to salmon, added an important technique to the salmon fisher's bag of tricks. He did not work alone in these developments—salmon fishing has a list of ''hallowed names'' almost as long as does trout fishing—but his work was usually in the vanguard.

It often *was* the vanguard in rod selection. He led the fight to reduce the size of salmon rods, in the process becoming a virtuoso at handling fish. Arnold Gingrich was fond of using musical analogies, calling someone the Stradivarius of this or that; I think a dancing analogy is appropriate in dry-fly fishing. LaBranche, with his delicate precision, was sort of the Fred Astaire of the dry fly, and Wulff, with his athletic power, was the Gene Kelly. Combining his own exceptional gifts for fishing with an almost religious devotion to experimentation, he has had a career whose highlights seem to have served as proof that the impossible is possible. His book *The Atlantic Salmon* (1958) described how he showed the extent to which rod size could be reduced, also describing one of the most impressive stunts in American fishing history, a stunt that was something more than just a stunt because it helped prove his point:

> As a pioneer in the use of extra light tackle for salmon, by 1940 I had come down to a seven-foot, two-and-a-half ounce fly rod, and since then have rarely used anything heavier. In 1943, in order to demonstrate to the most confirmed doubter, I eliminated the rod entirely from my tackle. Casting some thirty-odd feet by hand, I hooked a ten-pound salmon and played it by holding the reel in my right hand, reeling with my left, until I could finally reach down and tail it with my own hand, ten minutes later. Witnesses were present and pictures were taken to prove that a salmon rod may be as light as one wishes, even to the point of none at all. This experiment was the basis of an article in *Field and Stream.*

Of course fishermen did not flock to fish without rods, any more than they have flocked to use rods of less than eight feet in length. But Wulff showed what *could* be done, and strengthened American convictions that rods of ten feet or less were all that were necessary.

This separation from British salmon-fishing traditions reached its symbolic peak in 1962, when, after a couple years of occasional debates between various British and American authorities over rods and flies, Lee Wulff and "Jock Scott" (Donald Rudd, the eminent British salmon fisher) held a match on the Scottish Dee. Rudd fished a twelve-foot glass rod with low-water flies, and Wulff used a bamboo rod half as long with a weight-forward-taper floating line and either dry flies or wet flies on a riffling hitch (nice touch, I think, that the British fisherman was using synthetic fiber and the American was using cane). It was a good-spirited match, and though Wulff was the only one to take a fish, there was no clear sense of someone having won, beyond the important proof Wulff provided that he could do what they apparently were not sure he could. He may have done as much good in exposing the British audience to various other aspects of American fishing, such as landing the fish with his bare hand (according to a correspondent in *The Field*, that caused "something like a sensation"), and releasing all three fish he caught during his visit.[1]

A few years ago I happened, in the course of a conversation with an eastern salmon fisherman, to mention the name of a prominent western guide. My companion, for reasons I'm still not sure I understand, felt compelled to announce, "I never heard of him." It is that sort of regionalism that often keeps anglers of different regions from respecting another region's traditions. Just as the Catskills, or the Pennsylvania limestone country, or the Rangeleys, have their "household names" of important fishermen past and present, so does the western steelhead and salmon tradition. They are, perhaps, harder names to learn or hear about outside the region, if only because they have been less featured in books, but they are there just as surely. Salmon fishers will have heard of the exploits of Bill Shaadt on northern California salmon streams. They will be familiar with the writings of Enos Bradner, a giant figure in Northwest angling and author of what has been for years the standard all-round text on fishing Washington, Oregon, and southern Canada. Steelhead fly fishers will have their lexicon of great names to intone at appropriate conversational occasions—Al Knudson, Lloyd Silvius, Ken McCleod, Russ Tower, Fred Burnham, Clarence Gordon, Frank Moore . . . the list goes on and on. Each river has its heroes, its legends, and its miles and miles of named pools and glides, each evoking some community memory about fish and history. Such traditions are well known throughout the East, but are a surprise to newcomers in the West. I mention them here only to redress the balance a bit before moving on to the fishing. When Zane Grey wrote his popular book *Tales of Fresh-Water Fishing* (1928) glorifying the steelhead fishing of Oregon's Rogue River, he left the impression at times that his was the only civilized party there. In fact, the locals thought his manners left something to be desired, and had been fishing Oregon steelhead for decades already. They just hadn't written any best-selling books about it.

I believe it was Alec Jackson, a Washington-state angler well versed in the history and literature of both Atlantic salmon and steelhead fishing, who first pointed out to me that steelhead flies have undergone an evolution rather like that of the Atlantic salmon fly, except reversed. He has pointed out that in the most general of terms the steelhead fly started out simple and has in many of its forms (though the simple ones have not disappeared) tended toward more elaborate, even elegant designs.

When I first began to read about steelhead fishing, in the early 1970s, there was only the slightest of popular literatures, and most of the books were not even in print.

Copies of Claude Kreider's *Steelhead* (1948) and Clark Van Fleet's *Steelhead to a Fly* (1951), as well as the few other books that dealt with fly fishing for steelhead, were prized by those lucky enough to find them, and as for the Pacific salmons, most tackle-shop owners would tell you that you just couldn't catch them on a fly. As I found my way to the older sporting periodicals I discovered that both steelhead and salmon fishing had long histories, but that tradition was largely forgotten except in a few places. The Oregon Flyfishers, for example, through their journal *The Creel*, kept alive the memory of earlier generations of anglers, as did Frank Amato's various magazines and books, with occasional articles on old timers and their flies. More recently, western fly fishers have had appreciation of their angling tradition made easier by Trey Combs's books *The Steelhead Trout* (1971) and *Steelhead Fly Fishing and Flies* (1976), and Ferguson, Johnson, and Trotter's *Fly Fishing for Pacific Salmon* (1985). After all these years of studying western fly fishing, it still seems remarkable to me that steelhead and salmon fishing on the West Coast got to be more than a century old before anyone bothered to look back and write its history.

Like the rest of fishing history, the story must be got from sources other than the occasional how-to book.

By the late 1850s, as I showed in Chapter 6, fly fishing had reached the West Coast in a number of places. San Francisco and smaller cities all the way to Canada and beyond were quickly well-enough established to allow their citizens the leisure of an occasional fishing trip, and as travel conditions improved (sometimes quite slowly), coaches, trains, and boats allowed the sportsman to travel to more isolated regions for good fishing. Once the number of sporting periodicals increased in the early 1870s, reports of salmon or steelhead (and it is often impossible to know which were meant, because the anglers themselves were uninformed) taken on flies appeared regularly. There continued to be many people who believed such sport impossible, while others enjoyed good sport year after year. *Forest and Stream*, on February 19, 1874, reported that "a Captain Ogden caught twelve fish with a fly" on the Navarro in 1872. On June 18, the same magazine carried a report by an angler who knew of only one instance of a "salmon" taken on a fly in the Columbia but claimed that they were taken more commonly on flies in the Puget Sound area, where "the water is beautifully clear and cold." On February 12 of the same year, a writer had reported taking a fifteen-pound salmon on "a heavy old fashioned trout rod, a good plaited silk line," and a heavy gut leader, on a creek somewhere up from Humboldt Bay.

The accounts continued in subsequent years, so I will only refer to one more, from *Forest and Stream* on August 5, 1875 (I don't mean to suggest by example that only *Forest and Stream* paid attention to the West Coast; I have other examples from *The Country* and *American Angler*). On that day the paper ran a report from no less a fisheries authority than Livingston Stone, who a few years later would manage the first transcontinental shipment of striped bass to the West Coast, initiating a great new fishery. In 1875 he was at the McCloud River Fish Hatchery, where he witnessed the capture of several large salmon by a few fly fishers there. These were fish up to twenty-one pounds, and were caught on "fine trout tackle." Stone, though he does not say what species of salmon they were, would have known a steelhead from a salmon.

Anadromous fish were being taken on flies from many rivers in California, Oregon (the Clackamas is mentioned most often in reports from this state), and Washington by the 1890s. Most of the flies were standard trout or salmon flies, but a few local and regional patterns were appearing. The best known of the early fly tiers may have been John Benn, or Bean, who developed a variation on the Coachman using a multicolored wing. Combs credits Benn, who settled late in life along the Eel River of northern California, with also developing the Railbird, and with providing many steelhead and salmon (often king salmon were caught accidentally by steelhead fishermen) fishermen with effective patterns of his own creation. Ferguson, Johnson, and Trotter believe that practically all of the fly fishing on the Eel near Eureka was for steelhead rather than salmon:

> Fly fishermen, still under the influence of eastern and European techniques, usually fished steelhead with small, brightly dressed wet flies. It must have been a sight to behold when a gentleman angler would suddenly find himself contending with a 40-pound chinook salmon that had grabbed his No. 10 Professor and chugged off across the pool. Most of these encounters ended with the salmon parting the gut leader with a casual shake of the head.

Since the 1920s West Coast fishermen have been more often than not the national leaders in developing big-river fishing techniques. They were, as shown earlier, pioneers in distance casting, shooting heads, and the double haul, and West Coast rod builders such as Winston built the rods for the job. They were at the same time coming up with many new flies for their fishing.

Some went for bulk and weight. Jim Pray's Optics, as well as his other metal-bodied flies, were terrific fast sinkers that would have horrified many Atlantic salmon fishermen. One of the most interesting differences between Atlantic salmon and

At the opposite extreme from the complex and even elegant Atlantic salmon flies are the early steelhead patterns of C. Jim Pray of California. His "Optics" were simple, heavily weighted patterns that became popular in the 1940s. *Photos by C.M. Haller, courtesy of The American Museum of Fly Fishing.*

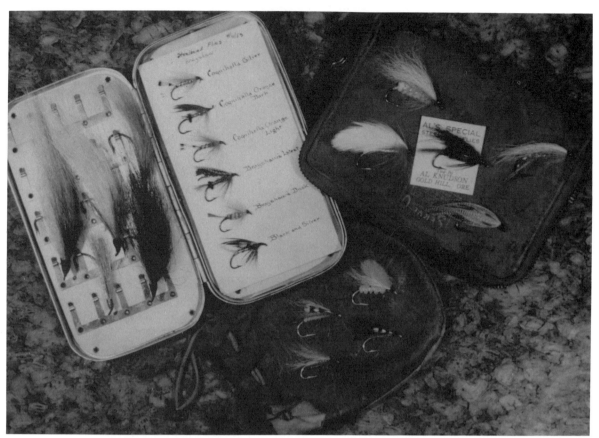

An assortment of steelhead and salmon flies by west coast masters: far left, some of Letcher Lambuth's coho streamers (of polar bear hair) from the 1930s; several of Tommy Brayshaw's British Columbia patterns from the 1930–1950 period; below them, a few of Enos Bradner's patterns from the 1940s and 1950s; on the right, some of Al Knudson's patterns for Oregon and Washington. *Photo by the author, courtesy of The American Museum of Fly Fishing.*

steelhead is in the attitudes of their anglers. Atlantic salmon fishermen approached the sport with an already established European code of conduct that both informed and restricted them. The steelhead was, to practically everyone, a new kind of fish with no such sporting tradition or dogma surrounding its pursuit. It demanded of fishermen certain things in order to be caught, and later it would demand other things of fishermen in order to be preserved and managed under "sporting" conditions that we are still trying to define. In the meantime, Pray, Peter Schwab, and many others were tying flies with a variety of weighting techniques. The first comets, for example, were tied in the late 1940s; the fly uses a pair of bead-chain eyes to increase its sink rate.

Many others (and sometimes the same people as were tying the weighted flies) tried other directions. The Atlantic salmon influence was often felt, and was sometimes directly present in the form of anglers, such as General Noel Money, so well portrayed in Roderick Haig-Brown's books, who came to the Stamp River in British Columbia shortly before World War I; Tommy Brayshaw, who arrived in British Columbia to stay after World War I; and Haig-Brown himself, certainly the dean of western fishing writers and the foremost literary interpreter of western fishing, who settled on his cherished Campbell River in the early 1930s. All three were British, and all three combined British tradition with American sporting opportunity.

But it isn't fair to trace the refinement of steelhead flies merely to former British citizens. Steelhead anglers were often avid readers of Atlantic salmon literature (the most recent reprinting of Jock Scott's classic salmon fishing book *Greased Line Fishing* was by Frank Amato of Portland, Oregon, due to many years' interest in the technique among steelhead fishermen). We see, especially in the past forty years, steelhead flies that, if they are not as complex as traditional Atlantic salmon flies, are every bit as graceful. Syd Glasso, Harry Lemire, Walt Johnson, and many others have done credit to the various esthetic standards of fly dressing in other parts of the world with their creations. I have occasionally been struck with the similarities between low-water steelhead flies as tied by these recent masters and their Atlantic salmon counterparts.

Those flies tied specifically for the Pacific salmons have for the most part not reached this stage of development. They are still primarily (I refer to the freshwater patterns rather than the baitfish imitations used most often in saltwater) "old" steelhead flies in form, due in great part to the necessity of getting such flies deep. Greased-line techniques that work so well for steelhead are less often applicable to the salmons, who require a presentation less distant from their resting positions. In fact I have wondered at the success of early salmon fishermen who were most likely using techniques much like they would have for Atlantic salmon, not fishing very deep. Most of their fish seem to have been steelhead and coho salmon, the latter being the salmon most traditionally identified with fly fishing on the West Coast (Haig-Brown, writing in *The Western Angler*, 1968 edition, knew of river fishing for coho as early as 1905, and there are earlier accounts that were probably coho).

The first angler to hook a steelhead on a dry fly may well have been a trout fisherman out for resident rainbows or cutthroats, and the odds are good that most such episodes were as brief as they were startling. Frank Steel, in *Fly Fishing* (1946), reported that he had taken steelhead on dries some years earlier, up to twenty-two pounds. Since then dry-fly fishing has become a part of the sport almost as well established as it is for Atlantic salmon.

What may most set the West Coast steelhead and salmon fisherman apart from his eastern and European counterparts who fish for Atlantic salmon is not the fish. The fish have now shown that they succumb to the same techniques, including the riffling hitch, "damp" flies, and the other approaches popular in both regions. What is different is the legal and social status of the waters. Atlantic salmon fishing in the New World is virtually always a fly-fishing proposition, even on public waters. Steelhead and Pacific salmon are most often pursued not by fly fishers but by a variety of bait and hardware fishermen. Pioneering efforts by fly fishers have resulted in a good many stretches of steelhead water being set aside for fly only; the first was the Stilliguamish in Washington, set aside in 1941 in the face of considerable public opposition. Such situations are the exception, however (as they still are with trout fishing), and most steelhead and salmon waters are still open to many kinds of tackle.

Among many other things, that openness has meant that the fly fisher operates with far greater creative leeway than does the Atlantic salmon fisher. That freedom has had a lot to do with the development of such eminently practical fishing tools and techniques as the lead-core shooting head, the various pram-fishing approaches, and many tricks for weighting flies, including the use of bead-chain, fuse wire, metal bodies, and so on. The first rivalry you are likely to hear about between steelhead and Atlantic salmon fishermen involves which is the "better" fish, a happily irresolvable debate that will never end. But beyond that there is a more complicated rivalry, a philosophical one, over just what is, and what isn't, fly fishing. How we have attempted to resolve that debate is the subject of a later chapter.

One thing that has given the Atlantic salmon fisherman at least a psychological edge in the debate over which is the "better" fish (putting aside who is fly fishing more properly) is the terrible shortage of good writing about steelhead and Pacific salmon. If the fish are so great, this line of reasoning might imply (without saying it out loud), why have steelhead fishermen been so slow to praise them in good writing?

That's a good question, one that westerners used to respond to by pointing to their one truly world-class fishing writer, Haig-Brown. It is generally agreed that American fishing has produced no one more capable at celebrating the pleasures of angling than Haig-Brown, but we ask a lot of even him when we expect him to stand up alone against a century and more of Atlantic salmon writers. He is much better than most of them, perhaps better than all of them, but he's mightly lonely as an example if we're trying to prove that steelhead inspire great writing. After all, he got his start as a fisherman in England. That may not disqualify him, but it doesn't strengthen the steelhead's case. Of course now the West has a number of very good writers. Steve Raymond and Russell Chatham, both natives and both critically admired, come to mind right off. But they just appeared in the last couple of decades. What about the previous century? The good steelhead writers are pretty rare during that hundred years.

I suppose there are lots of reasons, and none of them have to do with the relative sporting qualities of the two fish. For one, fishing-book publishing was essentially an eastern industry; publishers knew the eastern market and rarely showed interest in the western market. Something like that may be self perpetuating; fishermen who grow up with no books about their fishing may well not learn to see fishing as a reader's sport. For another, if you look at the short biographies of famous pioneer steelheaders in Trey Combs's book, you'll notice that a great many of them were blue-collar workers; this was a different social group than the one that gathered along the shores of the exclusive salmon rivers of eastern Canada, and it was a group much less likely to have the leisure and inclination to write books, especially books of gracious, companionable prose. Those two reasons probably carry the explanation far enough for our purposes. It should be enough that the steelhead was Haig-Brown's chosen fish, and that over the years a great variety of famous fishing writers, ranging from Ray Bergman to Ernest Schwiebert, have found time to celebrate it in writing, and that these days it appears that its best writers are the match if not the superiors of their brothers on the Atlantic salmon rivers.

17

Jennings Fished Here

A slender rod, a silken line, an invisible leader of hairlike
fineness, a counterfeit fly cunningly devised of fur and feath-
ers and steel, a surface-feeding trout, the cast, the strike,
the net, and another trout goes the way of all flesh.
Preston Jennings, *A Book of Trout Flies* (1935)

"The Derrydale Press has the honor to announce the publication of the most important book to the American Fly-Fisher ever published." With that statement, on the cover of a handsome pamphlet, American anglers were informed of the imminent appearance of Preston Jennings's *A Book of Trout Flies*. It was 1935.

Jennings's book was immediately recognized—and widely hailed—as just what the announcement claimed it to be: an angler's entomology that had long been needed by American fly fishers. The book eventually earned Jennings the title of "the American Ronalds," for having provided the outline of trout-stream insects for America that compared with what Ronalds had given England ninety-nine years earlier.

The book was most heavily devoted to the mayflies that were of greatest importance to fishermen on eastern streams in the Poconos, Catskills, and Adirondacks. The mayflies got ten chapters, while stoneflies, caddisflies, ants, midges, variants, and minnow imitations each got one. There were discussions of how to collect insects, understanding various elements of fly tying, trout vision, conquering the problems of drag, and the history of angling entomology. Though the book would eventually be improved upon by later writers, and though it had its specific faults (some reviewers immediately questioned Jennings's disinterest in caddisflies, for instance, and there are a few minor historical errors), it was an extraordinarily important work, and is still of great interest to fly fishers today. Jennings had recognized the importance of the task, he had undertaken it with suitable energy and thoroughness, and he had done the whole job right.

For one thing, he had the rare wisdom to realize that he could not do it alone. He knew he was not an entomologist, so he sought help in identifying the insects collected over several years of work by him and his friends. The insects were identified with the help of several people, including Herman Spieth (who also provided the book with a foreword, some measure of his respect for Jennings's methods), James Needham, Cornelius Betten, C. H. Curran, and William Creighton. All were established scientists, and few fly fishers have so intensively involved scientific authorities

Jennings on the Ausable in New York, shortly before the appearance of *A Book of Trout Flies* (1935). *From the Preston Jennings Collection, The American Museum of Fly Fishing.*

in their writing. For that reason his entomological information was uncommonly reliable.

He also knew he was not the only good fly fisher, and that in many ways others could help. His specimens were collected with the help of a number of friends, and the list he gives in his preface reads now a little like a Catskill hall of fame: Willis and Marjorie Stauffer, Roy Steenrod, Raymond Caunitz, William Henninger, Byron Blanchard, Arthur Flick, Eugene Connett, and Francis Rawle. As important as the help he got in collecting was his willingness to build upon the already-growing Catskill fly-tying tradition. He built as well upon useful elements of the British tradition, so that *A Book of Trout Flies* contains, first, accurate entomological profiles of the important emergences, and then his personally developed patterns—the American March Brown, Grey Fox, Grey Fox Variant, and so on—as well as those originated earlier. Steenrod's Hendrickson, Gordon's Quill Gordon, Hewitt's Bivisible, the Light Cahill, and other more or less "American" flies were joined where necessary by such British patterns as the Little Marryat and the Whirling Dun. There was a short chapter on nymphs, those just then becoming well known among American anglers after about twenty years of occasional references in the periodicals; like the caddis and stoneflies, few specific nymph imitations were given.

A Book of Trout Flies was the long-awaited codification its promotion claimed it to be. Previous attempts, including Louis Rhead's *American Trout Stream Insects* and George Parker Holden's loosely organized yet highly informative *Streamcraft* (1919), were quickly forgotten as the Jennings book, at first available only in a limited edition of 850 with seven hand-colored plates, was reprinted in a trade edition and became more generally available. The book followed and helped formalize the Catskill style of dry fly as defined by Harry Darbee (see Chapter 11). It cleaned up a century's accumulated fly-pattern confusion, discarding most of the old patterns that were

In the 1920s and 1930s George Parker Holden was a major influence in promoting the Catskill school of fly tying. *From the George Parker Holden Collection, The American Museum of Fly Fishing.*

nonimitative (it kept the Royal Coachman in concession to its immense popularity, though Jennings was at a loss in 1935 to call it imitative). It set a standard for subsequent books of angling entomology, in terms of system and in terms of book production. As a production, one of several important books from Eugene Connett's Derrydale Press, it has rarely been matched.

Last, it paved the way for a growing interest in serious angling entomology in this country, entomology that was to form the foundation for further American efforts at imitation. It did this in the face of a general attitude among the leading authorities that such imitation, though interesting, was not really necessary. Jennings was not working in a theoretical vacuum in the 1930s; his imitative work was simply not the mainstream. His book was a significant step in making imitation more important, and since then it has gradually occupied more and more of the attention of American fly fishers.

A term like "imitation" is ultimately unsatisfactory for a discussion of most periods of American fly-fishing history because most fly fishers would acknowledge that their flies imitated insects. That is why it is a little unfair to say that Jennings was espousing imitation while others were not. The others also held a view of imitation; it was rather less demanding in terms of fly pattern, but in other ways it was really quite demanding.

Perhaps the finest statement of an alternative to Jennings's approach was offered by LaBranche in *The Dry Fly and Fast Water* (1914). His chapter "The Imitation of the Natural Insect" dispels the common notion that anglers before Jennings were fishing British flies and "general" flies out of ignorance. LaBranche was far too thoughtful for any such carelessness. His imitative theory emphasized presentation over pattern detail:

> My own experiences have convinced me that imitation of the natural insect is absolutely necessary, and I put the forms this should take in the following order—the order of their importance:
> 1st—Position of the fly upon the water.
> 2nd—Its action.
> 3rd—Size of the fly.
> 4th—Form of the fly.
> 5th—Colour of the fly.

It appears to me that this degree of interest in imitation, and this approach to imitative theory, was the most common type before the 1940s. There is talk in the periodicals in the 1920s and 1930s about the importance of imitating stream insects, but most of the talk does not extend to a commitment to knowing the scientific designation of each major emergence and developing a specific artificial for each.

Ray Bergman was by far the most influential fishing writer, but by most accounts, the most influential fishing writer who wrote only of fly fishing between the wars was Edward Hewitt. In *Hewitt's Handbook of Fly Fishing* (1933), he listed five winged flies and five hackle flies, each in a variety of sizes, as being all the trout fisherman needed in the way of dry flies "for the general run of streams." At the conclusion of the lists, he said that even that many were probably more than necessary:

> Personally, I would not want any more patterns of dry flies than the above, and if finances interfere take only the first one or two on the list and you will probably catch just as many trout. Don't get a raft of patterns. They are not necessary *at all* and only confuse the fisherman into thinking he must have a certain pattern instead of studying what general shade and size should be used to get his fish.

Hewitt believed that fish discriminated wet-fly pattern far better than dry-fly pattern, and recommended a basic list of six patterns. He used only one style of nymph, his famous hardback nymphs, tied in a variety of shades, claiming that he reached that simple approach by "experimenting with about six hundred varieties of nymphs purchased, and making almost an equal number." His approach to midges, streamers, and spiders was equally simple. Hewitt, like LaBranche, caught his fish more through skill as a caster than through any serious attention to pattern. Both, it hardly needs saying, are regarded as among the most skilled and successful American anglers of this century. Jennings had his work cut out for him when he emphasized pattern.

A case could be made, of course, that Jennings, like Gordon before him, over-emphasized pattern to the cost of effectiveness. Gordon had resisted using the Royal Coachman, for example, because he couldn't imagine what it imitated. Lee Wulff, in his memoir *Lee Wulff on Flies* (1980), tells of Dan Bailey introducing Jennings to the Wulff flies:

> Preston looked at them and said that they imitated no insects, and he couldn't believe that they were actually good trout flies.

A last vote representative of anglers of that era who were at best casual about imitation comes from Ray Bergman. If anyone was of greater influence than Hewitt in the 1930s and 1940s, it must have been Bergman, who wrote much more often for the mass of fishermen than did Hewitt. In his books *Just Fishing* (1933) and *Trout* (1938), Bergman acknowledged that to some degree imitation was a good idea, and said, in *Just Fishing*, that his own approach was to try to keep an open mind:

> I have had many experiences supporting both views. Frequently I have found it necessary to select a fly in imitation of the natural fly on the stream in order to catch the rising fish. At other times I have readily taken trout with a fly that not only did not imitate the insects on the stream but which did not represent a natural fly of any kind.

Having allowed that much, he concluded that "in a general way I think it is possible to get along with half a dozen patterns ranging from sizes 10 to 15." This was a discussion of dry flies, and his approach to nymphs was similar. Bergman illustrated hundreds of flies in his books, and they remind me in a way of Marbury's earlier giant catalog of favorite flies. Bergman's color plates, though not nearly so well drawn, show row after row of bright little wet and dry flies, colorful as Christmas tree ornaments, showing little sympathy for the actual form of the insects they are supposed to imitate. They remind me as well of Louis Rhead's complaint in *American Trout Stream Insects* that most commercial plates of flies were all of identical form—same wing shape, same body thickness, same proportions, same hackle style—no matter what member of the diverse species of insect society they were

Ray Bergman's wet fly box, with 88 of his flies, as he used it in the 1950s. *Photo by the author, courtesy of The American Museum of Fly Fishing.*

Edward Hewitt on the
Neversink about 1950.
*Photo by John Atherton,
from the John Atherton
Collection, The American
Museum of Fly Fishing.*

intended to imitate. Bergman's fly plates, painted by Dr. Edgar Burke, are not quite as uniform as some of the earlier, similar catalogs, but they are not particularly dissimilar, either.

Still in all, the years between the wars were an exciting time in American fly-tying theory because so many unusual and fresh approaches were being tried. If the Catskill fly fishers were not in agreement over imitation, they were still contributing more to fly-fishing theory than any other region, at times more than all other regions. Edward Hewitt alone took several significant steps in those years. His Bivisibles, already mentioned, were and are useful searching flies (Jennings thought them an

Herman Christian's home at Neversink, a gathering-place of Catskill anglers, about 1916. *From the George Parker Holden Collection, The American Museum of Fly Fishing.*

excellent sedge imitation). His spiders, introduced in his little catalog of "Trout Fishing Specialties" in 1936 and announced in an article in *The Sportsman* the following year, have found a secure place in American fly fishing. At first he claimed they were imitations of butterflies, but the fly became best known for its ability to raise or turn fish that could then be taken on other flies. Its effectiveness was praised by many later writers, including Charles Fox and Vincent Marinaro; being essentially an oversized hackle of up to two inches in diameter on a small (Hewitt preferred size 16) hook, it was quite a break from tradition in dry flies, even from the British flies with very large hackles developed by Dr. Baigent earlier. Since his time various definitions and name variations have occurred, so that now "spider" and "skater" are more or less distinct names for different flies, but Hewitt seems to have used the terms less formally (he even said, at one point, that he "revived" the fly rather than originated it, though he did not say who originated it).

Hewitt at times approached the tackle manufacturer George Leonard Herter in opinionated crankiness, a characteristic that is probably more endearing in retrospect than it was in real life. He was, however, an original, creative angler. Few writers have contributed even one new fly style; Hewitt popularized several, including his spiders, Bivisibles, and nymphs, though later writers have tended to discount the nymphs. They seemed to work just fine for Hewitt, however. He was also often instructive in his manner of fishing flies, saying, for example, that he frequently gave a drifting dry fly a little twitch to bring up trout (and explaining that this was different from LaBranche's "bump cast," whereby the cast fly was made to bounce across the surface as it landed). On the other hand, he has occasionally been criticized, or even ridiculed, for his conviction that his new nymphs were so deadly that he could more or less clean out a stream with them.

The Catskills and Poconos took an impressive lead in developing fly-fishing theories in the first decades of this century. I suppose there are many reasons for

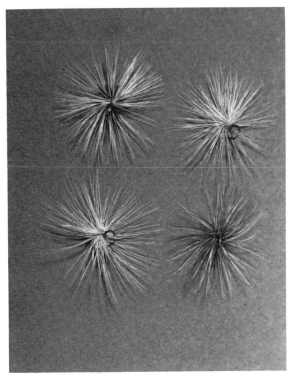

An assortment of Hewitt's spiders, in size sixteen. *Photo by the author.*

Edward Hewitt first marketed his flying ants in about 1934, in two sizes, fourteen and sixteen. *Photo by the author.*

that: they were close to several major urban areas with a large body of enthusiastic sportsmen to draw from; their aquatic insect fauna were abundant and well suited for angler study; they were the site of important plants of brown trout in the 1880s and later; they were close to the primary publishing center and thus may have been more "available" for book-length study (as well as for the recreation of periodicals editors, most of whom were located in the New York area). On the other hand, the lead they took was confined to certain kinds of fishing: fishing for trout on streams. Other fishing advanced more quickly in other places (Maine streamers are a good example).

It's worth a brief tour of some of the other major fly-fishing areas, many of which, by 1940, had more than half a century of local experience to generate new developments. It is this coevolution of fly fishing in many locations that has, in the long run, made modern American fly fishing so rich in technique, theory, and lore.

Michigan, for example, was also busily developing its own fly patterns. The hundreds of miles of superb trout streams touted by Thaddeus Norris and others starting in the 1870s (but fished earlier) have been a testing ground for many important fly theorists. Art Winnie of Traverse City was one of the most successful; his attempts to imitate the lumbering "Michigan Caddis," which was actually a huge mayfly, were well received by Michigan fly fishers, and his Michigan Hopper was for many years one of the most popular grasshopper imitations in the country. Winnie, who was best known in the 1930s, was not the first Michigan tier to develop a nationally prominent fly, though. In 1922 Leonard Halladay of Mayfield, Michigan, tied a dry fly that was first used on the Boardman River that year. An Ohio attorney, Charles F. Adams, was the first to use it, and when he reported to Halladay that the fly was a good one, the tier named it for Adams. As far as I have been able to determine, the Adams is easily the most popular (that is, best-selling) dry fly in North America. Paul Young, best known for his fine rods, also wrote a useful little book called *Making and Using the Fly and Leader* (1933). The Detroit-area craftsman produced a number of regionally important patterns, including his own version of the Michigan Caddis and his Strawman, a clipped-deer-hair fly that could be used both as caterpillar imitation and as a caddis-case imitation. Young, like other northern fly tiers, seems to have gotten the idea for this fly from Canadian Indians. Sid Gordon, in *How to Fish from Top to Bottom* (1955), gave the fly (in his own version) national attention.

Across Lake Michigan in Wisconsin, fly tying gave us both originality and volume. The nationally prominent trout fly to come from there in this period was the Hornberg, named for a local game warden; it has been one of few fly patterns of national popularity (the Muddler Minnow is another) to be commonly used, in one form, both wet and dry. But what Wisconsin should be best remembered for now (aside from

An original Adams tied by Leonard Halladay. *Photo by John Merwin, courtesy of The American Museum of Fly Fishing.*

being the home of Helen Shaw, who Arnold Gingrich appropriately called "The First Lady of Fly Tying," and who came of age as a professional tier in this era) is its unparalleled success in turning fly tying into an industry. Research by Susie Isaksen has shown that the Stevens Point, Wisconsin, area was, by 1940, the "fly tying capital of the world." Major companies, such as Weber and Worth, were joined by smaller businesses there to produce more flies than any similar area has produced (annually) since that time. It began in the late 1890s with a woman named Carrie Frost, a local fly fisher who hired a few girls to tie commercially under her direction, but, as Isaksen reported, the final stage of growth was something Frost couldn't have imagined:

> By the mid-1940s over 500 local tiers, mostly women working in factories, made over 10 million flies each year. It was a phenomenal total considering that Orvis, one of the (if not the) biggest contemporary fly sales outfits, last year [Isaksen was writing in *The American Fly Fisher* in the spring of 1981] sold 480,000 flies—more than in any of its other 125 years in the business.

Though some of the companies survive from that golden era, the Stevens Point fly industry largely folded up following World War II when spinfishing became popular.

Minnesota, among many other things, gave us George Leonard Herter, who became a serious part of the fly-fishing business in the 1930s. Generations of anglers ordered an astonishing assortment of gear from his catalogs, and I imagine a case could be made that the catalogs themselves were a notable contribution to angling literature; they were certainly colorful and opinionated enough. It was through his book *Professional Fly Tying, Spinning and Tackle Making* (1941), however, that Herter dealt angling historians a real wild card, for it confuses a host of otherwise clear stories.

In the first place, the book must rank among the most successful of all fly-tying books. The nineteenth edition appeared in 1971, and Herter claimed (in an interview in the *Minneapolis Sunday Tribune*, May 3, 1953) that in its first twelve years the book sold 400,000 copies. I doubt that many would take that claim seriously, partly because the book itself is so full of erroneous information; each new edition claimed for Herter the origination of more and more fly-fishing ideas—catching sailfish on flies in the 1940s and bonefish in the 1920s, "inventing" dozens of flies universally accepted as the work of others, and so on—so that the book's overall credibility is quite low. On the other hand, nineteen printings, even if they were comparatively small, is still a lot of books, and there is a wealth of information in this one, including a large section on aquatic entomology that no doubt introduced many thousands of fishermen to the subject, and ample instructions on fly tying. His lists of patterns are at least long, if the information is often unreliable.

In the second place, because of the book's undeniably wide readership, and because of the immense popularity of the Herter's catalog, the man deserves a much more prominent place in fishing history than he has been given. He has not been so much neglected as ignored, possibly because his claims and pronouncements, however true or untrue they may be (and most have not been absolutely disproved), are awkward to deal with. He promoted himself and his fishing products even more aggressively than did Rhead or Hewitt, but even the promotional hype makes for fun reading. He is an American original, and should not be forgotten.

Montana took fly tying in some unorthodox and highly successful directions in the 1920s and 1930s. The region, even now sparsely settled, was then practically deserted, and the introduction of brown and rainbow trout had by 1920 produced fishing that even by today's standards sounds to have been incredible. Isolated from other fly-tying traditions, the local tiers took fly tying in intriguing directions that, even if they never became important nationally, reveal just how many unexplored courses a craft can take even after several centuries of refinement.

Norman Edward Means, who became known to local sportsmen as Paul Bunyan, was a Missoula tier who developed a series of "Bunyan Bugs" in about 1927. These were cork-bodied floating flies with horsehair wings, intended to imitate the larger western stoneflies. Norman Maclean, in his evocative book *A River Runs Through It* (1976), has his narrator recall his first sight of a Bunyan Bug more than sixty years ago: "I took one look at it and felt perfect." The flies were constantly in demand on Montana streams.

But the most distinctive Montana fly-tying tradition was established by a Missoula barber and wig maker named Franz Pott. He was not the only man to be weaving hair into trout flies in the 1920s, but he was the leader, and the later refinements are based on his work. Pott worked out a series of patterns based on his techniques of cross-weaving animal hair (badger, skunk, deer, and others) into segmented bodies for wet flies, and of weaving hair hackles for the same flies (he held two patents on the techniques). The Pott flies, especially the Mr. Mite, Sandy Mite, Lady Mite, and a few others, were the most popular flies in Montana for decades. They were not strictly imitative of anything, but George Grant, heir to the Pott tradition and Montana's leading fishing historian, believes that the "Mite" name came from helgram-mite, that being the common term for the large stonefly nymphs so important as trout

The 1934 patent of F.B. Pott, for weaving hair hackles and flies.

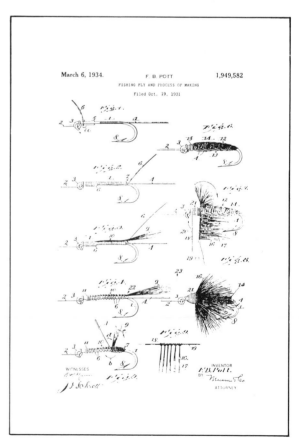

Some famous Montana fly patterns from the past sixty years: top, one of Dan Bailey's Mossback nymphs; right, a Bunyan Bug; below, two of George Grant's monofilament-wrapped stonefly nymphs; left, two of Pott's woven-hair flies on their card with patent information. *Photo by the author.*

food in Montana streams. Records kept at Sax & Fryer's, a little Livingston store that distributed the flies, reveal that most of the larger trout caught from the Yellowstone River in those days (fish up to ten pounds) that weren't taken on bait or hardware were caught on Pott's hair flies. Others shared in the woven-hair-fly market, including Butte dealer Wilbur Beatty, who set up a small factory to tie his own versions; but George Grant, who started fishing the Big Hole in the 1920s, has been the foremost popularizer and interpreter of woven-hair techniques, taking the Pott style far beyond its originator's abilities.

In the 1930s, outside influences were felt more strongly in Montana. In about 1933, Californian Don Martinez began spending his summers at a tiny shop in West Yellowstone. According to some accounts Martinez actually had a degree in limnology, but at least he had a full acquaintance with such worldly notions as dry flies and accurate imitation. He developed many patterns, including cranefly larvae, stone fly nymphs, and caddis dries, but is now best remembered as originator of the modern form of the Woolly Worm. In 1940 he sent one to Preston Jennings, and his notes to Jennings on the fly are part of one of the most fascinating correspondences in American angling history:

> This horrible looking grub—"Wooley-worm" is a made over bass and croppie fly. Properly fished it is murderous all season long. I made and sold as many of these things as all other flies combined last summer. I hate the looks of them and consider them more a lure than a fly, but they have had a boom for the two seasons last past with no sign of a let up. They should be used only in still or very slow water, fished deep, with a twitching of the line by the left hand. The movement of the hackle is what gets 'em, suggesting perhaps the waving breathing apparatus of the May-fly nymphs and others.

An original Don Martinez Woolly Worm, from the Preston Jennings Collection, the American Museum of Fly Fishing. *Photo by John Merwin.*

Martinez would probably be pleased to know that, as far as the Woolly Worm's popularity, there is still "no sign of a let up."

Ironically, the man who would become the most famous western fisherman of all was originally an easterner. Dan Bailey also started coming out to Montana, in his case from New York, in the 1930s, bringing with him a keen awareness of eastern fly-tying traditions and an open mindedness about what would take trout. His "moss-back" nymphs were another approach to woven flies, his dry flies soon sported hair tails to increase bouyancy, he tidied up and helped popularize the Muddler Minnow, he named and then expanded the Wulff series, and he adapted all he knew to western waters. Preston Jennings's widow, Adele, in a remembrance published in *The American Fly Fisher* in the spring of 1984, commented on Bailey's unrestricted viewpoint:

The Jenningses visited the Baileys in Montana in the 1930s on a fishing trip; pictured, from left, are Adele Jennings, Ken Reid (a Chicago sportswriter), Helen Bailey, Preston Jennings, and Dan Bailey, at the Bailey's camp. *From the Preston Jennings Collection, The American Museum of Fly Fishing.*

Dan wasn't much interested in this technical side of fly-tying. He was an empiricist who loved the fishing—and *big* attractor flies.

Bailey himself, writing to Jennings in 1954 when Jennings was corresponding with many people about imitative theory, had made that clear:

> My idea of flies is quite different from yours, so I doubt that any of my contributions would suit you. My theory which is borne out in practice is that the trout's version [probably should read "vision"] is so different from the human's that there is little value in working from the naturals. As long as a dry fly floats well and comes fairly close to imitating a large group of insects it does the trick. Changes which I have made in flies have been based on the trout's acceptance. That being the case, my patterns might look less like the natural than English or Eastern flies.

Bailey's sort of empiricism was the order of the day in many parts of the country. I wonder if Jennings got tired of hearing about how unimportant his imitative work was, especially from friends as good as Bailey.

This brief survey of a few important trout regions has been, like most good flies, more suggestive than exact. Regional progress was occurring, in many directions, from the Sierras to Alaska and from Newfoundland to the Smokies. The few regions I've discussed offer sufficient evidence of variety, and they also show how truly national our modern fly selections are. The Catskill dry flies have been joined by the Adams from Michigan, the Woolly Worm from Montana, the Wulffs from the Adirondacks, and by the various other types of flies discussed in the three previous chapters. The demands of geography—of different waters and their fish—enabled American anglers to create a selection of flies that were adaptable and enduring. The process was not a simple one, of each region coming up with its own; it was instead

Preston Jennings examining one of his Iris streamers and a minnow through a prism as part of his studies of the reflection of light from the sides of fish. *Photo from the Letcher Lambuth Collection, The American Museum of Fly Fishing.*

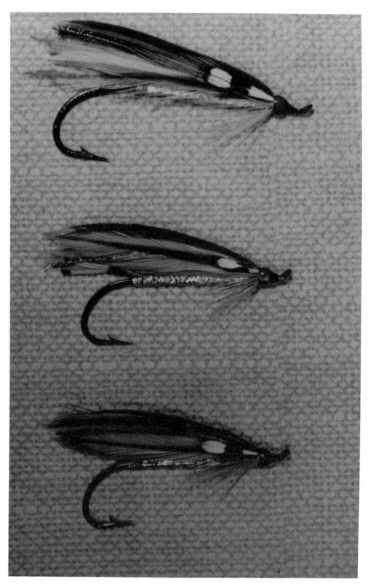

From the top, a Lady Iris, Lord Iris, and Murky Iris, tied by Preston Jennings during his years of experimentation with the effects of light on fish vision. *Photo by the author*.

a sort of cross-pollination process. Bailey took Catskill learnings to Montana. Weber sent Hornbergs everywhere. Martinez sold Woolly Worms to visiting fishermen from Pennsylvania. New York fishermen ordered books and materials from Herter. Fly fishing experienced a dynamic national evolution that is still going on today.

But I still think of this as Jennings's chapter. Most of these people may not have had much truck with his insistence on imitation, but his book, though it sold poorly despite great reviews, was in a way a refinement of the principles they were working by. They wouldn't have known it, but *A Book of Trout Flies* was a logical outgrowth of the creative process fly fishing was undergoing then.

Jennings did not rest on his laurels after 1935. He launched a letter-writing campaign of international scope. He requested lists of favorite fly patterns. He recruited many anglers—including Martinez and Letcher Lambuth, whose pioneering insect collections in Washington never developed into a publication that would surely have been of great value—to collect insects for him. He studied the effects of light on trout perception of minnows, and developed (and patented) his Iris streamers, designed to duplicate the colors reflected from the side of a baitfish under varying conditions. He was well along on his second book, *The Fish and the Fly*, at the time of his death in 1962, and it has been my pleasure over the past few years to shepherd some of that material into print. He did not live to produce a nationally comprehensive *Book of Trout Flies*, but he will never be faulted for that. In his later years he seemed to realize that the job was too big, and a paragraph from one of his manuscripts, now at The American Museum of Fly Fishing, is touching in its melancholy about that goal:

> And for myself, if in trying to break through the barrier that divides the known from the unknown I leave any sign of the struggle, I hope that it will signify to the friendly eye that sees it that ''Jennings fished here—he didn't catch much, but he tried—God how he tried.''

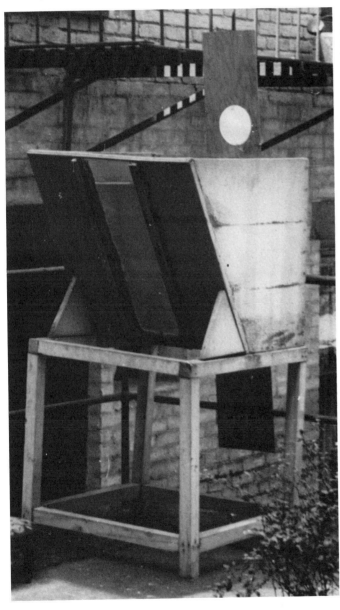

Like H.P. Wells, Edward Hewitt, and other anglers before him, Jennings was fascinated by the trout's view of the world. He built this tank for viewing flies from underneath, as part of his studies. *From the Preston Jennings Collection, The American Museum of Fly Fishing.*

18

Decline and Rise

*Now you may argue successfully for a "strict imitation,"
but obtaining it is another matter. The rejectionists would
have had the better of the dispute had they based their
argument solely on the difficulty of accomplishing such a
thing rather than upon denying its necessity. Worse, far
worse is the problem of defining the term, for if he is aware
of all the implications, he is a brave man who attempts such
a definition. It cannot be done in the dictionary way; above
all, it cannot be done in the way of Halford, Ronalds, and
others of ancient fame, for they spoke of imitation in terms
of human vision and comprehension, supported only by the
prop of entomology. That way alone lies grave error, since
it does not take into account the vision of the trout and the
geometry of the underwater world; and the study of entomology stops short, far short, of the approaches to these
considerations, which are the dominant factors in devising
imitations.*

Vincent C. Marinaro, *A Modern Dry-Fly Code* (1950)

"I hate this whole spinning business," declared Edward Hewitt in an interview a
few weeks before his death in 1957. "It will absolutely ruin all fishing in trout
streams. I'd outlaw it if I could. They're using lures and spinners, and they can reach
out farther and catch the big ones. And the spawn of big trout is worth five times as
much as the spawn of small ones. They can wipe out the trout. In a lot of English
streams they outlaw everything but fly fishing. And they ought to have a law like
that in every state."[1]

Spinning, by which we now usually mean the use of a casting reel with a fixed
spool from which line can run freely during the cast, is much older than its sudden
popularity in the United States would suggest. Fixed spool reels of various sorts
began to appear in England before 1900, but it wasn't until about 1935 that the reels
were commercially introduced here, and it wasn't until the late 1940s that they had
a chance to catch on.

With the close of World War II America experienced a recreation boom that
strained land management agencies all over the country with a sudden flood of

enthusiastic outdoorsmen. Fishing was typical, and the availability of spinning gear made fishing just that much easier for beginners. Later fly-fishing writers would grumble that a lot of people who should have known better turned to spinning as the new angling fashion, and immediately, and for reasons rather beyond the scope of this book, a rivalry developed between fly fishers and spin fishers that had long existed between fly fishers and everyone else. In the history of fly fishing, at least since the Civil War, the period between 1945 and 1955 is considered almost a dark ages, when only the most devoted of anglers continued to use their fly rods.

If it was a dark ages in terms of the numbers, or the commercial success, of fly fishers, it was a period of great productivity in fly-fishing theory. A number of men who had been gathering wisdom and experience through half a lifetime and more brought forth their findings in a series of books that are still in many respects as current as fly-fishing thinking can be. Fly fishers may or may not have been reduced in numbers, but they were not reduced in intellectual energy. The work symbolically begun by the publication of Jennings's *A Book of Trout Flies* was carried on and expanded by several others, some of whom knew him and some of whom did not. They were products of different waters, and, significantly, some were products of far wider fishing experience than previous generations of theorists.

When I suggest that the flies we use are the products of the waters we fish, I am not proposing that *only* those flies could have developed on those waters. It is true

John Atherton on the Battenkill. *From the Atherton Collection, The American Museum of Fly Fishing.*

that a stream whose trout dine heavily on stoneflies and sculpins will incline its anglers to imitate those life forms, but even at that much is left up to the angler. There are still many variables. The angler's education, or esthetic leanings, or available fly-tying materials, or even tendency to whimsy, will all affect the flies that result from a sustained acquaintance with a certain water. Another of the nice things about fly fishing is that, aside from obeying certain laws, we don't have to do anything we don't want to. Fly fishing is supposed to be fun, and every person has a slightly different definition of that. John Atherton, of whom more will be said momentarily, captured that attitude as well as anyone has, in his book *The Fly and The Fish* (1951):

> The fisherman who takes what sport he can find, who is not apt to devote much time to the collection of natural insects while on the stream and who prefers to let others do his research and experimentation is the man we most frequently meet with a flyrod. He may be allowed only a few week ends in the entire season, and he prefers to devote them to actual fishing rather than to the note-taking and close observation of the naturalist.
>
> Many anglers feel that anything resembling work, other than wading a stream and hiking to and from their automobiles, is something to avoid if their fishing is to be pure pleasure. I fish only for fun myself and refuse to stop fishing to capture a natural unless I feel like it, or to take any notes whatever on the stream. So I can sympathize with these anglers who so seldom are allowed the opportunity of catching trout. Being a fortunate individual who spends on the average at least part of three or four days a week on the stream, I can hardly find reason for my laziness other than to say that if one does enjoy fishing for its own sake he should avoid any suggestion of making it a chore. As soon as the sport becomes a pursuit, or resembles anything other than sport itself, it loses its main attraction.

These are deeper waters than at first they might appear to be. Fun really does mean many things to many people. For some anglers, the collection of insects and the rabid pursuit of accurate imitation are a very high form of fun.

Since World War II the serious angler-entomologists, as represented by some of the authors discussed in this chapter and many others, have held a sort of moral high ground in fly-fishing writing. They have written the most, and they write with an underlying insistence that this is the only way to be a serious fly fisher. Perhaps they are right; it surely is about time that angling entomology got more attention than it did in the first 150 years of American fly fishing. But Atherton's ''man we meet most frequently with a flyrod'' is still out there, and at times I suspect that the entomologists are too hard on him. The ''average guy'' buys their books in good numbers, and he seems to put a good bit of time in on getting his fly patterns right, but we can hardly blame him if he does not wholeheartedly embrace the role model of the few fishermen who are serious amateur entomologists. He is probably more suited, temperamentally, to the code expressed by novelist Thomas McGuane in *An Outside Chance* (1980). McGuane admitted to fishing most of the time with the Adams dry fly ''in about eight different sizes'' because it's ''gray and funky and a great salesman.''

> In the future, I mean to be a fine streamside entomologist. I'm going to start on that when I am much too old to do any of the two thousand things I can think of that are more fun than screening insects in cold running water.

There's that word fun again.

Though it was at least implicit—and I have occasionally pointed it out in previous chapters—in American fly fishing since the early 1800s, it is in this period since

1945 that we begin to see the diversity of courses taken even among the serious students of imitation. As I have already suggested, few fly-fishing writers have espoused a *non*imitation theory that completely disregards the need to use flies that somehow suggest insect or other life to the trout. The differences are a matter of degree. Among the serious imitationists, moreover, the differences are not only a matter of degree but of emphasis. Some of those differences of emphasis surface clearly in the decade after the war.

But I am not yet prepared to let go of Atherton's "man we meet most frequently." He is revealing, and he is important, partly because he is most of us, and partly because he can explain to us how fly-fishing writing works.

We dare not say, for example, that because Atherton's average guy does not collect insects that he is not a serious fly fisher. We dare not say that most of all because it is almost impossible to define "serious" in this context; he may have just as much fun as the insect collector. But we also dare not say it because that average guy is a product of the same traditions as the insect collector. He has the assurance that in most places he fishes, someone else has already studied up on the hatches and worked out the information he needs; this is more true in the 1980s than it was in the 1950s, and it will continue to improve the average guy's likelihood of having the right fly at the right time. Because of it, he no more needs to know the names of any insects than he needs to know the names of the grasses he walks across getting to the stream. He can learn those things if learning them is fun for him.

As long as the insect collectors and pattern theorists are having their fun in collecting, keying, and matching, the average guy's sport will continue to improve at little expense to him. In this way the two viewpoints—the anglers who care about entomological detail and imitation accuracy on one extreme and the anglers who just pick up some flies and go fishing on the other—have a symbiosis of ironic proportions. We are not yet close to having a complete catalog of North American hatches, but for the purposes of the casual angler the works of Jennings, Flick, Wetzel, Schweibert, Swisher and Richards, Caucci and Nastasi, Hughes and Hafele, and others are sufficient. If he chooses to build on them in some personal, informal manner—by tilting the wings back over the body on his Adams, say—he is exercising his prerogatives as a fly fisher who, ultimately, must decide for himself what is the most fun.

Ernest Schwiebert has a wonderful story—one of several, in fact—in his book *Nymphs* (1973), about encountering an aged wet-fly fisherman at nightfall on the Beaverkill. Both he and the other angler had been catching fish, and the old man challenged Ernie's "matching-the-hatch" theories, pointing out that a rough Cahill wet fly worked well that evening. Ernie took him to the shallows and, with a flashlight, showed him the empty shucks of newly emerged *Potamanthus* mayflies, revealing to the old man that his wet fly was in fact a good imitation of the emerger. We are all imitationists of some sort, I think. Even as seemingly iconoclastic a position as McGuane's—and it is a common position—reveals considerable imitative sympathy. The Adams is such a great salesman because it looks enough like a lot of things to work well. Fly fishing has always thrived in an atmosphere of ambivalence.

It thrives as well in an atmosphere of inquiry, and if the decade following World War II was one of commercial decline, it was also one of theoretical freshness. It is too simple to say that what happened was entirely the result of seeds sown by Jennings, because the authors involved had mostly begun their fly-fishing thinking by the time his book was published.

The book that was most directly a descendant of Jennings's work was Art Flick's *Streamside Guide to Naturals and Their Imitations* (1947). Flick was one of the

Art Flick and one of his
Gray Fox Variants.
Photos by Tom Rosenbauer.

anglers who helped Jennings collect the insects for his book, and, after years of encouragement and prodding by friends, especially *The New York Times* outdoor editor Raymond Camp, Flick was persuaded to produce his little book. It has since been heralded as a small masterpiece, plainly spoken and accurately presented, that made life simple for countless eastern anglers who were overwhelmed by the proliferation of fly patterns. Though his book was grounded in entomology, with helpful emergence charts for the major mayflies, Flick kept his list of necessary patterns to less than a dozen dry flies, and argued that a fly fisher could do well through the season with only three: his Dun Variant, Cream Variant, and Grey Fox Variant. The practical, warmhearted tone of his book has added measurably to its success:

> Having nothing definite to go by on this subject of vision and selectivity, I will continue to flounder along according to the experiences of others, and my own, until such time as a talking trout will be discovered that can give me the right dope. Possibly someday a mere mortal may discover the answer, but I hope that day never comes. Think of all the swell arguments we would miss!

Since its publication in 1947 the book has sold about 85,000 copies, an outstanding success for a book as narrowly focused as this one, but some proof that its focus was appropriate. By comparison, Ray Bergman's *Trout*, first published in 1938 and continuously in print for nearly half a century now, and aimed at all trout fishermen (fly, spin, and bait), has sold about 98,000. Ernest Schwiebert's *Matching the Hatch* (1955) has sold perhaps a few thousand more copies than Flick's book. Swisher and Richards's *Selective Trout* (1971) has sold about 85,000.

The product of a much broader experience than Flick's, but still a book firmly rooted in eastern fly-fishing traditions, was *The Fly and The Fish* (1951), by John Atherton. Atherton was a successful commercial artist whose paintings had appeared on the covers of *Fortune*, *The Saturday Evening Post*, *Holiday*, and many other magazines, and he had fished in many parts of the country. His work in fly-pattern theory, however, seems mostly to have been an outgrowth of his experiences with Vermont's Battenkill and New York's Neversink, where he informally apprenticed himself to Edward Hewitt, and visited often to fish with the master. Atherton's work in flies was most heavily influenced by his artistic background, leading him to an impressionistic approach. He developed a series of seven dry flies (as well as three nymphs and five wet flies) to serve most imitative situations. He had confidence "in the killing qualities of flies which are not exact imitations of any one insect but an approximation of several."

Atherton's flies are a testament to his theories. There is an indistinctness about them, for all their skilfull construction and fineness of proportion. His use of Bali-duck feather for the wings, his carefully blended dubbings of subtly different shades of fur, and his use of the traditional Catskill dry-fly form give, to the view of humans, anyway, the effect he desired to achieve with trout:

> As impressionistic color in flies is more apt to suggest life than solid tones, an
> impressionistic outline or silhouette suggests life more than a sharp outline.

It has been my great good fortune to see original flies tied by most of the anglers I have been discussing in the past few chapters. If you are a devoted fly tier, or at all attracted to fly tying theory, it is surprisingly easy to wile away many evenings in the presence of flies as interesting as these. And though I have happy memories of many flies and their characters—Preston Jennings's unexpected gift for married-wing wet flies, the stiff brilliance of Art Flick's perfectly trim Red Quill, the pioneering aura of Theodore Gordon's Quill Gordon, the fluttery taper of Charles Zibeon Southard's long-feather streamers, the unassuming plainness of a Skues nymph—there is something about the Atherton dry flies, some quality of indefinability that must have to do with his desire to keep the flies from looking too much like anything, that has caused me to remember them often. Unfortunately, not all that many others have remembered them, and these days it is only his general nymph patterns, the Atherton Light, Medium, and Dark, that are likely to appear in fly boxes or new books of popular patterns. His book had much more limited sales than many books of pattern theory, and except among Battenkill anglers who must contend with the descendants of the same trout that shaped his thinking, and an occasional angler elsewhere, it is not often consulted.

A much more far-reaching influence was had by a group of Pennsylvania anglers who were responding to the challenges of that state's diverse collection of trout streams. It could be said, in fact, that in the production of original and enduring fly theory, Pennsylvania occupied in the 1940s and 1950s a position of leadership not unlike that occupied by the Catskills earlier. Much more than Atherton, these few Pennsylvania anglers seem to have spoken for many of their colleagues alongside whom they worked out their theories (and that, perhaps, is why Atherton's book languished; it grew out of one mind rather than out of a wider "public mind" that was struggling with a set of common problems).

The streams of Pennsylvania have an unusually long documented history in American fly fishing; we saw fly-tackle dealers in Philadelphia, early in this book, active two centuries ago, and George Gibson was fly fishing the Letort in the 1790s. As with the Catskills, there are far too many excellent anglers and writers for me to describe here, and there is little point in simply listing a lot of names. It is more useful to mention a few outstanding achievements, those by Charles Wetzel, Alvin Grove, and Vincent C. Marinaro.

Wetzel, for many years editor of *Pennsylvania Angler*, among the most important of state fishing magazines in this country, first wrote his *Practical Fly Fishing* (1943) as articles in that publication. In it he listed the emergence dates and imitations of some fifty trout-stream insects, establishing an outline for Pennsylvania waters much like the one Jennings had produced for the waters farther north. Wetzel revised the entomological information and incorporated it in *Trout Flies, Naturals and Imitations* (1955), along with information on insect collecting and discussions of nymphs, dry-fly techniques, transplanting stream insects, and less formal material on his fishing experiences. I agree with Arnold Gingrich, who lamented in *The Joys of Trout* (1973) that Wetzel was too hard to find:

> Wetzel's name would be far more widely known than it is today if one of the reprinters would pick up any or all of the above-mentioned books, none of which had any appreciable circulation, and all of which contain information that is worth having in far more common supply. A one-volume Wetzel would be wonderful.

Fortunately, *Trout Flies* was republished in 1979, but Wetzel's major work of angling bibliography, *American Fishing Books* (1950) remains almost impossible to come by.

Wetzel's list of flies in *Trout Flies* is quite modern, including not only the routine mayflies, caddisflies, and stoneflies, but alder, ant, scud, cranefly, midge, beetle, and a number of other less traditional patterns. In these listings he showed something of the Pennsylvanian inclination toward terrestrial imitation that was to become such an important part of Marinaro's work.

Alvin Grove's *The Lure and Lore of Trout Fishing* (1951) has been regarded as important not only in imitation theory but in literary quality. Gingrich, in his entry on the book in *The Joys of Trout*, devotes the majority of his discussion to the book's typographical and editorial errors, but did find time to allow that the book was the fullest, in both instruction and writing quality, of this late-forties to early-fifties era.

Ed Shenk, one of Pennsylvania's modern fly fishing legends, on the Letort. *Courtesy of Bud Lilly*.

Alvin Grove fishing Slate Run, Pennsylvania, 1969. *Photo by Harry Groome, courtesy of Alvin Grove.*

That would surely be an unprovable point, but it suggests at least the general stature of what Grove achieved. Charles Fox, who could not have been unaware that he and Vincent Marinaro were destined to be subjects of an identical comparison, said that Grove and the great fishing instructor George Harvey were the American equivalents of Halford and Marryat of late-nineteenth-century England. Grove, in short, has been placed in the best company by his readers.

Grove displayed, as have many of the best American fly theorists before and since, a thorough acquaintance with British fishing literature. The book has less of the "over there they did it that way, over here we do it this way" tone than most of its predecessors; Grove wrote as an angler whose interests and lessons were international, and who went wherever wisdom could be found. The more he learned, the more cautious he became about being sure of any point, so that the book has a pleasant restraint on most points, including the necessity of imitation and the values of the so-called attractor patterns. The chapters "Food for Fish" and "Naturals and Artificials" were inquiries into the scientific knowledge and personal preferences involved in intelligent fly selection; in their fundamental lessons, they are hard to improve upon, however much more we may know now about any specific topic. The entire book had that quality of durability that makes even the outdated information forgivable (though Gingrich was right on one point: the copy editing and proofreading were abominable).

But for sheer originality and literary quality, no book of this era approached Vincent Marinaro's *A Modern Dry-Fly Code* (1950). Marinaro and Charles Fox, whose books *This Wonderful World of Trout* (1963) and *Rising Trout* (1967) would take their own honored places in the Pennsylvania tradition, have become the foremost angling heroes of Pennsylvania trout theory. Marinaro's book, based on his decades of experience on the Letort, Big Spring, and other south Pennsylvania streams, amounted to a substantial rethinking of traditional dry-fly definitions. Not only did he espouse a much broader imitation base including many terrestrials, he reconsidered the structure of the dry fly as it had been developed for mayflies. In all cases his modifications, though they may not have converted the majority of anglers, found enduring niches in fly theory. Rarely has a fly-fishing writer ventured to change so much and lived to see his work recognized and incorporated into the body of fly-fishing practice.

The imitation of terrestrials was not new; it has a history of several centuries, and has included most of the common insects. Some British writers were obviously serious about it and, judging from fly catalogs, Americans had some interest even in the days of the Victorian wet fly. But nothing had been attempted that would solve the singular problems of the smooth-currented limestone streams Marinaro fished, the meadow waters coated with minute ants, beetles, and aquatics. Marinaro, Fox, and their companions broke new ground by encountering a water type not unlike that which had inspired Halford and Marryat:

> . . . for there are trout and there are waters which differ greatly from those which established early American practice, and the character of the stream and its fish always establishes the best pattern of fly and the best manner of fishing it, not the fisherman.

He could have added, in fairness to what he and Fox accomplished, that the character of the fisherman establishes to what extent he meets the challenge.

A Modern Dry-Fly Code documented the development of practical ants, beetles, and hoppers. It also documented the development of a truly American dry fly. Marinaro, though not the first to suggest moving the hackle back from the hook eye, brought the idea to successful fruition. The thorax style of tying moved the wing back on the shank of the hook, introduced a different hackling technique that acted as support without obscuring the wing (which Marinaro thought of primary importance in duns), and introduced the widely split tails that added so much to a floating fly's stability and were later incorporated into the famous Swisher and Richards No-Hackles.[2] Marinaro's book did this in a spirit of inquiry, and with a literary intelligence that has rarely been equaled in American fishing writing. With frequent reference to the appropriate British authorities—Harding on trout perceptions, Dunne on insect and imitation translucency, Mottram, Halford, Ronalds, and others as needed—Marinaro conducted an eloquent dialogue with his ancestors on the needs of imitation. He introduced numerous tricks and innovations, such as the porcupine-quill extended body for large spinners, and he initiated a study of riseforms that would find fuller expression in his second book more than twenty years later.

The publication of *A Modern Dry-Fly Code* is now seen as at least the symbolic beginning of American fly fishers's fascination with what Marinaro called "minutae," those hordes of tiny insects that had always interested a few fishermen but were ignored by most. The limestone streams of Pennsylvania provided the impetus for this development, as Marinaro, Fox, Ed Shenk (who called it "fishing with next to nothing"), Dr. Bill Pfeiffer (who Fox credited with pioneering fishing to the minute *Tricorythodes* mayflies), Ed Koch, and others worked out imitations and techniques

Vincent Marinaro late in life. *Courtesy of Datus Proper.*

for extending their fishing season to include these hatches. Marinaro, in the *Code,* provided a good introduction to the challenges of fishing with the tiny flies, one more reason the book was such a virtuoso performance.

A performance of equal stature, though in another direction, was accomplished by a very young Ernest Schwiebert in *Matching the Hatch* (1955). The book whose name became a common expression was most impressive for its breadth. Still in his early twenties, Schwiebert had managed to fish or gather information on trout streams from coast to coast. His book was the one book to have if you were a transcontinental fly fisher. It was in the vanguard of future books on angling entomology, whose scope became necessarily national as more and more fly fishers became widely traveled.

Gingrich, who in the 1970s became established as the foremost commentator on fly fishing and its personalities, did not approve of the style of *Matching the Hatch.* He said that Schwiebert "used to come on like a juvenile Hewitt, without the saving grace of the latter's venerability to alleviate the stiffness of his know-it-all posture." I find the book nowhere near as opinionated or intolerant as Hewitt could be. Schwiebert was extraordinarily well informed, and spoke even then from an experience few fishermen today could match at twice his age.

He did not advocate slavish attempts at greater and greater precision in imitation. Recognizing the trout's abilities to be selective, he also recognized the limitations of our patterns:

> Still, the most casual eye can see that our carefully tied imitations are far from being exact replicas of the naturals. This point is often stressed by opponents of the imitation theory. But do our flies have to be exact replicas? The idea of exact imitation is preposterous.

Like most books of its type then, *Matching the Hatch* was devoted mostly to mayflies, but the sections on caddisflies and stoneflies were substantial. There were

Vincent Marinaro. *Courtesy of Datus Proper*.

several color plates with very small portraits of naturals, but no illustrations of imitations. There was an extensive catalog of fly patterns and emergence charts, and a discussion of streamside ethics that, though sound, may have been the source of Gingrich's disapproval for its preachy tone (I happen to think that streamside ethics need to be preached, and that this was one of the better sermons on the subject). With its national emphasis, based on the author's national experience (rather than on second-hand information from correspondents), *Matching the Hatch* was the prototype of many later books.

The books by Flick, Atherton, Wetzel, Grove, Marinaro, and Schwiebert were hardly the only books being published that had to do with fly fishing for trout. Leonard's *Flies* (1950) was a comprehensive encyclopedia of patterns that has been more popular than many of the books just discussed; Bill Blades's *Fishing Flies and Fly Tying* (1950) is still a coveted book on technique, with many fresh ideas and approaches; Sid Gordon's *How to Fish from Top to Bottom* (1955) was an unparalleled popularly written view of fishing waters, their character, and how to approach them; and McClane's *The Practical Fly Fisherman* (1953) exceeded all of the above as an introduction to the sport of fly fishing. McClane deserves further mention in the context of this chapter to show that entomology, though getting its fair share of attention in the early 1950s, was not universally regarded as essential:

It isn't the least bit necessary to be able to identify the naturals; just find out what's crawling around or drifting with the current and match it for color and size as best you can [discussing nymphs].

It is generally accepted that an angler can get along with four or five different fly patterns and catch trout anywhere. You can do a very competent job with an Adams Quill, a Light Cahill, Brown Bivisible and Royal Coachman (hairwing), for instance, provided the fly behaves like an insect after you throw it on the water [discussing dry flies].

These books and others also influenced and guided fly fishers, but they did not so clearly represent a new movement as did the books discussed in this chapter.

It could be that the spinning boom so despised by Hewitt and others really did reduce fly fishers in numbers enough to do harm to the sport. It is curious that there should have been this explosion of books devoted to imitative theory, some of them striking in their originality and most of them showing extraordinary energy in their entomological studies, all within a few years with no followup. After *Matching the Hatch* appeared in 1955, things quieted down, with few exceptions, until 1970. Did the spinning revolution distract enough fly fishers to result in a generation gap in entomological works? Or did the war simply remove the next generation? Or did it seem, contrary to what these authors themselves were preaching, that we knew enough on the subject for a while?[3] Or did preoccupations with other changes just then taking hold in fly fishing occupy our attention for a while until we could adjust and return to the work so well begun by Jennings and the postwar writers? Those changes may have had a lot to do with it. They were part of a revolution in technology even greater than the one that occurred following the Civil War, when bamboo replaced solid wood and silk replaced horsehair.

Four

THE MODERN
FLY FISHER

19

The Synthetic Angler

*The age of synthetics has greatly expanded the art of fly
fishing from top to bottom.*
A. J. MCCLANE, *The Practical Fly Fisherman* (1975)

The fly fisherman at the close of World War II, if he was at all tradition conscious,
was in for a series of shocks over the next fifteen years. Most of his outfit was going
to change.

His rod was by all odds six-strip bamboo, though there were still a few makers
tinkering with four- or five-strip construction. It was Tonkin cane, which began to
replace Calcutta cane in the late 1890s and was used by most respected makers after
about 1910. The rod was probably between eight and nine-and-a-half feet long.

If he had the money for a good rod, he had many opportunities to exercise the
personal taste that has made rod selection (and debates over it) such a mystical matter.
The tradition of bamboo-rod quality established in the era of Murphy, Green, Leonard,
Krider, and Orvis was in good hands. Payne, Thomas, Edwards, and Hawes, all
names originally associated with the Leonard operation, became distinguished independent firms, some through two generations. Lyle Dickerson and Paul Young
developed their rod-building businesses in Michigan, Dickerson in the 1930s and
Young in the 1920s. The R. L. Winston Company and E. C. Powell both began
production in California in the 1920s. Everett Garrison and Harold "Pinky" Gillum
began building rods about the same time, and produced a small number of rods that
were highly prized.

If, on the other hand, the fisherman had to shop more frugally, he still could do
well by getting a rod from Granger, South Bend, or Heddon, the best of which, some
experts now maintain, were as good as the best of the more expensive rods. If he
had even less money, he could take potluck (which often was pretty good luck) and
get rods from Sears or Wards or some less known and perhaps less trustworthy maker.

He had an equally broad set of choices in reels. He might have chosen one of
the expensive models—a Vom Hofe, or Leonard, or perhaps a Hardy—or he might
have preferred one of the less costly brands—a Pflueger, a Martin, or a
Shakespeare—or, again, there was always Sears and Roebuck and similar companies
that could provide you with fishing tackle for remarkably low prices.

His line was silk, and was identified by a bewildering and troublesome system of letter designations that were supposed to correspond to the diameter of the line. The smallest diameter customarily used was I, which was .022 inch. The largest you were likely to see anywhere was AAAAA, which was .080 inch. Most lines a trout or bass fisherman was likely to use had designations like HDH, or GBF, with no I's or A's. The code meant, in the example of the HDH, for instance, that the line began at H diameter, which was .025 inch, tapered up to D, which was .045 inch, and then back to H. As far as it went, the system wasn't all bad, but it just wasn't enough. Fly lines work or don't work depending not on their diameter, but on their weight. One manufacturer's H-diameter line might weigh half of another's, so that the angler had to do a lot of careful shopping and experimenting to find a line that really did match his rod.

His leader may have been either gut or nylon. If gut, it had the good and bad qualities discussed earlier. If nylon, it had a new set of problems. Nylon filaments had come out of research into synthetics by du Pont in the mid-1930s. The first were made using a hypodermic needle to push out long strands of molten nylon (known then as Polymer 66), but commercial manufacture was quick to follow, with huge amounts of fiber (most destined for brush bristles, hosiery, and other large markets) being produced. The material had obvious advantages over gut, but in its early years was often stiff and hard to deal with in casting or knot tying. It did not take long, however, for gut to vanish from practically all stores, especially as the spinfishing revolution got underway and there was sufficient demand to improve nylon fibers for fishing.

One other piece of equipment was appearing with increasing regularity, that being the fishing vest. A variety of fishing shirts and jackets had been developed in the late 1800s and early 1900s, but Wulff's vest, which he developed around 1930, was the impetus for the modern fishing vest without question; it is just one of many fishing ideas owed to this singular angler. I have no idea what percentage of fishermen were wearing vests by 1945, but today practically all fly fishermen you see on trout streams have one, though vests are much less common among bass fly fishermen.

The changes in fly-fishing tackle that have occurred since World War II have in some ways been similar to those that occurred following the Civil War. In both cases the changes did not happen all at once, nor were anglers uniformly happy about them; there was certainly plenty of disagreement over whether or not everything happening was really an improvement.

Unlike the solid-wood rods that it replaced, bamboo will never disappear from the hands of American fly fishers. Some of the reasons are subjective. Like so many things in fly fishing, it is a matter of personal taste, aside from economics, whether one favors bamboo or some synthetic material. Even in the 1930s, at least some anglers said that hollow-steel rods were just as good; though the steel rods never became favorites among most trout fishermen, their presence on the market for so long is proof of the loyalty of anglers to a chosen tool. Bamboo has always had a lot more going for it, both in its glamorous image and in its practical qualities, than did steel, so its future, if not bright with possibilities for increasing use, is at least secure in the hands of today's builders, some of them long established (Orvis and Winston), some of them relatively new (Thomas & Thomas, Walt Carpenter, Hoagy Carmichael, Gary Howells).

Though some experimenting had been done in the 1930s, credit for developing the first commercial fiberglass rods goes to Dr. Arthur Howald and the Shakespeare Company in the mid-1940s. The rods were at first built of fiberglass over a wood

Lee Wulff's first vest set the style for most later models; Lee designed and sewed it. *Photo courtesy of Lee Wulff.*

core, but soon a variety of solid, and hollow, rods were being produced as more and more makers became involved. Conolon has been given credit for the first hollow rods, which of course eventually became the standard construction for fly rods.[1]

Fiberglass, though truly a wonder for most anglers, went through a long period of refinement that, in a way, is still going on. By the mid-1950s it had not really "replaced" bamboo, but was preferred for any fishing that many anglers thought required power over finesse. Gradually, as craftsmanship and production improved, glass rods that would do much the same things as bamboo were possible, though many serious anglers still believe that bamboo has casting qualities, or sensitivities, that glass has not matched. After initial high prices, glass became cheap enough that any fine differences in quality between it and bamboo simply did not matter to most people. The late 1940s and early 1950s were a time of great growth in outdoor recreation, and the spinning craze brought many people to fishing who had no knowledge at all of the traditions of fly fishing; all they wanted were the most efficient fish-catching tools possible, ones that could take the abuse given by many clumsy beginners. Fiberglass was, in several senses, all they needed. Most did not even notice when snooty bamboo devotees looked down on them, and wouldn't have cared anyway. Ernest Schwiebert, writing in about 1974 (though not published until 1978) in his detailed history of fiberglass rods in *Trout*, estimated that by that time about three million rods were being bought annually by Americans and all but three percent were fiberglass. A reading of the fly-fishing books published between 1945 and 1975 would probably give the reader the impression that bamboo was much more common than it actually was, because the writers were often still devoted to bamboo, or were in a better position to afford it than most of the readers.

None of this takes away from bamboo its unique qualities for fly fishing; fiberglass's rise to popularity was in some ways a testament to the high standard set by bamboo, which all builders of synthetic rods are compelled to consider if not imitate.

Bamboo rodbuilding changed following World War II. Though expensive at first, fiberglass rods gradually occupied the lower end of the price range. The huge numbers of relatively cheap, mass-produced bamboo rods were no longer needed by the mid-1950s. When the Communists came to power in China, America lost its source of bamboo, and the flow would not be resumed even intermittently between China and America until the 1970s (though we did buy bamboo that had been purchased in China by other countries who then sold it to us). These factors, along with rising labor costs, turned the bamboo rod into what it is today: a premium, often custom, product of limited market. A few thousand are still sold new every year, but their high cost has turned them as much into investments as they ever were fishing rods. One industry leader has told me that though the rods still sell, repairs have dropped off dramatically, suggesting that people buy them but use them less than they used to.

Fiberglass's heyday was far shorter than bamboo's. By the early 1970s, when the material was being subjected to great craft at the hands of experts such as Russ Peak (who even as tradition-minded a fly fisher as Arnold Gingrich could not resist), the next so-called ultimate rod material appeared. Graphite rods were first publicly introduced by Fenwick in 1973, and, what with the far more sophisticated communication network then in existence among fly fishers (far more sophisticated than it had been in 1950, anyway), the new rods were a sensation. Their cost was not much less than some bamboo models, but there were many signs that, like fiberglass, introductory costs would soon drop. They didn't, at least not to the extent projected, but graphite conquered the market more quickly than fiberglass had. Graphite rods were lighter, smaller in diameter, and in many ways stronger than fiberglass; they were a revelation, and were promoted as almost guaranteed to add ten or fifteen feet to your casting distance. In 1975, when he put out a new edition of *The Practical Fly Fisherman*, A. J. McClane predicted that graphite ''will replace fiberglass during the next decade.'' Though the conquest was not as complete as fiberglass's had been over the previous two decades, his prediction came true. Early in 1986, Paul Brown of Fenwick told me that graphite rods made up eighty-four percent of their total sales. Others report similar figures. It is impossible now to come up with precise statistics, because few rods are pure graphite anyway, but fiberglass has lost out, and is now perceived among many fly fishermen as a low-budget second choice.

Like graphite, the most recently touted ''miracle'' fiber, boron, is a product of the aerospace industry. It was known to be stiffer, by far, than either graphite or fiberglass. Don Phillips, an engineer from Connecticut, worked out his first solid boron rod (it had a small wood core upon which he had mounted a boron tape) in 1972, and caught his first fish on it the following spring. Orvis had also been experimenting with boron in the early 1970s, and by 1980 several companies had begun commercial production, mostly of hollow rods. Boron showed promise of generating

Jim Green of Fenwick testing an early graphite rod model.
Ted Trueblood photo, courtesy of Fenwick.

the same kind of excitement that graphite had, but it did not prove to be the quantum leap in improvement that fiberglass and graphite had each seemed to be. Some of the largest manufacturers of high-quality rods now make no boron rods, or use boron fibers only to stiffen up rods primarily made of fiberglass and graphite.

An interesting stage was passed through in the late 1970s and early 1980s, during which claims and counterclaims flew among the manufacturers about whose rods—graphite or boron—were "pure" and whose were merely mixtures of fibers and therefore "not really graphite," or "not genuine boron." The best makers soon realized, though, that these three materials—graphite, fiberglass, and boron—were often better used in combination than alone, and that fly fishers would be best served by less emphasis on purity and more on practical fishing mechanics.

The development of synthetic materials revolutionized the fly line as it did the fly rod. Just after the war a polyvinyl chloride coating was developed with which tapered lines could be manufactured. The process, which has taken many forms, involves applying the plastic coating to some core fiber. The core may be braided nylon (now the most common), Dacron, or even fiberglass (the Rain-Beau Line Company used fiberglass on its plastic-coated lines in 1946). The Cortland 333 line, first produced in the early 1950s, had a tapered core over which plastic was placed, the thickness of any portion of line depending upon the thickness of the core material. Then, in about 1952, Scientific Anglers perfected a way of tapering not the core but the plastic coating itself so that a line with a single-diameter core could be given any combination of tapers and thicknesses desired.

Since that start, it has been mostly a matter of refining the materials involved for greater durability and variation in weight. The sink-tip fly line, also developed by Scientific Anglers, used plastic of a certain specific gravity for the first eighty or so feet of the line, then used plastic of a greater specific gravity for the last ten feet, which would sink. Many combinations have appeared, including what are called "intermediate" lines that have much the weight and sinking qualities of old silk lines and can be greased or left to sink slowly as the old lines did.

The ease of plastic-line production encouraged experimentation with taper. Though weight-forward lines (those whose forward, or front, ends were heaviest for greater distance casting) had been around since early in the century at least, modern fly-line manufacturers have offered a greater variety of such tapers, including very blunt, fast "saltwater tapers" for large flies or bass bugs. The old double-taper line, which tapered from a thick middle to equally light ends, has been losing popularity for twenty years now. Its advantages were that it worked well for normal fishing—casts under forty or fifty feet—and that it could be reversed once one of the ends grew old, worn, or weak. Plastics last much longer, making the reversal option less important, and can be cast as delicately under normal conditions, with the advantage that the modern weight-forward line can also be used for much longer casts when they are necessary.

Tournament casters and big-river anglers, especially in the West, had been making shooting heads (mentioned in Chapter 13) for decades, but these also became commercially popular after plastic-coated fly lines were common. By the 1980s a fly fisher had a choice of several tapers, many line sizes, shooting heads, and lines built so that part or all of them would sink, and several sink rates were available.

The plastic-coated fly line worsened the already troublesome line-designation problem. When all lines were made of silk, there was some variation in weight from one line to the next even if their diameters were identical. Once plastics made any line weight possible and did so in a dizzying variety of diameters, the old letter-designation code was worse than useless; it was perplexing. In about 1958, Myron Gregory, a leading California tournament caster, launched a campaign to develop a new designation system. Late that year the American Fishing Tackle Manufacturers Association established a committee that within two years proposed the current number-designation system. The system is based not on the line's diameter but on the weight in grains of the first thirty feet of the line, that being the portion most often of concern under normal fishing conditions. A 1-weight line is expected to weigh around 60 grains; a 5-weight around 140 grains; a 12-weight around 380 grains. As the line sizes increase, the amount of weight difference does too, so that in the smallest sizes, 1 to 6, there is only 20 grains difference between sizes, but in the larger sizes the differences gradually increase until there is a difference of 50 grains, for example, between an 11-weight (330) and a 12-weight (380). It hasn't proved to be a perfect system, but it was an immense improvement. There has been some complaint that sink rates need some kind of industry-wide standardization; one manufacturer's "fast-sinking" may be another's "extra-fast sinking," for example. Lately some manufacturers are listing sink rate in inches-per-second on their lines, which solves the problem for most people.

The A.F.T.M.A. line-designation system has been a special blessing for beginners. The code was soon found on all lines (some manufacturers continued to confuse things for some years by also trying to use the old letter designations on their lines, apparently for the information of anglers not yet used to the new system) and most rods. In principle all you had to do was match up a line with a rod and buy a reel that would handle the line and its backing. Scientific Anglers made the purchase of good fiberglass-rod outfits almost mindlessly easy in the late 1960s with their "System" outfits; you could buy a "System 4" or "System 7" or whatever your needs dictated, and have a perfectly matched outfit. But most other makers made it just as easy for you if you were willing to read the labels on the rods and lines. Myron Gregory believed that the old confusing letter designation, with its accompanying high risk of your getting a hopelessly unbalanced outfit, contributed to the decline in fly fishing that was caused by spinning. The A.F.T.M.A. line designation system, and the promotional use of it by tackle manufacturers, certainly helped reverse fly fishing's decline.

Thus armed with new rods, lines, ever more precise and tougher reels, and stronger leaders, and well stocked with flies that are themselves a testament to the synthetic age—some combination of natural materials and polypropylene, mylar, mohlon, orlon, antron, FishHair, flashabou, and on and on—the modern fly fisher moved toward broadening horizons.

On one extreme were the light-tackle anglers who found their fly-fishing season lengthening into the late-summer low-water days when feeding fish often concentrate on minutae in clear, still water. Nylon leader advancements made leaders of .005 inch diameter (6X) to even .003 inches (8X) more practical (if demanding of patience and skill), so that flies smaller than size 20 (that being the smallest hook commonly used before about 1960) could be reasonably cast. This change, and increasing availability of hooks in sizes 22 to 28, opened up a whole new fishing season for many anglers, and made practical fishing to extremely small insect emergences common.

On the other extreme, the power of fiberglass and graphite rods, along with stronger leaders and reels, finally allowed the capture of very large fish on a regular basis. The day I began work on this chapter I received by mail an advance copy of a revised edition of Lefty Kreh's *Fly Fishing in Salt Water*. This book, in its first edition, served as the guide to an entire generation of anglers and no doubt the new edition will do the same. It took up, in 1974, the sport when it had been the subject of few books (Joe Brooks's *Saltwater Fly Fishing*, 1950, and George Sands's *Salt-Water Fly Fishing*, 1969, were probably the two most important), and revealed just how far it had come since the late 1940s, when a fifty-pound tarpon was an unusual

The introduction of modern monofilaments and related tackle allowed for the practical use of smaller and smaller flies. Mounted on the matchstick is a set of five dry flies, four 28s and one 32, by Bing Lempke of Idaho, tied in the 1970s. *Photo by the author.*

conquest. The second edition revealed just how fast the sport had progressed in only twelve years, giving every indication that it will continue to expand its possibilities.

Though the advances in fishing to the minutae probably affected the angling habits of far more fishermen, it has been the advances in big-fish tackle that often get the most attention in the general outdoor magazines, probably because big fish are great press and undeniably spectacular. In the 1980s a small group of dedicated fishermen were vying to be first to catch a 200-pound tarpon on regulation fly equipment, and had already passed the 180-pound mark. In 1962 saltwater fly fishing took a significant step when Dr. Webster Robinson, fishing off Panama, boated a 74½-pound Pacific sailfish, the first taken on a fly. In the next few years, Robinson, Lee Wulff, Lee Cuddy (who took the first reported Atlantic sailfish on a fly), and a few others took a variety of billfish, including both Atlantic and Pacific sailfish and striped marlin, on flies, and now the feat is accomplished with at least a few billfish somewhere every year. On the West Coast, river anglers took advantage of the greater strength of fiberglass rods by casting homemade lead-core lines of five hundred or more grains, allowing them to cut through fast currents to reach deep salmon, and encouraging manufacturers to produce commercial versions of the same lines. Along both coasts, anglers (again following the example of Joe Brooks, who for some time held the world record with a striped bass of almost thirty pounds that he took on a fly in the late 1940s) developed techniques for taking larger and larger bass.

The technological changes in fly fishing between 1945 and 1980 were of course only a part of how the sport developed in those years, and they were, as usual, not accomplished evenly. We mustn't forget that it was in the late 1950s and early 1960s, while fiberglass was taking its lead in popularity, that Arnold Gingrich, Lee Wulff, A. J. McClane, and others were telling (and showing) the world just how much could be done with a midge or bantam bamboo rod of six feet or less in length. Synthetic materials did not so much make fly fishing a different sport as they accelerated processes already under way. By broadening the sporting opportunities of fly fishing, the new rods, lines, and other gear did much to revitalize the sport at a time when its popularity was fading. The new tackle simplified the sport for beginners, and it solved some of the most frustrating problems faced by veteran anglers, who suddenly found themselves able to fish flies both smaller and larger than they had before, to take fish both more finicky and more strong than had been imagined possible before World War II.

20

The Well-Published Angler

Perhaps the most remarkable aspect of our fishing is the explosive growth of American fly-fishing entomology. Less than a half century has passed since Preston Jennings published his Book of Trout Flies *in 1935, yet American writers have cataloged a galaxy of fly life in those brief years and their world encompasses an entire continent.*

ERNEST SCHWIEBERT, in *The Masters on the Nymph* (1979)

Despite all that has been published about fishing writing and writers, we still are without a good literary history of American fishing writing. Henry Bruns and Charles Wetzel have given us ample bibliographical background, but the formal critical study of fishing writing barely exists. What we have instead—and should probably be grateful for—are a number of informal, celebratory books and articles that talk about old fishing writing.

I judged it too large a topic to address more than peripherally in this book; like bamboo-rod building, or the development of synthetic fly lines, it is a fascinating story, but is only part of the greater story of American fly fishing. I have therefore used the books and periodicals primarily as sources of information rather than making them the central subject of the book.

The disadvantage of that approach is that I risk not paying sufficient attention to what fishing writing means in some broader sense—how, for example, it may serve to portray the spirit or the ideals of a generation of anglers. I have used fishing writing as evidence of such portrayals here and there, but do not pretend that more need not be done. It will take a larger, more concentrated effort to do justice to the topic than I can provide here. But I am not so immune from the topic that I can avoid it entirely. There are some intriguing ways in which fishing writing has reflected developments in the greater angling scene, ways that become especially apparent in recent decades.

We are perhaps too careless in our conversations about what we call ''fishing literature.'' For want of a better word, we refer to all of our writing, whether it be a paragraph published in a popular miscellany from the 1840s, or a letter from an amateur correspondent to *Forest and Stream* in the 1880s, or an essay by some acknowledged literary figure in the 1930s, or a how-to article by a modern-day professional sports journalist, as fishing literature. The different writers have different goals, to say nothing of different abilities. The modern sports journalist is usually writing for the fly-fishing audience; he writes ''inward'' to the fraternity. Ernest Hemingway, or William Humphrey, or any of the other famous writers who also fish, write ''outward,'' telling their broader public about fishing. All may instruct, all may inspire, and all may entertain, but we read them knowing who we are listening to, and knowing too that in each case we are part of a different audience.

Traditionally, at least up until the twentieth century, British fishing literature was dominated by brilliant amateurs. Now American fishing writing is more strongly dominated by professionals.

Like all generalizations, this one has its exceptions; several British fishing writers were in some sense professionals, either professional fishermen or professional writers. But most of the ones we revere, such as Halford, or Skues, or Ronalds, were not. They may have in some way cashed in on their prominence, as Ronalds marketed his published fly patterns, but their initial impetus was not commercial. There was not a living to be had in being a fly fisherman.

Now, in an accelerated and much larger market, there is at least a useful portion of a living to be made for the enterprising professional angler. That is not necessarily bad, though it can be, just as amateurism has its pitfalls. But good or bad, it does tend to give a different slant to a person's writing. It was not necessary for Halford to write any of his books, or promote any new ideas, in order for him to eat. When ideas and innovation become matters of personal urgency, more of them will appear. Volume can replace quality. Something like that, many observers have complained, happened to fly-fishing writing between 1970 and 1980. Volume increased tremendously, and quality, many now agree, declined. Volume often meant only repetition of the same information.

And yet the 1970s are certainly the most exciting and event-packed decade in American fishing publication. If there was a lot more junk, there was also a lot more good information. It probably wasn't a bad trade-off in the long run.

What follows is the story of a publishing phenomenon, perhaps several of them, and so I must brace myself for a good old-fashioned bibliographical essay. I don't like bibliographical essays as a rule, but I tolerate this one (and hope you will) because more than most it is about books I really enjoy. The only way to tell you about this part of our history is to name a lot of books. There are many things that distinguish the work of fly-fishing writers in the past fifteen years, but the one most immediately apparent is bulk. The technological revolution was accompanied by a publishing one that by its magnitude reveals just how popular fly fishing was, and just how enthusiastic its practitioners were about research and development. There is so much material to be introduced that it is impossible to do justice to its contents. We weren't just writing more books; we were thinking, creating, and arguing at an unprecedented pace. Anticipating the impossibility of doing justice to the contents of all the books and other publications you are about to read of in this chapter, I plan a more ruminative effort in the subsequent chapter, where at least a few of the intriguing recent developments in fly-fishing theory will be picked at in a more leisurely manner.

What happened to American fly-fishing theory in the years since 1970 could not have been imagined even ten years earlier. In the fifteen years following the publication of *Matching the Hatch* in 1955, some excellent books were published—Helen Shaw's *Fly-Tying* (1963), Haig-Brown's *A Primer of Fly Fishing* (1964), Arnold Gingrich's *The Well-Tempered Angler* (1965) and *The Gordon Garland* (1965), which he edited, Charles Fox's books mentioned earlier, most of Joe Brooks's books, including his *Complete Book of Fly Fishing* (1958), and Jim Quick's *Fishing the Nymph* (1960). The usual flow of how-to, where-to, and why-to fly-fishing articles appeared in the magazines, though Austin Hogan maintained that even here production was down, and that the "big three," *Sports Afield, Outdoor Life*, and *Field & Stream*, were publishing fewer than ten fly-fishing-related articles a year, which Hogan believed was a decline from earlier periods.

But imitative theory and fly-fishing entomology (and related pursuits, such as limnology and the study of baitfishes) had reached a stage where they were no longer easily advanced in a form short of a book. The books that did appear were for the most part either specifically directed (like Helen Shaw's book, aimed at fundamental fly-tying techniques) or general overviews (like Haig-Brown's and Brooks's manuals on the sport). Many were well written and quite valuable, and some pursued philosophical subjects and celebrated the sport rather than taught it (Gingrich's *Well-Tempered Angler* was probably his best book, certainly his best effort at explaining his own fishing code). But the theoretical leaps of the years between Jennings's book and Schwiebert's were mostly absent. That all changed in the 1970s, in a flood of new ideas, revived ideas, and, most of all, ever deeper information about what to imitate and how to imitate it.

If there was a single event that might be at least symbolically called the beginning of the new movement, it was probably an article written, appropriately, by Joe Brooks in *Outdoor Life* in August of 1970. In it, Brooks, by then perhaps the best-loved of American fishing writers and a leader of the old guard of fly-fishing generalists who understand the importance of some degree of imitation but do not usually apply much attention to entomology, told of meeting two young Michigan anglers who had developed some remarkably effective new flies. Brooks met them through a mutual friend, Scientific Anglers President Leon Martuch, and was unreserved in his praise (Brooks was always distinguished not only by his willingness to share his own knowledge but his instant recognition of the knowledge of others; he is one of few modern fishing writers about whom I have never heard *anyone* say anything bad). The anglers were, of course, Doug Swisher and Carl Richards, and when their book *Selective Trout* appeared the year after the article was published, it gave imitative theory a boost and started fly fishing on an entomological exploration that would have warmed the heart of Preston Jennings.

Selective Trout attempted much, and succeeded. It outlined many of the most important mayfly hatches in the best-known trout fishing regions, and from that solid entomological foundation it introduced a striking and still-provocative series of flies that were not so much new patterns as new types of flies. The most notable were the "No-Hackle" flies, prompted by the authors' realization that "hackle was a ridiculous imitation of legs." Other writers have pointed out that the "No-Hackle" was not truly original with Swisher and Richards, but the comment is vacuous; it is true that some flies as far back as the *Treatyse* seem to have been tied without hackles, but none were designed specifically to do what the Swisher-Richards flies did. The side-mounted wings and the Marinaro-style spread tails provided sufficient flotation to make these new dry flies extremely effective with their book's namesakes. But there was much more in *Selective Trout*. It contained the most detailed discussion of spinners

Arnold Gingrich shortly before his death in 1976. *Courtesy of The American Museum of Fly Fishing.*

Carl Richards (left)
and Doug Swisher.
Courtesy of Carl Richards.

yet to appear in an American book, it revived interest in parachute-style tying with
several new patterns of flies (parachute dry flies go back at least to the late 1920s;
William Brush's 1934 patented parachute hook had a short upward projection near
the eye upon which the hackle was wrapped), introduced several emerger patterns,
reacquainted anglers with hinged-body flies in its "Wiggle Nymphs," and by example
encouraged readers to break free from traditions, or at least reconsider traditions, in
developing their own imitations. *Selective Trout* has been one of the best selling of
American fly-fishing books; it has sold as many copies as *Matching the Hatch*, in
half as many years.

But in the long run it may be that the most important service that *Selective Trout*
provided fly fishers was in its illustrations. Here, at last, were sharp, large, color
photographs of the actual insects being imitated. Scientific works had contained such
photographs, but this was the first time they were made available in a fishing book,
and they were a significant advance over earlier illustrations. Some, such as those
in Wetzel's books, were often quite primitive. Even the illustrations in Schwiebert's
popular *Matching the Hatch* were small and vague, and are not now regarded as
especially useful even for color information. As well, the far more accomplished
insect portraits in the same author's *Nymphs*, for all their artistic interest, generally
show only the top or bottom side of the mayfly and stonefly nymphs, when fly tiers
are interested in both top and bottom sides. The photographs in *Selective Trout* and
subsequent books addressed those shortcomings with portraits of naturals from various
angles.

What followed the appearance of *Selective Trout* almost defies summary. It is

A Swisher-Richards No-Hackle.
Courtesy of Carl Richards.

like Theodore Gordon's wildest dreams coming true. The mayflies received unprecedented attention. Swisher and Richards were followed by several other books that concentrated most heavily on mayflies: Al Caucci and Bob Nastasi, two eastern anglers, produced *Hatches* (1975), an in-depth study of important mayflies from coast to coast, and introduced their "Compara-duns," hairwing dry flies (a pattern apparently borrowed from Adirondack fly tier Fran Betters; a similar style of fly had been suggested in *Selective Trout*, though its utility was not elaborated on) tied without hackle. Swisher and Richards were back with *Fly-Fishing Strategy* that same year, introducing their stillborn dun patterns to imitate flies unable to escape their nymphal shucks; the stillborn patterns were highly praised by fellow writers, but seem not to have caught on commercially or gained wide acceptance. If more information was needed, fishermen could add Fred Arbona's *Mayflies, the Angler and the Trout* (1980) or Charles Meck's *Meeting and Fishing the Hatches* (1977) to their shelves.

After far too long as the poor sisters of fly fishing, stoneflies and caddisflies received more attention. *Stoneflies*, by Richards, Swisher, and Arbona, appeared in 1983, the year after *Stoneflies for the Angler*, by Eric Leiser and Robert Boyle. Caddisflies received fresh treatment in Leonard Wright's *Fishing the Dry Fly as a Living Insect* (1972), in which Wright revived and refined techniques for twitching the floating fly to imitate the natural's motion on the water. *The Fly-Tyer's Almanac* (1975), edited by Dave Whitlock and Robert Boyle, contained two sections on the caddis, one by Larry Solomon, soon after coauthor of *The Caddis and the Angler* (1977) with Eric Leiser. Gary LaFontaine started modestly with caddis discussions in *Challenge of the Trout* (1976), then produced a much more substantial work, *Caddisflies* (1983), which seems to be comprehensive enough for almost all tastes.

The nymph had also arrived as a fit subject for repeated book-length treatments. It had been around for a long time, receiving much attention from British anglers because of the writings of G. E. M. Skues early in the century. His first two books, *Minor Tactics of the Chalk Stream* (1910) and *The Way of a Trout with a Fly* (1921), along with other writings of the period, established nymph fishing as an important part of fly fishing, even though many anglers on both sides of the ocean argued that the nymph was not as sporting as the dry fly. As pointed out in earlier chapters, occasional references to nymph imitation occurred in print in the United States well before the publication of Skues's first book, but interest in the imitation of immature forms of aquatic insects did not become anything like a movement in this country until after 1910.

In the teens, Louis Rhead occasionally wrote about nymph fishing, and soon after at least some other American anglers had begun to experiment with the flies. Samuel Camp discussed nymphs briefly in *The Angler's Handbook* (1925). Skues carried on correspondence with LaBranche, Hewitt, and other Americans, and hosted some of them when they visited and fished with him.

Eugene Connett, according to an article he wrote in the *Bulletin* of the Anglers' Club in 1959, had corresponded with E. W. Harding, author of *The Flyfisher and the Trout's Point of View* (1931) about nymphs, and in 1927 had even visited England and discussed nymph fishing with Skues. John Alden Knight occasionally wrote about it, and Bergman mentioned the nymph in *Just Fishing* (1933), then elaborated on his few simple patterns in *Trout* (1938). Articles in *Outdoor Life* in 1932 by Sid Gordon and *Field & Stream* in 1933 by Edward Hewitt helped, as did Hewitt's various books, mentioned in an earlier chapter. Jim Leisenring's little book *The Art of Tying the Wet Fly* (1941), with its brief instruction on imitating emerging nymphs, is often cited as an important step in nymph-fishing development, and by the 1950s, many writers, including Atherton, McClane, Ovington, Blades, Schwiebert, and others, were writing about the use of nymphs. At a time when western contributions to fly-tying literature were rare, Polly Rosborough's *Tying and Fishing the Fuzzy Nymphs* (1965) was an important exception, with its complete series of successful western patterns. Quick's manual on nymph fishing mentioned earlier was about the only all-around guide book, though, except for the excellent British works of Skues and Sawyer, which often had only limited application here. Of course many of the books already mentioned discussed nymph fishing, but nymphs usually took second place, at best, to dry flies, and even serious hatch matchers generally offered only a few generalized nymph patterns for all purposes. That changed dramatically in the early 1970s, primarily due to Ernest Schwiebert's *Nymphs* (1973). It has seemed to me that this book may well represent the most extraordinary one-volume accomplishment of any in the tradition of American angling entomology. Not only was it amazingly broad, the author's color illustrations were of a quality not previously seen in an angler's entomology. It was by any standard a mighty labor, and reaffirmed Schwiebert's position as the foremost spokesman of American angling entomology. Its depth might best be suggested by the expression of wonder I have heard from other experienced anglers, who can't imagine how one person could have managed to fish so many places in just one lifetime. Numerous other works followed it, including Charles Brooks's *Nymph Fishing for Larger Trout* (1976) and Gary Borger's *Nymphing* (1979). Brooks's book is often seen as the best companion for Schwiebert's; the latter is lacking in detailed instructions on fishing techniques, and the former contains a catalog of historically known and modern ways of fishing the imitations. J. Michael Migel and Leonard Wright edited *The Masters on the Nymph* (1979), a collection of instructions by some of the best-known writers of the day that revealed, among many other things, the amazing breadth of definition of what a nymph actually was, from Sid Neff's tiniest midges to Frank Sawyer's dainty British patterns to Charles Brooks's ''Maxi-Nymphs,'' large enough to be cast on spinning gear. The book had a high tolerance for diversity of approach.

A pleasant revival of a once-popular fly, the ''soft-hackles'' so often favored by W. C. Stewart and T. E. Pritt in the nineteenth century, was initiated by Sylvester Nemes in *The Soft-Hackled Fly* (1975) and subsequent writings. Nemes was inspired in part by the ''partridge spiders'' sold by Michigan tackle dealer Paul Young, and has become an ardent champion of these simple, traditional, and effective flies.

A number of the new books emphasized the importance of fishing a variety of ''midges''—that is, various insects in very small sizes—and Ed Koch codified his approach based on many years experience (and friendship with other such leading experts as Ed Shenk) in Pennsylvania in his *Fishing the Midge* (1972). The limestone country of south Pennsylvania (again, thanks to Koch, Shenk, Marinaro, Fox, and their colleagues) also had much to do with forming the attitudes and contributions of two authors writing on the imitation of terrestrials. Gerald Almy's *Tying & Fishing Terrestrials* (1978) and Loring D. Wilson's *Tying and Fishing the Terrestrials* (1978) revealed the breadth of opportunity now available to fly fishermen in imitating non-aquatic insects. Almy reminded readers that one of many reasons to look to terrestrials for good sport was that they were becoming increasingly important in trout diets:

> Terrestrials are the ardent dry-fly angler's ace-in-the-hole in the face of waning mayfly populations. Their resiliency and adaptability to changing environmental conditions is truly phenomenal.

There was no shortage of new books that introduced insects—dun, nymph, or other—in general. Borger's *Naturals* (1980) kept the discussion on a practically manageable level while maintaining scientific integrity. There was, at the same time that more and more nationally useful books were appearing, a fair production of regional books. Charles Brooks's *Larger Trout for the Western Fly Fisherman* (1970) and *The Trout and the Stream* (1974) concentrated on the Yellowstone country; Rick Hafele and Dave Hughes's *The Complete Book of Western Hatches* (1981) covered the area from the Rocky Mountains to the West Coast. All of these works showed a bright combination of awareness of eastern methods, fly patterns, and ideas with western adaptations where needed. Brooks has probably done more than any other writer to popularize extremely large and heavy stonefly nymph imitations, and Hughes and Hafele wisely built their book on some careful and impressively broad entomology combined with a reasonable survey of effective fly patterns, some historical, some the work of their contemporaries, and some their own. After many years of obscurity, George Grant brought out new editions of his two books, both first self-published, *The Master Fly Weaver* (1980) and *Montana Trout Flies* (1981), earning the recognition due him as one of the country's most original fly tiers; working with woven hair and monofilament, Grant has created flies of striking design, outgrowths of Montana's long tradition of fly-weaving. Regional fly-fishing books have found a sizable niche in the modern book market, though probably none of them are best sellers the way the occasional nationally oriented book may be. Books on Maine streamer trolling, or Michigan fly fishing, or the hatches of as small an area as Yellowstone Park are a healthy sign that the average fisherman will find fewer and fewer waters where the entomological homework has not already been done for him.

Gardner Grant, who has at various times been President of the Federation of Fly Fishers, Theodore Gordon Flyfishers, and The American Museum of Fly Fishing, told me a few years ago something I should have had the wit to see for myself, that saltwater fly tying is really the last great frontier of imitation. Traditional saltwater patterns (if something only thirty or forty years old can be called traditional) are mostly simple, not especially imitative of any one life form. That has changed dramatically since the early 1970s. Dan Blanton's Bay-Delta Eelet, Chico Fernandez's Glass Minnow, Dave Whitlock's deer-hair blue-crab imitation, and many others have come along in efforts to imitate saltwater fish foods more effectively. In the last few years anglers have been experimenting with epoxy-based bodies for permit and bonefish flies that Lefty Kreh believes will develop into a new generation of more effective patterns. Sea-life forms are almost as numerous as mayflies and other trout-stream insects, so there is indeed great room for exploring on this frontier.

Texts on how to tie flies have kept pace with books on what flies to use. Many of the books already mentioned deal to one extent or another with fly tying, but the modern era has produced a set of fly-tying masters as distinguished as its angling entomologists. Art Flick's *Master Fly-Tying Guide* (1972) followed the model of Helen Shaw's earlier book, with tier's-eye views of flies being produced by many of the best-known anglers, including Shaw on bass flies, Ed Koch on his famous midge series, Whitlock on his various western ties, Ted Niemeyer on his realistic nymphs, and Art Flick on his matchless Catskill dry flies. Most books on fly-tying since then have taken that same form. Some of the best are those by Poul Jorgensen, the gifted Denmark-born tier and author of several standard texts, Richard Talleur and Eric Leiser, whose books show immense sympathy for the beginner, and Jack Dennis, the Wyoming writer whose two books are an essential introduction to western fly tying.

Lefty Kreh with an
Atlantic salmon caught on
the Alta River in Norway.
*Photo courtesy of Lefty
Kreh.*

A fascinating book could be written about great American fly tiers. The craft
attracts many thousands of fishermen, it invites personal creativity as do few other
parts of the sport, and we never seem to get enough of new fly patterns and ideas,
however much we may stick with old favorites. There are so many outstanding modern
tiers that even a list of the ones that have received some national recognition would
take up several pages in this book, but in a chapter on fishing books I must at least
mention René Harrop of Idaho, whose superb ties graced the pages of Swisher and
Richards's *Fly-Fishing Strategy* and Whitlock and Boyle's *The Fly-Tyer's Almanac*,
Jack Gartside and Al Troth, both inventive and skilled tiers, and Ed Shenk, who has
mastered not only·tying but fishing of the entire range of fly sizes, from the smallest
dry flies to the largest sculpin imitations. There is an imbalance in our appreciation
of fishing history as long as we don't give credit to these and countless other skilled
anglers who would be much better known, but certainly no more skilled than they
already are, if they put their knowledge down in a book. As we already know from

the example of Theodore Gordon, you don't have to write a book to influence American fly fishing.

I do not consider the literature of entomology within the scope of this book (and will sympathize with those who think it should be), but it is worth pointing out that the science of entomology was moving along at an accelerating clip after about 1960; growing public interest in flies, along with an awareness of the importance of aquatic insects as indicators of environmental quality, had something to do with this, but ecological science publication experienced a rapid growth in many fields in that period. As more anglers became interested in entomology, there were more and more sympathetic scientists researching it.

At the same time, scientific understanding of trout ecology and behavior was improving. At least since 1836, when Ronalds introduced serious examination of the trout's vision to anglers, fly fishers have worked to understand what the trout sees and how it sees it, as well as to know as much as possible about the trout's world. The major books in angling literature that advanced appreciation of trout perspective include Ward's *Animal Life Under Water* (1919), Dunne's *Sunshine and the Dry Fly* (1924), Harding's *The Fly-fisher and the Trout's Point of View* (1931) from England, and books by Wells, Hewitt, and Connett here. More recently there has been much more produced, partly because the behavioral and ecological sciences allowed it. Of course most fly-fishing texts offer useful ecological information, but the scale of the presentation, as well as its sophistication, has been considerably increased in such popularly written books as Mark Sosin and John Clark's *Through the Fish's Eye* (1973), Vincent Marinaro's *In the Ring of the Rise* (1976), the British anglers Brian Clark and John Goddard's *The Trout and the Fly* (1980), Paul Johnson's *The Scientific Angler* (1984), and Leonard Wright's *The Ways of Trout* (1985). For the reader willing to wade through slightly more formal prose, and interested in the often greater rewards that come from formal quantitative studies, the scientific papers of Robert Bachman, C. E. Bassett, Neil Ringler, and others are exciting reading. Bachman and trout authority Robert Behnke have both contributed frequently to *Trout* magazine in recent years, lending a much-needed scientific perspective to the usual informal flow of information and opinion that appears in the fishing periodicals.

It is hard to overstate the contribution of these trout students to our fishing. Our awareness of trout response to light, temperature, turbidity, disturbances, and other environmental influences, and our understanding of how trout perceive food, fellow fishes, and predators, have been wonderfully improved. It is curious, I think, that advances in the study of trout behavior have not caught our imagination as anglers to the extent that entomological studies obviously have.

We have also been relatively slow to show interest in lakes; at least we have not matched British anglers in that regard, who have published profusely on lake flies and fly fishing. John Merwin's *Stillwater Trout* (1980) and Ron Cordes and Randall Kaufmann's *Lake Fishing with a Fly* (1984) are our two most important books on the subject, but we have far to go before we approach British anglers in understanding still waters, partly because we have had less need to do so. That is changing, however; as John Merwin and others have pointed out, we have more lakes and fewer streams every year.

I am not sure I would call it a trend, but it is at least a notable development that a number of writers in the 1980s have written advanced books on fly fishing that, though based on a solid knowledge of aquatic entomology, were nontechnical in approach. In a variety of ways these writers approached imitation seriously but without emphasis on keying insects. The most comprehensive in its coverage of natural trout foods was Dave Whitlock's *Guide to Aquatic Trout Foods* (1982). Whitlock, one of the best-known fly-fishing writers of the 1970s and 1980s and just possibly the most influential American fly tier since World War II, produced a portrait of the many kinds of aquatic creatures that was thorough and yet totally nontechnical, with virtually no dependence on Latin; simplifying the natural history and forms of these creatures, he succeeded in doing something very like what Louis Rhead had attempted, and, like Rhead, illustrated it with characteristic flair. One of the nicest of many touches was a fly-by-fly tour of what Whitlock carries in his own fly boxes, certainly something many readers wonder about their favorite writers. Datus Proper, in *What the Trout Said* (1982), explored both the history and the theory of trout-fly design (much in the tradition of Marinaro, who wrote the foreword for this book), concluding, among many other things, that the old imitation-versus-presentation quarrel is irrelevant because most fishing situations require some varying degree of attention to both. The book's unusually penetrating considerations of design (construction, proportion, and so on) of flies made it unlike many modern books, which concentrate on new fashions in patterns. Proper, instead, considered the elements of fly design as they have evolved, been tested, and accepted or rejected. Joe Humphreys, a Pennsylvania legend for his ability to take large brown trout on flies, wrote *Joe Humphreys's Trout Tactics* (1981), the consummate "no-nonsense" fly-fishing book, containing a host of re-finements on old techniques and introducing other techniques little enough known that they might as well be called new. This was almost exclusively a book about

Dave Whitlock demonstrating casting at a Berkley-Bud Lilly fly fishing program in West Yellowstone, Montana in the 1970s; the building in the background is now the International Fly Fishing Center. *Courtesy of Bud Lilly*.

locating trout and putting a fly in front of them, with heavy emphasis on special casting skills. Art Lee's *Fishing for Trout with Dry Flies on Rivers and Streams* (1983) was a comprehensive review of tackle and techniques that in some ways is sort of a grandson of LaBranche's book in its emphasis on a lifelike presentation (as opposed to a life-imitating fly). Like Humphreys, Lee relied on a general assortment of flies for most purposes, pointing out that some of the best dry-fly men he knows get along with only a handful of patterns. What makes the books similar, and what tempts me to call them evidence of a trend, is their reliance on fishing skill more than entomological studies. All four authors were well schooled in aquatic insects, and occasionally revealed their schooling in unavoidable Latin, but all expressed a viewpoint that was somehow beyond the insect-collecting passion (or fashion) of the 1970s. These books, and recent introductory texts by Craig Woods, Tom Rosenbauer, Dave Whitlock, Lee Wulff, and David Lee, seem to me a healthy direction for fly fishing to be going now that the hatches are getting well known.

At the same time that fly fishing for trout has experienced a boom in specialized studies, it has continued to inspire ''complete'' books that aim to do it all in one volume. There must be at least one new title of this sort a year, hopeful but short-lived books that lack either quality, marketing, or something else (author reputation seems important) and so are forgotten. Two have appeared since 1970 that seem to achieve something more permanent for themselves, though it still may be too early to tell.

The first was Joe Brooks's *Trout Fishing* (1972), an immensely popular book from an immensely popular fishing writer. It appeared only two years before his death, and is generally regarded as the culmination of his career as a writer. Produced in that now-lamented era when color printing was still reasonably cheap, it has more

Joe Brooks with an Argentinian trout. *From the Joe Brooks Collection, The American Museum of Fly Fishing.*

color illustrations—of flies, of happy people with obscenely large trout, of casting techniques, and of simply pretty fishing scenes—in one volume than usually appear in any ten today (the 1985 revised edition, though preserving Brooks's wisdom, lacks most of the color). With everything from a review of trout-fishing history to a gallery of mouth-watering trophy trout pictures, it was recognized as the true successor of Ray Bergman's *Trout*, and has sold well enough to earn that title.

Brooks was of the no-nonsense school of fishing instruction; this is above all a practical down-to-earth book, like Bergman's. It is strong on specific advice and, though Brooks obviously enjoyed fishing history and a good story as much as anyone else, you never forget you are listening to someone teach you how to fish. Perhaps it is just coincidence, but both Brooks and Bergman were the *Outdoor Life* fishing editor; maybe that desk brings out the "wise old uncle" writing style in anyone who sits at it. Whyever it occurs, the result is that Brooks introduced the reader to all the standard fly-fishing techniques, a remarkably broad array of flies, from ancient wet flies and South American streamers to the latest Swisher-Richards patterns, and all you really *had* to know about tackle, and did it with an utter lack of pretense or mystification. Ray Bergman would have loved it.

The second contender in the all-round trout fly-fishing book is in some ways nothing short of amazing. Already established, by *Matching the Hatch*, *Nymphs*, and *Remembrances of Rivers Past* (1973), as one of the giants of twentieth-century fly-fishing literature, Ernest Schwiebert saw his monumental two-volume *Trout* published in 1978. It was to be his greatest achievement. At nearly 1,800 pages, in two large volumes, it was by far the most ambitious trout-fishing (or fly-fishing) book ever attempted. It ranged, in unprecedented detail for a single book, through the history, tackle development, biology, environments, tackle, and techniques of fly fishing for trout.

Ernest Schwiebert, the well-traveled fly fisher, with a record Atlantic salmon from Iceland's Grimsa. *Courtesy of Orvis.*

The jury is still out on just where *Trout* fits in American fishing literature. The reviews were mixed. Many, including those in several prestigious publications not usually interested in fishing books, were effusive in their praise. Others were negative, some devastatingly so. The positive ones spoke vaguely (some, I must admit, suspiciously so; I would bet few reviewers of either position read the whole thing) of its hugeness, its great learnedness, its obviously tremendous research effort, and the author's winning literary style. The negative ones spoke of extensive sections paraphrased from technical publications, of embarrassing gaps in its research, of its excessive length, and of the author's awkward and annoying prose style. Rarely has a fishing book been the subject of such diversity of heated opinion. An extended study of the book's strengths and weaknesses is beyond me here; it is a massive, encyclopedic work, and I suspect that it will be quite some time before fly-fishing historians are able to judge where *Trout* will fit in angling's literary tradition.

But future historians may not judge us—whether as writers or as thinkers or as people—as much by our books as we have judged earlier generations. As the hundreds of pages you've already read (if you've gotten this far) suggest, fly-fishing history, at least its real day-to-day detail, is rarely found in books. It is found instead in other sources, including periodicals, catalogs, diaries, an assortment of other documents, interviews, and the vast attic-load of artifacts left behind. We have given future historians more to work with than previous generations gave me and my fellow historians, and nowhere have we been so generous with evidence in the past twenty years than in the production of periodicals.

Like the great sporting periodicals of previous ages, there is simply no summarizing what was said in this outpouring of millions of words on fly fishing. It is only practical to summarize how it happened.

Though it was not a fly-fishing magazine per se, the official publication of Trout Unlimited, *Trout*, started in the early 1960s. For many years its editor was Alvin Grove, whose high literary standards have been so roundly praised by several writers, including me, and whose obvious devotion to fly fishing had much to do with the magazine's direction toward fly fishers. The magazine has in recent years, under the editorship of Tom Pero, made a more self-conscious effort to be democratic, with lure- and bait-fishing stories given more prominence, but it also continues to be important to fly fishermen, not only for articles on fly fishing but for its excellent material on trout ecology.

But the acknowledged beginning of the fly-fishing-periodical boom occurred in 1969 with the first number of *Fly Fisherman*. Don Zahner, the founding editor, started the magazine in Missouri but soon moved it to Dorset, Vermont, where it resided for about a decade, when it was bought and moved to Harrisburg, Pennsylvania. *Fly Fisherman* lent fly fishing a sense of identity. As Arnold Gingrich observed in *The Joys of Trout*, "It says something about the status of our sport, if it shows that it can support a magazine that's devoted to it exclusively." Of course Zahner's magazine has done much more than that (though for most of its life there was real question whether or not the sport *could* support a magazine). It has served as a forum, an advertising clearinghouse, a newsletter for new ideas, and a sort of clubhouse-in-print for a generation of fly fishers. It more than any other one part of the fly-fishing revolution that has occurred since 1970 has been the unifying presence the sport needed to develop (commercially and theoretically) as fast as it has.

If nature abhors a vacuum, the magazine trade positively lusts after one, and *Fly Fisherman* could not hope to be alone for long. The first competition (I am not

Don Zahner *(left)* and John Merwin, founding editors of
Fly Fisherman and *Rod & Reel*. *Courtesy* Fly Fisherman *Magazine*.

considering various regional and local club publications, though some have been excellent and now approach venerability by magazine standards, especially Theodore Gordon Flyfisher's *Random Casts*, the *Bulletin* of the Anglers' Club of New York, and the Oregon Flyfisher's *Creel*), if it could be called that, came from *The Flyfisher*, the official publication of the Federation of Fly Fishermen. *The Flyfisher* was launched under the guidance of Arnold Gingrich, Jim Bashline, and Hermann Kessler in 1968, and though it has shared writers, advertisers, and most attitudes with the various commercial fly-fishing magazines, it has probably never been seen as much of a competitive threat because its circulation has rarely exceeded eight thousand. It has had a series of popular editors, with Joe Pisarro, Steve Raymond, Michael Fong, and now Dennis Bitton (who, in 1986, started an independent tabloid, *FlyFishing News, Views & Reviews*) in charge.

These two were more or less alone as "pure" fly-fishing magazines until the late 1970s. In 1977, Frank Amato Publications, already responsible for a general-interest magazine, *Salmon-Trout-Steelheader*, and a growing list of regional books, introduced *Flyfishing the West* under the editorship of Don Roberts. Within a couple years the magazine became *Flyfishing*, and it is now edited by Marty Sherman and has a national readership.

In 1979, then managing editor of *Fly Fisherman* John Merwin left that magazine, along with Kit Calabi and Charles Eichel, to establish *Rod & Reel*. At first a general-interest magazine aimed at the ''thinking angler,'' *Rod and Reel* eventually switched to fly fishing in order to find a market it could concentrate on successfully. In 1983, after several years of difficult struggle, the magazine was sold, equipment editor Silvio Calabi became editor, and John Merwin moved on to become my successor as Executive Director of The American Museum of Fly Fishing.

Fly tiers have been blessed with their own periodical since 1959, with the appearance of the United Fly Tyer's *Roundtable*. Primarily an eastern organization, United Fly Tiers has attracted writings from most of the famous American fly tiers over the years. Dick Surette published the first edition of his quarterly *Fly Tyer* in 1978, giving fly tiers yet another source of information on the latest fashions; that two such magazines could keep going is some testament to the hunger of fly tiers in this period for new patterns and more information on old patterns.

For those on the outside, the appearance of these magazines probably seemed like a perfectly natural thing; after all, look how popular fly fishing is becoming these days, right? Of course we can support a magazine. But it has rarely been that easy. *Fly Fisherman* survived, barely, hand-to-mouth for most of its life, and it was a hard climb to its present audited circulation of 137,000 (98,000 of whom subscribe, the rest being newstand sales). At that size it is the giant of the fly-fishing periodical world, more than twice as large as any of the others (and about one hundred times as large as the sport's most esoteric magazine, *The American Fly Fisher*, which was founded in 1974 by The American Museum of Fly Fishing to concentrate on the history of fly fishing).

Things do appear to have stabilized, as much as they ever do in the magazine business, by the mid-1980s. Real and perceived differences between the magazines are debated; *Fly Tyer* editor Surette (bought out by Dick Stewart in 1986) expressed defiant pride in his magazine's artless design; *Flyfishing* leans heavily to short, informational articles; *Rod & Reel* has its distinguished columnists—sort of anchor-persons—Lee and Joan Wulff; as does *Fly Fisherman* in Nick Lyons; and *Trout* with regular columns by Ernest Schwiebert, Dave Whitlock, Mike Fong, and Leon Chandler.

There is probably abundant room to debate whether the sport needs so many magazines. For some it must seem that one very good one would be enough, and for others twice as many as there are now would not satisfy their craving for reading matter. Like most other things in fly fishing, what you think is up to you, and whatever you decide there is probably someone ready to disagree.

As much as it pains a devoted bookman to admit it, the biggest advances in fly-fishing instruction in recent years have appeared not in print but on film. The appearance of videos—on fly tying, casting, stream tactics, exotic fishing trips, and most other topics previously covered by writers—are a significant event. No number of drawings, or even photographs, of something as initially confusing as fly casting can replace ten minutes of watching an expert, especially when you can stop his cast on the screen at any point for an extended meditation upon what he is up to at that instant. The same holds true for the mysteries of fly tying, or the intricacies of upstream nymph fishing. The videos have so far been the equivalent of the how-to and where-to articles in the magazines, but I have hopes that some adventurous filmmakers will try to evoke fly fishing's moods and joys, to do on film what fly fishing's best writers have done in print. There may be less of a market but there is surely no less of a need.

21

The Theoretical Angler

To aim flies at humans is to make fly-tying an art, or least a very clever craft. I have no philosophical objection to this. Certainly trout flies are decorative, and Salmon Flies more so. To make a fly well requires skill. With all these attributes, it is inevitable that flies should be tied for reasons other than fishing.

—Datus Proper, *What the Trout Said* (1982)

In his *A History of Angling*, Charles Waterman has a way of wondering about the evolution of fishing that often penetrates to fundamental issues. He wonders, for example, "about fishing lures and the mysterious ways in which they come and go." Recognizing that there really is something mysterious, in the sense of unsolved, about this, he suggests that there are at least several reasons we know of for the drifting popularity of lures. He includes some obvious ones, such as whether or not the lure is any good for catching fish, and some less obvious ones, such as whether or not the fish's habits change for some reason and lures simply won't work any more, or whether or not the manufacturer is able to market a lure, however effective it might be, successfully. More than we might be inclined to admit it, these same variables, and probably others, all act on the anglers of any era as they determine which are the "best" flies, which, I think, means which are the "favorite" flies. There is a difference between the two terms, but it is a little mysterious, too.

The "favorite fly" approach to fishing had its recognized heyday in the years between the Civil War and World War I. As we've already seen, it was not a simple movement, and its adherents did not attach their affections to certain flies *only* because they approved of them subjectively. But we have always seen that period as the time when the angler's choice of flies was least controlled by scientific awareness or imitative theory. There is something to the idea that the "favorite fly" period was different from ours, I will admit; there was a happy disregard among many anglers for any need to make their fly look like anything trout or bass eat. But the favorite-fly approach has not died. It has evolved, it has perhaps become slightly buried in

228

our decision-making processes when we choose our flies, but it is still there, and it is still common.

Fly theory is a complex blend of new ideas, resurrected old ideas, and fashion. In the great fly-fishing boom of the past fifteen years, a time of the brutal pummeling of certain popular adjectives, fly theory became, for many writers and commercial interests, of two parts. Everything new was "innovative," and everything else was "classic." Practically all announced innovations were in fact only modifications, and practically everything described as classic was in truth merely old. The rate of supposed change that the average angler, if he read a lot, would perceive was breathtaking. It looked as if everything, including rods and their design, lines and their floating or sinking capacities, and especially fly patterns, was becoming outdated on an almost yearly basis.

The perception was of course wrong. What was really happening was that minor modifications were being introduced at a wildly accelerated rate, and mixed in with them were a few real revelations, genuine innovations that because of the volume of the communication going on were difficult to sort out from all the chaff. This state of affairs was in good part the product of the communications revolution reported in the previous chapter, and of the intensification of recreational marketing of all kinds that necessarily thrives on the introduction of new products. Fishermen who tried to keep up with all the new stuff, though their fishing may well have benefited, were in good part victims of runaway fashions. To many old-timers the whole state of affairs was unseemly, but if you had the time it was also great fun and added zest to many a mailbox.

I was lucky enough to be new to fly fishing during that exciting period, and most of the time enjoyed being overwhelmed by information and advice from all these authorities. The trick that I and many thousands of others had to learn was that, though all these people—writers, tackle companies, speakers, shopowners—were as honest and sincere as any other group of people, it was essential not to believe any one of them blindly. In the last chapter I mentioned briefly the various modern approaches to fly casting. The newcomer could buy books by various experts and many others that would teach him to cast. Each had an approach that to some extent, sometimes to a startling extent, differed from the others, but *they hardly ever told you that*. Only the kindest would say that "here is something you must find a way to do that is comfortable for you." Fly theory has too often been approached the same way, and you must read a fair amount before you realize that you are hearing, in all these books, a disjointed and almost painfully polite debate. Swisher and Richards find Art Flick's Catskill dry flies ineffective with selective trout; British writers Goddard and Clarke find the Swisher-Richards No-Hackles impractical and awkward to use; John Betts finds an assortment of synthetic materials preferable to nonsynthetics that were being marketed as "premium"; you could leaf through that great and lamented repository of low-price fly-fishing gear, the catalog of the now-defunct Fly Fisherman's Bookcase and Tackle Service, and find book after book, each arguing its own approach over that of its fellows, page after page of published wisdom, and each one was touted (a word they loved) as the latest, freshest, *most innovative* thing. Definitiveness side by side with compleatness. Everything you needed. Everything you couldn't catch fish *without*. It was heaven, or hell, for the insecure angler.

By the early 1980s there was a fairly widespread feeling, apparently both among the public and in the fishing industry, that the boom of the 1970s had tended to hurry books and ideas into print, resulting in a glut that choked itself to death and a market that was more cautious about weekly miracles in fly theory. Now that things seem to have quieted down a little, we can even look back on the past fifteen years and make some tentative observations.

I realize that it's hard to know exactly what it is that most fly fishers think of fly theory, but we do have some hints. Some of the best have come from the nation's leader (in volume and probably in other ways) in fly sales, the Orvis Company.

John Harder has been in charge of the fly department of Orvis since the 1970s, and has described to me the usual trend (a good word for it, I think) of the waves of "innovative" new patterns. The year the book or article announcing the development appeared, orders came in by the hundreds. Within three years after that, the flies are hardly asked for. A rare one will last. Tom Rosenbauer, editor of the *Orvis News* and author of one of the best new general introductions to fly fishing, summed up the course of fly fashions in the 1970s in an article in *Sporting Classics* in March-April 1985:

> We can look back upon the 1970s as the decade of matching the hatch. Many writers began taking entomology and insect imitation very seriously, building upon the earlier research and writings of Flick, Jennings, Marinaro, and Schwiebert. Each new book claimed to have the ultimate insect imitation, the fly fishing public would go wild, and fly tiers would crank out thousands of dozens of No-Hackles and Comparaduns.
>
> By 1980, these flies were either absent from or reduced to a small corner of most fly catalogues. Effective patterns all, they are now kept in a small corner of most fly boxes for that difficult brown trout that resists all standard offerings.

Where this leaves the "average angler" we've been considering for some chapters now is hard to say. John Harder tells me that Orvis's national sales of traditional trout flies still dominate their categories. Far and away the best-selling fly (and dry flies are still the best sellers of all, however much we may have learned about trout preference for underwater foods) is the size 14 Adams. It, the Light Cahill, the Royal Wulff, the Black Gnat, the Hendrickson, the Quill Gordon, and others have weathered the onslaught of new flies with little damage. The only newcomer to join this list of big-selling dry flies has been Al Troth's Elkhair Caddis, which seems to be here to stay.

Orvis sales are certainly not the only way to measure fly popularity. We don't know what people who don't buy flies, who tie their own, prefer. As well, as John Harder points out, there are many excellent new patterns, including the No-Hackles and Comparaduns, that have found enduring niches in regions where such flies are especially useful. Enter a fly shop along the Henry's Fork, or in Sun Valley, or near the Letort, and you won't see the same selection you see in the Orvis catalog. The local shop, having less to be concerned with volume on special patterns, is more able to carry unusual or "exotic" or unusually complicated patterns than is a large retail-catalog outfit.

Of the several tackle dealers I have talked to, as well as among various writers and others well informed, most agree that the Hare's Ear nymph is easily the most popular of all trout nymphs. It is probably here, rather than in dry flies, that the commercial market has changed a lot. The variety of nymph patterns, including numerous giant stonefly nymphs and dragonfly and damselfly nymphs, seems to have increased dramatically over the years before 1970. Even here, though, you will find many fishermen willing to admit that the old Montana nymph, or the Woolly Worm, is probably as effective.

Tom Rosenbauer believes that the 1980s are revealing a greater emphasis on "meat flies," those being the large-fish flies—streamers, bucktails, bass bugs, and so on—and this fits with my own feelings about saltwater flies being something of a frontier for fly theory:

> Endless variations on the Muddler Minnow and Sculpin for trout, and a wide-open field in the area of bass and saltwater flies are creating a host of big, hairy flies. Many have strips of rabbit fur or marabou for wings, clipped deer hair heads, big doll eyes that actually roll around when the fly moves, and some colors that rival a freshly caught dolphin.

The new developments and directions in fly tying may not be so much a reaction against the 1970s and insect imitation as a growth in new directions. There is still ample interest in entomology, judging from the continued sale of the hatch-matching books, though it seems we can always carry our efforts further than we have; Ernest Schwiebert, in an article in *Fly Fisherman* in 1978, gave us forty different ant imitations, each aimed at a certain specific type of ant.

Trends in fly patterns or in fly design will always be a matter of subjective preference as much as technical advances. Make no mistake; we improve our flies. We do it slowly, and unevenly, and we make many false starts and take many wrong roads, but just as we improve our casting techniques, or our rods, we improve our flies. Even if an author's flies do not catch on, he has contributed to a sort of community consciousness—which is how I see the books, magazines, speeches, catalogs, and other forms of communication between fly fishers—and something more durable may pop up somewhere else because of what he did. If you read *Selective Trout*, even if you go back to your Red Quill and your Adams, you will never think of fly fishing quite the same as you did before.

On the other hand, what with so many flies that work so well, we need feel no special obligation to any traditionally proven pattern. The Muddler Minnow is recognized as the leading fish imitation, praised by countless writers as one of the most versatile and reliable of flies in the whole overstuffed fly box of history, and yet I know one thoughtful western guide and shopowner whose bins are loaded with progressive, exciting fly patterns who says, simply, "I don't sell 'em and I don't use 'em." He enjoys the variety of new flies, and knows that one of the things that makes customers buy flies is new ideas; everybody has heard of the Muddler, but these white Zonkers have been working just as well for us . . .

Fly fishers have outlived many a cracker barrel on the topic of new flies versus old. We know we improve flies sometimes, but it is problematic whether a new fly is better because "the fish hasn't seen it before," that being a common explanation of why we have to have new flies sometimes. Now that more fish are managed by catch and release, a fish that falls for a fly may live to make another decision, and so maybe we should be studying the trout's capacity to learn. Informal experience, as I read and hear it, suggests that many trout can be caught by the same fly repeatedly, but informal experience leaves a lot to be desired. New flies may work (or seem to work) better for many reasons. They may actually be better. We may, to borrow an idea from Charles Waterman, have used a certain fly pattern so much that the fish most susceptible to it (for whatever combination of reasons) have all been taken, leaving less willing fish. We may fish new flies with more enthusiasm and more concentration, and thus more effectiveness; renewed confidence is a great killer of fish. We may fish the new fly with greater skill than we had most of the years we fished the old fly, and our average score may be improving. Some combination of these reasons and others may cause us to catch more fish. We're probably better off not knowing for sure, and that is an attitude I hardly ever take about anything, so don't think I am offering it lightly. Intangibles are important to fly fishing, and so are imponderables.

But we have several centuries of fly theory to ponder; it is a gloriously tangible record in some ways, and there is a lot we can do with it even if we can't agree on whose ideas were best of all. The American literature of fly theory offers lessons for embryonic experts who intend to burst upon the world with their system. Some of the lessons have to do with flies, and some with fishermen's attitudes. Most of the time the two topics cannot be separated anyway.

Rule One: Don't insult the past. You may never realize the extent to which you are a product of it, and if you cut yourself off from all that tradition, learning, success, and companionship you cut yourself off from all the other people who are still attached to it. Louis Rhead is the best example of someone who broke this rule. Vincent Marinaro is a superb example of someone who broke with tradition without offending it; in *A Modern Dry-Fly Code* and *In the Ring of the Rise* he listened closely to his predecessors, he talked things over with them, and he built on what they had learned as he discarded some of what they believed. I'm not yet sure if Swisher and Richards were impolite to the past, partly because they were probably unaware of much of it; they used Marinaro's split-tail approach without acknowledging that he preceded them, but they also reintroduced hinged-body flies, popularizing them after Keene and Rhead were unable to.

Rule Two: Keep it Simple. This applies to individual flies and to any overall system. Again, Marinaro: "I am continually astonished by the fact that the most killing flies in fly-fishing history are of very simple construction." There is more truth there than there might appear to be. It is true that simple flies are killing. It is also true that simple flies become successful for other reasons. Incredibly involved flies, like the Victorian salmon flies, are not susceptible to widespread use because they are too hard or too time-consuming to make. Louis Rhead cut himself off from the self-sufficient fly tier partly by not giving those tiers a chance to tie his "nature flies," which he manufactured for sale, apparently in the hope of cornering the market on them. He cornered the market all right, but nobody cared. Rhead's mistake was compounded by his flies being complicated to tie, even had he decided to tell readers how to do so.

This rule should not be seen as a bad reflection on those gifted patient craftsmen who build incredibly realistic nymphs and perfectly accurate traditional salmon flies. They are contributing greatly to the craft, both by keeping precious skills alive and by constantly inventing techniques that can be applied to more easily tied flies. J. Harrington Keene's attempts at ultrarealism, at least as they appeared in the drawings in his publications, were striking, but they are nothing compared to the works of modern masters like Ted Niemeyer and Poul Schmookler. And a host of modern tiers—I think immediately of Bill Hunter, Ted Godfrey, Poul Jorgensen, and the late Syd Glasso, but there are many more—are keeping alive the full-dress Atlantic-salmon-fly craft. My point is not to say these people are not doing something important. It is instead to suggest that the future expert will not build his following and reputation if his theory requires two hours per fly.

So this rule, or your compliance with it, depends upon how widely you want your brainchild to appear on the streams. If you are content to know that a few fishermen believe in your flies, go ahead with individually attached gill filaments and articulated claws on the size 18 nymph.

Rule Three: But don't make it *too* simple. This one has little to do with fly effectiveness on fish. It has to do with what most fly tiers want to do. They like variety. *Fly Tyer* magazine proves that every time it appears, and various fly-pattern dictionaries, the biggest of which lists about fifteen thousand flies and variations on flies, prove it even more completely.

If you claim your technique can take every fish in the stream (The Hewitt Fish Magnet, let's call it) on a Zug Bug tied backwards on a size 17 Partridge hook, at least two things will happen: (1) hardly anybody will believe you; (2) nobody, or almost nobody, will be interested in fishing that way. Fishing's variety—a suite of factors ranging from water-type variation to the joys and frustrations of trying to find out which of a thousand insect species is of interest to the trout and then trying to imitate it—is one of its essential qualities. The significance of that quality was captured in G. E. M. Skues's wonderful tale of Theodore Castwell, an obnoxious sport who upon dying was condemned to the fly fisher's hell: a beautiful chalkstream whereon he was obliged to make perfect cast after perfect cast with perfect equipment, and each cast yielded a perfect two-and-a-half pound trout. No change from perfection, no change in the rise or the hatch or the tackle. Castwell, when he saw the water, thought he'd gone to heaven, but after several hours he grew weary and asked to rest, but his "guide" would not permit it:

> "Then do you mean that I have got to go on catching these damned two-and-a-half pounders at this corner forever and ever?"
> The keeper nodded.
> "Hell," said Mr. Castwell.
> "Yes," said his keeper.

Most fly tiers have some touch of Midas in their soul—they hoard materials, they look for new ones, they listen eagerly to new applications for old ones. They may be interested in synthetic materials, but the advent of synthetics proved that even fly-tying materials generate loyalty in fly fishers, who show every sign of increased enthusiasm for chicken necks, duck flank and wing feathers, deer hair, and dozens of other organic materials, an enthusiasm supported by such impressive advances in fly-tying materials as the stunning "genetic" hackles produced by Henry Hoffman, Robert "Buck" Metz, and others who are mass-producing feathers of a previously unimagined quality. There are probably many more amateur fly tiers tying full-dress Atlantic salmon flies today than there have been at any other time in this century; they are doing it out of a sense of craft and tradition, both of which are great fun for many people. A fly theory that either eliminates the need for all this frivolous exercise, or openly rejects it, is not going to get very popular.

Rule Four: Don't expect too much. Fly-tying conventions, and favorite fly patterns, have shown an incredible resilience in the face of new ideas. There is an unrespected inertia in public taste in flies that appears to give way to new ideas but really only absorbs the shock and returns to the old way. Enough shocks and the taste will be noticed to have taken on some new moods, but the bulk of the thing stays the same for decades, even centuries. It is fifty-two years since *A Book of Trout Flies* was published, and in that period millions of people have fly fished, thousands of them chattering away at each other in print and meetings on the subject of the dry fly, and yet the basic design of the dry flies used by most people, the well-known "trout flies" of standard pattern, has not changed at all. I think we have overstated just how much they changed even in the previous fifty years, during which we took Halfordian theory and modified it to American purposes. The form is tough. Most fly theorists, and I think most fly tiers, however interested they may be in new ideas, have a fundamental, perhaps even subconscious, sense of what is merely fashionable and what is actually an enduring form. The faster new ideas appear, the more difficult it is for any one of them to get enough attention and respect to be incorporated into the lasting body of fly theory. The near-impossibility of proving to the public that a new fly pattern or new design is significantly better than old patterns and designs makes it hard for the best new ones to get a toehold. We get comfortable with what we know. We enjoy trying new things, but we don't forget our roots.

Rule Five: Do your homework. If my reading of fly-fishing history has shown me anything, it has shown me that we are much better reinventors than inventors. That is probably because fly tying is for all its excitement a relatively narrow craft. Sam Slaymaker, author of one of the nicest of the modern simple introductory books on fly fishing, *Tie a Fly, Catch a Trout* (1976), has written that "After all, there are only so many ways to catch a fish on flies, and each has been exhaustively explored." To that I add this: There are only so many ways to tie materials on a hook, and though they have not all been exhaustively explored, many thousands of reasonably intelligent fishermen before you have thought hard about them. I am a mediocre fly tier at best, and even I have personally discovered several techniques a century old. It was very exciting. It made me feel, well, "innovative." Later I discovered I was only "classic." The discoveries were still just as much fun even if they weren't genuine discoveries, but I wasn't planning to write a book about them.

Before announcing that you have perfected a new fly theory, at least look at some of the better reviews of past theories. Datus Proper, in *What the Trout Said*, Ernest Schwiebert in *Trout*, Vincent Marinaro in *A Modern Dry-Fly Code*, and Lee Wulff in *Lee Wulff on Flies* will give you a start, and tell you the names of many others you should read next. They will also disagree, you may notice, about who before them was right, and what past theories should be most useful to us now.

If these rules are discouraging, if they make the American fly-fishing scene appear chaotic, undisciplined, and full of eccentricity and stubbornness, they are also a cause for celebration. Fly fishing is practiced by a lot of people who, like John Atherton, don't want to turn a sport into work. For one of them there may be no greater joy than the study of hooks, no more exciting development in the past twenty years than the "Flybody Hook" that had brief fame in the 1970s. For another the arrival of the Matuka-style wing from New Zealand may be the answer to his lifelong perplexity with streamer wings that get hooked underneath the body. For another the mere purchase of neat stuff may be the best part of the sport; John Harder tells me that though Orvis gets frequent requests for hackle necks with size 20 to 28 hackles on them, the company receives so few orders for hooks in those sizes that it's hardly worth keeping them in stock. His opinion is that precious few people actually get around to tying up many size 24s compared to the attention those small flies get in the magazines. There are probably many reasons, and different ones for every fly fisher, why fly theories come and go in such mysterious ways. Some of them have to do with fashion, some with the actual fish-catching qualities of the flies, and I'm sure there is much more to it than what I have suggested in these few rules. Perhaps most important of all, I have neglected the whole subject of how we define fly fishing, considering that topic, with all its semantic splendor and religious intensity, worthy of a chapter of its own.

22

The Organized Angler

We, in conclave assembled, out of a firm and abiding conviction that fly fishing as a way of angling gives its followers the finest form of outdoor recreation and natural understanding, do hereby join in common effort in order to maintain and further fly fishing as a sport, and, through it, to promote and conserve angling resources, inspire angling literature, advance the brotherhood of angling and broaden the understanding of all anglers in the spirit of true sportsmanship.

Preamble to the Constitution of the
Federation of Fly Fishermen, 1965

We have more information on the "average" fly fisher now than we have had at any time in the past. It may not be enough to generalize too broadly from, but it's probably more than most of us want to know anyway. The commerce of fly fishing, especially the burst of new businesses and expanded old businesses, has had the nice side effect of studying what before had been a pretty loosely identified group of people.

Even at that, it is impossible to know how many fly fishers there are. It depends partly upon who should be included. If you include everyone who has bought a fly line, there may be six million. If you include only those who are serious about it (whatever that means; let's say it means people who consider it one of their two or three favorite pastimes), maybe there are one million. *Fly Fisherman* editor John Randolph has had as much reason as anyone to think about these numbers:

I estimate 1 million committed fly fishers and 500,000 who identify themselves as fly fishers as a lifestyle commitment—they are our potential readers, for they use their leisure time for fly fishing and their perspectives are those of a fly fisher. Ninety-eight percent of our readers are male, and I suspect that carries throughout the sport. Leon Chandler has estimated 500,000 fly fishers in Japan, where the sport exploded into popularity in the '60s and '70s. France and Germany are currently experiencing the explosive growth in fly fishing, perhaps because the post-war generation is experiencing the same pursuit of the upscale or the excellent as we are in the U.S.

John's comment about women in the sport is revealing. While some organizations, especially the Federation of Fly Fishers, have devoted considerable energy to encouraging women to fly fish (though mostly reaching only wives of men who already fish), there are still fly fishing clubs in this country that do not allow women even to speak to them, much less join. Since at least the 1880s, the sporting press has contained hopeful announcements about the increasing numbers of women who were becoming fly fishers. In the absence of any evidence to the contrary, and in the face of considerable evidence to support me, I must say that John is right. If there has been an increase in the percentage of women fly fishers even in the past twenty years, their total is still tiny, and the sport does not show signs of changing that. A panel of sociologists could probably give us a list of reasons why the sport is so determinedly male dominated. An interesting book could be written on the power of sexism in field sports like fishing and hunting, but I'm not about to write it here. I suspect that the percentage of women will continue to increase, very slowly, but that fly fishing will continue to be a male activity for a long time. Overt sexism has declined some in fishing writing and, presumably, among fishermen too, but fly fishing, unlike the business world, is not a widely recognized and attractive bastion of maleness. The feminist movement has had more important things to do than redress imbalances among recreationist anglers.

Who, then, are the fly fishers? The best source of information on them is probably what comes from *Fly Fisherman's* reader surveys. Here are some statistics from a 1983 survey. I realize that readers of *Fly Fisherman* may in several ways be untypical because anyone interested in subscribing to a sport's magazine may be a little different, on the average, from all those who don't bother. The average income among those surveyed in 1983 was $62,590. That's a lot of graphite rods. The average value of their homes was $135,903. It is important to point out that average is higher than median, by the way. The median value of their homes, for example, was only $92,030. Their average age was about forty-five. One percent were women. Seventy-nine percent attended college. Eighty percent were married, and forty-two percent said someone else in the household also fly fished.

Ninety-five percent fished for trout, sixty-nine percent for bass, fifty-nine percent for panfish, and forty-five percent for salmon or saltwater fish. They averaged 22.5 fly fishing days per year, spending an average of $962 per year on the trips. They averaged 2.4 companions when they fly fished.

According to a 1985 study, 23.9 percent fly fished exclusively, using no other method; roughly three-quarters of the readers were multimethod fishermen, which surprises me, at least. Eighty-five percent of them had fly fished at least six years, and sixty-five percent at least eleven years. The 93.8 percent of them who owned single-action fly reels owned an average of 3.6 of them, and the 72.7 percent of them who owned graphite rods owned an average of 2 of them.

The biggest shame, of course, is that nobody took this survey thirty years ago. Many people, including John Randolph and me, believe that many changes have occurred in fly fishing in the past thirty years that are not easily quantified but that are significant. My own involvement in fly fishing is too short—fifteen or so years —for me to be entitled to the "things ain't what they used to be" attitude because I wasn't there when they used to be, but I hear from people who were that, indeed, things ain't. The boom in fly-fishing popularity had many effects, including a rising popularity of fly fishing as a fashionable recreation. The sport, for all the reasons it has attracted people for centuries, was "discovered" by new groups of people.

Fly fishing has caught the imagination of the same "upscale" recreational market

that latched onto backpacking, crosscountry skiing, and other relatively noncon-
sumptive sports in the period since 1970. Again I relinquish the floor to the greater
experience of John Randolph:

> The over-achiever: It has been my observation that Jimmy Carter is almost our
> archetypical new FFM reader—the new Catholic, so to speak. He proselytizes, spouts
> fly-fishing cant, buys all the new equipment, reads all the books (old and new), and
> must fish all the hallowed waters. And he cannot understand why *everyone* does not
> fly fish. We get them as an avid reader when the bug bites that hard, and we hold
> them until everything they read becomes *deja vu*. When one man becomes jaded
> versus another is a function of his mental state: some are jaded by age 30; others
> (Lee Wulff, for example), are still young and looking for new ways at age 80.
>
> During my lifetime, fly-fishing sportsmen have changed the way they view the
> sport, just as blood-sport hunters have changed since I grew up on the farm (and in
> the city). The new upscale fly fisherman may not be a yuppie (with all that connotes)
> but he is very often an over-achiever (as is Carter, believe me). He (the new over-
> achiever) worked too hard from grammar school through grad school and thence into
> business or the professions. He is typically the head of a business, a doctor or a
> lawyer, and as a member of the top 30 percent of our demographic profile he brings
> his zealous nature into his recreation—fly fishing. He often seeks to devour the craft
> and science and techniques of the sport, including the ultimate in-group club card,
> bug latin. It's heady stuff for the relatively small group of males who thirst after all
> the laurels. The rest I think are satisfied with fishing home waters and doing, in a
> relaxed way, things that matter, either onstream or at the tying vise at home. They
> are more like the old-fashioned sportsmen that I grew up with, and am more com-
> fortable with.

One interesting facet of this growth, even its inclusion of the "over-achievers"
described by John, is that it has tended to open up the sport in some ways. A lot of
these people have attended fishing schools, the first established by Orvis in 1966,
with Bud Lilly, Fenwick, and then many others following. There is an egalitarianism
in this sort of setting that, though it will never suppress fly fishing's snobbish tendencies totally, does even things out a bit and expose more people to certain standard
codes of behavior and certain relaxed approaches to the sport. As John also points
out, this new fly fisher is less likely to be hidebound about something like the dry
fly, and willing to fish nymphs or try other techniques, than someone who came to
the sport from some closed circle of relatives or companions.

The evening out is also carried on by the incredible ease with which the modern
fly fisher can travel and be exposed to many different kinds of fishing and many
different fishermen. Only money—not in short supply among fly fishers, judging
from the surveys—stands between him and Argentina, New Zealand, Alaska, Nepal
. . . The choices are as wide as the world. Thanks to travel, as well as to continuing
commerce and its published communications, there is an interchange of information,
ideas, and values among fly fishers in all parts of the country, an interchange that
has never before approached its current level. All fly fishers do not participate in it,
and many still go along doing "things that matter" on their home waters with no
real interest in all this activity, but the opportunity is there, and the opportunity is
improving.

Perhaps the most significant way it has improved is through organization. Anglers
have long enjoyed joining clubs, and there were growing numbers of fly-fishing clubs
by the early 1960s, when the idea of a national organization appeared.

Depending upon whom you ask—easterner or westerner—you will be told that the idea originated in the councils of the Theodore Gordon Flyfishers of New York or the Evergreen Fly Fishing Club of Washington or The McKenzie Flyfishers of Oregon. It appears to have been an idea that many people recognized as a good one at about the same time. Ed Strickland, secretary of the Federation of Fly Fishers, which resulted from the first meetings in the early 1960s, also wrote a short history of how it happened:

> It is easy to pinpoint the first overt move. The McKenzie Flyfishers of Eugene, Oregon, were organized in May, 1964, and announced that one of their goals would be to promote a national organization. The club sent a task force of William Hilton, William Nelson (who had moved from Everett, Washington, to Eugene), Webb Russell and Stanley Walters to Aspen, Colorado, in September, 1964, for a meeting with [Gene] Anderegg, who had been authorized by the Theodore Gordon club to talk with various fishermen across the country. After an extended discussion at Aspen, agreement was reached on a possible plan for a national organization, and the McKenzie Flyfishers volunteered to host a national convention.

Gene Anderegg is the acknowledged leader of the national communications that took place, with Lee Wulff and Ed Zern providing substantial support in New York. About a dozen clubs were represented at the first Conclave in 1965; all but one, T.G.F., were from California, Washington, or Oregon, and the resulting Federation of Fly Fishermen (changed to Fly Fishers in the early 1980s) has always been perceived as a western organization though gradually its representation in the East and South has increased.

The Federation developed around a loosely connected administrative structure where it was, truly, a federation of clubs. By 1969 there were fifty-nine clubs and 3,500 members sending in their money to receive *The Flyfisher*, which had begun publication the previous year. By 1974 there were 120 clubs and seven thousand dues-paying members, and today there are more than twice that many clubs and something less than nine thousand members. The disparity in growth between number of clubs and number of members is because a club can become affiliated with the Federation though none of the club's members are necessarily members of the Federation.

The early Conclaves were a revelation in many ways; they quickly became known as the premier opportunity for fly fishers to meet the various famous anglers of the day (the "greats and near-greats," as they have so often been called in promotional mailings). They also became, like any other convention, an annual show of new products. Most of all, however, they were the American fly fisher's first chance to recognize his power. The Federation's preamble, quoted at the beginning of this chapter, summed up the variety of goals.

Having had the opportunity to look over many of the Federation's past publications and learn about their work, and having worked with the Federation when I was at the Museum and later as a member of the Executive Committee and a Senior Advisor, I find it difficult to summarize what it has done. It has been by choice (though not with unanimous agreement among its leadership over the years) an organization that emphasized work on the local and regional level—what has often been called a grassroots organization. The clubs of the Federation have, with the support and sometimes the guidance of the national leadership, accomplished hundreds of important projects in conservation, public education, and so on, as well as having an inordinate amount of fun in their respective groups. The Federation's enormously successful Whitlock Vibert Box program, put to use by Federation clubs in many states and other countries, is one of their true showpieces of conservation work. The Federation has, in short, had a huge effect on the fly-fishing subculture, in good part because it provided a way for that subculture to focus on itself. There are now several regional conclaves besides the national one, each emphasizing and promoting the types of fishing (warm-water, saltwater, cold-water) available in each region.

On the other hand, with its club-oriented administrative structure, the Federation has more or less eliminated itself from the possibility of becoming a large, powerful national organization such as Trout Unlimited has become in the past few years. It is not impossible for a grassroots organization to be a powerful national presence, but experience in the conservation business suggests that it is very difficult. Arnold Gingrich commented on this problem in *The Joys of Trout*, and his remarks are essentially valid more than a decade later:

> Meanwhile TU has become, of late years, a great empire, with professional expertise and a proliferation of offices, while FFF remains a small republic, staffed and manned exclusively by volunteers, most of whom would appear to be descendants of Henry Clay, the man who would rather be right than president.

Gingrich wasn't being cranky; he was, through the Federation's first decade, one of their most visible and ardent supporters, and regularly served as emcee at important conclave functions. He was merely commenting on a problem that the organization has never come to terms with, though it has frequently tried.

In the meantime the Federation has taken an ambitious and promising step to increase their influence in another direction, through the establishment of the International Fly Fishing Center. The Center also has a long list of paternity claimants, people who had the idea first. In the late 1970s the idea began to surface formally in meetings of the national executive committee: the Federation should have a permanent home, and it should be in West Yellowstone, Montana, site of most conclaves by then. At the 1980 conclave, the new President of the Federation, Errol Champion, announced the campaign to raise money for and then build an International Fly Fishing Center. The town of West Yellowstone, at the West Entrance to Yellowstone National Park, offered a long-term lease on a prime building site, a fund-raising firm was hired, and hopes were high.

The Museum of American Fly Fishing (now the American Museum of Fly Fishing) was invited by the Federation to join in the campaign, and after a good deal of soul searching, the Museum's Board of Trustees voted to take part in a campaign to build a center that would house not only the Federation but the collections and exhibits of the Museum. It was a grand dream, and it never looked grander than at the 1981 conclave in West Yellowstone, when former President Jimmy Carter and numerous other luminaries, including Lee and Joan Wulff, honorary cochairpersons of the drive, broke ground for the building. The groundbreaking looked justified because the fund-raising firm was already reporting pledges and donations of several hundred thousand dollars.

The project didn't work, and it is still hard to say why. There was widespread conviction, with considerable evidence, that the fund-raising firm fell flat on their faces (or the Federation's faces, I suppose); by early in 1982 it was clear that the pledges were not firm or mounting up as announced. Various attempts in 1982 to regroup and initiate a new fund-raising campaign never got far enough along to make a difference, and the economic climate reduced donations further. Early in 1983 the Museum announced that it would stay in Vermont and provide the Federation with

The International Fly Fishing
Center, West Yellowstone,
Montana. *Courtesy of the
Federation of Fly Fishers.*

extensive exhibits if the Center was built. There was, after the great start, confusion, disappointment, and some bitterness. By August of that year an alternative plan had been developed that redirected fund raising toward renovation of an existing building, the very large and historic Union Pacific Railroad dining hall, known in West Yellowstone as the Convention Center. This building, long the site of conclaves anyway, became the International Fly Fishing Center, with a ribbon-cutting ceremony in August of 1984 attended by the Governor of Montana and other regional figures. With seventeen thousand square feet of floor space, this building has met most of the needs anticipated by the planners of the Center that was never built. There is a modest but promising library, extensive exhibits of the Federation's fly collection, the Pat Lilly Art Gallery, and remodeled meeting rooms besides the large convention space/banquet hall. With a second-wind fund-raising effort that brought in substantial support, and with volunteer help from nearby fishing clubs, the Federation has made a start at realizing the dream of a nationally visible fly-fishing center that would give the sport not only a pulpit but a symbolic home.

The Opening gala dinner at the dedication of the International Fly Fishing Center, West Yellowstone, Montana, August 1984. *Photograph by Larry Aiuppy.*

Efforts to establish an institution devoted to fly fishing history began almost as early as effort devoted to creating the Federation. There are now several fishing museums in North America, including the Freshwater Fishing Hall of Fame in Hayward, Wisconsin (this is probably the largest) and the Gladding International Sport Fishing Museum in South Otselic, New York, but these are general-interest museums devoted to all kinds of sport fishing. There are also many substantial (not to say spectacular) private collections, such as that held by the Anglers' Club of New York, where some of eastern fishing's most revered relics are stored. A public fly-fishing museum was apparently first thought of the same year that the Federation held its first conclave, and in this case it is clear who had the idea.

It started, like so many other good things in fly fishing, at a meeting of the Theodore Gordon Flyfishers. Hermann Kessler, then art director of *Field & Stream* (and designer of the Federation's symbols and letterheads at about this time), had just the previous year overseen the production of an article by Harold Blaisdell on the "Americana of Angling" for his magazine. Part of the research was conducted at the old Orvis building in Manchester, Vermont, where some amazing items had survived stored for nearly a century in the attic. After thinking this stuff over for a few months, Kessler encountered Leigh Perkins, then new president of Orvis, one evening at the Williams Club after a meeting of T.G.F. Kessler told the story in a short history of the Museum in *The American Fly Fisher* in the fall of 1978:

> After that meeting, down in the bar, I offered my idea for a museum to Perkins. Present at the table were Lee Wulff, Helen Shaw, Richard Rossenbach, Wes Jordan and some other members of TGF.
> Six months or so later, Leigh came back to me and showed an interest in my developing the museum idea. Months later, after much correspondence and many phone calls, a meeting was called, at which time a board of trustees was formed. At this first meeting, Leigh suggested that a president should be chosen.
> It was Arnold Gingrich, bless him, who reminded Leigh that inasmuch as the museum idea was presented to him by me, I should be the first president.
> And so it was ordained. I am still pleased about it.

In the summer of 1967 the Museum opened its doors in rented space on one end of the Orvis store in Manchester. At first a showplace for what was primarily Orvis memorabilia, the Museum soon drew a flood of old tackle and books from many sources. By the early 1970s it was the only place the public could go to see the best craftsmanship of Leonard, Orvis, Payne, Gillum, and many other rod builders, as well as the tackle of many famous anglers. Since its incorporation in 1968 as a nonprofit institution it has not been an "Orvis Museum," though it has unfortunately labored under that public image sometimes. The support of such independent leaders in angling as Arnold Gingrich, Gardner, Grant, and Leon Martuch, all of whom served as president, demonstrated that the Museum really was a nonpartisan collection.

Those who were involved at the Museum knew all along it was a real museum, with a real mission. The guiding light for the first ten years, as far as museum management and historical accuracy, was Austin Hogan, who served as voluntary curator and, after 1974, as founding editor of *The American Fly Fisher*. Austin had devoted many years to researching fly-fishing history and was recognized as the leading authority on American angling history. The combination of his expertise and the public stature of Arnold Gingrich, Alvin Grove, Harry Darbee, Ernest Schwiebert, Steve Raymond, Charles Brooks, Ed Zern, and the many others who served on the Museum's board gave it public respectability and the kind of publicity needed to

The American Museum of Fly Fishing, Manchester, Vermont
Courtesy of the Museum.

attract donations of money and tackle. The collection grew quickly. There are now over one thousand rods, four hundred reels, and many thousands of flies and miscellaneous items, as well as a library approaching two thousand volumes. There is a microfilm reader-printer (donated by 3M) and complete runs on microfilm of *Forest and Stream* and *The Spirit of the Times*. There are the personal libraries of Arnold Gingrich, Theodore Gordon, Ray Bergman, and John Atherton, as well as the fly collections of Atherton and Preston Jennings. There are rods 150 years old, and prototypes of the first Fenwick graphite and Don Phillips boron rods.

Even more impressive, in 1983, after fifteen years as tenants, the Museum bought its own home, a lovely building on the old square in Manchester Village, and completed the move in time for a grand opening in 1984. After the disastrous initial fund-raising campaign to build the jointly backed International Fly Fishing Center, it seems nothing short of remarkable that by 1984 both the Federation and the Museum were in their own permanent homes. The Museum is now housed in a professional facility with full security and atmospheric controls and modern gallerys and storage spaces. Those who have seen the whole process shake their heads and say that it's been a long road from the Williams Club.

Like the Federation, the Museum has been the work of too many people to name. Leigh Perkins, Austin Hogan, and Gardner Grant have been the real heroes of the Museum's development, but dozens of names come to my mind, people who worked their tails off just because they knew that "this history stuff" was important. The Museum needed lots of labor and love. It needed, in the words of Arnold Gingrich, people willing to go out there and "rassle anyone in the crowd for five dollars." It has been blessed with good rasslers.

Part of the fly-fishing renaissance of the past twenty years has been a growth in

An exhibit from The American Museum of Fly Fishing at the International Fly Fishing Center, West Yellowstone, Montana. *Courtesy of Dennis Bitton.*

interest in fishing history. Nick Lyons, first at Crown and then on his own, Armand Frasca at Freshet, and several other publishers complemented the rapid production of new fishing books by reprinting many out-of-print books of value. The writings of Arnold Gingrich, Ernest Schwiebert, Martin Keane, John McDonald, Austin Francis, and many others have helped generate a fascination not only with the past practices and personalities of fly fishing but with the surviving artifacts. The Museum was a part of that process, both cause and effect in today's heightened appreciation for fly-fishing history. But the Museum has not been the only institution to result. There are at least two others that show great promise now, each for a distinct and important region.

Late in 1981 the Central Miramichi Historical Society received a grant of almost a quarter of a million dollars from the Canadian government to build The Miramichi Atlantic Salmon Museum, aimed at saving and interpreting the history of Atlantic Salmon fishing as well as the natural history and the needs of the fisheries. The museum is on the banks of the Miramichi River at Doaktown, New Brunswick. This is an especially important regional effort from the historical perspective because of the great age of Atlantic salmon sport fishing in the New World; it has perhaps the longest documented tradition except for those faintly known early-Pennsylvania fly fishers mentioned early in this book.

Also in 1981 The Catskill Fly Fishing Center was founded. It had been preceded by an earlier, less ambitious idea for a museum. The Center, much like the International Fly Fishing Center, aimed to include not only history but also conservation and fly-fishing education in its scope of operations. The Catskill Fly Fishing Center is the latest manifestation of one of American fly fishing's most dynamic and creative traditions, and has made a promising start. Land has been obtained along the Wil-

The new bridge over the Willowemoc at the future site of the Catskill Fly Fishing Center between Roscoe and Livingston Manor, New York. *Courtesy of the Catskill Fly Fishing Center.*

lowemoc between Livingston Manor and Roscoe, and a small museum has already been opened in Roscoe. The thirty-one-acre site on the river will eventually be home to a variety of facilities for historical exhibits and educational and recreational (or both at once) programs.

It was my good fortune in 1982 to attend an early meeting of the Catskill Fly Fishing Center as the guest of Lee and Joan Wulff. What I saw in the enthusiasm and dedication of this group, combined with what I already knew about the history and character of the Catskills and their anglers, convinced me that this center is at least as great an idea as the International Fly Fishing Center. I am sure that there will be times when this Center, the International Center, and the Museum in Vermont find themselves competing, however politely, either for funds or other forms of support, but that doesn't bother me. They overlap, but they are also distinct, and we need them all.

Fly fishing's new society—what amounts to a sporting subculture—has indeed changed the sport. In this publication-, organization-, and institution-oriented situation some elements of the sport are harder to find, and others are easier. Lee Wulff, who has a longer and deeper memory of fly fishing than practically anyone else, recently wrote an essay on the changes in fly fishing, in *Rod & Reel*, in which he remained optimistic. Speaking about the increase in such things as angling fashions, ''après fishing'' parties, ''colorful scarfs with the right flies,'' and many other things that horrify some fishermen, Wulff concluded that it's all right, that fishing has always been changing and always will:

> We will have long discussions on the merits of the old days versus the new, but whether we like it or not the old days are gone. Our new world is bright and beautiful—as well as different. We're building wonderful fishing close to home. We'll make all our good available water as productive as possible. The best fishermen will still catch the most fish. Laugh or cry over the changes, fly fishing will always be fun.

This may sound like a different attitude from that expressed by John Randolph at the beginning of the chapter, but in a way it isn't. There is still the essential freedom to do, as John said, "things that matter," and that freedom includes the choice to join or not join the society. It is true that many of the waters are more crowded, but it is also true that because of the intensity of communication among fly fishers the odds are good that they are crowded with fly fishers who know how to keep the fishing good.

Increases in numbers are always hard to rationalize. Wilderness advocates have long faced the dilemma of knowing that in order to preserve some special wild country it was almost essential to publicize it, flood it with people, and thereby create a constituency for it. In the process of saving it, some of its value as empty wilderness was sacrificed. Fly fishers wishing to protect good fishing and promote their sport face the same dilemma.

The past twenty-five years have been ones of enormous change for fly fishing. The establishment of a national fly-fishing organization, the creation of the sport's own museums and educational centers, and the publication of magazines devoted exclusively to fly fishing have all heightened the self awareness of fly fishers as a group of at least occasionally like-minded sportsmen.

Such changes are not uniformly accepted. Not everyone, for example, is a joiner; the Federation of Fly Fishers has a membership less than ten percent the size of the circulation of *Fly Fisherman* magazine. Not everyone is a reader; *Fly Fisherman* magazine has a circulation less than ten percent the size of most estimates of the number of fly fishermen in the United States.

Not everyone cares about expert opinion. For some people, the idea that the sport practiced by Cotton and Gordon should reach the point where it actually had fulltime celebrities who made their living from speaking and writing about fly fishing is disturbing. For others, access to those experts is the greatest development in the sport's history. For most, the rise of the professional fly fisherman has had at least modest benefits (and for a few others there is nothing wrong with lionizing great fishermen as long as they're really great; I believe it was Lefty Kreh who said that the definition of an expert is a guy with his own slide projector, more than fifty miles from home).

Fly fishing has not entered some new stable state. Just as we continue to produce new fly patterns, rod designs, and books of theory and instruction, so do we continue to evolve as an angling society. Our perception of that evolutionary process is the subject of the next chapter.

23

The Undefined Angler

Imagination is one of the greatest gifts of fishermen.
—ALVIN GROVE, *The Lure and Lore of Trout*
Fishing (1951)

"A gentleman," announced Frederick Skinner, a prominent sportsman of the 1840s, "never shoots at a still, living target nor angles for a sluggish fish." That statement is so loaded with judgments, and so perilous of evaluation that I could almost let the chapter go at that, following it merely with the suggestion that readers think it over for half an hour or so. Fly fishing, like other sports, is a complex blend of cultural values and natural circumstances.

The topic of sporting definitions—that is, how we determine what constitutes appropriate behavior in a sporting activity—also reminds me of a remark made by Wallace Stegner, a historian and novelist, about civilization (you may read "sportsmanship"): "Civilization is built on a tripod of geography, history, and law, and it is made up largely of limitations."

The most important thing to keep in mind when considering the subject of sporting definitions is that sporting ethics are rarely immutable. Most people who speak on "good sport" in any age do so with the presumption that sport is easily susceptible to absolute definitions: this is clearly sporting, and that is clearly not. Fly fishing, which I have already shown is always a fertile field for disagreement in other ways, is an excellent example of just how difficult good sport is to define. I am appalled at the frequency with which fly fishers pronounce on absolute good and evil in fly fishing, and am shocked at their willingness to do so with no reference to several centuries of accumulated tradition, to say nothing of their equal ignorance of the geography, history, and law that created their attitudes.

It is true that we define sport in terms of limitations. Most activities that are now considered unsporting are seen as making the capture of fish too easy. Dynamiting salmon rivers and snagging steelhead are two examples of many. Sport requires challenge, and challenge requires limitations on, in the case of fly fishermen, fishing techniques. In no two ages of society are anglers apt to have exactly the same concept of what is a sufficient limitation. There will be many similarities, and some nearly constant ideas, but sport is a notion in flux. There are few absolutes, and the person who looks upon past practices as unsporting merely because they are not like his own is being both unfair and naive. In my readings in and out of fly-fishing history I have been repeatedly struck by the arrogance of anglers who have so little sympathy with other kinds of sport that they will not even call them sports. The attitude, even if held by a minority of fishermen, is a little frightening. Consider this paragraph from a letter written to the editor of *Trout* magazine, published in the Winter 1986 issue, complaining about baitfishing articles in that magazine:

> While I do not deny anyone the privilege of using natural bait or food to catch fish, this is not sport. It may be recreation of the finest, but results are dependent on whether or not the fish is hungry and has little relationship to the art of fooling or enticing the fish to strike.

That expresses such a confusion of notions, such a jumble of contradictions (are not trout when rising to mayflies hungry? does not wormfishing require skill to place the bait in the trout's vicinity and thus entice it to strike?) that it is an embarrassment. But it is not a rare sentiment. A fisherman, like anyone else, can convince himself that any preferred method is the only "right" one; many fishermen do just that. Their evidence is rarely if ever empirical, however; it is subjective. It may be sophisticated, or it may simply be bigoted. But it will always remain unconvincing, or insulting, to other fishermen who have worked just as long developing their own creed, or who don't care about such things and just prefer not to be ridiculed by someone whose values are different. The agencies that create the regulations by which fishing is governed (the "law" by which we so often formally define good sport) are not establishing right and wrong; they are merely enforcing an atmosphere of tolerance. In that atmosphere, baitfishers, fly fishers, poachers, and nonfishers all may know where they stand. If they do not like where others stand, their legal relationships to those others are at least made clear.

The ways in which we define fly fishing, that actually being a process of constant evaluation and frequent *re*defining, reveal the mixture of values and traditions that go into our self image as sportsmen. I'm going to consider three different forms of definition in this chapter, not in the hope of offering new definitions (surely I've learned better than to try that) but in the hope of illuminating how it all happens. At my most ambitious, I hope also to suggest ways in which we get off track in our definitions.

The three ways are (1) how we define fly fishing relative to other kinds of fishing; (2) how we define fly fishing itself, internally, as a sporting practice; and (3) how we define fly fishing as a part of our lives.

How we define fly fishing relative to other kinds of fishing is, usually, as better. Even the most open-minded of modern anglers speak of having "graduated" from baitfishing to fly fishing, of having passed through an important, educational youthful phase as a "worm drowner" or "hardware flinger." As I have suggested here and there in this book, fly fishing has enveloped itself in an image of purity. It is seen as the highest form of angling, as the sport of the most intellectually sophisticated, and as the sport of the people with the most money. Those things all have some truth to them, and they all are oversimplifications. It is clear, however, that at least among the anglers who share the same quarry—trout are the best example—none are as likely to look down on the others as are fly fishers.

There are many sources of the fly fisher's oft-announced feeling of superiority.

Fly fishing does offer a huge assortment of sub-crafts and pursuits, most of which do not have real equivalents in, say, baitfishing. The potential for the study of trout-stream ecology is probably greater for the avid fly fisherman, especially if he is a hatch matcher, than it is for the worm fisherman. I say "probably" because there is nothing about baitfishing that would keep its practitioners from studying up on ecology to whatever extent they might like; it does seem that most of them do not like to do so. Fly fishing, then, might be called more "involved," or even more "sophisticated," though that is a dangerous term when what is really meant is "complicated."

There is also no denying that a lot of fly fishing's announced superiority is the result of social factors. Fly fishing has often enough been the favored sport of wealthy people so that it is socially identified with white-collar and professional rather than blue-collar people. Grouse hunting is fly fishing's equivalent in hunting; deer hunting is baitfishing's equivalent. A long chapter could be written on how this state of affairs came about. I have alluded to it here and there—John Brown's comments on the skills of the lumberjack fly fishers, for example—but have not taken it on in depth, thinking most readers would not be interested and those that would already have their minds made up one way or another (subjective reasons, I know, but they suit me well enough in this book, which I think has other, more important, missions). The social superiority of fly fishing has had to do with many factors, including the allocation of scarce (and therefore expensive) sporting re-sources, fly fishing's enormous potential for costly investment in gear and fishing rights, and the self-perpetuating image of superiority that surrounds the sport generation after generation.

Fly fishing's supposed superiority has been based on many other things besides its complication and its social status. Fly fishers have for centuries, both in the Old World and here, attempted to distinguish it from other forms of fishing. British writers in the 1700s said that it was better because it was not cruel to worms. It does not soil the hands with distasteful, smelly baits. It is only practiced in the most sublime surroundings. It is the most "natural" because it most closely seeks to imitate the fish's customary foods. It allows the angler to release fish rather than kill them with a deeply swallowed baited hook. It makes people into good conservationists. It promotes good ethical behavior because unlike other forms of sport fishing it does not encourage fishermen to snag or overharvest fish.

We have all heard these reasons or variations on them (though the one about cruelty to worms is pretty rare). Some are preached as gospel, some have the hollow ring of cant. Behind many hide other emotions, including pride and bigotry.

It puzzles me, even after years of total immersion in the literature, lore, and society of fly fishing, why so many practitioners of this glorious, absorbing sport need to shore themselves up with self-praise. The sport itself seems sufficient jus-tification for its practice. I say that without having ruled out the possibility that a lot of the pride could result from fly fishing truly being better. Maybe, somehow, it is true, and fly fishing is a superior activity. Maybe worm fishing's simplicity is a defect, or spinfishing leads to moral degeneracy. One need only read the modern fishing magazines to find that quite a few people think so.

A lot of the reasons I have given as possible causes for fly fishing's supposed superiority are based on subjective thinking. We decide worm fishing is not sport. We decide spinfishing inspires joykilling. We confuse cause and effect; fly-fishing writers tend to be more literate than bait fishing writers, therefore fly fishing is more inspiring. Or, fly fishing attracts more literate people than baitfishing, therefore fly fishing is better.

Recent changes in fishing regulations, as well as research associated with those changes, have created a new challenge to fly fishing's supposed superiority. The great increase in "quality fishing" regulations in the past twenty years have taught us much about the advantages and limitations of various kinds of fishing.

As we've already seen, fly-fishing-only regulations have a long history. Sometimes they were applied for social reasons, and sometimes because of their biological advantage of allowing the release of fish unharmed. Anglers have for many years known what fisheries management research has recently proven: bait-caught fish, by most popular techniques, have a far higher release mortality than fly-caught ones.

Various forms of "fish-for-fun" and "catch-and-release" appeared in this century, and as usual there are conflicting paternity claims. Readers of fishing books trace their origin to Lee Wulff and his oft-quoted wisdom about a game fish being too valuable to be caught only once. Fisheries managers generally give Dr. Albert Hazzard, a prominent Michigan fisheries authority and outspoken conservationist, credit for developing the "fish-for-fun" concept, often called the Hazzard Plan even in the 1960s. What appears to have happened is that in the 1930s and 1940s, increasing pressure on fishery resources made it obvious to at least a few forward-looking people like Wulff and Hazzard that the recreational part of the activity was going to have to be emphasized to the reduction or exclusion of the meat harvest. Little signs of progress cropped up here and there (among them, though some were probably inadvertent, were various fly-fishing-only waters, such as Washington's Stilliguamish River set aside in 1941, or Yellowstone's Firehole River a little later). In the late 1940s, for example, John Alden Knight, Ed Zern, and a few of their friends established an informal "Half-Limit Club," to encourage anglers to kill only half what they were allowed. By the 1960s and the popularization, first by T.G.F., of the "Limit your kill, don't kill your limit" motto, the concept of catch and release was rolling along pretty well. Now there are specially regulated waters in many states where some form of catch and release (and the term, which seems so clear, has many definitions) regulations apply.

At the same time that releasing most or all fish caught came into vogue, of course, America was experiencing the spinfishing revolution. In fact the increased attention to limiting kill is probably partly a response to the effectiveness of the new tackle. But life has become complicated for fly fishers who for so many years simply knew that their form of fishing was the best one for releasing fish. Numerous studies have proven that there is no statistical difference between the release mortality rate of fly fishing and that of spinfishing. Indeed, some studies even suggest that treble hooks may cause lower mortality because the fish are less likely to swallow them deeply.

Fly fishers have not received this revelation with uniform good grace. It means that there is no longer a biological reason (and never was) for excluding spinfishers from any trout streams. Now flyfishers who want to have their own waters, managed solely for fly fishing, must come up with other reasons. Those reasons are invariably social or esthetic, and in today's rights-conscious world it will be harder than in the past to set aside part of a stream for fly fishing just because that is judged, by some, to be the best way to fish that stream.

It must be said in the defense of fly fishers that there is more involved here than snobbery. The vast majority of fishing waters in this country are open to all methods of sport fishing; even in the most sympathetic of states fly-only waters are rare. If fly fishers are right that their kind of fishing has a different enough esthetic base to require exclusive rights to some waters, then they really are getting a tiny slice of the pie.

On the other hand, most of the objections to opening up fly-fishing waters to spinfishing are either overtly or implicitly social. Spin fishers are perceived by fly fishers as lacking in manners or respect for law or esthetic sensibility or all three. Special regulation experience in some places has already shown that robust wild-fish populations can be maintained in the face of considerable pressure by both spin and fly fishers. If, as some fly fishers believe, spin fishers lack the necessary social graces (such as knowing when to pass another angler who has ''right-of-way'' to a pool, or knowing what are the proper distances to leave between fishermen, or even knowing not to litter or otherwise abuse the resource), there is no reason to believe they cannot learn them. Excluding them from waters that require them to learn is no progress at all; it simply reinforces old habits and maintains old prejudices. From my perspective, having fished on most kinds of special-regulation trout waters, it appears to me that human nature is human nature, and that spinfishers have no corner on the discourtesy market.

But there are other objections to spinfishing. As Edward Hewitt suggested in the quotation at the opening of Chapter 18, spinfishing allows anglers to reach fish that cannot be reached by traditional fly-fishing methods. Changes in fly-fishing techniques have in recent years given fly anglers just about as much versatility as spin fishers, but that is a subject I will turn to later. For the moment, consider the spin fisher. He can reach several feet down into a deep pool, perhaps a place where for hundreds of years trout have found shelter from fly fishers (though certainly not from worm fishers). He can have an effect on the overall fish population far greater than that had by the flyfisher, it seems.

But if the water is regulated to limit the kill, so that the trout population is not threatened, what difference does it make, biologically, if the fish have fewer or more absolute refuges from fishermen? The question does not have an easy answer. Lee Wulff, in *Lee Wulff on Flies*, suggests that excluding spinning, and thereby increasing the number of safe refuges trout have in a stream, will reduce the overall number of catches and thereby reduce the incidental mortality that exists on any catch-and-release stream. It appears, from the experience managers have had with fly-fishing-only, catch-and-release waters, that fly fishers alone can apply fabulously intense pressure on a fish population, repeatedly catching most fish in the water in a season.

At best, fly fishers do not have a strong case biologically or socially for excluding law-abiding spin fishers from catch-and-release waters. Pennsylvania, recognizing the unique historical contributions fly fishers have made to fishing on certain waters in that state (such as the Letort), has chosen to maintain a few waters for fly fishing only. Many other states that have long-established fly-only waters would probably do well to treat them the same. But we fly fishers have some serious thinking to do about just what it is that makes our sport special enough to exclude other fishing methods from some waters. For subjective reasons of my own, I hope we come up with some good answers, but we're not doing too well yet.

This leaves me only one other topic to mention before moving on to the next type of definition. That topic is the barbless hook. Barbless hooks of one sort or another have been recommended to fly fishers for more than a century. The Izaak Walton League has long been a champion of them. This statement by Harold Pulsifer, in *Outlook* on August 6, 1919, is typical of many since:

> I am only a passing angler, yet I have landed without any great difficulty pound-
> and-a-half trout on a barbless number 10 in quiet water, and have even brought safely
> to net several landlocked salmon of no great size, but with all the pyrotechnic instincts

of their athletic clan. I lose only a few more fish on a barbless hook than I do on its barbed cousin . . . What I catch I deserve. What I do not wish to keep I know I can release without damage.

The barbless hook is, along with catch and release, the new cause of fly fishers. But just as fisheries managers object that catch and release is not a panacea, certainly not the best management for all species in all waters, so do they wonder about the barbless hook. The studies to date do not prove that it reduces release mortality. Some biologists wonder about the "stiletto effect," the deeper and more harmful penetration of the fine barbless hook; barbed hooks tend to make a wider, shallower wound.[1] In special regulations and barbless hooks, fly fishers—because of their zeal to make things better—risk outrunning their scientific support.

I have devoted about a quarter of this book to showing the ways in which fly fishing in America has evolved as the fish and their waters required. That evolution has gone in many directions at many times, and the result is a greatly broadened sport that has experienced extraordinary technological advances. If it was difficult to come up with one universally applicable definition of fly fishing a century ago, it is nearly impossible now. What is appropriate one place is absurd in another. We approach fly-fishing definition, for our own needs, from many directions.

The one that surfaces most often in the history of the sport before modern times centers on the fly. The most famous of all attempts to determine what is right and wrong, or appropriate and inappropriate, in fly-fishing practice probably occurred in the ascendancy of the dry fly. The Halfordian code, adopted with variations in parts of this country, ruled many minds and established to the satisfaction of its adherents the sporting and even the moral superiority of dry flies. Make no mistake; there were practical as well as esthetic objections to nymph fishing on British chalkstreams. But for my purposes here it is the choice of fly type that matters most. The dry fly did not gain in popularity for simple reasons; some believed it was better for catching fish, many were caught up in its fashionable newness and immense charm.

But it was a narrowly defined dry fly; not only was it to be cast upstream only to rising fish, it was usually restricted to imitating certain forms of life. As Marinaro pointed out in *A Modern Dry-Fly Code*, Halford would have been uneasy at best with using an imitation of so large an animal as a grasshopper. Marinaro himself commented that "aesthetic values are rather low where the use of Melanoplus is concerned, and its ungracefulness is somewhat aggravated by its terrestrial origin and lineage."

These are wonderfully stimulating remarks. We must make so many decisions in choosing our sport. Marinaro, Gordon, and others were not satisfied that something as large as a grasshopper could be imitated in true dry-fly fishing. Marinaro objected to the use of what he called "outrageous hook sizes—12, 10, 8, even 6—for dry-fly imitations. Size of the insect being imitated was important in defining good sport. But there was more; there was a feeling that somehow a landborn insect was not quite appropriate too. It was one of Marinaro's real accomplishments that he elevated terrestrials to first-class citizenship among purist fly fishers, yet even he had trouble with the grasshopper. The grasshopper was not a part of the trout's aquatic ecosystem; it was a sort of intruder.

I have lately wondered if this concern over fishing the right insect imitations does not go yet deeper than we have imagined. My readings in natural history suggest to me that in the nineteenth century, even among serious entomologists, there was a preoccupation with the final, adult form of any insect to the exclusion of the immature forms. The common term for an adult was the "perfect" form. What a weighted label that must have been for anglers, already inclined by fashion to ignore what was going on under the surface of the water. It would be useful for some angler-entomologist in the United Kingdom to look into this and see if, among other things, it was not easier to come by information about the duns than about the nymphs, and if there were esthetic biases against nymphs that went beyond the bounds of fly fishing.

American waters were hard on traditional or newly established British fishing dogma. American anglers in the 1800s developed approaches to imitate whatever they observed fish eating, from mice to terrestrial insects to other fish, and did so in the absence of any serious social or esthetic controls. We continue to do so, with imitations of saltwater crustaceans, salmon eggs, leeches, and a host of other fish foods. Practically all of these we cast with traditional fly-fishing equipment, that is with rod and line providing the impetus to move the fly to the water, and then we manipulate the fly (which is what I will call all members of our artificial menagerie here) in a way that imitates the motions of its real-life counterpart.

More than ten years ago, the Federation of Fly Fishermen set up a special committee to come up with a workable definition of fly fishing that might standardize fly practices—at least their legality—if management agencies could be persuaded to adopt it. Steve Raymond, writing in *Fly Fisherman* in December of 1985, summarized the outcome:

> The list was circulated among the Federation leadership—not as a proposal, for we were still a long way from that, but merely as a status report on the committee's work. Nevertheless, it set off an immediate furor, and angry letters quickly started flowing in. All had a common theme: Do as you please about everything else, but if you so much as even think of trying to draft a regulation prohibiting the use of (a) double hooks, (b) metal-core lines, (c) chumming, (d) weighted flies or leaders, or (e) practically anything else, then the letter writer promised to (a) resign from the Federation, (b) persuade all his friends to do likewise, (c) start a rival organization, (d) punch everybody on the regulations committee in the nose, or (e) carry out any one of a great number of other imaginative threats.

The Federation still hasn't finished its definitions, and there is no sign that anyone else will undertake the job. Except that it has been undertaken, repeatedly, by management and record-keeping agencies. Predictably, they disagree in some important ways.

The International Game Fish Association, for example, defines a fly line loosely: "Any type of fly line and backing may be used. The breaking strength of the fly line and backing are not restricted." But they place some limits, if vague ones, on the fly:

> The lure must be artificial and designed for fly casting, and must be of a type which can be false-cast in the generally accepted fashion . . . In the case of a weighted lure, the fact that it can be cast is not evidence, in itself, that the lure was designed for fly fishing. It must be light enough to permit repeated false casts without causing undue strain on the angler or his equipment.

Contrast those terms with the regulations for the state of Oregon, for example. In that state's regulations a fly is "a hook (weighted or nonweighted) dressed with conventional fly tying materials only, to which no molded plastic, spinner, spoon, or similar devices are attached.'' But ''Fly Angling'' is defined as:

> Angling with fly rod, fly reel (no spinning or fixed spool reels), floating or sinking line, any type of backing line, and an artificial fly. In waters restricted to ''fly angling only'' no additional weights or attractors shall be attached to the hook, leader, or line, and no metal core lines may be used.

You could conceivably go to the North Umpqua fly-only water and catch a fish that, though it qualified perfectly for an I.G.F.A. record, would get you arrested there on the river.

Most states are fairly open-minded about what a fly is, and what fly fishing is. In many places a fly cast on a spinning outfit with a plastic bubble for weight is perfectly legitimate. Weighted flies are almost always okay, probably in part because it would be a nightmare to prevent them or adequately define weighted (is metal tinsel ''weight?'' a 5X-strong hook might have more weight, unleaded, than a 4X-light hook with a fine wrapping of lead).

Weighted flies and lines have taken some of the bite out of criticisms of spinfishing as ''too deadly'' because on most fly-only waters it is now possible to fish very deeply and very far away with flies that if anything are even more effective than spinning lures. But the question of weight is not the only unresolved issue.

A variety of fish attractants are recommended for various fishing conditions. Trout fishermen use insect emergences as a sort of natural ''chum'' to bring fish on the feed and within reach of traditional fly-fishing gear. Saltwater fly fishers are in the habit of chumming various species of fish up to within reach. Chumming, which would probably be unacceptable on a trout stream (someone would immediately liken it to baiting deer), is the only way to get the attention of some fish in salt water, just as lead-core lines are the only way to get a fly through fifteen feet of fast-running river to a king salmon on some California streams. The question that gets asked so often is, in effect, at what point do our efforts to get a fly to the fish disqualify the act from the definition of fly fishing?[2]

A few writers have somewhat hesitantly proposed using chemical or natural scents on flies to increase their attracting quality, a proposal widely criticized as unsporting among fly fishers. But even here we face some unavoidable compromises. Frank Sawyer, in *Keeper of the Stream* (1952), supposed that a fly once taken by a fish had a ''fishy flavour'' that probably inclined the next fish to hold it longer and thus increased our chance of hooking it. Are we closer to baitfishing than we think when we use a fly that has been munched on by several trout?

There is also the issue of timing. West Coast steelheaders were incensed a few years ago to learn that Michigan anglers were fishing flies to steelhead (and salmon) on the spawning redds. Yet few people give a thought to fly fishing to Maine small-mouths in the spring when the fish come to the shallows to spawn.

I suspect, in all these cases and others, that fly fishers probably exercise at least as much intolerance and rage in disapproving of one another as they do in condescending to non-fly-fishers. While some say that we must honor at least a few traditions or risk losing our hard-earned bearings, others insist that we must all be open to every new development that comes along. Neither position, nor any of the ones between them, are going to win out; the best hope is probably for increased tolerance of other viewpoints so we spend less time arguing irresolvables and more time coming to terms with those elements of definition that can be settled. If there are any.

The man who chooses to be a dry-fly fisherman, and chooses further only to imitate mayflies or other small life forms, has made, to his own mind at least, a perfectly reasonable and admirable choice. He has defined his own sport based upon his awareness of traditions and his personal tastes (and probably also on the basis of what water he has available to fish). The man who chooses to fish salmon-egg imitations to steelhead over the redds can come up with equally good personal justifications. Within the broad range of practice allowed them by the law they are both doing just fine. Within the less objective, if no less important, realm of sporting ethics, how well either is doing depends entirely upon the person asked to judge them. It is fine for Lee Wulff to believe, as he does, that no tackle that cannot be false cast with forty-five feet of line ten times should be called real fly-fishing tackle. It is just as fine for Doug Swisher to attach fifteen feet of lead-core line to the end of his fly line so he can reach down to a salmon on a deep Michigan river. It does not appear that, even if by some miracle a uniform definition of fly fishing could be adopted by all record-keeping groups and management agencies, there will ever be anything approaching unanimity among fly fishers over the ethics of various practices. It is too personal, and too subjective, for agreement. That being the case, perhaps what is needed is a finer understanding all around of just how fundamentally subjective sporting ethics are. Lord knows what we will be disagreeing about fifty years from now, but it will certainly be different from today's debates. With America's wonderful range of sportfish—from sunfish to marlin—and water types, a single definition of fly fishing would have to be either so lengthy as to be unusable, or so brief as to be meaningless, to apply all around. Agencies and organizations must have formal definitions, and fly fishers have a role to play in developing those. There is probably general agreement, for example, that a fish must be hooked in the mouth, and that in other ways unfair advantage not be taken (fish concentrated at a dam, for example). But several centuries of varying opinion on every topic relating to fly fishing—the best way to cast, the proportions best for a wet fly, upstream or downstream fishing, and all the others—do not suggest to me that there is any hope for absolute agreement on such a difficult assignment as defining the sport.

There is yet one other way in which we define our sport. It is the way that has meant the most to me, but it is the way that I can least describe. It is even more subjective than determining what constitutes ''proper'' fly fishing.

I'm speaking of the bundle of emotional, esthetic, and physical responses that make up the satisfaction we get from the sport. For many of us, the most important definition of fly fishing—the definition that we fish by, so to speak—is that fly fishing is fun. Fun, as I've suggested, is a pretty complex idea, but the fun of fly fishing, however we perceive it, has had innumerable celebrations. We have spent much more time and energy defining what fly fishing is in this way than in any other.

We do it for ourselves all the time, around campfires and kitchen tables and fly-tying vises. We do it at T.U., F.F.F., U.F.T., T.G.F., and other meetings, and we do it every time we fish. We define it as we practice it, and may never adequately answer the question of why we fish—though most of us come to terms with the question well enough so that we don't spend much time wondering about it. We fly fish for all of Art Flick's ''swell arguments'' just as we fly fish to catch fish, whether we hold those arguments with the fish, ourselves, our friends, or the books and magazines we read.

My reading of the literature of fly fishing suggests to me that why we fly fish has not changed significantly through all the technological revolutions that have otherwise overhauled the sport. That may be the reason why fishing historians have had so little to say about the subject; it is infinitely easier to write about changes in angling practice than about esthetic sensitivities and quiet companionships. Those sensitivities and companionships, though they may be manifested differently in different ages, and written about in new ways to suit new societies, are about the least fluid element of fly fishing, just as they are of most pastimes.

The writers who do something to evoke the enduring joys of fly fishing are the ones most often likely to be read generation after generation. In American fly fishing, we've had many writers capable of sharing those joys, and at the same time helping us to explore the reasons the joys are so important to us. Thaddeus Norris's essay on fly fishing alone in his *American Angler's Book* captured moods echoed repeatedly by later writers, and remains one of our best statements on the solitary pleasures of the sport. Among fly fishing's writers are a wide assortment of perspectives, all of which inform the sport's opportunities.

Norris, who was known even in his own time as "Uncle Thad," was one of the first American fly-fishing writers who either adopted or were thrust into the position of venerable authority. Gordon, of whom I have spoken at length, became the sport's foremost martyr, and gave us a body of intelligent literary monologue that no future writer is likely to surpass. Bergman, virtually never rising above the pedestrian as a writer, became the experienced, relaxed uncle for thousands of fly fishermen whose own approach to the sport was molded by this man's utilitarian, homey attitudes. Odell Shepard, in his small volume *Thy Rod and Thy Creel* (1930), had given the few who read him a penetrating and eloquent statement about fly fishing as a life pursuit.

John Voelker, better known to fly-fishing readers as Robert Traver.
Courtesy of Fly Fisherman *Magazine*.

In the greater world of literary criticism, Haig-Brown has probably been the most respected of the life-long fishing writers; his season cycle and his *A River Never Sleeps* (1946) and *Return to the River* (1941), as well as parts of several other works, put him in what many consider to be the foremost position among American fly-fishing writers. He wrote with an elder statesman's polish and dignity, in strong, unadorned prose based on a remarkable experience of rivers and fish. Robert Traver, on the other hand, has given us the angler as curmudgeon, though a curmudgeon with both a good heart and keen wit, in *Trout Madness* (1960) and *Trout Magic* (1974).

Ed Zern and Nick Lyons have both shown that it's possible to laugh at oneself (and thus at the sport) without relinquishing self respect. Ed has been the most important outdoor humorist of this century, possibly in the history of American fly fishing, and Nick, among his other contributions, has perfected the image of the angler as beleaguered bumbler.

The list is a long one, and, as with so many other aspects of the sport, fly fishers disagree over favorites. Some prefer the dated charm of John Taintor Foote, under whom the tale of the city-bound angler who motored up to the mountains to have amusing encounters with the locals reached its modern form. Others like the lyricism of Dana Lamb, or the mannered prose of Ernest Schwiebert's many ''remembrances.'' Others are attracted to Palmer Baker, Howard T. Walden 2d, Steve Raymond, Charles Waterman, Arnold Gingrich, Russell Chatham, Sparse Grey Hackle, and many other people identifiable as outdoor writers, while others find increasing instances of fly fishing being portrayed, often very well, sometimes only because of its trendiness, in general nonfiction and fiction.

Fly fishing has appeared now and then in ''regular'' writing, that is to say in writing not aimed at only an outdoor audience, for a long time, as long as writers have enjoyed the sport. It is true that many of the writers we point to when trying to establish how good fishing literature is are not really fishing writers; they are writers who once in a while have used fishing as a subject for their writing. William Humphrey, Ernest Hemingway, Thomas McGuane, Jim Harrison, Richard Brautigan, and Craig Nova are all writers who have at some time written of fly fishing, some using it in fiction, some in personal narrative. But even here, in the bigger pond of American literature (in which fishing writing is only a small, not especially deep bay), fly fishing is being defined, if only as these writers demonstrate the sport's utility as a literary device or a recreation worth the attention of thoughtful (or fashion-conscious) people.

All these writers—the outdoor writers, the novelists, the journalists, and so on —are contributing to our attempt to explain or define why we fish. Granted that many of them are making a minute, or even negative, contribution, and granted also that they are not striving either for consensus or for some victory in the technical debates.

It is precisely because these literary celebrations of fly fishing have been so personal, and often so idiosyncratic, that they may take a back seat to the technicians in most written histories of the sport; the technicians make easily identifiable contributions, in terms of this fly pattern or that hatch chart or this casting technique. A writer who sets out to tell you a story about his fishing trip, and who has no intention of introducing you to a new miracle rod taper, is making very few promises; he may not intend to do more than entertain, or he may have ambitions to alter in some fundamental manner the way you perceive the sport. The sport's artists—whether masters such as Winslow Homer, A. F. Tait, Ogden Pleissner, Chet Reneson, and Eldridge Hardie, or the hundreds of anonymous illustrators whose work has brought so much writing to life—are usually no clearer in their intentions.

All of this leaves my last category of definition in an even airier and less resolvable state than the previous ones. Ours is a happily—at least I see it in such affirmative terms—loose pastime, one that appeals to us for many reasons and grants us many satisfactions. If we cannot agree upon where it places us in relation to other anglers, or upon just what it should legitimately include in its proper code of practice, then we certainly will never agree upon just why we find it to be so much fun.

A formal and ''proper'' history of fly fishing might have been written in a considerably more detached manner than I have written this one; it would be awkward for a writer trying to get in the last word to admit, as I have repeatedly done in this book, that there is much to be said for fly fishing's apparent lack of focus. But though I have attempted to apply a reasonable amount of scholarly rigor to the study of the sport's historical evidence, I'm no more able than were thousands of previous observers to clarify just which theory of dry-fly silhouette is most reliable, or just how much weight can be attached to a fly before it is no longer a fly, or just which literary evocation of the sport is most on target. In fact, I am positively delighted by these irresolvables and I think that most of us would not have the sport any other way than as it is: open-ended, uncertain of direction, and singularly provoking of mind. We are always learning, but we are rarely settling anything.

Furthermore, I will offer a parting opinion that it is when we wonder about such things that we are participating in what may be the most fulfilling element of fly fishing short of actually going out and putting a fly over a fish. The act of casting a fly to a fish, at first so simple-seeming a business, is of course a mightily involved thing, with repeated judgments of what is the right fly, what is the right action, what is the right way to make the cast, what is the right thing to do with the fish once it is caught (or what is the right way to feel if the fish is not caught), and what in the world has caused us to be out there in the first place. Every one of those judgments is based in good part on things we have learned from others, whether from the tackle shop clerk who showed us the fly or the culture that trained us how nature is to be appreciated.

As we cast the fly, we also angle, as Ken Cameron has said, in the past. Our fishing habits are the products of many centuries of sporting experience and thought. We don't angle with all of that constantly in mind, of course; we would never get around to making the cast if we first tried to sift all the competing theories, or puzzle out just why it feels so good to be casting over this pool on this day. But our history is there, in the tug that lifts the line cleanly from the pool, in the fly that for reasons of color and light and size and hope manages to engage the attention of the fish, and in the wonder we never cease to find in the moment of the strike.

Notes

To the extent possible I have attempted to give adequate information on my sources in the text, usually listing the volume referred to if a book, or the issue if a periodical. The footnotes that follow provide documentation in cases where it was not practical, for one reason or another, to provide it in the text. They also provide additional support for some points I make, additional background on various topics, and an occasional aside, all of which seemed too peripheral (or too digressive) to include in the main narrative.

References given in the footnotes are to titles listed in the bibliography, where full publication information may be found.

CHAPTER 1

[1] The search for the historical reality behind the name Dame Juliana Berners has been conducted by several angling scholars, including John McDonald in *The Origins of Angling*, whose work is the foundation for later scholarship. At present there is general agreement that, even if Berners existed, she probably did not write the *Treatyse*.

[2] Heimpel's statement is quoted from, and much of the accompanying treatment of medieval sport fishing is based upon, Richard Hoffmann's "Fishing for Sport in Medieval Europe: New Evidence," in *Speculum* (1985).

[3] Besides Braekman's *A Treatise on Angling in the Boke of St. Albans*, the antiquity of sport fishing literature is given substantial attention in numerous other books, including John Waller Hills's *A History of Fly Fishing for Trout*, Robert Marston's *Walton and Some Earlier Writers on Fishing*, and William Radcliffe's *Fishing from Earliest Times*. The first two of these are light, conversational treatments of the sport since medieval times. The last is a really extraordinary study of ancient fishing of all kinds, displaying a far deeper research effort than the others mentioned here.

[4] As quoted in Braekman, *A Treatise on Angling*.

CHAPTER 2

[1] Many fishing writers have commented on the appearance of sport fishing in the nineteenth century in America, stating that the sport did not exist, or was rarely enjoyed, here before that time. Typical of these statements are the following:

> In the United States, sport fishing had been practically unknown before 1830.
>> John McDonald, in *Quill Gordon*

> American fishing remained primarily a matter of seeking food rather than sport, and our eastern fly-fishing shrines did not really become focal centers of angling until more than a century after the Walking Purchase.
>> Ernest Schwiebert, discussing the Walking
>> Purchase of the 1730s, in *Trout*

> Sport fishing in America is a development of the nineteenth century. Before that fish were caught only for food, and refinements in tackle were almost unknown.
>> Joseph Bates, in *Streamers and Bucktails,*
>> *The Big Fish Flies*

[2] As quoted in Freame, "Letter of Margaret Penn Freame in Philadelphia, to John Penn," *The Pennsylvania Magazine of History and Biography* (1907).

CHAPTER 3

[1]Among the many intriguing historical topics yet to be fully studied are the sporting activities of the Penn family, mentioned briefly in the previous chapter. This family has left a sizable documentary legacy in Old World and New, and it would be worth the effort of some historian to study it for additional information on early sport fishing.

[2]As quoted by David Ledlie in "More on Sir William Johnson," in *The American Fly Fisher* (1984).

[3]As quoted by Austin Hogan in "An Introduction to the History of Fly-Fishing in America," in *The American Fly Fisher* (1985).

CHAPTER 4

[1]I don't mean to suggest that only America developed an idyllic image of fly fishing, for of course there was much that was idyllic in tone in Old World fishing writing. We were still relying heavily on British example in our approach to sport.

CHAPTER 5

[1]The remark by Dick Finlay is from the Museum's first catalog, *The Museum of American Fly Fishing, Manchester, Vermont, Acquisitions Catalog, 1969–1973* (1973).

[2]Mary Kelly's comments are from a letter to the author, July 26, 1980.

[3]At the time of publication of this book, Jim Brown of Stamford, Connecticut, was completing work on an extended history of American fly reels, to be published as part of a catalog of the reels held by The American Museum of Fly Fishing. A draft manuscript of that history was made available to me by the author, and seemed to me to be a major step in the development of our understanding of American fly-reel history.

CHAPTER 6

[1]Kenneth Shoemaker, in "Daniel Webster and the Great Brook Trout," in *The American Fly Fisher*, 1981, offers the most complete review of the evidence for and against the fish having been caught by Webster, if it was a trout at all, as some accounts suggest it was a salmon. Followup material on the trout story appeared under the title "Did He or Didn't He?" in *The American Fly Fisher*, 1984, a comment written by David Ledlie, who quotes a letter from the *Spirit*, September 14, 1878. The letter details the circumstances under which Sam Carman actually netted a large brook trout in a pond in 1828; the letter adds substantially to the case against Webster having been involved in the fishing episode at all.

The story will not die easily, however, and readers should probably expect to continue to see fanciful versions of it in books and magazines for many years to come. Its foremost defender appears to be Ernest Schwiebert, who presented a remarkably detailed telling of the story in *Trout*, and who later spoke in its behalf, and against Shoemaker's thesis that the story is apocryphal, in the afterword to the second edition of *Trout*.

[2]Austin told this story in "Another Time, Another Laughter," in *The Flyfisher* (1972).

CHAPTER 7

[1]Mary Kelly made this statement in her review of early Leonard development, "Early Leonard," in *The American Fly Fisher* (1979).

[2]Ken made these remarks in an as-yet unpublished chapter of his manuscript *Angling in the Past*. The chapter is entitled "Mr. Leonard and Friends." This book manuscript, much of which has already appeared in various magazines, though available for study at the library of The American Museum of Fly Fishing, is an important contribution to American fishing history and deserves publication.

[3]For more on American silkworm cultivation, see, for example, L. Trouvelot, "The American Silkworm," in *The American Naturalist*, 1868. Charles Orvis attempted to grow silkworms and reported on his inability to produce usable gut in *Forest and Stream* in December of 1886.

CHAPTER 8

[1]Austin made this statement in his "Introduction to the History of Fly-Fishing."

[2]Ken's comments are from *Angling in the Past*, the unpublished chapter entitled "Adirondack Fancies."

[3]John's remark was made in *Trout Bum*.

[4]Ken Cameron's article "Fly Styles," in *The American Fly Fisher* (1981), is an excellent review of the development of the commercial fly pattern in Victorian America.

CHAPTER 9

[1]I have refrained from attempting to impose a system of naming on the various types of flies, relying generally on the existing terms, such as imitative, attractor, and so on, even though I point out that these terms are not used consistently by writers. I have also avoided giving each of the existing terms definitions for the purposes of this book. I have not done either of these things for two reasons. First, I perceived my role here as that of reporter, telling what has been done and what problems have arisen from it. Second, having studied the history of naming flies, I have concluded that any names or definitions I might attempt to introduce would be no more widely accepted than those introduced before me.

[2]A copy of the letter is now on file at The American Museum of Fly Fishing. Austin reported on the letter in his ''Introduction to the History of Fly-Fishing.''

[3]Eyed hooks, and hooks with gut-loop eyes, certainly date to the 1700s and perhaps earlier in England.

CHAPTER 10

[1]I must not give the impression here that Marinaro's definition of the dry fly holds sway in all quarters. When Halford established his rules, he established them well and firmly. In his provocative *The Book of the Hackle*, published in 1979, Frank Elder held forth on the subject of the dry fly, and distinguished between the formal, Halfordian dry fly and all other floating flies. His comments merit quoting at some length:

> But let us be perfectly clear as to what we are attempting to do. We are attempting to represent the newly hatched dun as it sails down the river waiting for its wings to dry, before it lifts off the surface and flies to the comparative safety of the river bank. It is sitting *on* the surface of the water, not a single part of it is in the water. It is in fact *dry* and if we are to represent the insect in this stage of its life, our representation should also be *dry*. In fact we must fish a ''dry-fly.'' It may appear that I am labouring the obvious, but there has been a lot of muddled thinking since anglers first tried to produce a representation of the dun. For a true copy, it must be a *dry* fly, it cannot be a fly floating in the surface film. The artificial must sit *on* the surface. Not the tip of a single barb should penetrate the surface if it is to be a true imitation.
>
> Since the days of Halford, fly-tyers have produced many variations which they suggest are improvements on the original dry-fly tied with a cock's hackle. ''Parachute,'' flies, flies tied with two bunches of hackle spread out on either side to support the weight of the fly on the surface, flies with the bottom hackles cut away in a V and many other such ideas are examples. All these variations are supposed, by their inventor, to be a step forward in the evolution of the dry-fly. Of course they are nothing of the sort, all that they are attempting to do is to produce an alternative to the proper dry-fly. The dun sits *on* the surface of the water, so the imitation must do the same. The only substance so far known which is delicate enough and strong enough to attempt to resemble the legs of a dun are the barbs of a really stiff cock's hackle. Some day a synthetic substance may be produced which can improve on this natural material, but so far there is nothing which has this strength. The trouble is that these really stiff cock's hackles are not easy to obtain; they never have been and ever since dry-fly fishing became popular, there has always been a search for good hackles.
>
> A parachute fly or a fly tied with a bunch of hackles out on each side is not a representation of a newly hatched dun. It is simply a production which is easily seen and will float for a long period before becoming water-logged. The fact that it will catch fish and indeed at certain times may be more effective than the really good dry-fly is not the point. It may be taken by the trout as a dun at the moment of hatching or a dun which has become trapped in the surface film and if the trout at that time prefer a representation of that type then it would be stupid not to use such a fly. Only the purest of purists would refrain from doing so. But we should clearly realise that we are representing a dun in a special condition, we are not representing a dun as it sails down the stream waiting for its wings to dry.

This is a strong doctrine to promulgate today. It presumes, among other things, that Halford's understanding of trout perceptions—that is, of which form of imitation the trout assume to be the real dun—is the only admissable one. Of course in practice a great many other types of flies, including those with no hackles at all, appear to be taken regularly by trout that are feeding exclusively on duns. But Elder, like everyone else, is entitled to his definitions. He does not want to outlaw other imitations of the dun, even though he does not believe the trout mistake them for duns; all he wants is for only the traditional Halford dun imitation to be given the name ''dry-fly.'' He is not getting his way in North America, where Marinaro's definition is the one most commonly applied. Indeed, if American fly fishers were somehow challenged by someone holding the Elder position, I suspect that their response would be more than just to challenge the reasoning that Elder used in defending such a narrow definition of the dry fly. I suspect that Elder's position would be challenged as that of the "hackle snob," who can afford those best hackles and does not want to see the traditional stiff-hackled dry fly's social supremacy threatened by new innovations and alternatives.

[2]There is always difficulty in knowing how completely to trust the authority of a fishing writer when he or she speaks in terms as broad as these. How, for example, could Gill's friend in the New York tackle trade know the number of dry-fly fishermen in Pennsylvania, or Michigan, or California? When, for another example, George LaBranche calls Theodore Gordon the "best fly tier I have ever known," are we justified in assuming that LaBranche knew all the good fly tiers? Would LaBranche have wanted us to assume that? When Sparse Grey Hackle referred to Harry and Elsie Darbee as the world's best fly tiers, upon what authority did he base that judgment? Did he have the qualifications to entitle him to evaluate the work of hundreds of professionals, did he systematically study the work of all the likely contenders for such a title, and did he come up with a way of determining just what constituted the "best"? (Was "best" a measure of skill at tying a single perfect fly, or volume output, or business success, or creativity in developing new patterns, or some other quality or combination of qualities?) Of course Sparse made his statement without doing any of these things; he wasn't qualified to make the statement as a formal, proven fact, and he probably didn't intend it that way. It was probably more a kind gesture on his part, an expression of admiration for these two gifted fly tiers. But once the statement was in print, it gained substantially in authority, and became rather more definite than it deserved to be. Fishing writing is full of these kindnesses and overstatements; someone is the best nymph fisherman (according to his friend the writer), or the best writer (according to his admirer the reviewer), or the best fly tier alive (according to someone who at least is unwilling to compare him to all the dead ones).

CHAPTER 11

[1]Gordon's stature as the father of American fly fishing, and sometimes as more than that, is frequently reinforced by fly-fishing writers who are attempting to set the stage for their own discussions of some element of fly fishing. Most of these statements about Gordon are simply offered as pleasant introductory material. An example like many others is Richard Henry's comments in "The Truth About Fishing Dry," in *Field & Stream*, (June 1983):

> The dry fly originated in England and was introduced to this country by Theodore Gordon.
> Using English flies sent to him by Frederic Halford as guidelines, Gordon fashioned patterns
> that more closely resembled mayflies then plentiful on Eastern waters.

Most of these statements about Gordon originate from what has become "common knowledge" in fly fishing, knowledge based on the writings of several important writers who have established Gordon's place in our history. A few of the more important examples of these writings should serve to make the point that Gordon's stature has been repeatedly reinforced and, in fact, enlarged, over the years:

> As the principal creator of the structure and style of the American, imitation trout fly, and the
> one who introduced and adapted the dry fly to the U.S., he also occupies a unique position in
> the sport. This historical connection gives his work—despite the fact that he died in 1915—an
> authentic intimacy with our present practices. For it was he who developed much of what we
> now do. Time moves slowly in fly-fishing. The last time it moved appreciably in the U.S. was
> with Theodore Gordon.
>
> John McDonald, from the Introduction to The
> Complete Fly Fisherman (1947) (The last sentence
> in this quotation seems to leave no room for
> appreciating the contributions of Louis Rhead,
> Preston Jennings, Lee Wulff, George LaBranche,
> or Edward Hewitt, all of whom were active in
> fly fishing, and doing important work, before
> 1947 when the sentence was published.)

Call him the American Walton or not—though the American Cotton would be more appropriate, since old Izaak was not primarily a fly fisherman—but you can't really call anybody else the father of modern American fly fishing.

> Arnold Gingrich, from the Preface to the
> 1970 edition of *The Complete Fly Fisherman*
> (We are left to wonder, incidentally, why it
> is necessary to call anybody at all the father
> of American fly fishing, when so many people
> took part in its development.)

Gordon brought dry fly development to a level very near its current state, played around with Skues nymphs, revitalized the traditional downstream wet fly, and developed the streamer (his bumblepuppy).

> Richard Eggert, "The Theodore Gordon
> Heritage," *Fly Fisherman* (1969) (What
> is most remarkable about this claim, for all its
> other problems, is that Gordon, who came to fly
> fishing when wet-fly fishing was at its most
> vital, somehow revitalized that technique.)

He was the principal architect of American fly fishing. Gordon first matched American natural insects with furs and feathers. He was the first to suggest angling for salmon with the dry fly. He was an innovator, and originator, a master angler, our leading fly-tier, and the undisputed father of dry-fly fishing in America.

> Thomas Capstick and Don Zahner, "The Gordon
> Legacy," *Fly Fisherman* (1980)

Gordon fully deserves to be known as "the father of modern American angling."

> Austin Francis, *Catskill Rivers* (1983)

We see in this series of quotations (all from sources that would generally be regarded as authoritative) the rise of Gordon from a specialized leader to a near-messianic figure. It is probably true that reputation-building is a cumulative process in many historical fields. We enjoy admiration, and we seek figures to admire.

[2]McDonald, in his Introduction to *The Complete Fly Fisherman*, states that Gordon developed the use of stiffer hackles. Harry Darbee, in an interview by A. J. McClane published in *Field & Stream* in July of 1955, claimed that Gordon improved on British dry flies in several ways:

> He actually changed the anatomy of the fly. He set his wings with the butts toward the rear and placed his hackles at right angles to the hook. He was smart enough to use nonabsorbent materials, which made a big difference. English dry flies at that time were nothing more than modified wets.

Little of this is true. British fly tiers were writing about setting butts toward the tail in the 1880s; Keene illustrated the technique in his American magazine articles in the late 1880s, and perhaps that is where Gordon learned it. Many British patterns used nonabsorbent materials, and it is certainly a gross disservice to Halford to call his refined patterns nothing but "modified wets" when in fact Gordon's flies were often just modified Halford patterns.

[3]Other flies have been linked to Gordon, especially the Light Cahill and the Fanwing Royal Coachman. The Light Cahill as we know it (say, for example, in Art Flick's version) appears to have evolved from a period between 1890 and 1915, when many variations on the Cahill were in existence. Theodore Gordon's own writings speak of the fly with no noticeable feeling of propriety, and he never gives the dressing for it. The difficulty of establishing patrimony for a fly is that with only one or two changes—say a different color hackle or a different wing—one fly will become another. Gordon without question tied and used the Light Cahill, as did many others, but it appears to me, from a reasonably thorough examination of the claims made that he originated the fly, that they are without real basis. There were so many flies in circulation at that time called Cahills, with so many subtle variations between them, that it is obvious that many people were

experimenting with light-bodied dry flies similar to the Cahill. Gordon was certainly one of those people, and may have been a key one in some stage of the fly's development, but so far that is about all that the historical record will permit us to say. It would be nice to think that Gordon helped give us this fly too.

Two thoughtful comments on the origin of the Cahill fly (in its various forms, including its older, darker, wet-fly form) are Charles Brooks's ''The Case of the Two Cahills,'' in *The American Fly Fisher* (Winter 1980), and Thomas Capstick, ''More on the Cahill,'' in *The American Fly Fisher* (Fall 1980).

As to the Fanwing Royal Coachman, again we are relying on hearsay. Gordon was never fond of the Royal Coachman in any form and often said he would not use it, but he was a commercial fly tier, and had to produce what fishermen wanted. His surviving writings leave no reason to believe he developed this variation on the Royal Coachman, but of course he might have. John Alden Knight, writing in *Field & Stream* in September of 1952, said that ''Guy Jenkins saw Gordon use some Royal Coachmen that were tied with what we now know as 'fan wings.' These were the tips of small white feathers from the breast of a male wood duck. Jenkins took a fancy to this fly, and until Gordon died he ordered a supply of them annually.'' This winging technique predates Gordon, of course, but we are left to wonder if only Gordon was tying the fly then, and if it was because of his use of the flies that the Fanwing Royal Coachman became famous.

[4]The Jennings manuscripts were donated to The American Museum of Fly Fishing by Jennings's widow, Adele Jennings. Jennings was, according to information given to Nick Lyons (who gave it to me) by Arnold Gingrich, bitter in his later years because he believed his contribution had gone unnoticed. This might help explain his frustration at the adulation heaped on Gordon.

CHAPTER 12

[1]Jones's comments were part of his Preface to *The Best of the Angler's Club Bulletin* (1972).

CHAPTER 14

[1]Some of the best sources of information on the early development of bass bugs are the following books: Harold Smedley, *Fly Patterns and Their Origins* (1943); Larry St. John, *Practical Fly Fishing* (1920); George Parker Holden, *Streamcraft* (1919); and Samuel Camp, *The Angler's Handbook* (1925). Ray Bergman's books are also helpful.

CHAPTER 16

[1]Douglas Iron, ''Two Outlooks on Salmon,'' *Atlantic Salmon Journal* (1962).

CHAPTER 18

[1]Hewitt was interviewed by George Laycock, who wrote ''Passing of a Great Fisherman'' for *The Fisherman* (1957).

[2]Perhaps the first American writer of record to suggest moving the hackle on a dry fly a long way back away from the eye of the hook was Dr. Edgar Burke (best remembered now for his color illustrations of flies in Ray Bergman's books), who wrote a small book called *American Dry Flies and How to Tie Them* (1925). Burke did not develop anything truly similar to the Marinaro thorax tie, however; he just left the forward portion of the hook shank bare and tied the fly on the aft portion.

[3]There is reason to wonder if there was all that much more interest in angling entomology in the 1950s than there had been in the 1930s when Jennings's book was published. Marinaro's book sold very poorly, as apparently did Atherton's. Of these early-1950s works, only Schwiebert's seems to have found enough audience to stay continually in print (perhaps because of its national scope), the others finding their largest audience in the 1970s when they were reprinted for a new generation of readers.

CHAPTER 19

[1]There have been many fascinating and little-remembered digressions and dead ends in the development of fishing tackle, and fly fishing has more than its share. For example, just as in the days of solid-wood rods, when more than one wood was often used in a rod (one type for the butt, for example, and another for the tip), so too in the 1940s and 1950s was more than one material used in some rods. Rods were built of half cane and half glass (just as today some builders experiment with half graphite and half cane). Another curious variation in the early glass rods were those with intermediate wraps. Many anglers had the most faith in bamboo rods that had wraps of thread every so often down the length of the rod (because in the early days

of bamboo-rod building the wraps were added insurance against unreliable glues used to hold the strips of cane together), and so occasionally glass-rod builders put similar wraps on their rods. The wraps had no real function on a tubular fiberglass rod, but apparently were reassuring to some fishermen.

[2]The synthetic rods gave fly fishers a previously unavailable topic for debate. After a century of fireside arguments over which bamboo rod builder made the best rods, suddenly there was really something to argue about. Personal taste has had as much to do with preference in rods as has anything else, and that of course means the arguments are pretty much irresolvable. For fly fishers, it seems to me, the irresolvable ones are the best kind; we thrive on the imponderable.

We also thrive on feeling good about ourselves, and those feelings show some unhappy tendencies in the bamboo-vs.-everything-else arguments. I came to fly fishing from somewhere off the bottom end of the market, using a borrowed twelve-dollar discount-store glass rod because that was all I could get. I graduated, after a couple years, to the almost embarrassing luxury of a System 7 (though I could only afford the rod, and continued to use the cheapest reels I could find). I fished quite happily, and with growing success, for several years before I discovered that there were people looking down on me because of my willingness to use such cold, *chemical* fishing tackle. I was, I later discovered, part of the revolution brought about the development of synthetics, and I had no idea just how complicated fly fishing's self-image was, or how much animosity a fishing rod could generate. Bamboo-rod snobbery is not a big problem today, mostly because those who practice it are so few and, to the minds of most fly fishers, more or less laughable. That it exists at all still surprises me somehow, though. Bamboo itself is a relative newcomer in the six centuries or so of known fly-fishing history, and though it has served us well and given us great joy it has earned no historical title as the "Highest Step" in rod making. It just provides one of several wonderful choices to anglers who are exploring the sport and deciding how they personally will choose to enjoy it.

CHAPTER 20

[1]It is a sad truth that in the greater world of literary criticism, fishing writing is not as admired as it is by fishing writers. With a very few exceptions the outdoor press is not so much looked down upon as ignored. Thus it has been that very little in the way of formal literary criticism (I use the word in the sense of serious evaluation, not in the sense of finding fault) has been written about fishing writing.

But something occasionally is said on the subject. Two recent examples are Verlyn Klinkenborg's essay "Why Trout Don't Read," in *The American Fly Fisher* (Summer 1985), and my essay "Hope for the Hook and Bullet Press," in *The New York Times Book Review* (September 22, 1985). Both of these essays quote the American novelist and occasional sporting writer William Humphrey, from his book *My Moby Dick*, on fly-fishing writing as he discovered it:

> The angler had metamorphosed into the ichthyologist, and the prevailing prose reflected the change—if mud can be said to reflect. I found myself correcting it as I had done freshman themes in my years as a professor. You had to hack your way through it as through a thicket. Participles dangled, person and number got separated and lost, cliches were rank, thesauritis and sesquipedalianism ran rampant, and the rare unsplit infinitive seemed out of place, a rose among nettles. Yet, instead of weeding their gardens, these writers endeavored to grow exotics in them: orchids, passionflowers. Inside each of them was imprisoned a poet, like the prince inside the toad. What came out was a richness of embarrassments: shoddy prose patched with purple—beautifully written without first being well written.

CHAPTER 23

[1]I am grateful to Dr. Robert Behnke for acquainting me with the concept of the stiletto effect, which has not yet been much written about in either the technical literature or in popular fishing writing. Dr. Behnke's article, "Yellowstone Cutthroat," in *Trout* (Winter 1987) discusses both the stiletto effect and the problems of anglers wanting to spread catch-and-release regulations indiscriminately where they may not work as well as they have on some Yellowstone waters. Even in Yellowstone the results have not been uniformly encouraging, as brown trout populations have not responded to such regulations with increased size or numbers.

[2]One of the things that makes this question so intriguing to me is that in many cases the weighted fly is the only one that can properly imitate the behavior of the natural. Thus, Charles Brooks's heavily weighted stonefly imitations are fished in such a manner as to reach fish feeding several feet under the surface on real stonefly nymphs. In that sense, Charlie was being as true to a goal of accurate imitation as Halford ever was.

John Gierach wrote an excellent article exploring some of these issues, "Flies or Lures? . . . and does it really matter?" in *Fly Fisherman* in May of 1986. He discussed some of the flies that are more like lures (flies included were tied—or made—by John Betts, Hal Janssen, Tim England, and Sandy Pittendrigh, and included a variety of imitations of crayfish, frogs, fish fry, insects, and minnows), flies with balsawood bodies, flies with scoops to make them dive, flies with cork bodies, and all manner of other innovations. Most of them can be cast at least as easily as Charlie's big nymphs, and some are already famous for their effectiveness. Resort to the O.E.D. and the I.G.F.A. for definitions of the word "fly," or the term "fly fishing," did not clarify much for John, but neither was he prevented from writing an intelligent, inquiring essay that is worth the attention of anyone interested in the problems related to fly-fishing definition. And, as he so often does, John managed to entertain as he instructed. His concluding remarks capture much of the frustration and challenge of the task of defining our terms:

> Here's one for you: If you want to land a longnose gar on a fly rod, you attach a length of
> frayed nylon rope to your leader. No hook, just a hunk of rope. The fish's teeth get tangled in
> the braid and the fish can be landed. Is that a fly or not? Does a fly have to have a hook? Would
> two turns of light ginger hackle help?
> You decide, but don't expect anyone to agree with you.

Bibliography

This list is limited primarily to book titles mentioned in the text. I frequently quote periodicals in the text, and whenever possible I have given, along with the quotation, sufficient bibliographical information to allow the reader to track down those periodical sources. There is no end to the number of articles that could be included here, and so I have chosen not to include any except those that are themselves studies of fishing history. The periodicals mentioned in the text are some of the most important sources of fly-fishing history, and I recommend them.

If you're interested in learning more about American fishing books, you should start with Henry Bruns's immense *Angling Books of The Americas*, an invaluable reference source for all angling-book enthusiasts. The single best source of information on American fly-fishing history is *The American Fly Fisher*, the journal of The American Museum of Fly Fishing.

Alexander, A. I. "Maine's Greatest Flytier." *Trout* 13, no. 4 (1972): 17.
———. "Exploring Dry Fly Origins." *Trout* 15, no. 2 (1974): 12.
———. "Rangeley's Giant Brook Trout." *Trout* 15, no. 4 (1974): 10.
Alexander, James E. *Salmon Fishing in Canada*. London: Longman, Green, Longman & Roberts, 1860.
Anderson, Gary., and Ann Brimer. *Salar: The Story of the Atlantic Salmon*. New York: International Atlantic Salmon Foundation, 1976.
Arbona, Fred. *Mayflies, the Angler and the Trout*. New York: Winchester Press, 1980.
Ashley-Dodd, G. L. *A Fisherman's Log*. London: Constable and Company, 1929.
Atherton, John. *The Fly and the Fish*. New York: MacMillan, 1951.

Babcock, Louis. *The Tarpon*. Buffalo: the author, 1920.
Banks, Joseph. *Joseph Banks in Newfoundland and Labrador, 1766 (His Diary, Manuscripts and Collections)*. Edited by A. M. Lysaght. London: Faber and Faber, 1971.
Barker, Thomas. *The Art of Angling*. London: R.H., 1651.
Bartram, William. *Travels Through North Carolina and South Carolina*. Philadelphia: James and Johnson, 1791.
Basurto, Fernando. *The Little Treatise on Fishing* (1539). Translated by T. Cohen and R. Hoffmann. *The American Fly Fisher* 11, no. 3 (1984): 8–13.
Bates, Joseph D. *Atlantic Salmon Flies and Fishing*. Harrisburg: Stackpole, 1970.
———. *Streamers and Bucktails*. New York: Alfred Knopf, 1979.
Bergman, Ray. *Just Fishing*. New York: Penn Publishing, 1933.
———. *Trout*. New York: Penn Publishing, 1938.
Benjamin, Joseph. Letter to Durfee Hill, February 10, 1934. American Museum of Fly Fishing Vertical Files.
Beverly, Robert. *The History and Present State of Virginia*. London: Richard Parker, 1705.
Bickerdyke, John. *Book of the All-Round Angler*. London: J. Upton Gill, 1889.
Blades, William. *Fishing Flies and Fly Tying*. Harrisburg: Stackpole & Heck, 1950.
Blakey, Robert. *Historical Sketches of the Angling Literature of All Nations*. London: John Russell Smith, 1856.
Borger, Gary. *Naturals*. Harrisburg: Stackpole, 1980.
———. *Nymphing*. Harrisburg: Stackpole, 1979.
Braekman, William. *A Treatise on Angling in the Boke of St. Albans (1496)*. Brussels: Scripta, 1980.
Bridenbaugh, Carl. *Cities in the Wilderness*. New York: The Ronald Press, 1938.
———. *Cities in Revolt*. New York: Capricorn, 1964.
Brinley, Francis. *Life of William T. Porter*. New York: D. Appleton, 1860.

Brookes, Richard. *The Art of Angling, Rock and Sea Fishing*. London: John Watts, 1740.

Brooks, Charles. *Larger Trout for the Western Fly Fisherman*. New York: Barnes, 1970.

————. *The Trout and the Stream*. New York: Crown, 1974.

————. *Nymph Fishing for Larger Trout*. New York: Crown, 1976.

Brooks, Joseph. *Saltwater Fly Fishing*. New York: Putnam, 1950.

————. *Complete Book of Fly Fishing*. New York: Outdoor Life, 1958.

————. *Salt Water Game Fishing*. New York: Harper & Row, 1968.

————. *Trout Fishing*. New York: Outdoor Life, 1972.

Brown, Jim. "Side-Mount Fly Reels: American Classics." *The American Fly Fisher* 12, no. 1 (1985): 14–17.

————. *Fishing Reel Patents of the United States, 1838–1940*. Stamford: Trico Press, 1985.

Brown, John J. *American Angler's Guide*. New York: Burgess, Stringer, 1845.

————. *Angler's Almanac*. New York: R. Craighead, 1851.

Bruns, Henry. *Angling Books of the Americas*. Atlanta: Angler's Press, 1975.

Burke, Edgar. *American Dry Flies and How to Tie Them*. New York: Derrydale Press, 1931.

Butler, A. J. *Sport in Classic Times*. Los Angeles: William Kaufmann, 1975.

Cameron, Kenneth. *Angling in the Past*. Unpublished collection of articles and essays. American Museum of Fly Fishing Vertical File.

————. "The Murphy Rod." *The Flyfisher* 7, no. 1 (1974): 12–13.

————. "The Art of the Hook." *Trout* 18, no. 2 (1977): 18.

————. "The Girls of Summer—Part I." *The Flyfisher* 10, no. 3 (1977): 8–11.

————. "The Girls of Summer, Part II." *The Flyfisher* 10, no. 4 (1977): 15–17.

————. "Sara McBride: Pioneer Angling Entomologist." *The American Fly Fisher* 5, no. 2 (1978): 10–11.

————. "The Victorian Angler." *The American Fly Fisher* 7, no. 1 (1980): 2–7.

————. "Fly Styles." *The American Fly Fisher* 8, no. 1 (1981): 2–7.

————. "The Dry Fly and Fast Trains." *The American Fly Fisher* 10, no. 1 (1983): 2–8.

Camp, Samuel. *Fishing with Floating Flies*. New York: Outing, 1913.

————. *The Angler's Handbook*. Columbus: Hunter, Trader & Trapper, 1925.

————. *Taking Trout with the Dry Fly*. New York: MacMillan, 1930.

Carlander, Harriet B. *A History of Fish and Fishing in the Upper Mississippi River*. St. Paul: Upper Mississippi River Conservation Committee, 1954.

Carmichael, Hoagy. "George Parker Holden." *The American Fly Fisher* 8, no 4 (1981): 8–14.

Carrie Stevens. Booklet published as part of celebration of Carrie Gertrude Stevens Day, August 15, 1970.

Carson, Jane. *Colonial Virginians at Play*. Williamsburg: Colonial Williamsburg/The University of Virginia Press, 1965.

Caucci, Al, and Bob Nastasi. *Hatches*. New York: Comparahatch, 1975.

Chandler, Leon. Transcription of taped comments on the history of Cortland Line Company, 1984. American Museum of Fly Fishing Vertical File.

Chetham, James. *The Angler's Vade-Mecum*. London: Thomas Bassett, 1681.

Clark, Brian, and John Goddard. *The Trout and the Fly*. New York: Nick Lyons Books/Doubleday, 1980.

Combs, Trey. *The Steelhead Trout*. Portland: Salmon Trout Steelheader, 1971.

————. *Steelhead Fly Fishing and Flies*. Portland: Frank Amato, 1976.

Cooper, J. G. "The Fauna of Montana Territory." *The American Naturalist* 3 (1870): 124.

Cordes, Ron, and Randall Kaufmann. *Lake Fishing with a Fly*. Portland: Frank Amato, 1984.

Crossley, Anthony. *The Floating Line for Salmon and Sea-Trout*. London: Methuen, 1939.

Dankers, Jaspar, and Peter Sluyter. *Journal of a Voyage to New York in 1679–80*. Translated by Henry Murphy. Brooklyn: Memoirs of the Long Island Historical Society, vol. 1, 1867.

Darbee, Harry, and Austin Francis. *Catskill Flytier*. Philadelphia: Lippincott, 1977.

Dashwood, Richard. *Chiploquoargan, or Life by the Campfire in the Dominion of Canada and Newfoundland*. Dublin: Robert White, 1871.

Dawson, George. *Pleasures of Angling*. New York: Sheldon & Company, 1876.

de Bergara, Juan. *El Manuscrito de Astorga, Juan de Bergara, Ano 1624*. Copenhagen: Flyleaves, 1984.

Dennys, J. *The Secrets of Angling*. London: Roger Jackson, 1613.

Dimock, Anthony W. *The Book of the Tarpon*. New York: Outing, 1911.
Dotson, Thurston. "Mortalities in Trout Caused by Gear Type and Angler-Induced Stress." *North American Journal of Fisheries Management* 2 (1982): 60–65.
Dunne, W. *Sunshine and the Dry Fly*. London: Black, 1924.

Earle, Alice M. *Colonial Days in Old New York*. New York: Charles Scribner's Sons, 1896.
Eggert, Richard. "The Gordon Heritage." *Fly Fisherman* 5, no. 3 (1974): 50–63.
Elder, Frank. *The Book of the Hackle*. Edinburgh: Scottish Academic Press, 1979.

Ferguson, Bruce, Les Johnson, and Pat Trotter. *Fly Fishing for Pacific Salmon*. Portland: Frank Amato, 1985.
Finlay, G. Dick, and Austin Hogan. *The Museum of American Fly Fishing, Manchester, Vermont, Acquisitions Catalog, 1969–1973*. Manchester: The Museum of American Fly Fishing, 1973.
Fisher, Paul. *The Angler's Souvenir*. London: H. G. Bohn, 1835.
Flick, Arthur. *Streamside Guide to Naturals and Their Imitations*. New York: Putnam, 1947.
———. *Art Flick's Master Fly Tying Guide*. New York: Crown, 1972.
Fly-Fishing in Salt and Fresh Water. London: Van Voorst, 1851.
Foster, David. *The Scientific Angler*. Edited by W. Harris. New York: Orange Judd, 1883.
Fox, Charles. *This Wonderful World of Trout*. Carlisle: the author, 1963.
———. *Rising Trout*. Carlisle: Foxcrest, 1967.
Francis, Austin. *Catskill Rivers*. New York: Nick Lyons Books/Winchester Press, 1983.
Franck, Richard. *A Philosophical Treatise of the Original and Production of Things*. London: John Gain, 1687.
———. *Northern Memoirs*. London: the author, 1694.
———. *The Admirable and Indefatigable Adventures of the Nine Pious Pilgrims*. London: John Morphew, 1708.
Fraser, Perry. "History of the Anglers' Club of New York." *Anglers' Club Bulletin* 4, no. 1 (1926): 1.
Freame, Margaret Penn. "Letter of Margaret Penn Freame in Philadelphia, to John Penn." *The Pennsylvania Magazine of History and Biography* 31 (1907): 121–122.
Furman, G. *Long Island Miscellanies*. New York: Egbert, Hovery, and King, 1847.

Garlick, Theodatus. *A Treatise on the Artifical Propagation of Fish*. Cleveland: Thomas Brown, 1857.
Gierach, John. *Trout Bum* Boulder: Pruett, 1986.
Gerlach, Rex. *The Complete Book of Casting*. New York: Winchester Press, 1975.
Gill, Emlyn. *Practical Dry-Fly Fishing*. New York: Scribners, 1912.
Gillette, Warren. Diary . . . August 7 to September 27, 1870. Montana Historical Society, Helena, Montana.
Gingrich, Arnold. *The Well-Tempered Angler*. New York: Knopf, 1965.
———. *The Joys of Trout*. New York: Crown, 1973.
———. *The Fishing in Print*. New York: Winchester Press, 1974.
———, ed. *The Gordon Garland*. Hartford: Connecticut Press/Theodore Gordon Flyfishers, 1965.
Glauert, K., and M. Kunz. *Kittitas Frontiersmen*. Ellensburg, Oregon: Ellensburg Public Library, 1976.
Goodspeed, Charles. *Angling in America*. New York: Houghton Mifflin, 1939.
Goodwin, Maud, Alice Royce, and Ruth Putnam. *Historic New York*. New York: G. P. Putnam's Sons, 1898.
Gordon, Sid. *How to Fish from Top to Bottom*. Harrisburg: Stackpole, 1955.
Grant, George. "The Historic Montana Trout Fly—From Tradition to Transition." *The American Fly Fisher* 1, no. 2 (1974): 20–21.
———. "Franz Pott: Western Original." *The American Fly Fisher* 7, no. 2 (1980): 20–22.
———. *The Master Fly Weaver*. Portland: Champoeg Press, 1980.
———. "Bunyan Bugs." *The American Fly Fisher* 8, no. 3 (1981): 12–14.
———. *Montana Trout Flies*. Portland: Champoeg Press, 1981.
———. "Don Martinez." *The American Fly Fisher* 9 no. 2 (1982): 8–14.
———. *George Grant's Scrapbook*. Butte: the author, n.d.
Gregory, Myron. "Fly Lines." *Fly Fisherman* 9, no. 2 (1978): 52–58.
Grey, Zane. *Tales of Freshwater Fishing*. New York: Grosset & Dunlap, 1928.
Grove, Alvin. *The Lure and Lore of Fly Fishing*. Harrisburg: Stackpole, 1951.

Hafele, Rick, and Dave Hughes. *The Complete Book of Western Hatches*. Portland: Frank Amato, 1981.

Haig-Brown, Roderick. *The Western Angler*. New York: Morrow, 1939.

———. *A River Never Sleeps*. New York: Morrow, 1946.

———. *A Primer of Fly Fishing*. New York: Morrow, 1964.

Hallock, Charles. *The Fishing Tourist*. New York: Harpers, 1873.

———. *The Sportsman's Gazeteer*. New York: Forest and Stream, 1877.

Halford, Frederick. *Floating Flies and How to Dress Them*. London: Low, 1886.

———. *Dry Fly Entomology*. London: Vinton, 1897.

Harding, E. W. *The Fly-Fisher and the Trout's Point of View*. London: Seeley, Service, 1931.

Hardy, Campbell. *Sporting Adventures in the New World*. London: Hurst & Blackett, 1855.

Heddon, Jack. "An Attempt to Reproduce Early Nineteenth Century Fly Dressings." *The American Fly Fisher* 2, no. 2 (1975): 10–12.

Henderson, Robert. *Early American Sport*. New York: A. S. Barnes, 1953.

Henry, Walter. *Events of a Military Life*. London: William Pickering, 1843.

Henshall, James. *Book of the Black Bass*. Cincinnati: Robert Clarke, 1881.

———. *Camping and Cruising in Florida*. Cincinnati: Robert Clarke, 1884.

———. *Favorite Fish and Fishing*. New York: Outing, 1908.

Herbert, Henry William. *Frank Forester's Fish and Fishing*. New York: Stringer & Townsend, 1851.

———. *Complete Manual for Young Sportsmen*. New York: Stringer & Townsend, 1856.

Herter, George. *Fly Tying and Tackle Making*. Waseca, Minnesota: Brown, 1941.

Hewitt, Edward R. *Secrets of the Salmon*. New York: Scribners, 1922.

———. *Hewitt's Handbook of Fly Fishing*. New York: Marchbanks, 1933.

———. *A Trout and Salmon Fisherman for Seventy-Five Years*. New York: Scribners, 1948.

Hills, John W. *A History of Fly Fishing for Trout*. London: Allan, 1921.

Hoffmann, Richard. "A New Treatise on the Treatyse." *The American Fly Fisher* 9, no. 3 (1982): 2–6.

———. "The Evidence for Early European Angling, I: Basurto's *Dialogo* of 1539." *The American Fly Fisher* 11, no. 4 (1984): 2–9.

———. The Astorga Manuscript, 1624, ordered notes for a critical analysis, 1985. Manuscript loaned by the author.

———. "Fishing for Sport in Medieval Europe: New Evidence." *Speculum* 60, no. 4 (1985): 877–902.

———. "The Protohistory of Pike in Western Culture," in *An Annotated Bibliography of the Pike Esox lucius*, Crossman, E. J., and Casselman, eds. Toronto: Royal Ontario Museum, 1987.

Hogan, Austin. "Treasure Lore." *Trout* 13, no. 1 (1972): 14.

———. "Another Time, Another Laughter." *The Flyfisher* 5, no. 3 (1972): 14.

———. "Mainstream and Cross Currents: The Trout and Salmon Fly in America." *The Orvis News*, August, 1972.

———. *American Sporting Periodicals of Angling Interest*. Manchester: The Museum of American Fly Fishing, 1973.

———. "The Greatest American Brook Trouts." *The American Fly Fisher* 1, no. 2 (1974): 7–9.

———. "The Historic American Grayling." *The American Fly Fisher* 2, no. 1 (1975): 2–5.

———. "The Historic Striped Bass—A Brief Introduction." *The American Fly Fisher* 2, no. 3 (1975): 6–9.

———. "Bob Fly, Dropper—Tail Fly, Stretcher." *The American Fly Fisher* 3, no. 4 (1976): 11–22.

———. "An Introduction to the History of Fly-Fishing in America." *The American Fly Fisher* 12, no. 4 (1985): 2–9.

Hogan, Austin, and Paul Schullery. *The Orvis Story*. Manchester: The Orvis Company, 1981.

Holden, George Parker. *Streamcraft*. Cincinnati: Stewart Kidd, 1919.

———. *Angling Recollections and Practice*. New York: Appleton, 1931.

Holliman, Jennie. *American Sports (1785–1835)*. Philadelphia: Porcupine Press, 1975.

Humphrey, William. *Open Season*. New York: Delacorte, 1985.

Humphreys, Joe. *Joe Humphreys's Trout Tactics*. Harrisburg: Stackpole, 1981.

Hunt, Richard. "Brodhead's Creek." *The Angler's Club Bulletin* 8, no. 3 (1934): 3–8.

Isaksen, Susie. "Carrie G. Stevens, Originator of Modern Streamer Design." *The American Fly Fisher* 3, no. 4 (1976): 2–5.

Jennings, Preston. *A Book of Trout Flies*. New York: Derrydale, 1935.

———. *The Fish and the Fly*. Unpublished manuscript, American Museum of Fly Fishing Vertical File, n.d.

Johnson, Paul. *The Scientific Angler*. New York: Charles Scribner's Sons, 1984.

Jones, A. Ross, ed. *The Best of the Anglers' Club Bulletin 1920–1972*. New York: The Anglers' Club, 1972.

Jordan, Wesley. Interview with Austin Hogan concerning Jordan's career in rod building. American Museum of Fly Fishing Vertical File, 1973.

Kalm, Peter. *Peter Kalm's Travels in North America, the English Version of 1770*. New York: Dover, 1966.

Kaufmann, Randall. *The Fly Tyer's Nymph Manual*. Portland: Western Fisherman's Press, 1986.

Keane, Martin. *Classic Rods and Rodmakers*. New York: Winchester Press, 1976.

Keene, John Harrington. *Fishing Tackle, Its Materials and Manufacture*. London: Ward Lock & Co, 1886.

———. *Fly Fishing and Fly Making*. New York: Forest and Stream, 1887.

———. ''The Fishing Reel and Its Development.'' *The Sporting Goods Dealer*, September 8–16, 1901.

Kelly, Mary. ''Rods Before Bamboo.'' *Fishing World* (July/August 1976): 8.

———. ''Early Leonard.'' *The American Fly Fisher* 6, no. 1 (1979): 12.

———. ''Thomas Chubb.'' *The American Fly Fisher* 7, no. 4 (1980): 12–19.

———. ''Spalding and Kosmic Connection.'' *The American Fly Fisher* 11, no. 3 (1984): 2–7.

Kelson, George. *The Salmon Fly*. London: Wymans, 1895.

King, William R. *The Sportsman and Naturalist in Canada*. London: Hurst and Blackett, 1866.

Koch, Ed. *Fishing the Midge*. New York: Freshet, 1972.

Koller, Larry. *Taking Larger Trout*. Boston: Little Brown, 1950.

———. *The Treasury of Angling*. New York: Golden Press, 1963.

Kreh, Bernard ''Lefty.'' *Fly Fishing in Salt Water*. New York: Crown, 1974.

Kreider, Claude. *Steelhead*. New York: Putnam, 1948.

LaBranche, George M. L. *The Dry Fly and Fast Water*. New York: Scribners, 1914.

———. *The Salmon and the Dry Fly*. New York: Scribners, 1924.

LaFontaine, Gary. *Challenge of the Trout*. Missoula: Mountain Press, 1976.

———. *Caddisflies*. New York: Nick Lyons Books/Winchester Press, 1983.

Lanman, Charles. *Letters from a Landscape Painter*. Boston: James Munroe & Co, 1845.

———. *A Summer in the Wilderness*. New York: Appleton, 1847.

———. *A Tour to the River Saguenay*. Philadelphia: Carey & Hart, 1848.

———. *Adventures in the Wilds of North America*. London: Longmans, Brown, Green and Longmans, 1854.

Laycock, George. ''Passing of a Great Fisherman.'' *The Fisherman* (May 29, 1957).

Ledlie, David. ''William T. Porter, First of Our Sporting Journalists.'' *The American Fly Fisher* 1, no. 3 (1974): 2–4.

———. ''The American Editor and the Complete Angler.'' *The American Fly Fisher* 2, no. 1 (1975): 14–16.

———. ''Dean Sage—Part III The Years at Camp Harmony.'' *The American Fly Fisher* 3, no. 3 (1976): 2–8.

———. ''William T. Porter and the Origins of Imitation.'' *The American Fly Fisher* 6, no. 2 (1979): 4.

———. ''A Colonial Fly Fisher.'' *The American Fly Fisher* 7, no. 3 (1980): 14–15.

———. ''The Black Bass in Maine.'' *The American Fly Fisher* 9, no. 3 (1982): 7–9.

———. ''Louis Rhead and Forest & Stream.'' *The American Fly Fisher* 10, no. 2 (1983): 22–25.

———. ''More on Sir William Johnson.'' *The American Fly Fisher* 11, no. 2 (1984): 2–6.

———. ''Dry Flies on the Ondawa: The Tragic Tale of John Harrington Keene.'' *The American Fly Fisher* 13, no. 1 (1986): 8–17.

Lee, Art. *Fishing for Trout with Dry Flies on Rivers and Streams*. New York: Atheneum, 1983.

Leisenring, James. *The Art of Tying the Wet Fly*. New York: Dodd Mead, 1941.

Leonard, J. Edson. *Flies*. New York: A. S. Barnes, 1950.

Leiser, Eric, and Larry Solomon. *The Caddis and the Angler*. Harrisburg: Stackpole, 1977.

Leiser, Eric, and Robert Boyle. *Stoneflies for the Angler*. New York: Knopf, 1982.

Lilly, Bud, and Paul Schullery. *Bud Lilly's Guide to Western Fly Fishing*. New York: Nick Lyons Books, 1987.

Lyons, Nick. *Fishing Widows*. New York: Crown, 1970.

———, ed. *Fisherman's Bounty*. New York: Crown, 1970.

Marbury, Mary Orvis. *Favorite Flies and Their Histories*. New York: Houghton Mifflin, 1892.

Marinaro, Vincent. *A Modern Dry-Fly Code*. New York: Putnams, 1950.

———. *In the Ring of the Rise*. New York: Crown, 1976.

Markham, Gervase. *The Second Booke of the English Husbandman*. London: John Browne, 1614.

Marston, Robert B. *Walton and Some Earlier Writers on Fishing*. London: Elliot Stock, 1894.

Martin Reel Company. "Martin Reel History." Unpublished typescript. American Museum of Fly Fishing Vertical File, n.d.

Martuch, Leon. Transcription of taped comments on the history of Scientific Anglers. American Museum of Fly Fishing Vertical File, 1984.

Mascall, Leonard. *A Booke of Fishing with Hooke & Line*. London: John Wolfe, 1590.

Mather, Fred. *Men I Have Fished With*. New York: Forest and Stream, 1897.

———. *My Angling Friends*. New York: Forest and Stream, 1901.

Maxwell, Herbert. *Salmon and Sea-Trout*. London: Lawrence & Bullen, 1896.

McClane, A. J. *The Practical Fly Fisherman*. New York: Prentice-Hall, 1953.

McClean, Norman. *A River Runs Through It*. Chicago: University of Chicago Press, 1976.

McDonald, John. *The Origins of Angling*. New York: Doubleday, 1963.

———. *Quill Gordon*. New York: Knopf, 1972.

McDonald, John, ed. *The Complete Fly Fisherman: The Notes and Letters of Theodore Gordon*. New York: Scribners. 1947.

McGuane, Thomas. *An Outside Chance*. New York: Farrar, Straus, Giroux, 1980.

McNeilly, Dorothy. "Charles Lanman." *The American Fly Fisher* 11, no. 3 (1984): 14–19.

Merwin, John. *Stillwater Trout*. Nick Lyons Books/Doubleday, 1980.

Migel, J. Michael, and Leonard Wright, eds. *The Masters on the Nymph*. New York: Nick Lyons Books/ Winchester Press, 1979.

Miller, Alfred W. ("Sparse Grey Hackle"). *Fishless Days, Angling Nights*. New York: Crown, 1971.

Miller, Hazen. *The Old Au Sable*. Grand Rapids: William Eerdmans, 1963.

Mills, W. & Sons, Inc. William Mills & Sons, Inc. Typescript of chronological history of company. American Museum of Fly Fishing Vertical File, 1964.

Moon, Ralph. "A Frontier Fly Fisher, 1847." *The American Fly Fisher* 9, no. 3 (1984): 10–11.

Murray, William H. H. *Adventures in the Wilderness*. Boston: Fields, Osgood, 1869.

Nemes, Sylvester. *The Soft-Hackled Fly*. Old Greenwich: The Chatham Press, 1975.

Netherton, Cliff. *History of the Sport of Casting, People, Events, Records, Tackle and Literature, Early Times*. Lakeland, Florida: American Casting Education Foundation, 1981.

———. *History of the Sport of Casting, Golden Years*. Lakeland (Florida): American Casting Education Foundation, 1983.

Nettles, Richard. *The Salmon Fisheries of the St. Lawrence and Its Tributaries*. Montreal: John Lovell, 1857.

Norris, Thaddeus. *The American Angler's Book*. Philadelphia: Butler, 1864.

Orrelle, John. "Five of the Best." *The American Fly Fisher* 1, no. 1 (1974): 10–13.

———. "Meisselbach Reels." *The American Fly Fisher* 1, no. 1 (1974): 18–20.

———. "Two Early American Fly Reels." *The Flyfisher* 9, no. 2 (1976): 24–26.

———. "Automatic Fly Reels." *The American Fly Fisher* 13, no. 1 (1986): 2–7.

Orvis, Charles, and Albert N. Cheney. *Fishing with the Fly*. Manchester: Orvis, 1883.

Overfield, T. Donald. *G. E. M. Skues: The Way of a Man with a Trout*. London: Ernest Benn, 1977.

Ovington, Ray. *How to Take Trout*. Boston: Little Brown, 1952.

Phair, Charles. *Atlantic Salmon Fishing*. New York: Derrydale, 1937.

Prime, William Cowper. *I Go A'Fishing*. New York: Harper & Brothers, 1873.

Proper, Datus. *What the Trout Said*. New York: Knopf, 1982.

Pulman, G. P. R. *Vade Mecum of Fly-Fishing for Trout*. London: Longmans, 1851.

Quick, Jim. *Fishing the Nymph*. New York: Ronald Press, 1960.

Radcliffe, William. *Fishing from Earliest Times*. London: Murray, 1921.

Raymond, Steve. *The Year of the Angler*. New York: Winchester Press. 1973.

———. *The Year of the Trout*. Piscataway, New Jersey: Winchester Press, 1985.

———. "A Matter of Definition." *Fly Fisherman* 17, no. 1 (1985): 21–23.

Reiger, George. *Profiles in Saltwater Angling*. New York: Prentice-Hall, 1973.

Reiger, John. *American Sportsmen and the Origins of Conservation*. New York: Winchester Press, 1975.

Rhead, Louis. *Bait Angling for Common Fishes*. New York: Outing, 1907.

———. *How to Fish the Dry Fly*. Brooklyn: the author, 1912.

———. *American Trout Stream Insects*. New York: Frederick Stokes, 1916.

———. *Fisherman's Lures and Game Fish Food*. New York: Scribners, 1920.

———. *How to Fish the Dry Fly Floating on the Surface also How to Fish Various Nymphs from the Bottom Upwards*. Brooklyn: the author, 1921.

Rhead, Louis, ed. *The Basses, Fresh Water and Marine*. New York: F. A. Stokes, 1905.

———, ed. *The Speckled Brook Trout*. New York: R. H. Russell, 1902.

Richards, Carl, Doug Swisher, and Fred Arbona. *Stoneflies*. New York: Nick Lyons Books/Winchester Press, 1983.

Robbins, William, and Hugh MacCrimmon. *The Black Bass in America and Overseas*. Sault Ste. Marie: Biomanagement and Research Enterprises, 1974.

Rogers, John. *Sport in Vancouver and Newfoundland*. London: Chapman & Hall, 1912.

Ronalds, Alfred. *The Fly-Fisher's Entomology*. London: Longman, 1836.

Roosevelt, Robert Barnwell. *Game Fish of the Northern States of America*. New York: Carleton, 1862.

———. *Superior Fishing*. New York: Carleton, 1865.

Rosenbauer, Tom. *The Orvis Fly-Fishing Guide*. New York: Nick Lyons Books/Winchester Press, 1984.

Rosborough, Polly. *Tying and Fishing the Fuzzy Nymphs*. Caldwell, Idaho: Caxton, 1965.

Sage, Dean. *The Ristigouche and Its Salmon Fishing*. Edinburgh: David Douglas, 1888.

Sage, Dean, ed. *Salmon and Trout*. New York: MacMillan, 1902.

St. John, Larry. *Practical Fly Fishing*. New York: MacMillan, 1920.

Salter, Thomas. *The Angler's Guide*. London: Sherwood, Jones, and Company, 1823.

Samuels, Edward. *With Fly Rod and Camera*. New York: Forest and Stream, 1890.

Samuel, William. *The Arte of Angling*. London: Henry Middleton, 1577.

Sand, George. *Salt Water Fly Fishing*. New York: Knopf, 1969.

Satchell, Thomas, and Thomas Westwood. *Bibliotheca Piscatoria*. Reprint. London: Dawsons, 1966.

Sawyer, Frank. *Keeper of the Stream*. London: George Allen & Unwin, 1952.

Schreiner, William. *Schreiner's Sporting Manual*. Philadelphia: Douglas Wyeth, 1841.

Schweibert, Ernest. *Matching the Hatch*. New York: MacMillan, 1955.

———. *Remembrances of Rivers Past*. New York: MacMillan, 1973.

———. *Nymphs*. New York: Winchester Press, 1973.

———. *Trout*. New York: Dutton, 1978.

Scott, Genio. *Fishing in American Waters*. New York: Harper, 1869.

Shaw, Helen. *Fly-Tying*. New York: Ronald Press, 1963.

Shepard, Odell. *Thy Rod and Thy Creel*. New York: Dodd Mead, 1930.

Shields, George O., ed. *American Game Fishes*. Chicago: Rand McNally, 1892.

Shoemaker, Kenneth. "Daniel Webster and the Great Brook Trout." *The American Fly Fisher* 8, no. 1 (1981): 20–24.

Skues, G. E. M. *Minor Tactics of the Chalk Stream*. London: Black, 1910.

———. *The Way of a Trout with a Fly*. London: Black, 1924.

Slaymaker, Sam. *Tie a Fly, Catch a Trout*. New York: Harper & Row, 1976.

Smedley, Harold. *What's What and Who's Who in Fly and Bait Casting in the United States*. Muskegon: Westshore, 1940.

———. *Fly Patterns and Their Origins*. Muskegon: Westshore, 1943.

Smith, Jerome Van Crowninshield. *Natural History of the Fishes of Massachusetts*. Boston: Allen & Ticknor, 1833.

Smith, Onnie. *Trout Lore*. New York: Frederick Stokes, 1917.

Sosin, Mark, and John Clark. *Through the Fish's Eye*. New York: Harper & Row, 1973.

South, Theophilus. *The Fly-Fisher's Text-Book*. London: R. Ackermann, 1841.

Starkman, Susan, and Stanley Read. *The Contemplative Man's Recreation*. Vancouver: The Library of the University of British Columbia, 1970.

Steel, Frank. *Fly Fishing*. Chicago: Paul Richmond, 1946.

Stewart, William. *The Practical Angler*. Edinburgh: Black, 1857.

Sturgis, William B. *Fly-Tying*. New York: Scribners, 1940.

Suckley, George. "A Report Upon the Fishes Collected on the Survey." In *Reports of Explorations and Surveys to Ascertain the Most Practicable and Economical Route for a Railroad from the Mississippi River to the Pacific Coast*. Washington, D.C.: Thomas Ford, 1860.

Swan, James. *The Northwest Coast*. New York: Harper & Brothers, 1857.

Swisher, Doug, and Carl Richards. *Selective Trout*. New York: Crown, 1971.

————. *Fly Fishing Strategy*. New York: Crown, 1975.

Taverner, Eric. *Trout Fishing from all Angles*. London: Seeley, Service, 1930.

Tolfrey, Frederic. *The Sportsman in Canada*. London: Newby, 1845.

Traver, Robert. *Trout Madness*. New York: St. Martin's, 1960.

————. *Trout Magic*. New York: Crown, 1974.

Trench, Charles C. *A History of Angling*. Chicago: Follett Publishing Company, 1974.

Van Dyke, Henry. *Little Rivers*. New York: Scribners, 1895.

————. *Fisherman's Luck*. New York: Scribners, 1899.

Van Fleet, Clark. *Steelhead to a Fly*. Boston: Atlantic Monthly Press, 1954.

Venables, Bernard. *Fishing*. London: B. T. Batsford, 1953.

Venables, Robert. *The Experienced Angler*. London: Richard Marriott, 1662.

Vernon, Steven. *Antique Fishing Reels*. Harrisburg: Stackpole, 1985.

Walton, Izaak. *The Complete Angler*. Edited by G. Bethune. New York: Wiley and Putnam, 1847.

Ward, F. *Animal Life Under Water*. London: Cassell, 1919.

Waterman, Charles. *A History of Angling*. New York: Winchester Press, 1981.

Wells, Henry Parkhurst. *Fly Rods and Fly Tackle*. New York: Harper Brothers, 1885.

————. *The American Salmon Fisherman*. New York: Harper Brothers, 1886.

Wetzel, Charles. *Practical Fly Fishing*. Boston: Christopher Publishing House, 1943.

————. *American Fishing Books*. Newark: the author, 1950.

————. *Trout Flies, Naturals and Imitations*. Harrisburg: Stackpole, 1955.

Whitlock, Dave. *Dave Whitlock's Guide to Aquatic Trout Foods*. New York: Nick Lyons Books/Winchester Press, 1982.

————. *L. L. Bean Fly-Fishing Handbook*. New York: Nick Lyons Books/Winchester Press, 1984.

Whitlock, Dave, and Robert Boyle, eds. *The Fly-Tyer's Almanac*. New York: Crown, 1975.

Williams, Arthur B. *Rod & Creel in British Columbia*. Vancouver: Progress Publishing, 1919.

Wilson, J. *The Rod and the Gun*. Edinburgh: Black, 1844.

Woods, Craig. *The Fly Fisherman's Streamside Handbook*. New York: Ziff-Davis, 1981.

Wright, L. B. *The First Gentlemen of Virginia*. Charlottesville: Dominion Books, 1964.

Wright, Leonard. *Fishing the Dry Fly as a Living Insect*. New York: Dutton, 1972.

————. *The Ways of Trout*. New York: Nick Lyons Books/Winchester, 1985.

Wulff, Lee. *The Atlantic Salmon*. New York: Barnes, 1958.

————. *Lee Wulff on Flies*. Harrisburg: Stackpole, 1980.

————. *Trout on a Fly*. New York: Nick Lyons Books, 1986.

Yates, Norris. *William T. Porter and the Spirit of the Times*. Baton Rouge: Louisiana State University Press, 1957.

Young, Paul. *Making and Using the Fly and Leader*. Detroit: the author, 1933.

Zern, Ed. *To Hell with Fishing*. New York: Appleton Century, 1945.

————. *Are Fishermen People?* New York: Harper, 1955.

————. *A Fine Kettle of Fish Stories*. New York: Winchester Press, 1972.

Index

Note: page numbers in italics refer to illustrations